Also by Victor Sebestyen

Twelve Days: The Story of the 1956 Hungarian Revolution

REVOLUTION 1989

REVOLUTION 1989

The Fall of the Soviet Empire

VICTOR SEBESTYEN

Pantheon Books
NEW YORK

 Published in the United States by Pantheon Books, a division of Random House, Inc., New York. Originally published in Great Britain by Weidenfeld & Nicolson, Orion Publishing Group Ltd., London.

Library of Congress Cataloging-in-Publication Data

Sebestyen, Victor, [date]
Revolution 1989 : the fall of the Soviet empire / Victor Sebestyen.
p. cm.
Includes bibliographical references and index.
ISBN 978-0-375-42532-5
1. Soviet Union—Politics and government—1985–1991. I. Title.
DK288.S393 2009 947.085'4—dc22 2009023045

www.pantheonbooks.com

Printed in the United States of America

First United States Edition

2 4 6 8 9 7 5 3 1

In memory of my mother Éva
and Patricia Diggory

CONTENTS

PART THREE: REVOLUTION

ILLUSTRATIONS

SECTION ONE

SECTION TWO

ACKNOWLEDGEMENTS

I have been travelling to Central Europe for work and pleasure since the late 1970s when, to Westerners, cities like Prague and Budapest were considered mysterious, occasionally sinister, faraway places of which we knew little. It is directly because of the events I describe here that once again they are thriving cities at the heart of the European tradition. This book is the result of more than two hundred trips over three decades and it could not have been written without enormous help from a great number of people, some of whom in the dark days of totalitarianism risked a great deal to talk with me. I have space to mention just a few of them here. I have weaved into the narrative interviews and conversations from many years ago – a lot of them in 1989 – with more recent reflections. Often I talked to the same people again years later, who spoke with the benefit of hindsight.

In Poland I am grateful to Tadeusz Mazowiecki, Jerzy Urban, Lech Wałęsa and the Lech Wałęsa Institute, Anna Walentynowycz, Danuta Galecka and Jadzia Komornicka. While I was researching and writing this book three people died who, over the years, and during many visits to Poland, had been extremely helpful: Mieczyslaw Rakowski, Alina Pienkowska and Bronislaw Geremek. The Andrzej Stelmachowski papers were very useful, as were the staff at the Central Military Archives and at the Institute of National Remembrance in Warsaw.

In the Czech Republic and Slovakia I am particularly indebted to Ondřej Soukoup, Michael Kocáb, Jefim Fistein, Peta Brod, Jacques Rupnik, Dasa Antelova, Jiří Dienstbier, Anna Bryson, Peter Uhl, Tom Gross, Jan Urban, and the staff at the Archive of the President's Office, at the Home Office archive and at the Czech Parliament's archive. The Alexander Dubček Institute in Bratislava and surviving members of the late Mr Dubček's family were hugely helpful.

In Hungary Katalin Bogyay, Miklós Haraszti, Maria Vásárhelyi, László Rajk, Csilla Strbik, Adam LeBor, Imre Pozsgay, Ferenc Köszeg, Gábor Demszky, Béla Szombaty, Istvan Rév, Csaba Békes, Dominic Arbuthnott, Nora Walko, Andrea Kalman, János Kis, László Eörsi, Gábor Kélemeri, Károly Makk, Sándor Revesz and Nick Thorpe went out of their way to help me. I would like to thank the staff at the Hungarian National Archive, the archive of the Hungarian Parliament, the Institute for the Study of the 1956 Revolution and the archive of the Open Society Institute in Budapest.

In Germany I am immensely grateful to Dr Matthias Mueller, Reinhard Schult, Aram Radomsky, Rüdigger Rosendahl, Carsten Krenz, Christian Führer, Klaus Peter Renneberg, Philip Lengsfeld, Günter Schabowski, and the staff in charge of the Stasi Files, the Commission for Records of the State Security, Berlin, and the State Archive of Political Parties and mass organisations of the GRD, also in Berlin.

In Romania I want to thank Mircea Dinescu, Gheorghiu Constantinescu, Alex Serban, Pavel Câmpeanu, Sergiu Celac, Oleanna Tedescu, Petre Roman, and the staff at the Presidential Commission for the Study of the Communist Dictatorship, the archive of the Romanian Ministry of Home Affairs and of Foreign Affairs, and the Institute for the Investigation of Communist Crimes in Romania.

Ivan and Tanya Pojarleff and Lyubo Markov were exceptionally generous with their time in Sofia, where I am also grateful to Stefan Tafrov, Petar Mladenov, Blaga Dimitrova, Kalin Manolov, Krassen Stanchev, Rumen Danov, staff at the Institute for the Study of the Recent Past, the Archive of the Bulgarian Council of Ministers and of the Files Commission, the Inquiry into the records of the Bulgarian State Security Service.

In the US, James Baker III was immensely generous with his time and I would like to thank the office of General Brent Scowcroft. Charles Gati, Jamie Dettmer, Rebecca Mead, Joan Stein and Christopher Hitchens were thought-provoking companions who gave me new ideas about American foreign policy. The Cold War International History Project in George Washington University, the Hoover Institution at Stanford, the Library of Congress and the US State Department were vastly helpful.

In Moscow, I am indebted to staff at the Russian Presidential Archive, the Gorbachev Foundation and the Centre for the Preservation of Contemporary Documents. Many people in Russia were extremely helpful over the years. For depressing reasons to do with politics in Moscow now, most of them asked not to be mentioned by name. But you know who you are and how much I owe you.

Two books in particular were inspirational: Timothy Garton Ash's *We the People* and Michael Dobbs's *Down With Big Brother.*

In England I am immensely grateful to Lord Powell, Simon Sebag Montefiore, Maria Stanowski, Mitko Dimitrov, Annabel Markova, Joachim von Halasz, Anjelica von Hase, John Hamilton, Lucy Perceval, Christopher Silvester, Mátyás Sárkozi, Sir Bryan Cartledge, Peter Unwin, Anna Reid, Amanda Sebestyen, Tira Shubart, Mark Jones, Anne McElvoy, Daniel Johnson, Boris Marelic, Marina Daskalova, my sister Judith Maynard and brother John Walko. The staff at the London Library, at Chatham House, the British Library and the Bodleian Library were ever useful, as were the staff at the library of King's College, London, where the Liddell Hart Centre for Military Archives houses a set of invaluable transcripts of interviews for two TV series: Brian Lapping Associates' 'Fall of the Wall', and CNN's 'Cold War'. The constant support of Paul, Wendy, Peter and Jayne Diggory and Adil Ali has been vital.

I must praise the deep, reassuring calm of my friend and my editor at Weidenfeld & Nicolson, Ion Trewin. The word 'sage' might have been invented just for him. It is a joy to work with my enthusiastic and tireless assistant editor Bea Hemming, and with my exceptional copy-editor Linden Lawson. My agent Georgina Capel was ever optimistic, encouraging and generous.

But most of all I am indebted to Jessica Pulay. Without her loving support, wise counsel, clear mind, imagination and editing skills I could not have completed this book. Her informed understanding of Central Europe has been invaluable. At many stages she pointed out new ideas and new avenues to explore. Her constant encouragement has been my beacon.

Europe in 1989
0
250
500 miles
0
400
800 km
NORWAY
SWEDEN
North Sea
Copenhagen
DENMARK
IRELAND
Dublin
BRITAIN
London
Amsterdam
NETHERLANDS
Berlin
EAST GERMANY
Leipzig
BELGIUM
Bonn
Prague
CZECHO
WEST GERMANY
Atlantic Ocean
Paris
LUX.
Vienna
FRANCE
SWITZ.
AUSTRIA
ITALY
Rome
PORTUGAL
Madrid
SPAIN
Lisbon
TUNISIA
ALGERIA
MOROCCO

Members of Nato
Members of Warsaw Pact
Boundary of EEC
FINLAND
Baltic Sea
Moscow
U. S. S. R.
Gdańsk
Warsaw
POLAND
Krakow
SLOVAKIA
Bratislava
Budapest
HUNGARY
ROMANIA
Timisoara
Belgrade
Bucharest
YUGOSLAVIA
BULGARIA
Sofia
Black Sea
ALBANIA
Istanbul
Ankara
GREECE
TURKEY
Athens
SYRIA
IRAQ
IRAN
Mediterranean Sea

It is impossible to predict the time and progress of revolution. It is governed by its own more or less mysterious laws. But when it comes, it moves irresistibly.

Vladimir Ilyich Lenin

Ideas that have outlived their day may hobble about the world for years, but it is hard for them ever to lead and dominate life. Such ideas never gain complete possession of a man, or they gain possession only of incomplete people.

Alexander Herzen

God preserve me from those who want what's best for me.
From the nice guys
always willing to inform on me
from the priest with a tape recorder under his vestments
from the blankets you get under without saying good evening
from those angry with their own people. . . .
now when winter's coming.

Mircea Dinescu

INTRODUCTION

This is a story with a happy ending. Nobody who witnessed the joy on the streets of Berlin, Prague or Budapest at the end of 1989 will ever forget those extraordinary scenes of celebration. The people's will had triumphed over tyranny in a dizzying few months of almost entirely peaceful revolutions which changed the world. That is where this narrative finishes, at a point of bright hopes, intelligent optimism, sincere thanksgiving – and great parties. One of history's most brutal empires was on its knees. Poets and philosophers who had been languishing in jails became presidents and government ministers. When the Berlin Wall fell on a chilly November night it seemed as though the open wounds of the cruel twentieth century would at last begin to heal. These were not entirely foolish dreams. Some pundits – most notably, but not uniquely, Francis Fukayama – became carried away and predicted the end of history and of future ideological conflicts.

The pundits were right about the scale and importance of the changes in 1989 – if not about the end of history. An entire way of life and of looking at reality – communism as inspired by Marx, Lenin and Stalin – had been exposed as a gruesomely failed experiment. Freedom and independence for a large part of Europe that had been imprisoned for four decades became feasible within weeks. At the start of 1989 neither seemed possible for years ahead. The Cold War was declared over. There remained two powers which possessed enough nuclear weapons to destroy civilisation several times over, but neither now looked like using them. The Year of Revolutions appeared as a beacon of hope for oppressed people elsewhere who dared to dream that they too could free themselves.

The sudden collapse of the Soviet empire was entirely unexpected. After the event, many sages in academia, the military, the media, politics and diplomacy boasted that they had seen it coming. But it is hard to find any evidence, least of all from inside the intelligence agencies. Espionage played a vital role in the Cold War – in reality as well as in the imagination of a public in East and West fed on a diet of thrillers and spy movies. Despite the huge resources lavished on the intelligence services in both camps, spies were not telling their masters in Washington or Moscow or London how weak the Soviet system was. Before it happened, nobody of significant influence proposed that the entire monolithic structure feared by so many for so long would disintegrate – and within a matter of months. I discount the late British journalist Bernard Levin who at the end of 1988 wrote an unusually prescient piece that foreshadowed events with bizarre accuracy, but at the time even he said that he was indulging in fantasy, not prophecy. Received wisdom was that the USSR faced a long, slow and painful decline and it would be many years, maybe decades, before the satellite states of Central and Eastern Europe escaped the Soviet orbit. As James Baker, the US Secretary of State during part of this story, said: 'Anyone who tells you they knew it was going to happen – well, they're blowing smoke at you.'

For nearly half a century, the Soviets had held on firmly to their spoils of war. The Red Tsars in the Kremlin saw possession of their satellite states as proof of their power and a vindication of their Communist faith, though by the 1980s nationalism had become a stronger impulse than ideology. They had crushed any potential rebellions with ruthless savagery – in Budapest in 1956 and Prague in 1968. It looked as though the Iron Curtain, 300 kilometres of concrete walls and wire fences dividing a continent, was permanent. Many revisionists since have argued that it was inevitable the Soviet empire would fall the way it did. They claim it was a classic case of imperial 'overstretch'; the USSR could not afford to hang on to its burdensome outposts. To the brave Czechs, East Germans and Bulgarians who demonstrated in their hundreds of thousands demanding freedom, the fall of their oppressive regimes did not seem inevitable at the time. If the police answering to their own dictators did not shoot at them, the Soviets might. The Russians had done so before, many times and at a high cost in blood. It was not beyond the realms of possibility that the Red Army, with an occupation force of more than half a million soldiers, would revert to traditional methods. An entire way of life was swept away along with a half-dozen incompetent, corrupt and at times vicious tyrannies. It happened with little violence, apart from a few days in Romania. But it was not a given that these revolutions would be peaceful. There were many occasions when one spark could have lit a fuse that set half a continent ablaze.

No other empire in history had ever abandoned its dominions so quickly or so peacefully. Why did the Soviet Union surrender without a fight? And why at the end of the 1980s? Archives in the USSR and Eastern Europe show how exhausted, bankrupt and painfully aware the Soviets were that communism had failed. The USSR lost its will to run an empire. The imperialists in the Kremlin could have expired slowly, over many decades, like the Ottomans. The Soviet Union could have limped along for a long time as 'Upper Volta with Nukes'. The Soviets chose not to do so.

I have written extensively here about Afghanistan. Some readers might ask why I have set so much of a book that is principally concerned with Central Europe in the hills around Kabul? Losing the war in Afghanistan during the 1980s caused Soviet leaders to abandon their 'outer empire', though at the time they did not see the consequences so logically or clearly. The Soviets' disastrous military campaign in Afghanistan made them reluctant to send troops into battle anywhere else. Without the implied threat of force, they were in no position to hold on to their empire in Europe. The crippling foreign debts incurred by the satellite states, some of which by the late 1980s could barely meet their interest payments, was one of the main factors. The Soviets were no longer prepared to guarantee them, particularly as the collapse in oil prices during the mid-1980s triggered a crisis in the USSR from which the state never recovered. Communism in Europe survived only as long as capitalist bankers from the West were willing to bankroll it.

The human factor is the principal answer, as so often. The last Soviet leader, Mikhail Gorbachev, was a contradictory figure. A new kind of Kremlin chieftain, he could walk, talk and think on his own, unlike the geriatrics who preceded him, whose physical decay seemed to symbolise the condition of their country. He and a few of his advisers thought that the Soviet Union's satellite states were not worth keeping if they could only be held with tanks. He did the right things, but for the wrong reason. His overriding aim was to save communism in the Soviet Union. He believed the people of Eastern Europe would choose to stay allied to the Soviets in a socialist commonwealth. His miscalculations were staggering. Given the chance, the East Europeans joyfully abandoned communism. Nor was Gorbachev able to save it in the USSR. By his own lights he was a failure, but millions of people have cause to be thankful to him. He was consoled for his errors when he was awarded the Nobel Peace Prize in 1990.

A few of the other big personalities who emerge from these pages had a much clearer and more realistic grasp of events than the Soviet leader. The Polish Pope John Paul II, Lech Wałęsa, the workers' leader who defeated the workers' state, Václav Havel, the playwright/philosopher who turned himself into a man of action, and the hard-nosed East German despot Erich Honecker all knew communism was doomed if it was pushed in the right way. As this was the first fully televised revolution in history they became familiar faces. Television had a powerful effect in this drama. When people in Prague saw the Berlin Wall come down, they began to believe they too could overthrow their rulers. Ten days later they did. Nicolae Ceaușescu lost power the moment his face was seen on Romanian television looking confused, then petrified and finally weak as crowds booed him at a Bucharest rally. Four days later he was dead.

East Europeans liberated themselves, but the West played a vital part. The United States 'won' the Cold War and victors tend to write history. The classic narrative is that the toughness of Ronald Reagan brought down the evil empire of the Soviet Union. But Reagan was misunderstood. It was forty years of Western 'containment' that weakened the Soviet Union, and Reagan made no progress whatsoever in his first four years. It was only after Gorbachev emerged and Reagan tried a new, more conciliatory approach that a process began which ended the Cold War. Reagan was admirable in many ways, as this story will I hope show. But his cheerleaders praise him for the wrong things. That is less of an irony than the fate of his successor, George H.W. Bush, a cautious, moderate and sensible man. He valued 'global stability' as one of his primary aims. During periods of 1989, when revolutions were happening so fast, he feared the globe might become seriously unstable. He had been a Cold Warrior in his time and a former head of the CIA. He was leader of the Free World. As documents now show, as well as interviews with his aides, there were times in the middle of the year during which he tried desperately to keep Communist governments in power when he felt that Eastern Europe might be careering out of control.

A word on geography and terminology. This story is about the fall of what the Soviet Union called its 'outer empire' – the six countries that comprised, under the USSR's tutelage, the Warsaw Pact. They are very different places with vastly contrasting histories, cultures, religions and experiences. In the past they had as many antagonisms as alliances. I have not attempted to lump them together to invent a monolithic whole. But one thing they shared historically is that for forty-five years they were joined together, effectively under one ruler. It made sense to stick with the Warsaw Pact countries because they, in the 1989 story, formed a discrete whole. Nor have I covered Yugoslavia, which had begun its agonising death throes in 1989 but was not part of the Soviet sphere. That tragedy requires a book of its own.

Throughout this narrative I have used the terms Central Europe or Eastern Europe interchangeably, and I realise that is a liberty. I do not wish to tread on toes. Entire books have been written about the 'meaning' of Central Europe as an idea and as a place, where it ends and Eastern Europe begins. I intend them to mean the same thing, purely to avoid repetition of the same phrase too often. Similarly with Soviet Union, the USSR and Russia. Obviously I know 'Russian' is not the same as 'Soviet'. I use them loosely solely in the interest of style.

As a journalist in the 1980s I covered many of the events described in this book. It was more than just a story for me. My family had fled Hungary and, a tiny child, I was a refugee from 'behind the Iron Curtain'. From my earliest memories people around me were speaking as though the all-powerful Soviet empire which had transformed our lives would be there for ever. It turned out to be far weaker than everybody supposed. I am lucky that I was there at some of the crucial points as it fell, amid the excitement and drama that I describe here.

London, December 2008.

REVOLUTION 1989

PROLOGUE

Târgovişte, Romania, Monday 25 December 1989.

AT 11.45 A.M. TWO MILITARY HELICOPTERS landed outside the army barracks in Târgovişte, a bleak steel town 120 kilometres north of Bucharest built in the brutalist style favoured by Communist dictators from Stalin onwards. From the larger aircraft emerged six army generals in immaculate uniforms weighed down by gold braid and medals. They were followed by three lower-ranking officers attached to the Romanian General Staff, along with a group of four civilians.

One man, clearly in charge, began to bark orders as soon as the delegation touched down after its thirty-minute flight from the capital. He was silver-haired, fifty-three-year-old General Victor Stănculescu, representative of the newly formed National Salvation Front government that had yet to win complete control over Romania. That morning he had been given an urgent task that required some delicacy and plenty of ruthlessness: he was told to organise the trial of Nicolae Ceauşescu, Romanian dictator for almost a quarter of a century, and his wife Elena. Three days earlier, amidst jubilant scenes of revolutionary fervour, the couple had been forced to flee their capital. They had been captured within a few hours and were held at the Târgovişte barracks while their fate was decided in Bucharest. Forces loyal to Ceauşescu – the Securitate secret police – were still fighting to reinstate him as President. The uncertain revolutionary government finally decided it had to act speedily to bring the Ceauşescus to justice and to show Romanians who was now in charge of the country.

Stănculescu was chosen as the fixer. A tall, elegant man, he was known as a smooth and subtle operator. In the old regime, until 22 December, he had been Deputy Minister of Defence, a long-time friend of the ruling family, regular dinner companion at the Presidential Palace and one of the chief sycophants of the Ceauşescu court. But he was quick to see the wind change and was among the first senior army officers in Romania to pledge loyalty to the revolution. Along with his political flair for timing he was also a meticulous organiser. He had brought with him from Bucharest the judges, prosecutors and defence lawyers needed for a trial. Stănculescu had also attended to other details. In the second helicopter, he had placed a specially selected team of paratroopers from a crack regiment, handpicked earlier in the morning to act as a firing squad. Before the legal proceedings began the General had already selected the spot where the execution would take place – along one side of the wall in the barracks' square.[1]

A 'court room' had been hastily prepared in a shabby lecture hall with rust-coloured walls. Five plastic-covered tables served as the bench. A dock had been set up with two tables and chairs in a corner. The squalid surroundings may have lacked the dignity usually thought necessary for such a momentous event, but from Stănculescu's point of view they served their purpose. When the delegation from Bucharest arrived in the room just after midday the accused were already sitting down, flanked by two guards. Three days earlier Nicolae and Elena Ceauşescu had been the most feared and hated couple in the country. They had the power of life and death over twenty-three million Romanians. They ran the most brutal police state in Europe. Domestic television and the press hailed them each day as virtual demigods. Now they were simply a querulous and confused old couple, exhausted, nervous, bickering together gently. They were dressed in the same clothes they wore when they made their escape from the capital – he in a black woollen coat over a crumpled grey suit, looking older than his seventy-one years. Elena, a year older, was wearing a fawn-coloured fur-collared coat, with a blue silk headscarf covering her grey hair.

That morning in Bucharest, the prominent lawyer Nicu Teodorescu was having Christmas breakfast with his family when he was telephoned by an aide to the new President, Ion Iliescu, and asked by the National Salvation Front to be the Ceauşescus' defence counsel. He replied that it 'would be an interesting challenge'. After thinking it through for a few moments he agreed. The first time he met the couple was in the Târgovişte 'court room' when he was given ten minutes to consult with his clients. The interview did not go well. With so little time to prepare any defence he tried to explain to them that their best hope of avoiding the death sentence was to plead insanity. The idea was brushed aside gruffly. 'When I suggested it,' said Teodorescu, 'Elena in particular said it was an outrageous set-up. They felt deeply insulted . . . They rejected my help after that.'[2]

The 'trial' began at around 1 p.m. There were five military judges, all generals in uniform, and two military prosecutors. It was public in the sense that a junior officer filmed the event, but he was ordered only to show the defendants. At no point were the judges, prosecutors or defence counsel recorded on film. It lasted fifty-five minutes. The ousted dictator snarled throughout most of the proceedings. On occasions he angrily picked up his black astrakhan cap from the table in front of him and threw it back down again as if to emphasise a point. She was far less demonstrative, looking straight in front of her most of the time. Occasionally they would hold hands and whisper to each other, always addressing each other as 'my dear'.

There was no written evidence produced against them and no witnesses were called. From the beginning the ex-President rejected the court's right to try him. 'I recognise only the Grand National Assembly and the representatives of the working class,' he said repeatedly. 'I will sign nothing. I will say nothing. I refuse to answer those who have fomented this *coup d'état*. I am not the accused. I am the President of the republic. I am your commander-in-chief. The National Treason Front in Bucharest . . . usurped power.'

The charges were read out by the prosecutor. Ceauşescu's bravado remained consistent throughout:

PROSECUTOR: These are the crimes we charge against you and ask this tribunal to sentence both of you to death.
1. Genocide.
2. Organising armed action against the people and the State.
3. The destruction of public assets and buildings.
4. Sabotage of the national economy.
5. Attempting to flee the country with funds of more than US$ 1 billion, deposited in foreign banks.
Have you heard this, accused? Please stand up.

CEAUŞESCU: (remains seated) Everything that has been said is a lie. I do not recognise this tribunal.

PROSECUTOR: Do you know you have been dismissed from your position as . . . President of the country? Are the accused aware they face trial as two ordinary citizens?

CEAUŞESCU: I do not answer those who, with the assistance of foreign organisations, carried out this coup. The people will fight against these traitors.

PROSECUTOR: Why did you take these measures of bringing the Romanian people to this state of humiliation today . . . Why did you starve this nation you represented?

CEAUŞESCU: I refuse to answer questions. I do not recognise you. Everything you allege is a lie . . . I can tell you that never in Romania's history has there been such progress. We have built schools, ensured there are doctors, ensured there is everything for a dignified life.

PROSECUTOR: Tell us about the money that was transferred to Swiss banks?

CEAUŞESCU: I do not answer the questions of a gang which carried out a coup.

Elena was restrained, remaining mostly silent except when the prosecutor asked: 'We in Romania could not obtain meat. What about the golden scales your daughter used to weigh meat she got from abroad?' She exclaimed loudly, 'How can you say such a thing?' At one point Ceauşescu said, 'Let's get this over with' and looked at his watch.[3]

The court had a recess of just five minutes to consider its verdict and sentence. Ceauşescu refused to rise when the judges returned. While the death sentences were read out – along with the confiscation of all their property – neither the president of the court nor the prosecution looked directly at the couple. Asked if they wanted to appeal, they remained silent. Under Romanian law death sentences could be carried out no earlier than ten days after they were promulgated, whether there was an appeal or not. But Teodorescu did not raise this in court. Possibly, the Ceauşescus, though they had sent unnumbered people to their deaths, were not aware of this technicality of the law. But it was not a day for legal niceties.*

Justice was summary, squalid and clumsy. Inside the court room, the Ceauşescus' hands were tied behind their backs with rope. Nicolae was dignified and fairly brave in his last few minutes. 'Whoever staged this coup can shoot anyone they want,' he said. 'The traitors will answer for their treason. Romania will live and learn of your treachery.

* The president of the tribunal, Colonel Gică Popa, was well known as a Ceauşescu courtier. A paunchy fifty-seven-year-old, he was a good friend of the dictator's brother, Ilie, who was a Deputy Minister of Defence. On 1 March 1990, less than three months after the trial, Popa shot himself in a mysterious suicide. The causes have never been entirely clear. Popa was not the kind of man to have developed a conscience about the way the court proceedings were run or about his past relationships with the Ceauşescu circle. At the time of his death he was facing investigation on a range of criminal allegations from embezzlement to murder.

It is better to fight with glory than to live as a slave.' Elena wept, and was shrill to the end. Almost in hysterics, she shouted, 'Don't tie us up. It's a shame, a disgrace. I brought you up like a mother. Why are you doing this?' They were escorted forty metres along a corridor into the courtyard of the barracks. As they were being led along, one of the soldiers who had tied their hands said, 'You're in big trouble now.' Elena snarled back at him: 'Go fuck your mother.' Nicolae began singing the first few bars of the *Internationale*. They seemed to have no idea they were to be executed immediately – until they were outside in the courtyard. Then they looked terrified. 'Stop it Nicu,' she shouted. 'Look they are going to kill us like dogs. I don't believe this.' Her last words were 'If you are going to kill us, kill us together.'[4]

The firing squad had been made ready around halfway through the trial. Eight paratroopers had originally been selected by Stănculescu and were flown from Bucharest. They did not know what their mission was until they arrived at Târgovişte. Now three were chosen to perform the deed: Dorin Cârlan, Octavian Gheorghiu and Ionel Boeru. Armed with AK-47 automatic rifles, they were standing by a flower bed waiting for the couple when they reached the courtyard. The executioners' orders were not to fire at Nicolae above chest level. He had to be recognisable in pictures taken after his death. No similar orders were given regarding Elena. The firing squad marched the Ceauşescus to a wall, he on the right, she on the left, a pathetic-looking elderly couple. 'She said they wanted to die together so we lined them up, took six paces back and simply opened fire. No one ordered us to start, we were just told to get it over with,' Gheorghiu said later. 'I put seven bullets into him and emptied the rest of the magazine into her head.' He buckled backwards on his knees. She slumped sideways.[5]

Chaos ensued. Almost the entire complement of the base had watched the execution. Once the firing squad had completed its business, everyone in the courtyard with a weapon began shooting with abandon at the dead bodies until the barracks commander, Lieutenant-Colonel Mares, ordered them to stop. For many years afterwards there were impact holes of over a hundred bullets along one of the walls in the courtyard and window frames more than ten feet above ground.

The corpses were wrapped in tent cloth. They were taken to the capital by helicopter, guarded by the paratroopers who had executed them. They were unloaded on to a playing field at the Steaua Bucharest football team's practice ground, in a south-western suburb of the city. In a macabre twist, their bodies were mysteriously mislaid at some point that evening. Frantic army search parties scoured the area all night before finding them the next morning near a shed within the stadium grounds. What happened to the corpses during those few hours remains a mystery. The next day they were buried at the nearby Ghencea cemetery. In death they were laid fifty metres apart, separated by a pathway, and given new names. Plain wooden crosses were found and hastily painted over in simple lettering with false identities – Popa Dan for the feared dictator Nicolae Ceauşescu and Enescu Vasile for his wife.

PART ONE

COLD WAR

ONE

THE WORKERS' STATE

> They ran to us shouting,
> 'Under Socialism
> A cut finger doesn't hurt.'
> But they felt pain.
> They lost faith.
>
> Adam Ważyk, 'Poem for Adults'

THREE YEARS AFTER the Berlin Wall was built in 1961, the German Democratic Republic's ruling regime devised an unorthodox but lucrative business scheme to earn convertible currency from the West. It started trading in human beings. Officials from the East offered to release political prisoners to West Germany in return for a fee. The traffic began on a small scale, a handful at a time. The first few were prominent dissidents, 'troublemakers' whom the East Germans did not mind packing off into exile. Within a few years it became a well-oiled business with an infrastructure of its own. A few days before each sale the prisoners were taken to a special, highly secret, jail in Karl Marx Stadt (now Chemnitz) run by the GDR's intelligence service, the Stasi. A fleet of buses had been built by a West German contractor just for the purpose of ferrying this precious cargo. The vehicles were fitted with revolving number plates – East German for the return trip from the prison to the border and Federal Republic of Germany (FRG) registrations for the time they were in West Germany. Around twice a week groups of ten or so would be driven, early in the morning, to a border post near the city of Jena, where, unusually, they would be waved through by guards without any document searches. They would be in the FRG by lunchtime, on the road to Hanover.[1]

Over the years around 34,000 people were 'sold' in this way and the trade was sensitive to free-market economic laws. In the mid-1960s the price per head was around DM 40,000; by the mid-1980s, inflation and hard bargaining by the East had pushed that up to more than

DM 100,000. The GDR soon saw it as a way of maximising income. The state made nothing from people who legally applied for visas to see their relatives in the West. So the police arrested thousands of them on trumped-up charges, called them 'political prisoners' and promptly sold them to West Germany. Egon Bahr, for many years the administrator who handled the sensitive business on West Germany's side, said it was clear to him that 'it was part of the GDR's general budget'. Usually payments were made in hard cash, but on occasion the East received bartered goods. In one year, as part of the agreement, the GDR was sent shiploads of bananas, a luxury item in the East at the time, extremely hard to obtain in the shops of Berlin, Leipzig or Dresden. According to one of the most senior East German economists, this 'business venture' netted his massively indebted nation a total of around DM 8 billion. It was the kind of sum without which the country could not survive.[2]

The trade depended on conditions of high secrecy; it depended on a quiescent population in East Germany desperate to leave the country; and it depended on a regime cynical enough to believe it could sell and buy citizens at will. The sales were never officially admitted by the GDR. The authorities of course recognised that it was not the best advertisement for life in the countries that Erich Honecker, East Germany's supreme leader then and for more than two decades, liked to say operated 'actually existing socialism'.

It was socialism as the Soviet Union saw it, imposed at gunpoint on a half-dozen states that did not want it. The empire Joseph Stalin built after World War Two extended as far as the Russian armies reached in the final onslaught against the Nazis in the spring of 1945. There was no other logic to it. By agreement with the Allies at Yalta, the Soviets were essentially allowed to do what they liked in their 'sphere of influence'. Stalin treated the entire region as one vast dominion, barely recognising any national identities in countries of extremely diverse cultures. The Red Tsar in Moscow imposed as his consuls in Prague, Warsaw and Sofia his own henchmen, whose prime loyalty was to the USSR and then to a Communist ideology. They were chosen for their unswerving allegiance to him. Most of them had spent fifteen or twenty years in exile in Russia and had taken Soviet citizenship. They had lost contact with the lands of their birth. The Soviet Union had given them shelter and a cause to believe in. Most were from countries where Communist Party membership had been illegal between the wars and they had spent long periods in jail. When they returned on Stalin's instructions after the war, they were not going home. They went to Hungary or Czechoslovakia or Poland as representatives of a foreign power, to serve the interests of the Soviet Union. They knew what was expected of them: they were to build a socialist imperium in Central and Eastern Europe, with barely any deviation permitted from the Stalinist model. These countries in 1945 had important things in common: they were overrun and occupied by the Red Army and Stalin was about to transform them utterly in his image. Otherwise there were substantial differences, occasionally antagonisms, between them.

The Soviet attempt to turn the region into a stable, reliable and monolithic whole would be a hard task. There was some idealism to begin with. The majority of people who had endured the Nazi occupation were simply relieved the war was over. The experience of the 1920s and 1930s had turned many Central Europeans into socialists, though never anything like as many as the Communists imagined. Only in one country, Hungary, did Stalin permit a genuinely fair election. In November 1945 the Party won 18 per cent of the vote, while the main centre/right party received 51 per cent. The Soviets insisted on a coalition government, while the power of the police and 'state security' was placed in the hands of the Communists. In Czechoslovakia there had been a large industrial working class during the 1920s and 1930s; immediately after the war the Communists were supported by about 35 per cent of the voters. But if democracy would not give them power, the Soviets were determined to take it – one way or another. Using a mixture of bribery, intimidation, deceit and, finally, terror, within three years the Soviets had asserted full control over their new colonies. All other political parties were abolished by the end of 1948, or subsumed into the Communist Party and ceased to exist independently.

The occupation had been accompanied by atrocities from Russian troops who had seen some of the most brutal fighting in the war. It will never be known exactly how many women were raped in Germany, Hungary or Poland after the Soviet 'liberation', but the number certainly ran into hundreds of thousands. Desperate, conquered, exhausted, most people were prepared to put up with the new reality as long as a few improvements came along. Some of these countries were massively unjust peasant societies where serfdom had been abolished less than a century earlier. In large parts of Romania, agriculture had barely changed since medieval times. Generally, they lagged behind Western Europe. The Communists promised to transform all this, eradicate the injustices, start from scratch andbuild a dynamic new commonwealth of equals through rapid development.

For a while it worked. Immediate postwar reconstruction was as fast as in the Western half of Europe. But it started from an extremely low base of devastation and destruction. While in Britain there was still food rationing until the early 1950s, Czechoslovakia and Romania began exporting food fairly soon after the end of the war. The new regimes were given some praise for getting bridges and city centres rebuilt, transport links running again. Initially, at least, peasants were handed small pockets of land taken from the vast *latifundia* estates that stretched through tracts of Eastern Europe. Then the land was taken away again in a rush to organise great collective farms owned by the state. Any enthusiasm there may once have been did not last beyond the purges of the last insane years of Stalin's life.

The Communists had eliminated or cowed into submission their real enemies soon after the war. Opposition politicians were murdered en masse, Church leaders were intimidated into silence and on occasion collaboration. The bourgeoisie had their homes dispossessed and artists were told by commissars of culture what kind of music or painting or literature would henceforth be permitted. All businesses employing more than a handful of people were nationalised and in some countries – Bulgaria for example – no one other than the state was allowed to be an employer of any kind.

Relations between East and West had reached freezing point soon after the war – accelerated by Winston Churchill's 'Iron Curtain' speech in Fulton, Missouri, in 1946. Then, in the winter of 1948–9, a Cold War broke out within the socialist bloc. A leader in one of the 'liberated territories' dared to challenge Moscow. During the war Josip Broz Tito had been a partisan leader in Yugoslavia's struggle against the Nazis, earning respect, and material support, from anti-Communists. He established a Marxist dictatorship in Belgrade but resisted Yugoslavia's descent into the slave status of his Central and East European neighbours. He identified various paths towards socialism, declared himself a 'national Communist' and saw the future for his country as 'non-aligned'. All this was heresy in the eyes of Stalin, who once boasted 'I could smash Tito with a snap of my fingers.' It proved to be not quite so easy. Stalin thought he could afford to show no crack in Communist solidarity in case it was exploited by the West. Tito's defiance could not go unpunished. Anyone in the empire inclined to show sympathy with the Yugoslavs had to be crushed. Stalin organised a campaign against the 'nest of Titoist Trotskyite spies' throughout the satellite states which for the next few years convulsed all of Eastern Europe as Communists devoured their own children in an orgy of bloodshed.

Famous names who had been hailed in the Bolshevik pantheon as heroes suddenly faced arrest on bogus charges, terrible tortures, show trials and, after a ritual 'confession', execution. Such was the fate of loyal Communists like Rudolf Slánský, second in command of the Czech Party, László Rajk, the heir apparent in the Hungarian leadership, and the impeccably Stalinist Tchaiko Kostov in Bulgaria. Scores of thousands of lesser-known comrades were shot in the back of the neck, in the classic Bolshevik manner, or rotted away in prison camps. Often Communists who had survived Hitler's camps and came out as faithful believers in socialism, died at the hands of their comrades – for example Slánský's co-defendant Josef Frank, who after three years in Buchenwald returned to Czechoslovakia as an honoured figure in the ruling regime but was murdered four years later in a Communist-run camp. In turn, those same executioners a month or a year later would themselves be executed. This was the method by which 'socialist order' was imposed. Who was or was not a traitor did not matter – the argument was semantic. Stalin believed in constant purges as the most effective way of retaining power and, when things were not going well, he required a regular supply of scapegoats. The system as created by him could not be in error: *someone* had to be responsible for its failures.[3]

The great monster died in 1953 and his crimes began to be exposed by Nikita Khrushchev three years later. Over time the violent excesses were removed, but essentially the system that Stalin created survived barely reformed for another three and a half decades under various successors. It became less vicious, but through bureaucratic inertia and stagnation just as rigid, inflexible and hungry for control over its subjects. 'Society is the horse and the Party is the rider,' Stalin had said. The horses of Eastern Europe were ridden extra hard and would prefer to have been stabled elsewhere.

Life in the colonies was modelled on the Soviet Union. Anyone living from Varna on the Black Sea to Gdańsk on the Baltic would have recognised how the system worked. It had next to nothing in common with the concepts of socialism defined by any of the faith's idealistic founders. Traditionally, the main principles of socialism involved a commitment to equality, social justice, freedom, new opportunities for the poor, widening choice, respect for the individual and extending democracy. The Soviet model paid no more than lip service to any of these ideals. The rulers used the language of socialism entirely devoid of its content as a means of giving themselves bogus legitimacy. Soviet communism was not a classless society. Theoretically, under Marxism-Leninism, the working class was supposed to be dominant. The proletariat was the dynamic force that drove history, the textbooks said. The workers operated through a 'vanguard' – the Communist Party. It was not like that in real life. In practice, the leaders of the Communist Party sat at the top and did not trust the workers below. Leninists believed that the working class did not know what was in their best interests – they might, after all, if given the choice, allow the bourgeoisie to rule. So the Party would decide what was good for them.

The basis of Soviet communism was the system known as the *nomenklatura*, which is how the Party maintained its power. It was an elaborate network of political patronage on a scale unknown in pluralist societies. Its result was that every important job in the country was held by a member of the Communist Party. Centrally and locally, a series of lists were maintained of all the positions that required Party membership – and of the people fit to hold them. This did not apply only to the top government and economic positions, but in every field: judges, head teachers at big schools, managers of football clubs, the fire service bosses, senior army and police officers, newspaper editors, hospital administrators, college lecturers, theatre and concert hall directors. The lists were enormous – in Czechoslovakia, a country of about nine million people, there were something like 450,000 nomenklatura jobs in every conceivable walk of life. Politics became paramount.*

The Party enforced rigid hierarchical discipline on members rather like the army. The high ranks formed a closed elite, a self-perpetuating oligarchy. They had monopoly power and sole access to the fixed list of the top jobs. They rewarded themselves handsomely – luxurious houses, domestic staff, cars, the best medical care. They could travel occasionally to the West. They had access to a range of goods denied to others, from foodstuffs to furniture, at special shops where they paid

* In ancient Rome a *nomenclator* was a slave whose duty was to remind his or her master of the names of people with whom to exchange greetings. It was particularly important in the rampant office-hunting in the late days of the Republic. The word had good Polish ancestry, according to the *Great Polish Encyclopedia*. In medieval times, it was the Latin term for the list of properties owned by the great landed magnates, and of the tenants who lived in them. The Communists simply borrowed it with no sense of historical irony.

with hard currency to which only they had access. Their children enjoyed all the class privileges of background and a relatively high standard of living. They went to the best schools and universities; they had far better job opportunities than the children of average workers. The children of the nomenklatura did very well – as long as they were obedient and dutiful. The privileges depended on loyalty to the Party. One false step politically, and the job, the car, the nanny, the maid-servant and cook, the children's university education, could all disappear overnight. Every rung of the Party ladder was formally required to execute the orders of the rung above, on the absolute Communist golden rule called, with no hint of irony, democratic centralism.[4]

The rules applied right to the top. The Soviets had ultimate control as they chose – or at any rate approved – the senior political figures throughout their domains. After Stalin died, Moscow interfered just as directly, replacing people whose loyalty they thought suspect, or installing their own Russian-trained favourites. But the Soviets' reach also went down to relatively low levels. Each government minister in every country throughout its empire, each senior army officer, each police chief, each senior judge, had a Soviet 'adviser' with a direct line to the Kremlin.

Navigating these labyrinthine bureaucracies required certain characteristics. Once idealism or revolutionary fervour had disappeared – certainly by the Soviet invasion of Czechoslovakia in 1968 – the system stagnated. The talent pool in the various Communist Parties diminished. Advancement was not on merit, but on obedience and loyalty to the Party. Discretion was rewarded, initiative, originality and brainpower frowned upon. Occasionally some highly intelligent, creative and efficient *apparatchiks* reached senior positions, but they were exceptions. Cynicism ate into the soul of communism. Belief grew irrelevant to Communist functionaries. 'Little by little it became a more or less theoretical thing . . . like the second coming of Christ,' said Oleg Troyanovsky, who had been a diplomat in several of the satellite states after 1945. 'You preach it; you are supposed to believe in it, but no one really takes it seriously. Ideology took second place to national interests, sometimes it was just a cover for national interests.'[5]

The Party had to protect itself from the people. In 1917 the first thing Lenin did was to set up a secret police force, the Cheka. Upon Soviet 'liberation' after World War Two, each of the new Communist regimes had established within weeks similar organisations, all carbon copies of the Soviet model. By the end of 1945 in Budapest there were already hundreds of full-time officers of the hated Államvédelmi Osztály (AVO, the State Security Authority) before work had begun on rebuilding even *one* of the bridges across the Danube blown up in the war. The Stasi in East Germany was called the 'sword and shield of the Party'. Erich Honecker was fond of telling its senior officers later: 'We did not seize power in order to give it up.' Over time the methods of all these agencies became less violent. Torture chambers were turned into filing rooms. The task was still essentially the same, though: to ensure the supremacy of the Party. But there were subtle differences. For the most part, the secret police and their political masters ceased to think they could make people believe in communism. All citizens had to do was pretend they believed and outwardly conform. It became increasingly a spiritless charade.

In the early 1970s the Polish regime hushed up the results of a research project conducted by some government economists. It is easy to see why the information was kept secret. The survey found that the average female Polish worker got up at 5 a.m., spent more than two hours a day travelling to and from work, fifty-three minutes queuing for food, nine hours a day working, an hour and a half a day cooking and on housework and less than six and a half hours a day sleeping. After more than a quarter of a century of socialism, the system was evidently failing. Unlike most religions, which offered rewards in heaven to come, communism promised earthly relief from miseries here and now. It was not delivering.

In the 1950s, after the recovery from war, and the early 1960s there had been spectacular growth throughout Europe, East and West. The socialist countries kept pace with the West. Some of them, such as Czechoslovakia and East Germany, did well. But then began a long slide backwards. Growth peaked at 4.9 per cent between 1970 and 1975, dropping to 2 per cent in 1975–1980 and then continued to fall. In the West, surging inflation and mass unemployment posed problems which more flexible economies managed to deal with effectively. Prosperity returned – on a scale and in a way unimaginable under the Soviet system. The Soviet model was rigid. It was directed for political rather than economic ends, according to a centrally calculated Plan that bore no relation to the market. Prices and wages quickly turned out to be unrealistic, but no matter. They couldn't be changed because they were in the Plan, approved by the bureaucrats in the Party. It led to absurdities big and small. For example, there were no hairpins made in Poland throughout most of the 1970s. The Plan had of course been produced by men and no mention in it anywhere was made of hairpins, so there were none produced. Some women in the Economics Ministry pointed this out but were told it was too cumbersome a matter to change the Plan for such a relatively minor item. Hence – no Polish hairpins. In liberal democracies, and under market capitalism, businesses respond to consumers if they want to stay afloat and politicians respond to voters' demands for better standards of living if they want to stay in power. In one-party states that operate command economies none of these pressures apply.[6]

For a couple of decades communism managed to provide the basics in most parts of Eastern Europe, though in some places only just. But even the showplace countries were never effective at providing consumer goods, which as time went on was what people wanted. From the mid-1960s the gap with the West began to widen, then grew further rapidly. From the start, the new Communist rulers made catastrophic mistakes. The worst was to try to turn light industrial and agricultural economies almost overnight into 'nations of iron and steel'. They did so because that is what Stalin had done in the USSR and the Soviet experience was dogma in all things.

A prime example was the construction from the early 1950s of Dunaújváros (originally Sztálinváros), a vast steel plant and new town on the Danube fifty kilometres south-east of Budapest. It required large amounts of coke and iron ore, neither of which existed in Hungary and had to be imported thousands of kilometres at vast expense from Soviet Central Asia. Of course it made the plant hopelessly uneconomic and a drain on scarce resources. But such practical considerations did not concern the regime. Dunaújváros had to be built, because the Plan said it would be built. Anyone who pointed out the craziness of these grandiose ventures was branded a 'saboteur'. Theory held that the system was perfect, the planners at the centre were omniscient and therefore if anything went wrong it had to be the fault of someone or some group – enemies of the state, terrorists, imperialist agents. The obsession with heavy industry lasted throughout the Communist years. For most of them, the value of the natural resources mined and exported was considerably more than the finished goods produced in East European factories. Many manufactured products were made at a phenomenal loss.

Marxists argued that the absence of private property would abolish corruption. The opposite happened. In economies dominated by shortage, the only way to obtain a vast range of basic goods was through connections. A sophisticated system of barter and favours operated. If a doctor's family needed the fridge repaired an electrician, moonlighting almost certainly illegally from his normal work, would do the job in return for, say, a hospital appointment. A new part was needed for the fridge and there was only one place that could come from. Theft from the workplace was common. An acute observer who knew many of the East European Party leaders thought that one of the worst aspects of communism was a new amorality. 'Many people believed embezzling from the state, from big frauds to petty larceny, was OK. It was argued it was even a way of fighting back, of resistance.'[7]

Eastern Europe was an environmental disaster zone. The great Czech writer Ivan Klíma began one of his finest stories, 'A Christmas Conspiracy', with a description of stepping out into the streets of his beloved Prague. 'The dark, cold, mist smelled of smoke, sulphur, and irritability.' The state was the big polluter. The People's Democracies did not care about the people's environment. In Slovakia, according to the government's own figures, 45 per cent of the country's 3,500 kilometres of river were 'dangerously polluted' in 1980 and 80 per cent of the well water was unusable for human consumption. The fertiliser in the collective farms 'was over-used and poisoned the soil'. Bohemia had the worst air pollution in Europe – the cheap local coal had a dangerously high sulphur content. More than a third of all Czech woods and forests were already dead or dying. In East Germany the authorities banned the publication of pollution levels after some brave journalists found that in the Leipzig and Lausitz regions skin cancers, respiratory ailments and skin diseases were well above the national average and many times higher than the worst levels recorded across the border in West Germany.

The subject people in the People's Democracies hated communism. They hated their own rulers. But they hated the Soviet occupiers most. Russian influence was everywhere and burned as a profound national grievance in proud countries that cherished their independence. The Soviets displayed their power in numberless ways, small as well as big. Naturally the major decisions about war and peace and the deployment of sensitive military hardware were the prerogative of the Soviets. That would have been so in any empire. But even the loyal satraps imposed by Moscow were occasionally offended by the brusque insensitivity with which they could be treated by their masters. The Czechoslovak Foreign Minister in the early 1980s, Bohuslav Chňoupek, was surprised he was not even told when a new range of nuclear missiles was based on his country's soil. 'We got a note from the Soviet Embassy, containing no more than 50 words, saying that medium range nuclear missiles were . . . deployed on the territory of Czechoslovakia and the German Democratic Republic. I called the Prime Minister Lubomír Štrougal to ask if he knew anything about it. He said "No, that's the first I've heard of it." I called Berlin and an official confirmed that the same message had been received there. The deployment had not been discussed with us.'[8]

The Russians seemed unconcerned about trampling over delicate national feelings and symbols. National flags were changed, always with Communist hammer and sickle or steel and hammer emblems replacing old, traditional ones which had existed before. Public holidays conformed with those in the USSR. Children were taught Russian at school as the only foreign language offered. A new constitution in Hungary was introduced, with gross insensitivity, on 20 August 1949 – the traditional Feast Day of St Stephen honouring the country's first king and patron saint. The first line of the constitution contained profuse thanks to 'the glorious Soviet Union for its historic role in liberating our country'. All these slights rankled deeply.

The Russians understood this not only from the major acts of rebellion that would explode every few years when people would declare en masse that they had had enough – Budapest 1956, or Prague 1968. But there was an undercurrent of resentment that seethed daily. The KGB was intensely aware of this hatred. Usually, its permanent spies based in Eastern bloc countries – called 'residents' – wrote reports that their bosses wanted to hear, containing flattering accounts of local reactions. Occasionally, the Soviets sent spies on short fact-finding missions throughout their territories designed to gauge the truth. They would produce a far more accurate picture, filled with small but telling details. A KGB officer in supposedly 'friendly' Bulgaria, where it was said the people liked the Russians, commented that 'Anti-Sovietism flourishes on Bulgarian TV . . . though it is not expressed.' How could he tell, when it wasn't expressed? Most nights on Bulgarian television there were short films about life in the USSR, but the local electricity authorities told him that the power supply was massively increased suddenly, at exactly the time these were broadcast, when the public switched off their sets.[9]

After Soviet tanks crushed the Prague Spring in 1968, the defeated Czech leader, Alexander Dubček, whose dream was to give communism a human face, was summoned to Moscow at gunpoint and given a lesson in great-power politics. The Red Tsar in the Kremlin, Leonid Brezhnev, explained that idealism was irrelevant.

> Your country lies on territory where the Soviet soldier trod in the Great Patriotic War. We bought that territory at the cost of enormous sacrifices and we will never leave it. The borders of your country are our borders as well. Because you do not listen to us, we feel threatened. In the name . . . of the dead who laid down their lives for your freedom too, we are therefore fully entitled and justified in sending our soldiers into your country, so that we may feel secure in our common borders. It is immaterial if anyone is actually threatening us or not. It is a matter of principle. And that is the way it will be – until eternity.

It was from this lecture that the Brezhnev Doctrine came to be developed. Although nobody stated it as a 'doctrine', everybody in Eastern Europe understood its force and what it meant. The Russians would not relax their grip in any of their domains. A threat to the political system in any of the socialist countries would be seen as a threat to the security of the empire as a whole.

The Soviets controlled everything of importance in their territories. But on the other hand it was an extremely curious empire, perhaps unique in history. The imperial power was far poorer than many of its colonial possessions. Soviet soldiers based near Berlin, Prague or Budapest could not help noticing that from their provincial homes in the USSR they were considerably worse-off than their East German, Czech or Hungarian 'hosts'. In traditional European empires, the colonial powers bought, or took, raw materials from the colonies in exchange for manufactured goods. Under the Soviet system – which operated under a trade agreement imposed on the satellites known as COMECON (the Council for Mutual Economic Assistance) – the reverse happened. The Soviet Union supplied large amounts of oil, gas and other raw materials in return for engineering products, consumer goods and food. This caused resentment the other way, as Soviet citizens believed the colonies were getting the best of the deal. When the future Party leader of Hungary Károly Grósz met the Soviet Communist Boris Yeltsin – then a senior Kremlin apparatchik – in Moscow, he recalls: 'I remember visiting Yeltsin . . . We had a quarrel – in the literal sense of the word – because in . . . a blunt, ill-mannered way . . . he told me that the Hungarians should no longer treat them as a milch cow, living off them.'[10] Of course, there were jokes about Soviet colonialism – a Russian agronomist boasted that in the Soviet Union 'we have five crops a year'. Impossible, he was told. 'Not at all. Here we have one in Russia, one from Poland, one from Hungary, one from Czechoslovakia . . .' But it was no laughing matter.

The Russians were able to keep communism in place in this ill-assorted half-dozen countries only as long as they showed readiness to use force. But each separate 'police action' demanded greater effort while yielding fewer satisfactory results. Nowhere were the results as poor as in Poland, the largest of their satellites, with nearly forty million people bitter at the poverty around them and the slave status their old traditional enemy imposed on them.

TWO

A MESSAGE OF HOPE

The Kremlin, Monday 16 October 1978

IT WAS LATE in the afternoon Moscow time that the head of the KGB, Yuri Andropov, was first told the name of the new Pope. White smoke above the Sistine Chapel had signalled the election of Karol Wojtyła, who had adopted the papal title John Paul II. The Soviet spy chief realised immediately the importance of the news. In a sombre mood he began calling his fellow magnates in the Kremlin and repeated to each a prophetic warning: 'Wojtyła represents a menace to Soviet security'. Angrily, that evening, he phoned Boris Aristov, the Soviet Ambassador in Warsaw, and demanded an explanation of 'how could this have happened? How could you possibly have allowed the election of a citizen of a socialist country as Pope?' He said again that the new Pope was 'dangerous for us'. Aristov blamed 'politics in the Vatican' for Wojtyła's elevation, but Andropov was not mollified. He ordered a full and urgent report into how 'this disaster for Soviet interests' had occurred.[1]

Andropov called for as much information as he could obtain on the new Pope. The KGB had bulging files on Karol Wojtyła, dating from the early 1950s when he was a young lecturer in ethics at the Jagiellonian University and a regular contributor of pithy articles in the Catholic press. He was watched more carefully after he was appointed Archbishop of Kraków in 1963. Routine surveillance reports by the Polish secret police, the Slużba Bezpieczeństwa (SB), show that the regime in Warsaw had considered his sermons to be 'subversive'. He was investigated by the State Prosecutor, who thought of charging him, but dropped the idea. Andropov was not unduly disturbed by any of this. He had read countless reports over the years on sermons preached by turbulent priests and he knew most of them could be discounted as no real threat. He was far more concerned by what was said about Wojtyła's character. Even the dry, monochrome dossiers produced by intelligence agents told of the force of Wojtyła's personality, his extraordinary charisma, his messianic fervour and the power of his intellect. Andropov was not cheered by the telegram received at the headquarters of the KGB, from their top man in Warsaw, Vitali Pavlov. Within a few hours of the new Pope's election he reported to Moscow Central: 'Wojtyła holds extreme anti-Communist views. Without openly opposing the Socialist system, he has criticised the way in which State agencies of the People's Republic function.'[2]

Just days after Pope John Paul's enthronement, Andropov and his deputy, Viktor Chebrikov, presented the Soviet leadership with a highly secret plan to counter the threat they now perceived from the Vatican. They urged a propaganda campaign in the Eastern bloc designed to scare people into believing there would be a Soviet backlash against religion of all kinds. In the West there would be 'active measures ... to demonstrate that the leadership of the new Pope is dangerous to the Catholic Church'. In addition, the KGB managed quickly to bug the Pontiff. Sophisticated listening devices were twice found by the head of Vatican security, Camillo Cibin, in the rooms most frequently used by Pope John Paul: his private office, his official office, known as the library, where he held most of his meetings, and his bedroom. Cibin naturally had his suspicions about who was responsible, but the Vatican did not learn until much later that it was certainly the handiwork of Soviet intelligence.[3]

Stalin once famously asked: 'How many divisions has the Pope?' His successors were disturbed by a different question: what if this Pope should embark on an all-out ideological struggle against socialism? This is something none of the religious leaders had seriously attempted anywhere in the Soviet empire. Most of the churches had been suppressed without much of a struggle in the late 1940s and 1950s. There had been a few high-profile 'martyrs' such as the Hungarian Cardinal Mindszenty, who had been tortured and jailed *pour encourager les autres*. But with a mixture of brutality, coercion and subversion in most of Eastern Europe the churches had been driven underground and were not seen as centres of resistance. The Vatican since the war had generally compromised with the Communists. Pope John Paul's predecessor, Paul VI, confessed, almost proudly, that he was pragmatic and had 'hardly followed a policy of glory' in his relations with the Soviets. His duty was to save what could be saved, he said. Communism would be around for a long time to come and Catholics unfortunate enough to be living in the Soviet empire would have to accept it.[4]

But in overwhelmingly and enthusiastically Catholic Poland there was an uneasy truce between Church and State. Though modelled as rigidly on the Stalinist colonial system as elsewhere in the Soviet empire, there were some important differences between Poland and most of the other socialist bloc countries. There had been bloodletting after the Soviet 'liberation' of Poland in 1945. The Communists took over at the point of a gun, as they had done everywhere. Most of those who had returned to Poland after fighting with the non-Communist resistance led by General Władysław Anders were murdered. But later the purges were less vicious. Poland did not suffer the same terror as Hungary, for example, where more than 10 per cent of the population had either been murdered or, after torture by the secret police, the notorious AVO, rotted in internment camps.

The Polish comrades were given more leeway by their masters in the USSR. Only a tenth of the land was collectivised, by far the lowest proportion in the socialist bloc. The Church was allowed a degree of independence. The Party made a historic compromise with the Catholic hierarchy. The Church was permitted to run a few schools. In early 1975 the Polish Church establishment numbered two cardinals, forty-five seminaries, seventy-three bishops, 13,392 churches, 18,267 priests, 35,341 monks and nuns and twenty million weekly communicants. This was considerably more than officially Catholic countries with similar populations. The Catholic University of Lublin was world-famous, with more than 2,000 students. The Polish Church sent large numbers of missionaries to Asia and Africa. About one half of the country's Communist Party members said that they were also regular church attenders, according to an opinion poll. The true number was probably greater, as many would go to mass but not admit it.[5]

Such paradoxes abounded in Poland. The erstwhile Communist fellow traveller Jean-Paul Sartre described it as the land of 'socialist surrealism' and said when he visited in the early 1970s he discovered a world of 'perfect absurdity'. Poland, he said, was

> a country torn from its past by violent measures imposed by the Communists but so bound to that past that the capital demolished in the war was rebuilt from the pictures of Canaletto . . . it has a capital where the citizens have taken up residence again in the 'old city' which is entirely new . . . a country where the (official) average monthly remuneration does not exceed the price of two pairs of socks, but where there is no poverty . . . a socialist country where church festivals

are public holidays . . . a country of total disorganisation where nonetheless the trains run on time . . . a country where censorship and satire both flourish . . . the only country in the socialist bloc whose citizens are freely allowed to buy and sell US dollars but not to possess them . . . a country where one can talk with the waiter in English or German and the cook in French, but the Minister only through an interpreter.'[6]

Poland seemed as anarchic to an orthodox Marxist as it did to a capitalist brought up on free markets. It limped along from economic crisis to crisis, utterly dependent on Western loans guaranteed – and this was another surreal part of Polish socialism – by Communist Party bosses in the Kremlin. Now there was a Pope who understood communism from first-hand experience, and this worried men like Yuri Andropov.

One of the first decisions Pope John Paul made was to visit his homeland. If his election had been a shock to the men in the KGB headquarters at the Lubyanka it had also come as an enormous surprise to the Faithful. The Catholic world for centuries had been used to elderly Italian popes. Here was a vigorous fifty-eight-year-old, a man who still looked athletic, a Slav, an inspirational pastor rather than a Curia politician. He believed God had selected a Polish pontiff for a purpose, and that Poland's suffering in the twentieth century was for a purpose. His own tragic childhood and youth typified his country's painful history. Karol Wojtyła's mother died when he was eight; he lost his only sibling, his elder brother Edmund, three years later and his only other close relative, his father, died in the war when the future Pope was in his teens. He had to train as a priest underground during the Nazi occupation.

Pope John Paul had a natural gift for timing. He wanted to make a substantial difference quickly with a grand, symbolic evangelising mission that would set an early seal on his papacy. In Poland his election had been welcomed with extraordinary scenes of joy. The authorities knew better than to suppress any of the huge public celebrations. Even some among the Communist leadership were secretly proud that a Pole now sat on the throne of St Peter. On the day after the election the Polish Party boss, Edward Gierek, messaged Moscow, probably more in hope than with any real conviction. 'It is good that Wojtyła has left for Rome,' he told Vadim Zagladin, the highly influential senior man at the Soviet Communist Party's International Department.

'Here, in Poland, he would be a disaster. He could create great difficulties for us. In Rome, he is less dangerous . . . to some extent he can even be useful there. After all, he has "exported" a lot of ideas and considerations inspired by communism.'[7]

In early November 1978 the Pope ordered his officials to start negotiations with the Warsaw regime for a papal visit as soon as it could be organised. The talks were delicate. The Polish Communists wanted to refuse, but thought they could not. Denying Poles a visit seemed politically impossible. They believed they would be taking the lesser risk by letting him come on a carefully controlled tour and thought they could even gain some credit for allowing Poles to see their national hero. Some more far-sighted figures warned of the consequences, but they were voted down. The Soviets had to be persuaded to let the tour go ahead. Grudgingly, they agreed. Soviet leader Leonid Brezhnev told Gierek: 'Take my advice, don't give the Pope any reception. It will only cause trouble.' Gierek spoke of the domestic pressures on him and said he couldn't risk vetoing the pilgrimage. Brezhnev reluctantly gave his approval: 'Well, do as you wish. But be careful you don't regret it later.'[8]

The lacklustre Polish leaders regretted it almost as soon as Pope John Paul's Alitalia Boeing jet arrived on the tarmac at Warsaw airport at about 11 a.m. on Saturday 2 June 1979. The Pope knelt, kissed the ground in a gesture that became famous on all his many future foreign tours, opened his arms in a blessing and was greeted by rapturous applause from an adoring crowd. A heatwave hit Poland that summer. Temperatures soared to more than 40°C. The Pope criss-crossed the country for a week. A third of the entire population went outside to see him in person at some point during the visit. People waited for hours in boiling conditions along his route just to catch the briefest glimpse of him. His visit was proof that after three decades, the Roman Catholic Church commanded far more loyalty among Poles than Communism ever had. More than two million people attended some of his outdoor masses. His final address on 10 June, in Kraków, was by the government's own admission the largest public gathering ever held in Poland. His addresses were carefully scripted. Vatican officials had agreed with the Soviets and the Polish regime that at no point would Pope John Paul say anything incendiary or anything that could be taken as an anti-Communist crusade. But they were amazingly powerful speeches that resonated with everyone who heard them. 'I have come to talk about the dignity of man,' he said at one of them. 'Of the threat to man, to the rights of man. Inalienable rights which can be easily trampled on – by man.' Everyone understood what he meant, though technically he never broke the terms of his agreement.

The Pope ran rings around the regime, who had no answer to the sensational power of his appeal and his message of hope. He grasped the nature of public relations instinctively. State television, in a typically cack-handed way, tried to show that the crowds were mainly swooning nuns or elderly peasants. All Poles had to do was go outside on street corners to see otherwise. Their efforts brought more people out to meet the Pope. 'Why did I go?' one congregant managed to tell the Pontiff. 'To praise the mother of God – and to spite those bastards.'[9]

He inspired and galvanised people as nobody had before and he fatally wounded communism – a fact acknowledged by the grim-faced Polish Defence Minister, General Wojciech Jaruzelski. The Pope never said so openly but his triumphant return home amounted to an unmistakable call for resistance to oppression rather than compromise. The call was heeded a few months later.

THREE

SOLIDARITY

Gdańsk, Poland, Saturday 9 August 1980

ANNA WALENTYNOWYCZ was a diminutive woman. In her fifty-first year she was beginning to put on a little weight, but throughout the vast, sprawling Lenin Shipyard she was still called 'Tiny' Anna. Everyone in the shipyard knew Anna, one of the most popular workers in the plant. A bustling figure full of energy and warmth, she had worked there for thirty-three years. Now she was just five months short of retirement.

Orphaned in the war during the occupation of Poland, she became a convinced Communist. Her dream from adolescent years had been to build socialism and the place she would start was at the Lenin Shipyard. She was a model worker, a welder who because of her size was often sent into the most remote and narrow crannies of a ship's frame where other workers could not reach. At twenty-one years old, a proud member of the Rosa Luxemburg work brigade, she won a 'Hero of Labour' award. During 1950, according to the citation, she had increased her work productivity by 270 per cent – 'one of the proudest moments of my life'.[1]

After sixteen years with the blow-torch, Anna rose to the more responsible position of operating a crane. Only a handful of women at the yard – which mostly made cargo vessels for export to the USSR – were qualified to handle such valuable and potentially dangerous machinery. She was married, briefly, in 1964, though the relationship did not last. The following year she was diagnosed with cancer and given less than five years to live. Later, after radiotherapy, the doctors told her they had been entirely wrong and gave her a clean bill of health. Throughout these personal crises she had been a hard worker, patriotic, loyal to communism. She was so well respected that, increasingly, co-workers brought their problems to her. She would try to help in practical ways or, more often, just listen sympathetically to moans and complaints. Gradually, she began to open her eyes and see how short of the ideal socialist paradise her new model Poland had fallen. But Anna was no natural rebel.

In 1970, anger erupted in Poland when, with unerringly crass timing just a fortnight before Christmas, the government increased prices on staple foods like meat, bread, milk and eggs by 36 per cent. There were riots in several Polish cities. The worst were in Gdańsk where police fired on unarmed demonstrators outside the Lenin Shipyard. Forty-four workers were killed.

Anna had then stayed out of trouble, as she did in the next big wave of Polish unrest in 1976, during which thousands of people were arrested. But, like so many of her compatriots, she was becoming radicalised the more she saw of everyday life in People's Poland. She always referred to the workers who had died in 1970 as 'martyrs' and was one of a steadily increasing number who would ensure there were candles and flowers by their gravesides on the anniversary of their deaths. She uncovered a racket involving a large-scale fraud from which some leading figures in the official trade union at the plant, run by the Communist Party, personally profited.

On May Day 1978 she took the first step that marked her out by the Communist apparatchiks in Poland as a potential problem. She joined a group created that day with the cumbersome title 'A Founding Committee of Free Trade Unions on the Coast'. Soon it would gain a more catchy and famous name, Solidarność, or Solidarity. It started a magazine, *Robotnik Wybrzeża* (*The Coastal Worker*), that declared on the front page of its first edition its principal, overriding aim: 'Only independent trades unions, which have the backing of the workers they represent, have a chance of challenging the regime. Only they can represent a power that the authorities will one day . . . have to deal with on equal terms.' Anna Walentynowycz was one of sixty-five activists who signed the magazine's charter on its founding day.[2]

A new round of industrial unrest engulfed Poland in spring and early summer 1980. Strikes hit dozens of factories throughout the country. The railway workers of Lublin, in eastern Poland, blocked the main line that took passengers and goods to the Soviet Union. The strike was settled when the Deputy Prime Minister, Mieczysław Jagielski, went personally to make peace by announcing a government climb-down. But the pattern throughout the 1970s in Poland had been that every time the regime made a concession with one group of workers, it would deal harshly with others somewhere else. This time the regime's eye alighted on Walentynowycz.

At around noon she was summoned to the shipyard's personnel department and fired. The pretext was that she had been spotted over the last few nights at various graveyards around Gdańsk gathering candle stubs. She was planning to reuse them as fresh candles to light at a memorial ceremony for the forty-four 'martyrs' of the 1970 crackdown. A police report accused her of stealing. If she was fired for a disciplinary offence she would lose her pension, even though she was so close to retirement. A low-level official apologised to Anna with the weasel words of cowardly apparatchiks everywhere: 'I'm sorry, but I have no choice. If I don't do it I'll be sacked myself and then somebody else will sack you anyway.' She replied with the spirit of Solidarity: 'Well that other one should refuse to do it, then the other one and the one after that. They can't sack everyone can they?'[3]

The reaction was swift and bold. Five days later a petition called for a strike at the shipyard 'to defend the crane operator Anna Walentynowycz . . . If you don't, many of you will find yourselves in the same dire straits as her.' The petition was signed by seven people who workers would have recognised as campaigners for better working conditions and, especially, for free trade unions outside the control of the Communist Party. The final crisis of Polish communism had begun, typically in a workers' state, with a grievous injustice to an honest worker.

FOUR

THE ELECTRICIAN

Gdańsk, Thursday 14 August 1980

THOUGH ANNA WALENTYNOWYCZ was such a popular figure and her treatment had been so clearly unfair, the activists in Gdańsk who issued the strike call were uncertain how the workers would react. The big towns on the Baltic coast were relatively quiet throughout the summer. Party chieftains locally were beginning to think that perhaps the worst of the troubles were over. In the days since Walentynowycz was fired, hundreds of copies of the strike appeal had been distributed on the trams and trains which brought workers to the yard from the outlying housing estates. The strike was due to begin at dawn.

At six a.m., when the first shift clocked on, about 100 workers began to march through the shipyard. Some held banners demanding the reinstatement of Walentynowycz and others were shouting to their workmates to join them. There were not many, but the management was beginning to feel worried. A half-hour later around 500 had joined the demonstration. They reached the shipyard Gate Two, one of the main exits, and were ready to march into the city. There they hesitated, remembering it was when they marched into central Gdańsk that the forty-four workers were killed in December 1970. During this pause the director of the shipyard, Klemens Gniech, climbed on to a crane to address the strikers. Gniech was an energetic, tough but generally fair-minded man who was respected, even well liked, by his workforce. In a smooth speech he promised that he would discuss their demands as long as the workers returned to their jobs. For a while it seemed as if his audience would be appeased. There were mutterings amongst them that they might as well return to work. At this point, a short, squat man with a large moustache clambered up on to the crane next to Gniech. He tapped the manager on the shoulder and began to improvise: 'Remember me?' he asked. 'I worked here for ten years and I still feel I'm a Lenin Shipyard worker. I have the confidence of the workers here, though it's four years since I lost my job.' He went on to talk about Walentynowycz and about the need for an independent trade union. To resounding cheers and applause Lech Wałęsa called for an 'occupation strike'. Immediately, a strike committee was formed – with Wałęsa at its head – and Gniech beat a retreat. He agreed to negotiations and as a signal of good faith he dispatched his own shiny black Volga limousine to collect Anna Walentynowycz from her home to take part in the negotiations.[1]

The occupation strike was one of the most successful weapons used by Solidarity over the succeeding years. It was a carefully calculated tactic designed primarily to protect strikers from being attacked on the streets by police. Taking over a factory filled with hundreds of workers would require a military operation – a costly and potentially bloody enterprise only the most brutal governments would adopt. It had other advantages too: in effect, it holds valuable machinery hostage and it prevents the management employing 'blackleg' labour. Psychologically, it turned out to be vitally important by holding strikers' morale together in siege-like conditions and reminding workers that they could control the workplace.

The strike spread rapidly. Within hours workers at factories in Gdynia, a few kilometres away, joined in. They were soon followed by all the other 50,000 workers in the Gdańsk region. The government had immediately cut all telephone lines between the Baltic coastal towns and the outside world, in a futile attempt to contain the protests. Naturally, neither television nor radio mentioned the strikes, but everyone in Poland knew about them.

While Wałęsa and the other strike leaders were closeted in a lecture room in the shipyard's health and safety centre negotiating with Gniech, conditions in the rest of the yard were growing increasingly uncomfortable. On the first night more than 2,500 strikers slept on foam mattresses and across benches in the main halls or in the hospital. The mood was uneasy, expectant and fearful. It was not revolutionary. 'We're thinking about better working conditions, more money and the right to strike,' Wałęsa declared. Nobody was talking about challenging communism. Support for the strike wavered, depending on the news from the negotiating room. Gniech was under instructions by the Party bosses in Warsaw and locally to play for time, but eventually to make enough concessions to secure a deal. Their aim, as so often in the last decade, was to divide and rule. They wanted to reach separate agreements with different groups of workers so that at no time could they feel united. In August 1980 it nearly worked.[2]

The key moment came on the third day, the 16th. Early that morning Wałęsa's strike committee accepted a package offered by Gniech. It included the reinstatement of Anna Walentynowycz and Wałęsa to their shipyard jobs, a pay rise of 2,000 złoty a month (about 7 per cent), an increase in various family allowances roughly on a par with the police and immunity from prosecution for all the strikers. The major sticking point had been a demand that a memorial should be built to honour the dead workers of December 1970. On that Saturday, with tension growing throughout Poland, the Party bosses were so desperate to reach a settlement that even this big symbolic concession was made.

But almost as soon as hands were shaken on the deal it fell apart amidst confusion and chaos. Gniech announced on the shipyard's loudspeaker system that the strike was over. Wałęsa punched his fist in the air and declared: 'We've won.' He quickly sensed something was wrong. Scores of workers started to head for the gates – and home. But some people in the crowd began yelling 'traitor' and 'sell-out'. The crowd was wavering. They were swayed by a representative of other local workers who were also on strike. They depended on the Lenin plant – the region's biggest employer – as the flagship of Gdańsk industry to secure a deal that would be favourable for all of them. A big, burly woman with short cropped hair, Henryka Krzywonos, had been leader of the Gdańsk tram drivers for years. She was not a great speaker but she was able to make her point forcibly. She pleaded with the shipyard workers not to 'sell out too cheaply and leave your comrades in the lurch'. She said they must not allow workers in different industries to be picked off by the regime one by one. 'If you abandon us we'll be lost. Buses can't face tanks.' Cheers echoed throughout the yard.

'All right then,' said Wałęsa, 'if the majority decide then we'll carry on striking. Who wants to carry on?'

The entire hall resounded with the cry 'We do.'

'Who does not want to strike?' There was silence.

'So we will strike . . . It will be a solidarity strike. I will be the last to leave the yard.'[3]

Lech Wałęsa led the first real workers' revolution in history. The Bolsheviks in October 1917 had grabbed power for themselves in the name of the proletariat. It took Wałęsa, an ordinary worker with extraordinary gifts, to see how authentic workers' power could be used against the Bolsheviks' heirs.

He was born on 29 September 1943, in the small village of Popowo, about 150 kilometres north-west of Warsaw. He never knew his father. Soon after the baby's birth, Boelek Wałęsa, a carpenter, was hauled off to a Nazi labour camp, where he died eighteen months later. Lech's mother, Feliksa, remarried her late husband's brother, Stanisław, as was quite common practice in Poland at the time. Lech loathed his stepfather, whom he used to call a 'money-grabber'. He and his three natural siblings got on badly with his three stepbrothers. The split in the family 'was a burden that cast a shadow over my whole childhood', he said.

Feliksa was extremely devout. Wałęsa used to say repeatedly, 'I sucked in religion from my mother's breast.' He hated the countryside from an early age. His maternal grandparents had originally bought 150 hectares of land, but it had all gone during the German occupation. He was brought up in peasant poverty. Home was a shack with a wooden roof that was cracked but was never repaired. There were just two rooms for all of them – two adults and seven children.

Wałęsa was a typical child of the People's Republic, with all its soaring hopes and bitter disappointments. The relationship started with a seemingly sweet deal. He, along with so many young Poles, wanted to get away from rural misery. The Party/State dreamed of reordering everything and aimed to depopulate the countryside to create an urban working class which, unlike the peasantry, would be loyal to communism. The first part worked – Poland industrialised at breakneck speed. The second never did.

Wałęsa did badly at school. He had quick intelligence but poor powers of concentration and was demotivated. As soon as he could after graduating – just – from elementary school, he left Popowo, never to return. He went to the nearest big town, Lipno, where he attended a vocational school to learn a trade. He trained originally as a mechanic and later as an electrician. In Lipno, he found work at the POM, a depot that serviced farm equipment. In 1964 he started two years of military service during which he rose to become a corporal. He toyed with the idea of staying in the army but decided against it. Instead, he moved to Gdańsk – formerly the free-port of Danzig – in the footsteps of millions of Poles who went to the city in two waves of postwar migration. The first, immediately after 1945 when the territory was reclaimed by Poland following Nazi occupation, resettled Poles into areas where the German population had been brutally forced out. The second, in the 1960s, brought people like Wałęsa into the city as part of the Communists' programme to transform Poland into a modern, industrial socialist state. In 1967 Wałęsa found work at the fast-expanding Lenin Shipyard. People who knew him then remember an energetic, talkative, wise-cracking young man, with few political opinions. He had some basic ideas which had not changed much from his teens. He was a strict Catholic, instinctively anti-Russian like most Poles, and sceptical of official propaganda. In those days he was a socialist, but not in any ideological way. He would not, probably could not, spout Marxist-Leninist dogma. Yet he took seriously one part of socialism and the ideology of the workers' state. He believed in the primacy of the working class and continued to do so for two decades.

When he began work at the Lenin Shipyard, Wałęsa was amongst the aristocracy of the Polish proletariat. Workers there received the highest industrial wages in the country, but conditions were woeful. Most Polish factories and mines resembled Dickensian England rather than a Marxist utopia. The Lenin Shipyard, said Wałęsa, 'looked like a factory filled with men in filthy rags unable to wash or urinate in lavatories. To get down to the ground floor, where the only lavatories were situated, could take at least half an hour, so we just went anywhere. You can't imagine how humiliating these working conditions were.'[4]

Safety standards were appalling. Accidents were common. There seemed to be no regard for the welfare of workers. Soon after he started at the shipyard there was a serious incident on the *Konopnicka*, a trawler ship that was being fitted throughout 1967. The job was heavily behind schedule and 2,000 workers were labouring to get the vessel completed. Safety regulations – theoretical at the best of times – were entirely ignored in the final rush. Fuel leaked into the hull and, sparked by a welder's blowtorch, there was a devastating explosion. Twenty-two of Wałęsa's fellow electricians were burned alive. He was unharmed, but the accident changed him profoundly. He grew more serious and took more interest in politics, especially workers' rights. For the first time, he became active in the official trade union and joined the health and safety committee in the plant. Living conditions outside the shipyard were equally poor. Younger, unmarried workers lived in hostels, three or four to a room. Kitchens and showers were shared with other dormitories at the end of a long corridor. They were ugly, miserable, squalid places. Fights broke out regularly in the male blocks – particularly on paydays, when in time-honoured fashion Polish workers would drown their sorrows in vodka. Surrounding the hostels were depressing residential zones with unlit, unpaved streets, wastelands of broken glass and uncollected rubbish. Basic public services were scandalously poor.

In 1969 Wałęsa met and quickly married a slender, petite, dark-haired woman who appeared frail and fragile but had a strong and determined personality. Mirosława Golos, brown-eyed and pale-skinned, was just twenty but looked even younger. She worked in a florist's shop near the shipyard. She came from a poor peasant background similar to Wałęsa's in a tiny hamlet, Krypy, a few kilometres from Gdańsk. She often missed school because she had to help on the family farm and she barely completed elementary grade. But she was intelligent, practical, down to earth. She too was an extremely devout Catholic and at that time hated communism rather more than he did, principally on the religious grounds that it was an atheistic creed. Soon after their first meeting, Wałęsa asked her to use her second name, Danuta (Danka for short).

Wałęsa was a new father when the food riots erupted in December 1970. He was a shop steward with the official union, but played a minor role in the strikes. He was not a radical voice, though he was determined to keep alive the memory of the Gdańsk shipyard 'martyrs'. Those protests toppled the Communist Party leader since 1956, Władisław Gomułka, and shook the regime. Gomułka was one of the most interesting of all the East European Marxists – a fiercely intelligent man who began his rule with a courageous effort to steer an independent path from Moscow, but ended as an even more orthodox figure than his masters in the Kremlin. He failed to deal with the systemic disasters of the Polish economy and its state of near-bankruptcy.

When Gomułka was ousted, Wałęsa had high hopes for the new Communist oligarch in charge of Poland, Edward Gierek. He admired the straightforward, no-nonsense style adopted by Gierek, who had been a manual labourer. Most leading Polish Communists came from the intelligentsia – a class which on the whole Wałęsa treated with contempt and used often to label 'those stuck-up, snobby jerks'. But Wałęsa quickly became disillusioned with Gierek, despite the leader's proletarian credentials. He could do no more than his predecessor to halt the country's slide into ruin. Gierek tried to win support by bringing the population a steadily improved standard of living and stable prices. For a while he succeeded. Cynically he would tell his aides in private: 'Right, we will give them meat and promises and that will shut them up ... stuff their mouths with sausage.' But he could do it only for so long and his sole method was by heavy borrowing from the West, which subsidised food and increased workers' wages.

It could not last. In June 1976 Gierek was faced with a fresh cash crisis. Although he knew the political risks involved he could think of no alternative but to raise prices – by 60 per cent on bread and milk, 69 per cent on meat, 100 per cent on sugar. Even on official calculations the cost of living would rise by nearly a fifth. Predictably, a wave of strikes began, along the Baltic coast, in Warsaw and elsewhere. This time Wałęsa was at the centre of events. He began to speak regularly in front of large crowds and found that for an uneducated man he had a gift of eloquence. He was shrewd, witty, coarse at times, passionate at others and always sounded like an average worker, a man of the people. He was brilliant at off-the-cuff extempore performances. But when he tried to read from a prepared text he sounded curiously wooden and stilted. He loudly criticised the official trade unions, which he said were representing not workers but the bosses. One particularly fiery speech that summer landed him in trouble. He was summoned to the director's office where Klemens Gniech, then new to his job, was flanked by two officers from the SB, the Polish Secret Service. They told him to keep quiet in public. He refused. Shipyard security guards arrived and dragged him out of the main gate. His dismissal notice arrived a month later.[5]

Elsewhere in Poland, industry was in a state of siege. Workers from the vast Ursus tractor plant in the suburbs of Warsaw, one of the biggest factories in the country, marched to the transcontinental railway lines and halted the Paris-to-Moscow Express. In Radom, a city in south-west Poland, workers from the weapons factory struck. On 25 June, when they demonstrated on the streets demanding negotiations with their management, police opened fire with semi-automatic rifles. In the riot that followed a huge crowd went on the rampage and burned down the Communist Party headquarters. Seventeen people were killed and more than 2,000 arrested. That evening the Prime Minister, Piotr Jaroszewicz, looking deeply worried, appeared on television and announced he was withdrawing the price rises 'for more consideration and consultation with the workers'. That restored the peace and workers drifted back to their factories. But the police and security services took their revenge on the Ursus and Radom workers. During the following weeks, at various prisons and hastily established 'centres of special rehabilitation', most of the thousand or so who had been arrested were beaten and tortured. Hundreds were forced to run a gauntlet through two lines of truncheon-wielding thugs, called with a deliberately malicious irony the 'path of health'. Wałęsa escaped that punishment but in the next few years, by his own admission, 'I must have been picked up by the police at least 100 times.' Usually it was for short periods of interrogation; sometimes, along with scores of other trade union activists, he would be locked up on forty-eight-hour warrants. He found odd jobs as an electrician, but it was a struggle making ends meet for his growing family. Eventually, he landed regular work as an engine mechanic with the ZREMB works, which made agricultural machinery. To raise extra money he moonlighted, repairing old cars.

He began to educate himself – in political theory, economics, history and law. Though contemptuous of intellectuals, he had a strong belief in learning. He was much cleverer and better-informed than he looked or sounded. Wałęsa began to attend meetings organised by a group of dissident thinkers, KOR (Komitet Obrony Robotników), the Committee for the Defence of Workers. KOR's leading figures were the brilliant philosopher Jacek Kuroń and the historian and journalist Adam Michnik. Both had been Communists but were jailed on charges of sedition, principally for criticising the Party from the idealistic left. Kuroń, for example, argued that the Soviet empire was in the hands of a new class of bureaucrat whose efforts were benefiting no one but themselves. He wanted a revolution that would rid society of 'parasitic apparatchiks' and create a true workers' state. The parasites took their revenge and he was sent to prison for three years.

The immediate aim of KOR was to help the Radom and Ursus workers who had been jailed after the 1976 riots. It was the first organisation of its kind in the socialist world. KOR activists – there were quickly about 150 – offered the families financial help and legal assistance. The organisation's longer-term vision was to forge a unity between intellectuals and workers – the only way Kuroń and his associates believed that the Communists could ultimately be challenged. It was an idea that appealed strongly to the fledgling workers' leader Lech Wałęsa. One of KOR's most successful ventures was to establish 'flying universities'. Teaching at the official universities was rigidly orthodox and the lecturers were carefully watched. KOR established a roster of supportive writers, academics and thinkers who toured the country holding discussion groups with workers. 'Lectures' were held unofficially at private homes.

Karol Wojtyła and a few other Catholic priests began to forge links with KOR leaders – the Archbishop used to travel regularly from Kraków in plain-clothes disguise to meet them at the Warsaw flat of the writer Bohdan Cywiński. This was significant because clerics from a church that was traditionally conservative, and leftist intellectuals, often Jewish, were generally wary of each other. Word of the Archbishop's support gradually became more public. In May 1978 when Stanisław Pyjas, a student KOR activist in Kraków, died in the custody of the secret police, the Archbishop held a special mass for him in front of a congregation said to number 20,000 people.

KOR was the godfather of the Free Trade Union organisation which Lech Wałęsa joined, along with Walentynowycz, as soon as it was founded. But although he was well known among workers in Gdańsk, at first Wałęsa was not marked out as the obvious leader. That seemed to be Andrzej Gwiazda, a reserved, unbending forty-five-year-old who had planned the shipyard strike and laid most of the groundwork for it. Over the last two years he was the main spokesman for the free trade union movement in Gdańsk. The two men hated each other on sight. They could not have been more different. Gwiazda had intense, piercing eyes, a passionate nature and was a true radical. Wałęsa's relaxed, hail-fellow-well-met manner revealed a pragmatic man who could cut deals and who understood the art of compromise. 'Lech's 100 per cent a politician,' Michnik used to say.[6] Gwiazda and his equally inflexible wife Joanna organised the Union meetings, worked the phones, operated copying machines. He wrote the rousing call urging workers to support Anna Walentynowycz and he ensured people knew about it. He imagined he would be the strike leader. But all that changed the moment Wałęsa climbed over the perimeter fence of the Lenin Shipyard early on the morning of 14 August 1980 and returned to his former workmates. Now and for the next decade he was the unchallenged leader of Polish labour.

It had been easy to outmanoeuvre Gwiazda. The far harder task was to come. Wałęsa's goal was to inflict enough damage on the regime to win the right for free trade union recognition, but not to bring down the system. His main fear was that the Soviets would intervene with tanks as they had done every other time since the war when they felt their empire was under serious threat. Wałęsa and his advisers were careful not to demand too much. They emphasised they were not leading an insurrection, but essentially an industrial dispute and they had no wish for yet more Polish workers to become martyrs.[7]

Over the next three weeks Poland practically ground to a halt in a general strike. With no trains working or lorries on the roads, Warsaw and the other cities were receiving no food deliveries. This time the strike was solid – the regime was unable to split the workers, as always before, or reach separate local settlements. An increasingly desperate Gierek, nervous about his own position, dispatched his top officials to Gdańsk to negotiate a deal. This gave Wałęsa status as the acknowledged leader of the strikers. He proved to be a shrewd, wily deal-maker. Despite his own personal views on intellectuals, he summoned two of them from Warsaw to act as advisers and check on the small print of the agreements. 'We are only workers,' he used to say with *faux* modesty and purely for public consumption. 'These government negotiators are clever men. We need someone to help us.' Bronisław Geremek, a pipe-smoking scholar of medieval history, and Tadeusz Mazowiecki, editor of the Catholic magazine *Więź* who had good relations with the Pope, went to Gdańsk and began acting as Wałęsa's close advisers.[8] A historic agreement was finally signed on 31 August. The Gdańsk Accords gave workers, for the first time in the Soviet bloc, the right to be led by representatives they chose for themselves, the right to form free associations, and the right to strike. To Wałęsa, these were the vital concessions by the Communists. 'We wouldn't have risked our necks for a few thousand złoty. But this was really worth winning,' he said. A month later the Polish government legalised the new free trade union, which now called itself Solidarity. Wałęsa had won a unique victory and become a household name throughout the world.

The magnates in the Kremlin were appalled. The Poles were challenging the most sacred myth which underpinned their empire – that the Soviet Union acted for the working class. They were horrified and scared by the slogan adopted by Solidarity, with its deliberate echo of Marx and Engels: 'Workers of all enterprises – Unite'. They were furious with the satraps they had installed in Warsaw, supposedly to rule on Moscow's behalf. The Polish Communists were showing weakness and incompetence. There was nothing unusual in that, from the Kremlin's point of view. For years Poland had been their most troublesome colony, the hardest to keep in any sort of socialist order. But it was the biggest, with a population of forty million, and it bordered neighbouring Soviet republics whose loyalty to the Union was suspect. The Party chieftains were worried that the 'contagion' of Solidarity would spread and take root inside the USSR itself. Already in Lithuania and Latvia there were some dissidents uttering heresies such as demands for free trade unions in the Baltic republics. By the military, Poland was seen as vital strategically as the main supply route for the Soviets' 200,000-strong army in East Germany.

But they were tired old men who lacked the energy, will and imagination to deal with a crisis they knew was upon them. The decision-makers in the Kremlin were all in their late sixties or seventies and mostly in poor health. The Boss – more *capo di capi* than Tsar – was still Leonid Brezhnev, now seventy-six. The others all deferred to him, even when he was in his dotage and unable to work more than an hour or so a day. No major decisions were taken without his approval as General Secretary of the Soviet Communist Party. Towards the end of his life he appeared a ludicrous figure to be in charge of one of the world's two superpowers. But he had not always been so. For more than a decade after he took power in 1964 from Nikita Khrushchev, he was a vigorous and impressive man, gifted in many ways. He may not have been much of an intellectual but he understood intuitively the nature of power and nobody knew better than he how the Soviet system worked.

Brezhnev had been a great bear of a man, immensely strong and physically fit. But from 1974 he began developing arteriosclerosis of the brain and suffered a series of strokes. He stumbled as he walked and slurred his speech. At moments of high stress he blacked out. The disease profoundly changed his personality. In his prime he had an easy-going charm, a cheerful disposition and a good sense of humour. He became a peevish old man as his nervous system collapsed. He was now prey to deep black moods and would often burst into tears for no obvious reason. He started to suffer from chronic insomnia. Brezhnev's condition was aggravated by an addiction to sleeping pills and opiate-based tranquillisers. Occasionally he would take too many and end up comatose, followed by days of severe sluggishness. His doctors stopped prescribing the drugs, but his retinue of sycophantic cronies slipped him the pills without the physicians' knowledge. Invariably he took them with his favourite Zubrovka vodka. The doctors and his more devoted security guards realised what was happening and would dilute the vodka with boiled water. Brezhnev sometimes looked at the glass and said: 'There's something not quite right about this vodka.' The

Kremlin's chief physician, Yevgeni Chazov, concluded that Brezhnev's addiction 'contributed to the collapse of the national leadership'.[9]

He spent his days reclining on a divan closeted away with his cronies, the chief of whom was his long-time friend, Konstantin Chernenko, whom Brezhnev had made head of Communist Party appointments. Brezhnev used to love driving fast cars. He had a large collection of BMWs which he would steer at dangerous speeds on the narrow corniche roads around his villa in the Crimea. Now his favourite pastime was playing dominoes with his bodyguard Alexander Ryabenko. He displayed ever-increasing vanity. By the time he died he had accumulated more medals and honours than Lenin, Stalin and Khrushchev combined. Entire history books were written about his war record – in truth undistinguished – which hagiographers absurdly presented as the crucial contribution towards the defeat of Hitler.

It was evident that Brezhnev was in serious decline but the truth about his health was a state secret known only to a few Kremlin insiders, close family members and some bodyguards sworn to silence. Elaborate efforts were made to hide the full extent of his infirmities from the Russian people and to prepare him for public appearances. On the big holy days of Soviet socialism, May Day and 7 November, the official anniversary of the Bolshevik Revolution, special escalators helped him climb up to the Lenin Mausoleum in Red Square. He was determined to be seen and to show the world that the Soviet Union was in safe hands. He even managed to make fairly frequent speeches, though his doctors admitted later that they were never sure that he would make it back from the podium. Speechwriters were told to ensure that they never used words he had trouble pronouncing. Doctors with resuscitation equipment travelled with him wherever he went. Chazov, as Brezhnev's personal physician, went along with this charade reluctantly. The effort 'to hide the General Secretary's state of health was not only hypocritical but sadistic', he said later.[10]

A troika of Party oligarchs ran the Soviet Union's day-to-day affairs. Yuri Andropov was heir presumptive. No previous head of the KGB had climbed to the very top in the Soviet Union, but the devious sixty-nine-year-old spy chief had been carefully plotting for years to gain the prize. He was a man in a hurry, already diagnosed with a serious kidney condition, who knew his own time was limited. He was the first to be told of the details and extent of Brezhnev's illness, but kept the information to himself for a long time, justifying the subterfuge to Chazov. 'For the sake of peace in the country and in the Party, for the well-being of the people, we must keep silent,' he told the doctor. 'If a struggle for power begins in conditions of anarchy, at a time when there is no strong leadership, it will lead to the collapse of the economy and the entire system.'[11] Andropov had a sharp analytical mind and was deeply sensitive to the dangers of 'losing' any of the satellite states of Eastern Europe. He had been Soviet Ambassador to Hungary in 1956 and played a prominent part in the brutal response to the uprising, when 2,500 Hungarians died. In 1968 he was a strong voice in favour of suppressing the Prague Spring. Andrei Gromyko, seventy-one, had been Foreign Minister for a quarter of a century, the stern, unbending face of Soviet diplomacy, known by successive Western governments as 'Comrade Nyet'. Marshal Dmitri Ustinov, seventy-two, the Defence Minister, was a martinet with deeply orthodox views. He had been a bemedalled hero in World War Two, the Great Patriotic War, but not for fighting. He was the efficient organiser of the evacuation of the Soviet defence industry eastwards to Siberia, which contributed hugely to Russia's victory. He still saw it as his job to speak for the military industrial complex – by 1980 the Soviets were producing 350 fighter planes, 2,600 tanks and heavy guns and 350 nuclear missiles each year.

A key decision facing the Soviets was what to do about Poland. It had to be referred upwards to the highest level. Though Brezhnev's attention span was brief and his powers had waned, the major decisions were left to him. The Soviets were well aware at every stage of the deal Gierek was making with Solidarity. They had been kept well informed by the Polish Communists and by their own man on the spot, Ambassador Boris Aristov. They did not like it, but grudgingly they accepted it. As Aristov reported, it was the only way to get Poland back to work.

The ink on the Gdańsk agreement was barely dry before the Soviets started looking for ways to subvert it. They regarded the Accords as merely a tactical retreat. Andropov ordered his own aides in the Lubyanka to draw up a response to the comrades in Warsaw. Just three days after the Gdańsk agreement was signed a highly secret message was sent to Gierek and the Polish leadership. The text had been approved by Brezhnev, Andropov and Gromyko and seen by only a few Kremlin aides outside that trusted circle. It was meant as a rap across the knuckles and a warning that the Polish Communists had to crack down on Solidarity, whatever deal may have been reached with them. The Gdańsk agreement, it states:

is a very high political and economic price for the 'settlement' you have achieved. Of course, we understand in what conditions you have had to take this difficult decision. The agreement practically means legalisation of the anti-socialist opposition ... Now your task is to prepare a counter-offensive, and to win back the lost positions in the working class and among the people ... To make efforts to restrict the activity and influence of the so called 'self governed' trade unions ... To actively infiltrate the so called 'self governed' trade union with people loyal to the Party ... In these conditions, you should clearly indicate the limits of the permitted. You should say openly that the law forbids statements against socialism.'[12]

But Gierek and his entourage were reluctant to embark on a renewed conflict with Polish workers which they thought they would lose. Instead they breathed a sigh of relief that the strikes were over – and proceeded to drift. In Moscow the magnates were losing patience. They met inside the Kremlin on 29 October amid general agreement that there was a 'counter-revolution' in Poland, which had to be reversed. Brezhnev felt this was important enough for him to be there in person. He complained that 'Wałęsa is travelling from one side of the country to the other and they honour him everywhere across Poland. The authorities are doing nothing to stop this outrage ... Polish leaders keep their mouths shut and so does the press. Not even television is standing up to these anti-socialist elements.' The newest and youngest member of the Soviet leadership, Mikhail Gorbachev, agreed. He said: 'We should speak openly and firmly with our Polish friends. Up till now they haven't taken the necessary steps. They're in a sort of defensive position and they can't hold it for long – they might end up being overthrown themselves.'

Gromyko was still furious about the rapturous reception the Pope had received in Poland the previous year. He accused Polish priests of inciting people to 'political hooliganism' and inciting 'counter-revolutionary disturbances'. He said: 'The Polish Communist Party isn't putting much effort into the struggle ... things have reached the point when thousands upon thousands of people are crawling on their knees before the Roman Pope.'[13]

Instinctively, the Russians thought of a military answer, the kind of brutal solution they had adopted at other times they perceived a threat to the socialist bloc. Their first reaction was to order the Soviet General Staff to lay plans for a full-scale invasion of Poland. But they swiftly decided against military intervention. The difficulties were immense. They did not want worsening relations with the West and they knew the Poles would fight back. Instead the Soviets tried to bluff the Poles into thinking that they *would* send in tanks, hoping to make the Polish leadership act for themselves. It was an elaborate ploy. The most senior generals from all the Warsaw Pact countries were summoned to Moscow on 4 December to put the final touches to long-planned exercises, codenamed Soyuz, which were due to start at midnight four days later. During the meeting the Soviet delegation told the Polish generals, in private, that in fact Soyuz was not going to be an exercise, but a real invasion of Poland. They let the Poles see the maps which showed exactly where the Pact's armies would be deployed in a carbon copy of the invasion of Czechoslovakia a dozen years earlier. The Soviets let it be known that the East Germans were insistent on the invasion and had promised three divisions. The prospect of German invasion troops entering Polish towns, according to the Soviets, really worried the generals from Warsaw. Secretly, Russian officials were reporting back to the Kremlin what the real purpose of their plan was, so we know now that there was never a real intention to invade Poland. 'We must subject the Polish leadership to constant pressure,' Marshal Ustinov told Brezhnev, Andropov and other colleagues. 'We are planning manoeuvres in Poland . . . we should extend these manoeuvres so as to create the impression that our forces are ready to intervene.'[14]

The intimidation worked, up to a point. The Polish Communists drew up their own plans to introduce martial law and prepared a list of 4,000 Solidarity activists who would be interned immediately, with Lech Wałęsa's name at the top. Yet, maddeningly for Moscow, no action followed. In September the Kremlin bosses ousted Gierek. He was replaced by a new Communist Party boss, Stanisław Kania, and a new head of government was named, General Wojciech Jaruzelski, an experienced soldier who the Soviets hoped would be made of sterner stuff. But still the Polish Communists prevaricated.

The year and three months after Solidarity was legalised were, even by the anarchic standards of Polish communism, a baffling time. On the surface it remained a People's Democracy. But scratch the carapace and the country was transformed utterly. There was a revolution in thinking, during which Poles began learning the truth about their recent history. There was something like free assembly and free speech, for the first time in nearly half a century. A parallel society developed at breathtaking speed. Solidarity achieved something that was not just unique in Eastern Europe but seemingly impossible. 'I thought it was impossible, it was impossible. I still think it was impossible,' Kuroń said later. Communism did not disappear – far from it. But in many sectors of society the most repressive aspects corroded and fell into disuse. Within a few weeks Solidarity had more than eight million members, more than twice as many as the Communist Party. For a mass organisation – any organisation – to exist alongside the Party but outside its control was unprecedented.[15]

Samizdat publications had always existed in People's Poland. But now 'illegal' newspapers mushroomed and in effect they were permitted. The authorities made no serious efforts to halt them, though they still censored the official press as before. The Poles had another word for samizdat – *bibula* (lavatory paper), because that was the quality of the paper on which most of them were printed. Now twenty-five new magazines and newspapers of good quality were produced every week on decent presses with big circulations of more than 50,000 each. The Independent Publishing House NOWA run by Mirek Chojecki – a true hero of the struggle for press freedom – also published hastily produced editions of long-suppressed classic texts and modern masters. Orwell's *Animal Farm* was published in Poland for the first time, as was Polish exile Czesław Miłosz's powerful and compelling critique of communism, *The Captive Mind*. One of the most extraordinary events was the poet Miłosz's emotional return to Poland from Scandinavia after receiving the 1980 Nobel Prize in Literature. The film director Andrzrej Wajda's tributes to the Polish working class, *Man of Marble* and *Man of Iron*, used to be shown to small groups in private homes. Now they were on general release. This period was 'a revolution of dignity, a celebration for the rights of vertebrae, a permanent victory for the straightened spine', said Michnik.[16]

Solidarity thinkers now set out its aims more clearly. Kuroń had emerged from jail with changed views. He evolved into a kind of social democrat along Western lines, but forged by East European experience. He emphasised a peaceful transformation, which set the tone for all the changes in the socialist bloc over the next decade. It was predicated on the conviction that the Cold War reality was clear: nobody in the West would risk a confrontation with the Soviets by rushing to the assistance of any revolutionary movement behind the Iron Curtain. He did not urge all-out confrontation with the state. Workers and intellectuals had no prospect of winning a violent struggle with an opponent willing to use its power against *them*. A strategy far more likely to succeed was to bypass the Party as far as possible and set up unofficial structures alongside the totalitarian ones. 'Don't burn down Party Committees; found your own,' he wrote. He stressed the importance of Solidarity struggling for a 'self-limiting' revolution that did not make extreme demands which could provoke a Soviet backlash. Solidarity should say nothing about Poland's security alliances or foreign policy. Communist authority could be preserved as a figleaf, though in time Poland would become a pluralist society in all but name. Michnik echoed the crucial importance of peaceful change: 'A revolution that begins by burning down Bastilles, will in time build new Bastilles of its own,' he said in a celebrated essay.[17]

Solidarity was under the microscope as never before and Wałęsa became, in effect, the first Leader of the Opposition in the Communist world. He showed great skill as a negotiator but was soon being criticised for an overbearing manner. He did not operate openly or democratically. He infuriated the more radical wing of Solidarity by constantly urging compromise with the regime. During 1981 he stopped far more strikes than he started, repeatedly persuading workers to moderate their demands lest Solidarity risk a crackdown by the Russians.

Partly this was natural and sensible caution. Partly it is how the Pope advised him to proceed when Wałęsa had a private audience with John Paul II on 14 January 1981 – his first of many. The Pope initially had misgivings about Wałęsa. He knew that some members of the Polish episcopate were wary of Solidarity because of the socialist roots of some of its leading figures. The politicians in the Curia – mostly Italians – wanted to avoid any confrontation with the Soviet Union. But the Pope liked the idea of a genuine workers' leader, especially one who spoke about the Church at every available opportunity. After their audience he came out strongly in public support of Lech Wałęsa and never wavered.

But the Pope had heard the ever-increasing rumours about the hero-electrician who was defying communism. In particular, said Polish friends and priests, there were stories – never corroborated – about his infidelities. Anna Walentynowycz claimed categorically that he was having affairs. 'We all knew they were bringing girls for him – he had a sofa in his room. Outside, his bodyguard Henryk Mażul would block the door and say "you can't go in there now, he's sleeping". But once I managed to get in – and he had company – his hair was completely ruffled.' She and some assistants moved the sofa from his office. 'I scolded him, "You sinner how can you wear the Black Madonna on your lapel?" and he replied "I confess every week".' But she fell out with Wałęsa soon after the August strikes and she had been dropped as a Gdańsk representative of Solidarity.[18]

The stories were told and repeated by Solidarity activists. It was said at this time that beautiful, raven-haired student Bożena Rybicka was more than his assistant. The speculation was fuelled by an extraordinary paragraph in an article by Ewa Berberyusz in the Catholic weekly *Tygodnik Powszechny* in December 1980, who teased him about being a flirt. 'He likes women. With a kind of devotion that is disappearing amongst men and which is based on total lack of complexes, complete self-confidence, a shade old-fashioned courtliness and the rock-solid conviction that women will never harm him.' But all the gossip was entirely untrue. He was always very close to Danuta – and during this period he was being watched far too closely to risk any extra-marital indiscretions.[19]

The Soviets continued to wait for their Polish satraps to obey orders, fall into line and crack down on Solidarity as they were required to do as loyal Communists. Brezhnev met Kania in Moscow in March and again warned him that Moscow was prepared to act if necessary. 'OK, we won't go in. But if there are complications, if we see you being overthrown, we will go in.'[20]

A particularly disturbing report reached Andropov following a visit by his deputy, Vladimir Kryuchkov, and the KGB head of foreign counter-intelligence, Oleg Kalugin, who said the Polish 'SB were always difficult, not like the Czechs or the East Germans. They had to be handled with care.' On a visit to Poland for talks with the SB, the two intelligence officers, out of general interest, went to the Lenin Shipyard. Kalugin said:

> When we arrived we were greeted by the manager (Gniech) who asked us to leave our big limousines outside the gates. He explained there was a lot of unrest among the workers and that the sight of our . . . convoy might be too provocative. Naturally we complied. Far from being welcomed by the workforce, or clapped as was the convention during such tours, we met sullen stares and resentment. During a banquet thrown in our honour at the end of the visit to Poland I made a casual reference to the dissent in my speech. To my amazement their security minister reacted as if I had touched on a very raw nerve

and insisted there was only a handful of troublemakers and all of them were under control. I knew then there was a real problem . . .[21]

In October the Soviets removed Kania, whom they had installed as Polish leader barely a year earlier. He had made it plain he was reluctant to take the required brutal steps against the independent trade union. Naïvely, he had let himself be bugged by the KGB making criticisms of the USSR that were extraordinary coming from one their supposedly obedient quislings. He said: 'The Soviet model has failed the test. The fact that the USSR was systematically buying grain in the West is an indictment of serious errors in their management . . . The power of their regime is marked only through their army and powers of coercion. If the USSR still has some strategic advantage over the US, within two or three years they may lose it because [of the weakness] of the Soviet economy.' A transcript of the recording was sent immediately to Andropov and within days Kania was ousted. He was replaced as Communist Party leader and the ruler of Poland by Comrade General Wojciech Jaruzelski.[22]

FIVE

CIVIL WAR

Warsaw, Saturday 12 December 1981

COMMUNIST THEORY tells loyalists to be wary of military men. Armies are potentially an alternative source of power and must be firmly kept under the control of the Party. Yet the Soviets and the diehards among the Polish leadership saw Jaruzelski as the answer to their most urgent hopes. No professional soldier had become a Communist Party boss before – though several had worn elegant uniforms which they had never earned in the battlefield or barracks square. Jaruzelski was trusted, loyal, reliable and thought to be the man who would offer the smack of firm government. He would solve the chaos in Poland, which, as Moscow saw it, was threatening the security of all its possessions in Europe.

Wojciech Jaruzelski hardly seemed like a natural Communist. He was born on 6 July 1923, into a wealthy landed family of noble descent in eastern Poland near Białystok. He grew up on his parents' country estate of Trzeciny into a life of ease. He learned to fence, to ride horses and to waltz. The 'family tradition', as the General described it, was Polish nationalist and, especially, anti-Russian. His grandfather and two great-uncles took part in the 1863 rebellion against the Tsars, and when it failed were sent to Siberia for twelve years. His father fought for the Poles in the 1920 war against Russia – on this occasion the Poles won. He was sent to a strict Catholic school in Warsaw run by the Marian monks where, as he said, 'every subject – history, geography, languages – was linked to the tragic history of relations between Poland and Russia'.[1]

He was sixteen when the Germans invaded Poland and the family sought refuge with some friends in Lithuania. After the Hitler/Stalin pact – when the Baltic republics became part of the Soviet Union – they were all deported to Siberia. Their crime was his father's record of nineteen years earlier and their aristocratic pedigree. Jaruzelski senior was sent to a labour camp where, already in poor health, he was worked to death. Wojciech, still a teenager, his mother and twelve-year-old sister were sent to the Taiga, the icy Siberian tundra plain, and left to fend for themselves. The journey took nearly a month in an overcrowded goods train. He spent two years in forced labour, felling trees. It was back-breaking work, and in the winter the glare of the sun on the ice damaged his eyes. The trademark dark glasses he always wore dated from that time. 'In Siberia, the cold was indescribable. I worked very hard. All this should have made me hate the Russians. Paradoxically, the opposite began to happen. I fell in love with the Russians, with their indomitable spirit, with the country itself, with the ordinary people I got to know.'[2]

No doubt a psychiatrist could explain the phenomenon more fully, but Jaruzelski became a passionately committed Communist. After the German invasion of the USSR in 1941, he was one of the first to join the Polish ranks of the Red Army. This was another defining moment in his life. He fought alongside the Soviets, through to the siege of Berlin, in some of the most brutal battles in the war. 'I identified with them ... My superiors, my colleagues, all those who depended on me were Russian,' he said. They were the victorious power, he was convinced they had right on their side, they were building a great empire in Eastern Europe that would be there to stay. With a mixture of conviction and opportunism, Jaruzelski chose to serve them.

In Poland after the war, he became a military commissar. 'I was a fanatical believer. It went without saying that we had to defend our church and its dogmas,' he would say. His job was to establish a loyal Communist army that would look after Soviet interests. He was a highly political general, an efficient administrator, a deft tactician and he climbed steadily through the government ranks. He had little public exposure until December 1970, when as Defence Minister he was responsible for the troops who fired on the Gdańsk workers, though he did not give the order for them to shoot. He was loathed by most Poles from then onwards, who regarded this one-time aristocrat-turned-Communist ideologue as an enigma. He spoke with perfect old-fashioned, almost nineteenth-century diction, yet the words he uttered were orthodox Marxist-Leninist gobbledegook. He remained Defence Minister when he was made Prime Minister in February 1981 and, later, when he was appointed to replace Kania.

By now Poland's foreign debt had risen to US $25 billion, on top of the generous handouts it had received from the Soviets that went directly towards subsidising food prices. The country could barely afford to pay interest on the loans. Despite Wałęsa's appeals for calm and restraint, the more radical wing of Solidarity was making increased demands – for more pay, less government control in factories and for wholesale economic reforms. In concert with his Soviet advisers, Jaruzelski from the start played a double game to 'squash' Solidarity. In public he appeared to be emollient. On 4 November 1981, a fortnight after he took over as Party boss, he met Wałęsa and the new Primate of Poland, Archbishop Józef Glemp, who had become head of the Polish Church in the summer following the death of the respected and deeply mourned Cardinal Wyszyński. The General declared he wanted to establish a 'Front for National Unity' – a kind of coalition that would bring in the Church and Solidarity as junior partners in government. Wałęsa was in a conciliatory mood. 'We do not want to overthrow the power of the State,' he said. 'Let the Government govern the country and we will govern ourselves in the factories.' There was a second meeting a fortnight later, which broke down amidst rancour. Jaruzelski threatened to introduce emergency laws to ban strikes, prohibit public meetings and to use military courts to try some civilian offences. Wałęsa said he would call a one-day national strike followed by an unlimited general strike if those measures came into force. The two sides were set on a collision course.[3]

Secretly, though, Jaruzelski knew what he intended to do. Plans to introduce martial law if the regime felt it necessary had originally been laid months earlier. They were refined throughout 1981 under the direction of Jaruzelski's General Staff and a highly confidential National Defence Committee. They had the codename Spring and only a few members of Poland's political leadership knew anything about them. Kania had seen the plans but never agreed to implement them. They would not risk using Polish soldiers to shoot at workers. The troops might refuse. In the strictest secrecy Jaruzelski had organised a force of 15,000 specially trained riot police, known by the Polish acronym ZOMO, which he trusted would be absolutely loyal to the regime. They were paid several times more than regular police or troops and they were well equipped with the latest line in plastic shields, water cannons and state-of-the art truncheons.

Jaruzelski, as he had always intended, deliberately engineered a pretext to crack down on the union. On 15 September, when Prime Minister and Defence Minister, he chaired a meeting of his aides in which he said they needed an excuse to impose martial law 'which can in no way be assessed as a provocation by the government side but, rather ... will make it clear to everyone in society exactly why it is necessary'. He resorted to forgery. In early December the government claimed it had unearthed details of a violent plot to overthrow the state. As proof, it cited what it called the Radom Tapes – a recording of a meeting of leading Solidarity activists in that city. It turned out later that the tapes were fakes, crudely doctored by the Polish secret service to make the discussion look like a plan to mount an insurrection when it was not. But the damage was done. Jaruzelski had provided himself with what he thought was, and could explain to others as, a plausible reason to act.[4]

Despite the tense atmosphere, Solidarity was totally unprepared for martial law when it was imposed on the freezing cold night of 12–13 December 1981. Wałęsa repeatedly warned that 'we should never underestimate the enemy', yet he and his closest advisers had done so. 'We were simply not mentally prepared for it. Nobody imagined that this seemingly weak government would prove strong enough to turn the police, or the army, against us,' said Władisław Frasyniuk, a leading Solidarity organiser.[5] If Solidarity did not know the coup would take place, the US and other Western governments did. The CIA had an informer close to General Jaruzelski who had been giving the Americans valuable intelligence for several years. Colonel Ryszard Kukliński was a senior officer in Polish military intelligence, but reported to Washington under the codename Jack Strong. He had told the Americans about the invasion threat in December 1980, though he thought it was a real danger and not a bluff. Now he tipped off the CIA about martial law. The US and other Nato countries reacted calmly to the news, but nobody thought to warn Solidarity.*[6]

Most of the union's best-known figures were arrested in their beds. The regime had carefully planned the action for this weekend, Solidarity's annual congress. The entire Solidarity leadership was in Gdańsk, apart from a few who were on trips abroad. At two a.m. on

* Kukliński was one of the most valuable agents the CIA ran during the Cold War. In 1971 he volunteered himself as a spy for the Agency in a letter dispatched to the American Embassy in Bonn and for the next decade he passed on a series of vital military secrets to the West in more than 30,000 documents. They included Warsaw Pact battle plans, technical diagrams on new ranges of missiles and intelligence. He was active for nearly ten years until he defected in 1981. Three years later he was sentenced to death, in absentia. The sentence was rescinded in 1989, but Kukliński was never officially pardoned and many Solidarity supporters who loathed communism and the Russians – such as Lech Wałęsa – always regarded him as a traitor.

the Sunday morning, 2,000 ZOMO riot police, in their pale blue battle dress, surrounded the Monopol Hotel in the centre of the city, where most of the delegates were staying. They blocked the exits and searched all the rooms. They arrested every union official they could find, handcuffed them and piled them into waiting trucks where they were at first taken to holding cells at police stations and military barracks. The same happened at other guest houses and hotels.

Wałęsa was arrested at his home in a high-rise apartment block in Zaspa on the outskirts of Gdańsk. His doorbell rang at 3 a.m. It was the Gdańsk Communist Party chief, Tadeusz Fiszbach, along with six SB officers. Wałęsa was told to dress and he would be put on a plane 'for talks with Jaruzelski'. His first reaction was defiance. 'I told them . . . "This is the moment you lose. This is your downfall . . . the end of communism." Of course I was exaggerating a bit.' He was warned the police would take him by force if need be. He packed a few clothes and went with them. A few top figures managed to get away – such as the dynamic twenty-seven-year-old leader of the union in Warsaw, Zbigniew Bujak, who was up in a bar drinking brandies with some college friends most of the night while the raids were proceeding, and had been planning to take a dawn train back to the capital. But it had been a surgical operation carried out with efficiency.[7]

General Jaruzelski broadcast on television just after six that morning, looking solemn and stiff-necked as usual in his impeccably pressed olive green uniform. Two Polish flags were draped behind a desk as he spoke. He looked more like a Latin American dictator at the head of a military junta than a Communist apparatchik, as he explained that he had to take action 'for the good of the nation . . . Our country has found itself on the edge of an abyss . . . Poland's future is at stake, the future for which my generation fought.' Archbishop Glemp's sermon was shown on TV soon after the General appeared. He said martial law 'was to choose the lesser of two evils. Assuming the correctness of such reasoning, the man in the street will submit himself to the new situation. Do not start a fight Pole against Pole.' It was an extraordinary performance by the charmless, rotund former canon lawyer, whose calm appeal for compromise seemed to chime oddly with the Pope's inspiring calls for resistance to godless communism.

Jaruzelski always defended the imposition of martial law on the grounds that if he had not done so the Russians would have invaded Poland, which would have been worse for the country. For many years, however unpopular his regime became, he was believed by his opponents at home and abroad. But it is untrue. The Soviets ruled out sending a force into Poland – and Jaruzelski knew it. In fact, Jaruzelski desperately appealed to the Russians to send in their troops but was rejected.[8]

At the beginning of December Poland's then Chief of Staff, General Florian Siwicki, went to Moscow on the orders of Jaruzelski. The two had been friends as well as comrades-in-arms for years and Siwicki was a highly trusted emissary. The purpose of his visit was to persuade the Russians to intervene in Poland. Jaruzelski believed that martial law would not succeed without Soviet help and the Polish military on their own could not 'restore order'. According to Siwicki he was carrying a document drawn up in Warsaw which was 'a statement demonstrating that the Polish Communists do not stand alone and asked for a fulfilment of the obligations of the alliance as well as total support for the Polish government's struggle against counter-revolutionaries'. What it meant, of course, said Siwicki, was an absolute commitment by Moscow to send in their armies to Poland. The Soviets refused to sign the document. When Siwicki returned home empty-handed, the Polish leader looked deeply disturbed and said, 'Our allies have abandoned us . . . now we have exhausted the options available to us.' He made a similar remark to another old friend, Red Army General Anatoli Gribkov, the Warsaw Pact Chief of Staff, when he accused the Soviets of 'betraying an old friendship'.[9]

On 10 December the magnates in the Kremlin met urgently to discuss – yet again – a crisis in Poland. This is when a final decision was made not to dispatch Soviet troops there. Andropov said: 'We do not intend to introduce troops into Poland. That is the right position and we must stick with it to the end . . . I don't know how things will turn out in Poland, but even if it falls under the control of Solidarity, so be it . . . If the capitalist countries pounce on the Soviet Union . . . with economic and political sanctions, that would be burdensome for us. We must be concerned above all about our own country and strengthening the Soviet Union.' Gromyko agreed: 'We must somehow try to dispel the notions of Jaruzelski and other leaders in Poland . . . There cannot be any introduction of troops into Poland.'[10]

The next day Marshal Viktor Kulikov, head of the Soviet military delegation to Warsaw, passed on Moscow's decision to Jaruzelski. But the Polish leader still tried to change minds in the Kremlin. According to the KGB chief in Warsaw, General Vitali Pavlov, Jaruzelski telephoned Mikhail Suslov on the morning of 12 December, just a few hours before martial law was proclaimed. Suslov was the Soviets' chief of ideology, an inflexible diehard who had been a highly influential figure in the Soviet leadership for a quarter of a century. He had been one of the Soviet Union's troubleshooters on the spot in Budapest when the Hungarian Uprising was crushed in 1956 and he voted enthusiastically to send the tanks into Prague in 1968. But on this occasion he told the leader of the Polish Communists, 'under no circumstances will we send in our troops . . . You have always said that you can handle this with your own forces.' He did promise that if the Polish regime took action on its own, the Soviet Union would help to bail the country out of its economic mess. Yet that did not satisfy the General. He tried to call Brezhnev, who refused to speak to him. He decided to act on his own, and that night. If he delayed any longer he would have lost the element of surprise and the opportunity of finding the Solidarity ringleaders in one place at one time. The job of restoring 'socialist discipline' would be harder.[11]

Solidarity had disastrously miscalculated. Its leadership believed that if the moment ever came the police, army and security forces – many of them union members – would disobey their superiors' orders. They thought that even if there was a crackdown it would be only partial: the workers could shut the country down at will and the government would eventually cave in. The union was woefully ill-prepared. Even after all the leading figures had been arrested, no efforts were made to protect Solidarity's vital printing presses – or the considerable amounts of ready money it had raised over the last year, which were confiscated more or less overnight. It had naïvely prepared no network of safe houses or meeting places. Solidarity went underground, with no organisation, no money, and had to start again virtually from scratch.

Jaruzelski expected that Solidarity would instantly call a general strike, but the leadership were now behind bars. What was left of the movement was demoralised and nonplussed. A few isolated strikes were called but were brutally and speedily suppressed. ZOMO troops went into factories and arrested strike leaders. Nine miners in Wujek, near the industrial town of Katowice, were shot and twenty-one injured. At the Lenin Shipyard, birthplace of Solidarity, resistance lasted for less than a week. The majority of the workers were cowed into submission. In industries thought vital, like coal-mining and food distribution, the workforce was placed under army discipline.

Jaruzelski ruled with a Council for National Salvation comprising a group of senior officers, not Party apparatchiks. Polish martial law seemed in many ways as much a coup against the Communists as against Solidarity, though the declared object was to 'save socialism and national honour'. Marx and Lenin would have called Polish martial law classic 'Bonapartism'. Newsreaders now wore uniforms. A dusk-to-dawn curfew was imposed in all major towns. Strict censorship was placed on official newspapers. The junta tried to cut off Poland from the outside world, severing phone links. It attempted, in vain, to limit internal travel to prevent information moving around the country. In the first few days more than 6,000 people were arrested without charge and detained in dozens of internment camps. They included well-known writers, actors, academics, musicians and artists as well as trade union activists. The great philosopher Leszek Kołakowski said the martial law declaration was the moment the Polish Communists 'declared war on their own people' and the idea stuck. Everywhere Poles referred to the next few months as a period of war.

The Soviets fondly imagined that they had paid a relatively small price to pacify their perennially troublesome colony. Again they had reasserted their authority, and this time the Poles had themselves done the dirty work. In the Kremlin the sight of Polish tanks, patrolling Warsaw streets, commanded by a Polish Communist, was seen as a relief and a victory. But quickly it began to look like no sort of victory at all.

SIX

THE BLEEDING WOUND

Kabul, Sunday 13 December 1981

THERE WAS ONE overriding reason why Red Army tanks were not sent to Warsaw to suppress Solidarity. It was explained by Mikhail Suslov, perhaps the most hardline apologist for Russian imperialism in the entire Moscow leadership. 'We simply cannot afford another Afghanistan,' he said, when the Soviet magnates agonised over what to do in Poland. By December 1981 Soviet troops had been fighting the battle for socialism on their Central Asian border for two years and it was clear they had been led to a disaster. Already about 2,000 Russian soldiers had been killed – more than the number who had died on active service in the three and a half decades since the end of World War Two. The old men in the Kremlin searched for a way out, but could not find one that did not involve international humiliation. *That* they would not contemplate. They were trapped by Russian nationalism, and by their own ideology. They believed that the tide of history was with them, that communism must inevitably triumph, and that no country which had seen a socialist revolution – even one as unlikely for communism to take root as Afghanistan – must ever be allowed to slide back. In hard-headed terms, they felt that if they admitted defeat anywhere it would be a sign of weakness that would give encouragement to their opponents everywhere. They allowed themselves to be sucked deeper into an unwinnable conflict in hostile, mountainous terrain, surrounded by enemies they did not begin to understand.

The Soviets never planned a war in Afghanistan. Their intention had not been to occupy the country. The other occasions since 1945 in which Soviet troops had been sent into conflict abroad had been to Warsaw Pact neighbours, their satellite states, to reassert their dominion. Those – such as Hungary in 1956 – had essentially been police actions in countries they regarded as their possessions. Afghanistan was different. It was not in the generally acknowledged Soviet sphere of influence. Now it became part of the Cold War as a 'proxy' dispute between East and West. A war in Europe in the era of Mutually Assured Destruction was deemed unthinkable. But superpower rivalries spread to the Third World and, especially, to the Middle East, where both sides saw vital strategic interests at stake. If on their western flank the Soviets were worried about the Pope, in the East the leadership feared the mullahs. They were anxious about the rise of Islamic fundamentalism in Iran, as well as 'Western imperialism' in Afghanistan, which bordered its Central Asian republics.

At the end of April 1978 a small group of left-wing army officers seized power in the Afghan capital, Kabul. All the coup leaders were Communists, members of the People's Democratic Party of Afghanistan (PDPA), and had close links with Moscow. The Soviet Ambassador, Alexander Puzanov, had been told about the takeover plan and opposed it. So did Moscow. The KGB begged the plotters not to proceed, but was ignored. The first the Kremlin knew that the coup had taken place was from a Reuters wire report. Swiftly, the Soviets changed their tack, started referring to the Afghan leaders as comrades and hailed the revolution as a great victory for socialism. The Russians sent a contingent of advisers – engineers, doctors, road builders as well as intelligence agents – to advance the cause of international communism.

The new Afghan leader was a bookish sixty-one-year-old Marxist thinker, Mohammed Taraki. He began to put his theories into practice in the traditional way, despite the deeply conservative nature of the country's Islamic society. He rounded up and executed hundreds of opponents and trod on ancient customs. He tried to force farmers to grow other crops instead of poppy and had elaborate plans to collectivise agriculture. Women were sent to schools, given literacy classes and discouraged from wearing the traditional bhourka.* As Saher Gul, a mullah in the remote Laghman Province, explained: 'The Communists tried to change the law of God. They wanted to destroy Islamic traditions – to rid everyone of poverty and make everyone equal. This is against the law of Islam. God has decided who is rich and who is poor. It can't be changed by Communists.'[1]

Most of the country's population agreed with Gul. Over the next eighteen months the revolution fell apart. Resistance grew and the

* Most of the few women doctors, teachers and other professionals who qualified in Afghanistan were trained in the brief period the People's Democratic Party of Afghanistan (PPDA) were in charge of the country. Naturally none of them were permitted to practise their chosen professions after the Islamists came to power a few years later.

mullahs called for *jihad* against the atheistic Communists. Scores of thousands of Afghans joined the Mujahideen, the Army of God, and took to the hills or fled over the porous border to Pakistan. Kabul and a few of the bigger towns were controlled by Taraki's forces, but most of the countryside was in the hands of the guerrillas. He desperately pleaded with the Russians to send him help against 'the saboteurs and terrorists' who were endangering the revolution. He received a few fighter planes, some weapons and moral support. Even after a Mujahideen group killed seven Soviet advisers in March 1979, Moscow turned down requests for direct military help. Andropov said, wisely: 'There's a question, whose cause will we be supporting if we deploy forces into Afghanistan. It's completely clear ... that Afghanistan is not ready at this time to resolve the issues it faces through socialism. The economy is backward, the Islamic religion predominates and nearly all the rural population is illiterate. This is not a revolutionary situation. We can uphold [Taraki's regime] only by Soviet bayonets and that is utterly inadmissible for us. We cannot take such a risk.'

Gromyko agreed, using diplomatic and strategic arguments. If the USSR sent in an army it would be seen as an aggressor: 'All that we have done in recent years with such effort in terms of détente, arms reduction and much more would be thrown back. China, of course, would be given a nice present. All the non-aligned countries would be against us ... serious consequences are to be expected by such an action.'[2]

Two geopolitical considerations changed their minds – and the bloody result of one internal Afghan squabble. The collapse of the Shah of Iran's regime in February 1979 proved as great a blow to the Soviet Union as to the US. The Kremlin expected American intervention to prop up the Shah and, again, when dozens of American hostages were seized at the US Embassy. When no American intervention came and Revolutionary Guards began patrolling the streets of Tehran, the Soviet leadership could sense the danger posed by Ayatollah Khomeini's Islamic Republic. 'Our main concern was the security of the southern borders of the Soviet Union ... and the spread of Islamic fundamentalism,' according to Vasily Safranchuk, the Soviet Foreign Ministry's chief official responsible for the Middle East. The other strategic concern for the Kremlin was that détente and the process of disarmament talks seemed to be running into the sands. Neither East nor West appeared able or willing to halt a renewed arms race. Brezhnev had made agreements in the early 1970s with Presidents

Nixon and Ford to place limits on the number of intercontinental missiles in Soviet and Nato arsenals. But the Russians had developed a new range of intermediate range weapons, the SS-20s, which they had begun to deploy in Europe in 1978. Nato intended to counter with new land-based Cruise and Pershing missiles, though it was not clear when they would be deployed.[3]

The other conflict, in Kabul, required more immediate Soviet attention. There had been a power struggle among Afghan Communists since well before the revolution. Taraki's deputy, the regime's strong man and security chief, Hafizullah Amin, had always wanted power for himself and believed that he, a man of action, would be better able to lead the fight against the guerrillas. On 14 September he overthrew Taraki but the news was not made public until a fortnight later when the *Kabul Times* reported that he had 'died of an undisclosed illness'. A member of the palace guard – in exile some years afterwards – described what had really happened. Taraki was tied to his bed with a towel and then suffocated with a pillow. His death throes had lasted a quarter of an hour.

The vigorous and ruthless Amin, fifty, who had supervised the purges against the PDPA's opponents, was deeply distrusted by Moscow. The KGB thought that he was playing a double game and was making diplomatic overtures to the Americans. A report sent upwards to Brezhnev said Amin might even have been recruited by the CIA. There was never any evidence against him, but Andropov became convinced that Amin had to be removed. Whatever the reservations the KGB chief held a few months earlier, he now believed that Soviet troops had to be dispatched to Afghanistan to 'save the revolution' and defeat 'the terrorists'. His deputy Vladimir Kryuchkov said: 'He felt ... that if we didn't go into Afghanistan then some other countries would.'[4]

The two others in the Kremlin 'troika', Ustinov and Gromyko, agreed. The Foreign Minister's view now was that 'we cannot afford to lose Afghanistan'. The three of them talked round an initially reluctant Brezhnev, who still had enough faculties left to see the serious risks that he was running. He said that he had struggled hard to gain a reputation as a peacemaker and all that would be in jeopardy if the Afghan venture went wrong. The plan was to enter the country with a show of force, get rid of Amin, replace him with a more malleable and trustworthy puppet, support the Afghan army's operations for a few weeks, and then leave once the new regime had been established. It was supposed to be a quick, surgical intervention.

The top brass in the Soviet military were against the plan from the first and tried hard to stop it, even at some risk to their careers. The Chief of the Defence Staff, Marshal Nikolai Ogarkov and his deputy, General Sergei Akhromeyev – both highly decorated officers from World War Two – were the senior dissenters. They raised their doubts with the Defence Minister, Ustinov, pointing out that military experience from the British in the nineteenth century and the Russians in Tsarist days should encourage caution. They were reprimanded. 'Are the generals now making policy in the Soviet Union? Your job is to plan specific operations and carry out orders,' Ustinov told them. They produced a detailed plan which satisfied their masters, if not themselves. On the morning of 10 December Ogarkov told Brezhnev that most of his colleagues had 'grave reservations' about the enterprise because of the possible 'perils of being mired in unfamiliar and difficult conditions'. Ustinov told him to 'shut up and obey orders'. Later in the day when other Kremlin magnates met, the Marshal bravely tried again and warned of 'very serious fallout' from the venture. 'We could align the entire Islamic East against us,' he said. Andropov cut him off. 'Focus on military affairs,' he was told. 'Leave the policy making to us and the Party.'[5]

The final decision was taken on 12 December 1979. The scales were tipped by Nato's decision four days earlier to begin deployment the following year of 464 ground-based Cruise missiles and 108 Pershing missiles in Western Europe. 'After that decision by Nato, we . . . had nothing to lose,' one senior official commented. Brezhnev signed the order 'with a shaky hand', but he was optimistic in public. When a short while later he spoke to a sceptical Anatoli Dobrynin, the Soviets' vastly experienced Ambassador to the US, one of the Soviet Union's shrewdest servants, Brezhnev said: 'Don't worry, Anatoli, we'll be out of there in three or four weeks.'[6]

The operation began on Christmas Day and was bungled from the start. The initial plan had been to poison Amin, but he was left alive, albeit in pain. He strengthened the guard at his palace on the outskirts of Kabul. Soviet special forces – now without the element of surprise – eventually found him and shot him, though suffering severe casualties. What was supposed to be a swift and straightforward assassination, leaving few traces, turned into a bloodbath that produced two truckloads of corpses.

Amin's replacement was Babrak Karmal, who turned out to be a chronic alcoholic and occasional womaniser. Originally one of the leaders of the revolution, he fell out with both his predecessors. He was dispatched into exile as the Afghan Ambassador to Czechoslovakia, where he lived quietly until the KGB airlifted him out of Prague and smuggled him back to Kabul two days before the invasion. The city was not deemed safe as there were still pockets of resistance from Amin supporters who feared for their lives. Karmal was installed officially as Communist Party leader on 26 December at a hastily convened meeting of the Party, under the guard of the Red Army, at the Bagram military airport, which the Soviets were using as their main base of operations.

Two years later, around 100,000 Soviet troops occupied the country and the war continued to escalate. The Mujahideen were receiving massive shipments of arms and money from the US, whose principal aim, in which it was supremely successful, was to keep the Soviets tied down for as long as possible in a costly conflict. The Soviets changed their tactics over time. At first they engaged in large-scale armed sweeps in the most troublesome areas like Helmand Province in the south and the border areas with Pakistan, through which most of the guerrillas' weapons were flowing. But this was not working. As an observer of the conflict explained: 'About 99 per cent of the battles that we fought in Afghanistan were won by the Soviet side. But the problem was that the next morning we had the same situation as if there had been no battle . . . The Mujahideen were again in the village where they were – or we thought they were – destroyed a day or so before. It was . . . useless.' The Russians adopted more brutal methods and took to the air. They bombed and strafed towns and villages, sending in commandos to 'mop up' afterwards, but the results were similar. The Mujahideen would melt away temporarily and then return. But an estimated million Afghans were killed in the war and between two and three million refugees left the country.

The Russians could find no way out and their armed forces were so overstretched there was no question of deploying troops elsewhere. A junior member of the Soviet leadership, Mikhail Gorbachev, in charge of agriculture, was already in private calling the Afghan War 'our bleeding wound'.

SEVEN

THE POWER OF THE POWERLESS

Prague, June 1982

POLAND WAS IN MANY WAYS an exception, the semi-anarchic state that even one of the Soviet leaders recognised as 'the Achilles heel' of communism. But to most outsiders Warsaw looked as much a capital of the Communist world as Bucharest or East Berlin. One of the first things a stranger would note, in the early 1980s as in the 1950s, from Varna on the Black Sea to Vilnius near the Baltic, was the absence of advertising hoardings or displays in shop windows designed to attract customers. It was not just that there were fewer of these things. There were *none*. Arguably, a visitor from the West might have thought this was a blessed relief, but it certainly gave the streets in the socialist world an identifiable look. There was an eerie darkness at night in most cities. The roads were poorly lit and there were relatively few private cars on the roads. People were clothed well by the 1980s – nobody was in rags. But there was little variety and, for the fashion-conscious, little to buy in domestic stores. The height of luxury – and of longing – was a pair of American blue jeans. 'We pretend to work and they pretend to pay us,' was a well-worn saying throughout East/Central Europe – and it was not a joke. It was a fairly accurate single-line description of the system.

Politically, Eastern Europe was frozen in ice. Most regimes were dominated by men already in their second decade in power by the 1980s. A couple, Todor Zhivkov in Bulgaria and János Kádár in Hungary, had already lasted more than twenty years by the time of martial law in Poland. They had no intention of relinquishing power either for themselves or for their overlords in Moscow. These Communist potentates believed that the quiescence of their people meant the public had accepted them – grudgingly, sullenly and unhappily perhaps, but the important thing was that the people had submitted peacefully and ceased to give the rulers much trouble.

Generally, throughout the Soviet empire, this was so. There had been rebellions. They had ended tragically, with Soviet tanks patrolling the streets of some of the loveliest cities in Europe. The memories of the Hungarians and Czechs were still raw – in 1956 more than 2,500 people had died in Budapest in a heroic but doomed fight for freedom. The Czechs still felt crushed by the failure of the Prague Spring. The aftershocks of both experiences were deeply painful. Hundreds of Hungarians had been executed for daring to challenge the system and more than 15,000 imprisoned. In Czechoslovakia, the period of 'normalisation', as the regime called it, was less brutal – 'a process of civilised violence', the Slovakian writer Milan Šimečka called it. But it transformed the country and the ruling Party, which was thoroughly purged. Almost half the membership of around a million and a half were thrown out of the Party. All the leading academics, journalists or teachers had to sign 'loyalty' pledges to the State – i.e., the ruling Party – and if they refused they were fired. The Czech broadcasting station shed around 1,500 of its 3,500 employees. In the Czech capital during the 1970s and 1980s there were scores of stokers, janitors and mechanics who had been philosophers, history professors and newspaper editors before or during the Prague Spring.

The lessons were learned. People devised ways of living with Communist totalitarianism. They retreated into their private lives, where they hoped the Stasi or the Securitate could not follow. The Polish journalist and author Konstanty Gebert* said he built 'A small, portable barricade between me and silence, submission, humiliation, shame, impregnable for tanks. As long as this [exists] . . . there is around me, a small area of freedom.'[1]

It had been a joyous party – at least until three uninvited guests turned up towards the end of the evening and arrested the band. The musicians had just finished their set at an apartment in central Prague on 15 March 1976. The beer had flowed freely and the group were mixing with the partygoers, when a trio from the Czech secret police, the Státní Bezpečnost – StB – walked in. That night they took away members of the Plastic People of the Universe, Czechoslovakia's best known pop group, and locked them up, as well as several of the band's supporters – nineteen people in all – for 'disturbing the peace'. The next day they were charged with 'alcoholism, drug addiction and antisocial behaviour'.

* A cheerful, bearded, witty polymath, he wrote under the pseudonym Dawid Warszawski.

After the court case that followed, four of the group were jailed for periods of between one and three and a half years, including the Plastics' twenty-seven-year-old founder, lyricist and bass player Milan Hlavsa.[2]

They were not a great band musically. Compared with their heroes Frank Zappa, Captain Beefheart or the Velvet Underground, the Plastics were hardly innovative as artists. Nor, as their guiding spirit Hlavsa would repeatedly say, 'were we political . . . we didn't have a message, certainly we did not plan to bring down communism. We just loved rock and roll and wanted to be famous.'[3] Yet Gustáv Husák, the Soviet puppet leader installed by Moscow in 1969, was jittery. Deeply conservative in many ways, he was a humourless man who wanted silence and obedient conformity from his people. A stern, unbending figure from a small town on the Danube close to Bratislava, he had been jailed by the fascist regime that ruled in Slovakia under German occupation during the war. Later, when a fast-rising Communist Party apparatchik, he spent six years in a detention camp during the purge years in the 1950s on charges of 'bourgeois nationalism'. The experience scarred him. Aged sixty-three now, he felt threatened by anything he imagined was unconventional. He had recently prosecuted the Slovak writer Jan Kalina for editing and publishing a book called *1001 Jokes* – a collection of (mostly) anti-Communist gags that the regime believed were deeply subversive. Kalina's home in Bratislava was bugged so the intelligence agency could find out who was passing jokes on to him. Then he was jailed for two years.[4]

Pop music was perceived as a danger to the State. The Plastic People of the Universe had been founded in the late 1960s and at first were allowed to perform legally. But in 1973, along with some other Czech bands, they were forbidden to play at public events. They found a way to appear within the law at 'private gatherings' like weddings, anniversary parties, in people's homes or – as a loophole in the law allowed – in gardens. They quickly attracted a cult following. Young people thought that if Husák and the full force of the Communist regime were against them, the Plastic People must be doing something right. One of their great admirers was a man beginning to make his mark as a playwright, essayist and philosopher, Václav Havel, whose work was receiving some attention in the West.

The Plastics dressed in the same way as counter-culture bands of the time in the US or Western Europe – leather jackets, jeans, tie-dye T-shirts, lots of beads – and they wore their hair long. The police and the StB of course knew they were performing, but for some years let them carry on, not wishing to provoke a conflict between generations. The Plastics were more psychedelic than capitalist, but the popularity of the band was a constant irritant to the neo-Stalinist voices in the regime. The Communist oligarchs in Prague Castle ordered the security apparatus to arrest these 'work-shy people', according to a conversation at the highest level in the Czech government. 'Their music has nothing to do with art and seriously threatens the moral values of society. The lyrics . . . [display] extreme vulgarity with an anti-socialist and an anti-social impact, most of them extolling nihilism, decadence and clericalism.'[5] When they appeared at a show trial in October 1976 Havel, who loved the vigour and vibrancy of rock music, managed to watch the 'performance' from the gallery for part of the case. He wrote a brilliant essay with a title echoing Kafka, 'The Trial', which he published in samizdat, and which, much to the embarrassment of the authorities, was smuggled to the West. 'The Plastics were simply young people who wanted to live in their own way, to make the music they liked, to sing what they wanted to sing, to live in harmony with themselves in a truthful way,' he wrote. The Plastics represented 'life's intrinsic desire to express itself freely, in its own authentic and sovereign way'.[6]

Two months after the Plastic People were convicted and sentenced, Havel and a few other writers, artists, academics and musicians launched an organisation to campaign for the band's release and, more broadly, to call attention to the violations of human rights behind the Iron Curtain. It was 'a loose, informal and open association of people . . . united by the will to strive individually and collectively for human and civil rights in our country and throughout the world'. The document, known as Charter 77, was sent to West German TV and Deutsche Welle Radio, where it received modest coverage. Initially it was signed by 243 people.[7]

There was another catalyst behind the formation of Charter 77, which along with the Polish KOR became the best-known human rights group in Eastern Europe. The Helsinki Accords on Security in Europe, signed after lengthy negotiations in 1975, gave civil rights campaigners a powerful weapon they could turn against the Communist regimes. The 'rights' package within the Helsinki Treaty had a far more profound impact than any of the diplomats who worked on it could have conceived. Over time it helped to sap the confidence, the strength and the will of the Communists to govern.

Initially, the Soviet Union and its satellite states hailed the Helsinki agreement as a masterstroke of diplomacy for the Kremlin bosses. The Accords recognised the post-World War Two borders as inviolable and appeared to give the Communist regimes a legitimacy they had not possessed. In particular, the East German Communists were delighted. Previously nobody outside the socialist bloc had recognised the GDR as a country. Now the East Germans would have diplomatic links everywhere. But the Soviets paid a price. They agreed to a declaration on a range of rights about free assembly, free speech and democratic values enshrined in the United Nations Charter. 'All signatories agree to respect civil, economic, social, cultural and other rights and freedoms, all of which derive from the inherent dignity of the human person,' the preamble to the Treaty stated.[8] The Soviets thought that if the West agreed to recognise postwar borders it also meant nobody would seek to change the internal politics in the socialist countries. They believed it would make Communist rule in the satellite states permanent and put an end to any potential Prague Springs. They seriously miscalculated. It was

> a nail in the coffin of Communism ... Brezhnev looked forward to the publicity he would gain when the Soviet public learned of the final settlement of the postwar boundaries for which they had sacrificed so much. As for the humanitarian issues, those could be mentioned at home, just vaguely, without much publicity. He thought this would not bring much trouble inside our country. But he was wrong ... In the Kremlin, some amongst the old guard were stunned when they first saw the language of the Human Rights provisions in the treaty. Andropov, Suslov (and others) had grave doubts about assuming international commitments that could open the way for foreign intervention in our political life ... Many Soviet ambassadors expressed doubts because they correctly anticipated difficult international disputes later on. But Gromyko won the argument proclaiming 'we will be masters in our own house', thus admitting non-compliance with the treaty from the start ... The agreements gradually became a manifesto of the dissident and liberal movement – a development totally beyond the imagination of the Soviet leadership.[9]

The Soviets felt they could hardly say no to the Accords. The rights enshrined in them were, theoretically at least, guaranteed in the constitutions of the USSR and its satellite countries, in noble and uplifting prose. Nor could they easily just ignore the provisions, which clearly they had intended to do. The Treaty permitted the West to upbraid the Soviets and their allies when they failed to live up to its terms and gave civil liberties campaigners throughout the empire a legal basis on which to insist that their governments uphold the terms of the agreement. Helsinki Watch groups mushroomed throughout the socialist bloc, except Romania, where nobody dared to form one. The Czech historian Petr Pithart said the Treaty provisions armed the opposition with a new strategy. Rather than demand new rights they did not possess, the Helsinki Watch groups could claim that these freedoms were already enshrined in law, but not recognised in reality. The argument made the opposition sound reasonable and forced the Communist Parties on to the defensive. The Hungarian philosopher and human rights activist Miklós Haraszti agreed. 'Helsinki gave us a stick we could beat the regime with constantly. It was vital,' he said.[10]

Even cynics in the West became convinced. When it was being negotiated, US Secretary of State Henry Kissinger mocked the Helsinki agreement. His own chief aide on Europe, William Hyland, admitted his boss's attitude was one of 'disdain. He said "I don't care what they do ... they could write it in Swahili for all I care ... I don't believe that a bunch of revolutionaries who have managed to cling to power for 50 years are going to be euchred out of it ... by the kind of people negotiating in Helsinki'.[11] Later Kissinger changed his mind and recognised it as 'a political and moral landmark that contributed to the progressive decline of the Soviet system ... Rarely has a diplomatic process so illuminated the limitations of human foresight.'[12]

Václav Havel did not look the part of a charismatic leader. He was short of stature, with an awkward gait, and gave the air of a slightly diffident and absent-minded professor. He was a man who could not conceal his insecurities and self-doubts. He made a good living by writing about them with wit, charm and searing honesty. Yet when the time came he could act with certainty, boldness and speed. In many ways he was the archetypal Central European intellectual, at his happiest talking about philosophy, drama and politics late into the night in a bar with fellow writers. He spent, by his own admission, many months of his life at his favourite pub near the Vltava River in Prague's Old Town. By inclination he was a philosopher, but he loved the theatre and actors. Circumstances and accident turned him into a political leader, a man of action, but he found he had an aptitude for it almost as great as his skill as a writer.

Havel was born in Prague on 5 October 1936, into a prosperous family. He had a pampered, privileged early childhood. His grandfather had made a fortune in land speculation and built a famous and elegant art deco shopping mall, The Lucerna, just off Wenceslas Square in the centre of the Czech capital. It was one of the earliest ventures of its kind in Europe. His father was a famous Prague restaurateur. All the family property was seized in 1948 when the Communists took over. Havel and his kind were regarded as class enemies by the new power in the land. As the son of a bourgeois, he was denied any education beyond grammar school. University places were reserved for the sons of workers – or of loyal Communist Party members from whatever class. He got a job as a stagehand at Prague's Balustrade Theatre, where his passion for the stage was born. He started writing plays in his spare time, elliptical, absurdist work, most of which could not be performed in his own country because it did not pass the censor. His best plays began to be staged regularly abroad, though, where his reputation grew.[13]

Havel made a name for himself as an 'oppositionist' before he was twenty at a meeting of the Czech Writers' Union – an important organisation under communism, as nobody could get published without being a member. He made a speech criticising older, more established writers for 'hypocrisy', not so much because they did not tell the truth – a difficult and dangerous thing to do – but because they would not even listen to the truth. It was 'the truth' that exercised Havel more than anything else. His best-known works were essays of a discursive, philosophical nature about living as honestly as one could under oppression in a land where 'the State has an outpost in everyone's mind' and where 'real history has stopped . . . (where) all history has become pseudo history . . . the government, as it were, nationalised time. Hence, time meets the sad fate of so many other nationalised things. It has begun to wither away.'[14]

Havel became the chief spokesman for 'the Chartists' after the document was launched in January 1977. The group was tiny and at most a minor irritant. But Havel was arrested several times for short periods of twenty-four hours in the months afterwards. His repeated description of Gustáv Husák as the 'President of Forgetting' was among the reasons. In April 1979 the regime lost patience and decided to make an example of him. He was picked up by the StB, tried for 'slandering the

State' and sentenced to four and a half years in a tough prison with hardened career criminals rather than amongst gentle intellectuals. He was worked hard and his already poor health – he repeatedly suffered from chest and lung problems – deteriorated further. But this was Czechoslovakia, *Good Soldier Švejk* and Kafka territory, and there were moments of farce behind bars. Havel used to say that he recalled prison guards – called *bonzaks* – persuading him to write their reports on inmate Václav Havel. 'I had to write many confidential reports on myself,' he said. 'I wanted to help the bonzaks, and besides it was a chance to mystify the authorities.'[15]

After his release he was watched and followed, suffered many petty indignities, yet was allowed to make a good living . He was permitted to keep the money he earned from royalties abroad. In Czech terms he was a rich man. He spent long periods writing quietly at his country cottage in Bohemia two and a half hours from Prague. The secret police built a two-storey chalet nearby so that they could keep an eye on him. On a clear day he could see the officer on duty peering at him through binoculars. Havel simply ignored them, as he did the two StB goons placed permanently outside his apartment in Prague. He knew his phone and home were bugged; he ignored that too, as far as possible, and lived as 'normal' a life as he could, meeting whomever he wanted, whenever he wanted, and talking about whatever he wanted. He was developing a way of surviving under totalitarian conditions while maintaining his integrity intact. His message was that when you live *as if* you are free, you can learn *to be* free, whatever the totalitarian State throws at you.

The idea seems personal and moral, but Havel recognised it as supremely political. He explained it best in a classic essay, *The Power of the Powerless*. There was no point in confronting those in power or arguing with them, he said. The point was not even to *tell* the truth, though against a system based on lies that was important. The crucial thing was to 'live in truth' – all else was compromise. 'If the main pillar of the system is living a lie, it is not surprising the fundamental threat to it is living the truth . . . the very act of forming a political grouping forces one to start playing a power game, instead of giving truth a priority,' he wrote. People who can find no autonomy from the State 'confirm the system, fulfil the system, make the system, *are* the system'. It was a difficult concept to grasp – easily mocked by workers whose main worries were not notions about 'truth' or moral sensibility, but keeping a roof over their heads if they landed in trouble with the regime, or providing for their children's higher education. 'The moment someone breaks through in one place, when one person cries out "The Emperor is naked", when a single person breaks the rules of the game, thus exposing it as a game, everything suddenly appears in another light, and the whole crust seems to be made of a tissue on the point of tearing and disintegrating uncontrollably.' These were ideas totally foreign to the likes of Husák or his henchmen. Paranoid they may have been, but they could sense a real threat when they saw one: in a totalitarian society, bypassing the State is potentially a dangerous challenge to the regime. Havel recognised that on the surface it did not seem to say a great deal to a factory worker in the tractor plant in Brno. 'These are perhaps impractical methods in today's world and very difficult to apply in daily life,' he acknowledged. 'Nevertheless I know of no better alternative.'[16]

Havel was the most imaginative, eloquent and powerful critic of Soviet-style communism. He inspired and encouraged others. Yet he was always among a mere handful throughout the socialist empire. The importance of dissident intellectuals far outweighed their minuscule numbers. Writers, for example, had always been highly valued by communism as, in Stalin's phrase, 'engineers of the mind'. That is why the dictatorships over the years went to such elaborate lengths to seduce and use them. An artist who went along with the system, acted as a Party propagandist, wrote paeans of praise and birthday tributes for the dictator, as they were expected to do, could live in great comfort and achieve stardom. Historically in most of Central and Eastern Europe the intelligentsia was a class on its own, involved politically in a way unknown in the Anglo-Saxon world and rare in the rest of Europe. As Bronisław Geremek, one of the most influential advisers to Solidarity in Poland, used to say: 'The West is different, "normal". Here . . . an intellectual must be engaged . . . Because we are fighting for the very right to think.'[17]

Now it was far harder for the satellite regimes to deal with dissidents. The East was no longer cut off from the rest of Europe. Writers, journalists and artists had better contacts with the West than before. Gone were the days when a troublesome poet or painter could be hauled off and quietly executed or dispatched to the gulag to languish away for years. In September 1978 the Bulgarian secret service – with active help from the KGB – murdered the exiled writer Georgi Markov at a bus stop on Waterloo Bridge in the middle of London. He was poisoned with ricin which had been placed in a pellet on the end of an umbrella that was then used to scratch him, lightly, on the shin. Markov died after a few days in hospital and nobody knew the details of his murder until some years later. Two exiled Romanian journalists who worked for Radio Free Europe were killed in Germany by the Securitate. But these were crude exceptions from the cruder regimes. Elsewhere, dissidents were handled with more subtlety – or at least with less overt brutality. The satiric singer and songwriter Wolf Biermann had for long been a thorn in the side of the East German regime. His witty and wry ballads proved the point that bullies fear mockery above all things. When in November 1976 the regime wanted rid of Biermann, the East Germans waited until he was on a concert tour in West Germany. After a performance in Cologne the GDR government simply announced that he had been stripped of his citizenship and would not be permitted to return East.

Until 1968, most of the internal opposition to the regimes had come from within the Party. The anti-Communists had been suppressed or cowed into silence, so the thinkers who spoke up were careful to say they were examining from a Marxist perspective what had gone wrong with the system. There had been 'false moves along a true path' and they suggested liberalised 'socialism with a human face' reforms of the kind instituted by the socialist leader of the Prague Spring, Alexander Dubček. 'We were trying to find flaws in the blueprint,' as Milan Šimečka said. But after the Soviet invasion of Czechoslovakia it became clear that the Party would permit no challenges to strict orthodoxy. Among intellectuals, deep pessimism – deeper than usual in Central Europe – descended. Even true believers grew cynical, or despaired. The gloom was lifted by Havel and others who pointed a way which, as the novelist Ludvík Vaculík explained, allowed people to survive as 'a citizen of a state which I will never abandon but in which I cannot contentedly live'.[18]

Some could not see that 'living in truth' was much of a strategy at all, though. The Czech author Milan Kundera said that 'it was not only idealistic but stupid to confront an immovable regime with meaningless small deeds such as passing around carbon copies of manifestos'. He abandoned any form of hope and escaped to the Left Bank of Paris. Havel responded to Kundera's emigration with a typical comment. He too had been encouraged to go elsewhere, but he decided to stay. 'The solution . . . does not exist in leaving. Fourteen million people can't just go and leave Czechoslovakia,' he said.[19]

Most of the dissidents did not like the term, said Michnik. 'A dissident is a renegade, a rebel, a rare bird, whereas we ... believed we represented the majority of the nation.' Nevertheless dissidents are what they were called in the Western media and for the rebellious intellectuals who remained in their countries life was hard, though easier than it had been. The Hungarian philosopher Gáspár Tamás described their existence:

> Dissent was an anomaly. Dissidents ... led a life where satisfactions, successes, defeats and frustrations were very different from those felt by the population at large. While our academic or ... other colleagues looked for preferment, authorial fame, international travel, second homes and the like, our pride lay in our work appearing in smudgy, primitively stencilled little pamphlets ... and success as distributing a couple of hundred copies before the secret police arrived ... A secret police officer – unforgettably dressed in a University of Texas T-shirt – asked me once: 'You consider yourself an intelligent man I suppose? Then how can you explain that you are acting against your own interests?' The powers that be ... were puzzled, nay, appalled, at the phenomenon of dissidence. Non-conformism and eccentricity are conflated with madness even in freer and more permissive societies than in Eastern Europe. Dissidence was regarded as an expression of anomie by many and, well, I could not deny that there were a few strange types among us ... The dissidents said strange things. They began to talk about ... 'parallel public spheres' and 'dissident sub cultures' and the like, as though they were content with the murky underworld of political, artistic and moral avant-garde. Dissidents wore beards, did not save up to buy East German automobiles, spoke foreign languages and were the first to carry their children in pouches. Many were Jewish. In 1968, when many good Hungarians and East Germans drunk themselves into oblivion with happiness at the sight of the humiliation of their ancient foe, Czechoslovakia, the dissidents took the side of the foreigner. In short, they were a pain in the neck.[20]

The ruling oligarchs had more pressing problems than were posed by a few long-haired rock musicians or playwrights. Their regimes were going bankrupt – and they believed that they could only be rescued by Western capitalists. Leaders like Husák made a social contract with their people. 'If you conform outwardly and cause no trouble, we the Party will guarantee enough food, a reasonable, constantly improving standard of living and various social provisions. Just forget about freedom or other "bourgeois democratic" ideas, and there will be enough material benefits to satisfy you.' At this time, as the émigré Czech novelist Josef Škvorecký put it, 'the butcher's shop became the barometer of East European contentment'. The pact worked for a while, but began to unravel in the early 1980s. The Communist regimes could not keep their side of the bargain without massive borrowing from the West. Over time, the basic flaws in the system grew increasingly obvious. But although it had to change, it could not – for ideological and political reasons. The Party drew its authority from the conviction that it was infallible, that the tide of history was on its side. Problems began to be compounded when events failed to follow the script laid down by the socialist visionaries.

The rulers saw economic reform as dangerous. The system might have been hopeless and unworkable – but, they thought, it protected their hold on power. They saw, correctly, that their authority depended on maintaining a centrally planned economy where decisions were taken as much for reasons of political advantage as of economic sense. Above all, central planning ensured that the decisions were taken by them, the Communists. Decentralising decision-making – introducing a market – would disperse power and put in question the Party's claim to sole authority. The system was still no good at making consumer products. An example was motor cars – an obvious and visible sign of the differences between East and West. They were a symbol of consumerism, wealth, independence and economic efficiency. Everybody could see the difference between a Mercedes and a Trabant, which was a joke inside East Germany, let alone in the rest of the world. The Communist countries were bad at producing cars. The reason was not technical or even economic. It was the way they were 'sold'. Owning them had as much to do with official position as wealth. The state allocated cars – as it did all luxury items, homes and holidays. For instance, in Czechoslovakia the right to buy a car was withdrawn from purge victims after the Soviet invasion in 1968. It took several years before car ownership there returned to 'normal' – as in the rest of the socialist bloc. First for the nomenklatura; second to friends of the nomenklatura; and only third, those who could afford them.

The only way to stock shelves in the East was to borrow large amounts of money from the West. The new vision, as Adam Michnik put it, was 'to build Communism on the US dollar'. Communists and Western bankers fell into each other's arms in a bizarre *danse macabre*. The Communist regimes saw Western capital as a means of buying off public opinion at home and of delaying the introduction of much-needed radical changes. They used the foreign credits not on new investment in technology or diversifying their industrial base, but on food and consumer goods, which they could pass on to their own people at unrealistically subsidised prices. At first the East Europeans were content. As were Western bankers, who beat a well-worn path from the City of London and Wall Street to Warsaw, Berlin and Budapest. Half the loans were from private banks guaranteed by Western governments, which had encouraged them to lend behind the Iron Curtain. The other half was unsecured, but the East Europeans were regarded as responsible borrowers. The bankers with short-term memories saw the regimes as highly stable, with a well-trained workforce. Crucially, they believed that the Soviet 'guarantee' over the socialist bloc would rule out any chance of defaults.[21]

They were cynical and at the same time stunningly naïve about the political systems they were dealing with. In the long term the most realistic hope of getting their money back was to encourage a more open democracy, but that idea seemed never to have occurred to them. Instead, many of them greeted martial law in Poland as an excellent thing. The General would make the trains run on time. 'Who knows which political system works?' explained the head of Citibank's international division in a *Commentary* magazine article in 1982. 'The only test we care about is: can they pay their bills?'[22]

In the longer term the loans did not ease the plight of communism. They made it far worse. Poland was the most heavily indebted – or, as one Polish economist described it, 'addicted, as with the most dangerous of drugs'. In the six years leading up to the martial law declaration Poland's foreign debt increased fifteen-fold, to US$ 66 billion. But every East European regime began using these platinum credit cards, to ruinous effect. Paying interest soon began to consume national budgets. In East Germany, by the early 1980s, 60 per cent of income went towards loan repayment – a level that became impossible to maintain. Miklós Németh, the chief official in Hungary's Economic Ministry throughout most of the 1980s, and later to become Hungarian Prime Minister, explained, despairingly, how the credits were used: 'We spent two-thirds of it on paying interest,' he said. 'The remaining third went towards importing consumer goods to ease the impression of economic crisis.' Most of the ageing men in charge of these economies hid their heads in the sand. Naturally they never let on to their people how heavily in hock they were to those they were describing each day in the state-owned media as the hyenas of capitalism.[23]

The Soviets were in as bad an economic mess as the rest of their empire – far worse than some parts of it. Protecting their territorial possessions was becoming an increasing burden, though the exhausted men in the Kremlin refused to acknowledge it. They were not prepared to consider any sort of cost benefit analysis about maintaining the empire they had won just a few decades earlier. Their determination to remain a superpower – for ideological and prestige reasons – was resolute. It did not concern them that they were driving the USSR to penury. The Soviets were building bigger and heavier weapons on a vast scale. Soviet industry in the 1970s and early 1980s was still geared to military production, not to providing what consumers and Soviet citizens wanted – or, towards the end of the twentieth century, what they needed. The Plan still contained a 'dual purpose' element. Every factory which made industrial products like cars or electrical goods was required to have a military application, too, and could quickly be converted to a war footing. This distorted Soviet industry up to the end of the Union. Huge numbers of weapons of all kinds were produced. Hundreds of intercontinental missiles were made a year. They were called, strangely for a regime supposedly run by atheists, 'The Satans'. Thousands of tanks annually rolled off Soviet production lines. The Russians continually added to their arsenal out of ideology – and from an inferiority complex. They sought to catch up with the West's technological superiority by weight of numbers. Their military theory was that they needed superiority not just with the US, but with all of Nato, the British and French nuclear weapons, and also the Chinese. The Soviet military thought the quality of their weapons was almost certainly inferior to equivalent American armaments. So they were determined to compensate with quantity. As Viktor Starodubov, an assistant to Defence Minister Ustinov, said: 'We built so many weapons of mass destruction because they are one of the few things we can build well.'[24]

But the military and the industry that supported it appeared to have slipped out of any rational control. Vitali Katayev, an official in the Defence Ministry at the time, said the Soviets' military 'was a bull in a china shop, a sort of Soviet Texas. It always demanded as much weaponry as possible. A decision to introduce a new weapon was made not on the basis of military needs or technical merit, but rather on the basis of the authority of its sponsors and their relationship with the political leadership. Soviet military industry was supposed to increase by three per cent a year – it was in the Plan that it must do so – therefore "production of many types of weapons was not stopped even after the army was saturated with them".'[25]

The USSR was 'massively overproducing armaments', according to Georgi Arbatov, the influential head of the US and Canadian Studies Institute and chief adviser to a succession of top Kremlin magnates. 'It undermined Western trust towards us . . . our actions encouraged the Americans to intensify the arms race.' Accurate figures were extraordinarily hard to come by, but according to some numbers Brezhnev was shown in the last months of his life, direct military expenses such as the cost of armed forces and equipment were at least 15 per cent of the state budget, and direct defence-related spending was probably two and a half times that sum. A good estimate was that defence ate up around 40 per cent of the Soviet Union's budget – far more than when the USSR was preparing for World War Two. When the rest of the economy was stagnating, this was a huge drain on the nation's resources. Some of the leaders knew it. But there is no evidence they did anything about it – or even discussed it. There seem to have been no debates within the Kremlin on this most vital of issues for the country's future. Even some of the most senior men in the army realised the military budget had become bloated. In the early 1980s Marshal Nikolai Ogarkov, head of the Soviet General Staff, began to argue that there was too much waste in the military-industrial complex, too much inefficiency and far too many gigantic projects that did not seem worthwhile. He said it was 'suicidal' automatically to pursue the US in the arms race. Instead of initiating a debate on future Soviet military and geopolitical strategy, the Marshal was unceremoniously fired.[26]

EIGHT

ABLE ARCHER

Washington DC, Wednesday 2 November 1983

JUST A HANDFUL of people knew how close the world would come to nuclear obliteration over the next few days. The Cuban Missile Crisis of twenty-one years earlier was a drama played out in public. It had a gradual build-up, a centrepiece and a dénouement seen on live TV when a stunned and terrified world could breathe a sigh of relief. Everybody who lived through it would remember the fear and intensity they felt. The story of Able Archer 83 was entirely different. Barely anyone outside a few military bunkers and espionage headquarters knew anything out of the ordinary was happening. While the world went on as normal, the Soviet leaders in the Kremlin became convinced that the US and Nato were about to mount a surprise nuclear attack against them and ordered the Soviet military to begin a countdown to retaliate. Only since the collapse of communism have documents surfaced which establish that, through a series of misunderstandings and miscalculations, Armageddon was averted more by luck than sound judgement towards the end of 1983.

Yuri Andropov finally achieved his lifelong ambition about a year earlier, on 10 November 1982, when he succeeded Brezhnev as Soviet Communist Party boss. But he was already a dying man, bitter, frightened and deeply pessimistic. His character and political convictions had been formed as a rising apparatchik in the years of Terror. 'He was deeply traumatised by his years working under Stalin, like the majority of his generation,' a long-time colleague said. Andropov was a master of 'spin'. Somehow he had maintained a reputation as a 'liberal', though it is hard to see on what possible basis. It is true that he wrote some occasionally pretty lyric verse; in earlier days he liked to dance with attractive women – and they liked to dance with him. He had an entourage near him of bright, youngish cadres, some of them with progressive views, for whom he acted as mentor. However, he was a man of his era, austere, absolutely convinced in his own ideology and in the final victory of communism. He believed that for prestige and strategic reasons the USSR needed a 'buffer' zone – its European empire – and he was not going to be the General Secretary who lost any part of it. He was a resolutely orthodox Bolshevik. As KGB chief for nearly two decades it was he who enthusiastically orchestrated the campaigns against dissidents in the 1970s and Jewish refuseniks who wished to go to Israel. He had wanted to jail the novelist Alexander Solzhenitsyn rather than send him into exile. He supervised the trials of figures such as Yuri Orlov and Natan Sharansky, and approved the harassment of the physicist and human rights campaigner Andrei Sakharov, who was sent into internal exile with his wife Yelena Bonner. Much of this was down to Andropov's insistence that 'communism needed permanent vigilance'.[1]

Andropov as KGB boss knew the real and parlous economic condition of the Soviet Union. He proposed a few economic reforms and he launched a big public relations drive for more 'workplace discipline', but he was as closely associated with what some Soviets were already calling 'the years of stagnation' as any of the other old men in the Kremlin. He did nothing to challenge the basic flaws in the Soviet system – the dead weight of central planning, the dominance of politics over economic reality. He imagined that all he needed to do was cleanse the system of the corruption and indolence of the Brezhnev years, fire a few of the more sleazy bureaucrats, and communism would return to the true path for which it was destined by history.

Now he was unrecognisable as the forceful, tall, handsome, smooth, silver-haired dancer at parties. Ailing and skeletal, he barely moved from the special Kremlin hospital room designed for him where he sat in a dentist's chair with a high head-rest which enabled him to change position – and make telephone calls – at the press of a button. Three months after he became General Secretary his kidneys failed completely. He needed dialysis treatment twice a week, which exhausted him for two days at a stretch. He was never seen in public – the Moscow rumour mill had it that he was dead and the Kremlin was keeping the fact secret while a vicious power struggle was going in the high reaches of the Soviet Communist Party. He was alive – just. But he communicated through statements 'from the Soviet leadership' via the official state news agency, Tass, or by interviews in the principal Party newspaper, *Pravda*.[2]

Andropov had been convinced before he succeeded to supreme office that America was planning a sudden first-strike nuclear attack on the Soviet Union. The election of a tough-sounding conservative, Ronald Reagan, as President of the US was part of the reason, but not the only factor. He was receiving intelligence about American military manoeuvres throughout the globe, and, piecing all the clues together – wrongly – was persuaded that the Americans were preparing an attack. Nothing would dissuade him, certainly not the facts. Andropov believed Reagan meant his anti-Communist propaganda and viewed him with unrelenting suspicion. Soon after he was inaugurated as President in January 1981, Reagan wrote to Brezhnev proposing a meeting to discuss nuclear weapons. Andropov convinced Brezhnev it would be a waste of time. He said it was a 'phoney gesture' and he never changed his position.[3]

In May 1981 Andropov invited Brezhnev to a closed session of top KGB and military officers where he told a surprised audience of his conviction about the imminent first-strike threat from Washington. He ordered his officers at the KGB to co-operate with the Russian army in the biggest intelligence-gathering operation the Soviets had ever conducted in peacetime, codenamed (in English translation) RYAN – *raketno yadernoye napadenie*. Intelligence agents abroad were given orders which were, as they clearly stated, 'a permanent, operational assignment to uncover Nato preparations of a nuclear missile attack on the USSR'. RYAN created a vicious circle. Soviet spies were told to search out alarming information. The Kremlin was duly alarmed and wanted more.[4] Many in the KGB and the GRU military intelligence thought Andropov was exaggerating the danger – experienced agents in the field saw no evidence of any American attack.

But few voices dared challenge him. One who did was the British spy Donald Maclean, part of the 'Philby' espionage ring, who had dramatically defected to Moscow in the 1950s and later became a respected analyst on foreign and intelligence policy. He wrote a highly classified memo to his KGB superiors:

> During the last five years, at certain crucial turning points, the views of the military authorities, with their natural professional interest in maximising the armed strength of the country, have, with the support of the top leadership, prevailed over those who are called upon to assess the overall influence of military policy upon the international interests of the country . . . The result will be, unless the Soviet Union

> changes its policy, a rise in the level of nuclear confrontation in Europe with no compensatory advantage to itself – indeed, quite the reverse.[5]

Andropov was not listening to such sceptics. When he became General Secretary he gave RYAN a yet higher priority. Additional instructions went out to agents in Nato countries to 'watch for activity at places where government officials and their families are evacuated ... [identify] the location of specially equipped civil defence shelters ... [investigate] increased blood from donors and the prices paid for it'. The US had promised that it would not launch any medium-range weapons from European bases without consulting NATO allies first, so the instructions from Moscow to KGB agents in the field say that 'the most important problem ... for the apparatus of Soviet intelligence is to ascertain in good time the moment when nuclear consultations begin inside Nato'.[6]

In January 1983 Andropov summoned Communist Party chiefs from the Warsaw Pact for a hastily convened secret summit in Moscow at which he issued them with what he described as a direct warning that relations between the two superpowers were at their lowest point since the Cuban Missile Crisis. He told the East Europeans:

> Especially dangerous ... is the military challenge from the US. The new round of the arms race, imposed by the US, has major qualitative differences. Whereas before, the Americans, in speaking about nuclear weapons, preferred to accentuate the fact that it was above all a means of ... 'deterrence' now ... do not hide the fact that they are really intended for a future war. From here springs the doctrine of 'rational' and 'limited' nuclear war. From here spring the statements about the possibility of surviving and winning a protracted nuclear conflict. It is hard to see what is blackmail and what is genuine readiness to take the fatal step.[7]

In Washington President Reagan and his advisers had no conception of the fear and paranoia sweeping through Moscow, largely at the instigation of the Soviets' supreme leader. They did not realise Andropov was taking the presidential rhetoric so seriously. Reagan's famous speech in Orlando, Florida, on 8 March 1983, where he branded the Soviet Union an 'evil empire', ratcheted up the tension. Senior military men in the USSR responded. According to General Vladimir Slipchenko of the Soviet General Staff: 'The military ... used that speech as a reason to begin a very intense preparation for a state of war. We started to run huge strategic exercises. These were the first in which we really tested our mobilisation. We didn't just exercise our ground forces, but also strategic arms. For the military, the period when we were called the "evil empire" was actually very good and useful because we achieved a very high military readiness.'

Less than a month later the Americans began a series of military exercises which the CIA's leading Soviet analyst, Douglas MacEachin, called 'America's biggest exercise in history around Soviet waters'. He said 'the air force "tested" the Kremlin's defence systems and the navy ... its territorial waters'. During this huge exercise the US Pacific Fleet probed for gaps in Russian ocean surveillance and early-warning systems. The Americans practised simulated assaults on Soviet strategic submarines with nuclear missiles on board. The Soviets reacted with their own series of exercises introducing, for the first time, a rehearsal of a general mobilisation using strategic nuclear forces. The Americans increased the numbers of their spy flights and reconnaissance sorties – especially around the Soviet Union's far eastern border. The war of nerves was about to take a heavy toll.[8]

Colonel Gennadi Osipovich was a veteran pilot in the Soviet Union's Air Defence Force, the PVO, with more than ten years' experience in the Far East. The PVO was little regarded by the elite among Russian flying aces, but it was the first line in Soviet air defences. 'At this point, 1982 and especially 1983, we were flying more often than we used to,' he recalled. 'There were more spy planes provoking us. We were in a constant state of tension.' A few minutes before dawn on the morning of 1 September Osipovich was scrambled into his Sukhoi-15 interceptor and ordered to track an unidentified 'military' target which was approaching the island of Sakhalin in the Sea of Okhotsk from the direction of Kamchatka.[9]

The 'intruder' aircraft had already been flying above Soviet territory for over an hour. Four fighters had been following it but had managed to lose touch with it before they could execute their mission, which was to destroy the target. The Soviets believed the intruder was an American RC-135 reconnaissance plane that had been spotted earlier, sent with the Soviets' knowledge to monitor a Soviet missile test. The Russians had been told the American aircraft would leave the area by 05.00 hours. They thought it had overstayed its welcome on an espionage mission. In fact the American plane had accidentally crossed flight paths with a South Korean Boeing 747 passenger plane, Flight KAL-007, en route to Seoul from New York, having refuelled at Anchorage. There were twenty-nine crew and 240 passengers on board, including a US Congressman, Larry P. McDonald of Georgia, the chairman of the ultra-right-wing John Birch Society. Colonel Osipovich was now tracking the civil airplane, which he spotted after about fifteen minutes in the air. He and his superiors knew that he would have to act quickly. The Su-15s had limited flying range, and in any case they were deliberately kept short of fuel. Ever since, a couple of years earlier, a pilot of a state-of-the-art MiG-25 flew to Japan and defected there was a standing order that no PVO plane should be loaded with enough fuel to reach a foreign airfield. Osipovich had a maximum flying time of about forty-five minutes.

On board the 747 Captain Chun Byung-in and his colleagues on the flight deck had no idea they had wandered more than 300 miles off-course and had drifted over forbidden Soviet territory. The captain had mistakenly flicked a wrong switch. The Boeing was flying on its automatic magnetic compass rather than its more accurate inertial guidance system. The Korean pilot and his navigator believed they were in international waters 100 miles off the northern coast of Japan. They never knew what was about to happen to them.

Osipovich was ordered to flash the interceptor's lights to attract the Boeing's attention, but he was not spotted. Then he fired warning shots from his cannons – 243 rounds in all – but Chun did not hear them. For a short while, as Osipovich explained later, he was unsure about the 'target'. 'I could see two rows of windows which were lit up,' he said later. 'I wondered if it was a civilian aircraft. Military cargo planes don't have windows like that. But I had no time to think. I had a job to do. I started to signal to him [the pilot] in international code. I informed him that he had violated our air space. He did not respond.'[10] But, increasingly, the generals on the ground were convinced the Boeing was a military target. They worried that if they allowed it to get away they would be in trouble from their superiors and possibly lose their jobs. There was no time left before the plane left Soviet air space and Osipovich's interceptor ran out of fuel. At 6.21 a.m. the commander of air defence on Sakhalin Island, General Anatoli Kornukov, issued his order: 'The target has violated the state border. Destroy the target. Get Osipovich to fire and soon.'[11]

Osipovich spun around behind the 747 and at a distance of five miles stubbed his index finger to release the R-98 heat-seeking missile. 'I have executed the launch,' Osipovich radioed back to his base. About thirty seconds later he saw flame from KAL-007's tail section and as he veered off to the right, back to his base, he could see the plane disappear into the sea. 'The target is destroyed . . . I am breaking off attack.'

The destruction of a civilian aircraft was a disaster for the Soviet Union's reputation. It was compounded by the obtuse way the magnates in the Kremlin handled the aftermath. They lied and at no point accepted any measure of responsibility. There were many officials in the Soviet Foreign Ministry who urged the leadership to admit the truth. Sergei Tarasenko, for long a senior diplomat who later became an adviser to future foreign ministers, said: 'We came to the conclusion that we simply had to be honest and admit something along the lines of "an unfortunate incident has occurred. There was a pilot error, bad weather, one thing led to another. It was not a pre-planned action." We went to [Georgi] Kornienko, the Deputy Minister, who agreed with us ... But he was unable to convince the leadership. It was a question of prestige, and the military didn't like to admit mistakes.'[12]

The Defence Minister, Ustinov, categorically opposed admitting that the Soviet military had destroyed a civilian airliner. 'Don't worry,' he told Andropov, who was extremely ill in his hospital room. 'Everything will be all right. Nobody will be able to prove a thing. The Americans can never find out.' He might also have thought that it could be wise to deflect attention from his generals' role in the affair and what was revealed about air defence failures. The 747 had been in Soviet air space for over two hours before it was approached. Even more disturbing, eight of the eleven Soviet tracking stations on the Kamchatka Peninsula and Sakhalin had not detected the plane.[13]

Andropov was still in hospital the next day when the Kremlin magnates met in private to consider the consequences of the disaster. Konstantin Chernenko, Brezhnev's great friend, whose main function had previously been to keep Brezhnev amused and light his cigarettes, led the discussion. 'One thing is clear ... We cannot allow foreign planes to overfly our territory freely. No self-respecting state can allow that.' Ustinov was determined to defend the military and he told a bare-faced lie. He said the Boeing had been flying without warning lights, flatly contradicting the pilot. Nor was it true, as he claimed, that there were 'repeated instructions' to the Korean pilot to land at a Soviet airfield. 'My opinion is that in this situation we must show firmness and remain cool. We should not flinch. If we flinch it gives all kinds of people the opportunity to overfly our territory.' The Foreign Minister, Andrei Gromyko, did not stand up to this, though he might have done. He knew the damage that downing a civilian aircraft could do to the USSR's image abroad, but he did not challenge the military. He said it had been 'correct' to shoot down the plane, though he added that the USSR should anticipate what 'imperialist propaganda' would make of the incident.

One of the last to speak was the up-and-coming Mikhail Gorbachev, known to be Andropov's favourite and a strong candidate to succeed him. The rule in the Kremlin for an ambitious apparatchik trying to progress up the ladder was, when in doubt about what to say or do, attack the 'forces of imperialism'. Now Gorbachev said: 'The Americans must have been aware of the unauthorised incursion into Soviet territory. The plane had been in Russian air space for over two hours, showing clearly that this was a well-planned provocation ... It is no good keeping quiet now. We must go on to the offensive.'[14]

The rhetoric grew increasingly alarmist. A day after the plane was shot down President Reagan described it as 'an act of barbarism born of a society which wantonly disregards individual rights and the value of human life ... This was a crime against nature.' Andropov responded three weeks later, continuing to brazen out Soviet actions. He accused the US of an 'insidious provocation involving a South Korean plane engineered by US special services'. He blamed Reagan personally for a 'conspiracy that's an example of adventurism in politics' and for using 'inadmissible propaganda methods' and he warned that America was a country where an 'outrageous militarist psychosis is being implanted. If anybody ever had any illusions about the possibility of an evolution for the better in the policy of the present American administration they are completely dispelled.' The propaganda was noisier, echoing the worst days of the Cold War in the 1950s, but it was still rhetoric. Now the chilliness went beyond words.[15]

Towards the end of September Soviet satellite surveillance repeatedly picked up warnings of strategic missile launches from the US mainland. They were all false alarms – there was a glitch in the Soviet radar system that was quickly put right – but with the atmosphere between the superpowers so poor, they increased the tension. As did the American invasion of Grenada on 25 October to liberate the island from a coup by a Marxist guerrilla band. The Soviets did not care about a tiny Caribbean island, whose Communists they knew very little about. But almost at the same time the first Cruise and Pershing intermediate-range missiles began arriving at bases in West Germany. These were introduced in response to the Soviets' deployment of similar missiles in Eastern Europe, yet Andropov felt 'encircled'. His limited vision of the world was 'a bizarre mixture of grim realism and worst-case mentality', one of the most astute analysts of Soviet foreign policy observed. Now the latter took over.[16] He sent a message to Communist Party chiefs in the Warsaw Pact warning them that 'Washington has decided on a crusade against socialism as a system. Those who have now ordered the deployment of new nuclear weapons on our threshold link their practical policies with this reckless undertaking.' He summoned to his sickbed his most senior Kremlin and KGB officials. 'The international situation is very tense ... The US wants to change the existing strategic situation and they want an opportunity to make a first strike. The Soviet Union must prepare itself for every possible contingency in the short run.'[17]

Then came the Able Archer exercise, a nine-day-long test starting on this day of Nato's command and communications readiness for nuclear war. Andropov and his top intelligence advisers, hand-picked by him, were convinced that it was no exercise, but the real thing, a preparation for a strike against the Soviet Union or its East European empire. The Soviets had their own war plan which would disguise a move to the use of nuclear weapons with an apparently routine conventional exercise. The Soviet military assumed a Nato attack would begin the same way. But there were a myriad of other signs which the Kremlin and the KGB misread in 'the fog of cold war', as one intelligence analyst described it.

Able Archer 83 was on a far larger scale than previous war-game exercises. It was a more realistic drill than ever before. Nato leaders took part, including British Prime Minister Margaret Thatcher and the West German Chancellor Helmut Kohl. KGB spies discovered their participation and alerted Moscow. President Reagan, his Vice President George H.W. Bush and US Defense Secretary Caspar Weinberger were intending to be involved but withdrew at the last minute. Reagan's National Security Advisor, Robert McFarlane, was worried that superpower relations were so tense that their presence at the exercise could be misunderstood. Their non-participation was itself misinterpreted. Sudden disruptions to politicians' schedules and the swift movement of generals around Washington were precisely the kind of signs KGB officers were told to look out for as part of the RYAN project. Soviet military intelligence discovered that American communications formats had been substantially changed from previous exercises, which again was reported to the Kremlin as highly unusual.[18]

Andropov concluded that all this information could mean only one thing: that his fears and warnings about an American attack were coming true. He placed Soviet forces on the highest level of alert, and warned his Warsaw Pact allies that for the first time since the Cuban Missile Crisis the Soviets would deploy nuclear submarines along the US coastline.

The Americans could not believe the Soviet reaction to a straightforward drill. They assumed it was political posturing. One of the CIA's most senior Soviet experts, Melvin Goodman, recalls seeing some 'clandestine reports that suggested great alarm in Moscow. But frankly they weren't taken seriously by anyone except the analysts.'[19] A KGB officer working as a spy for the British, Oleg Gordievsky, urgently warned his controllers in London of the mood at the top in the Soviet Union. He recalled: 'When I told the British, they simply could not believe that the Soviet leadership was so stupid and narrow-minded as to believe in something so impossible . . . I said to them OK I'll get the documents.' His information went direct to Thatcher, who insisted that the Americans be told. 'Only a tiny handful of people knew the full details of how fearful they were,' said Thatcher's foreign policy adviser, Charles Powell. 'We knew then, through some extremely well-placed agents, that the Russians actually feared that the West was preparing for an aggressive nuclear war against them.'[20]

The CIA, late in the day, accepted that the Soviet fears may have been paranoid and misplaced but were for real. Former Director of Intelligence Robert Gates admitted: 'I don't think the Soviets were crying wolf . . . They did seem to believe that the situation was very dangerous. And US intelligence had failed to grasp the true extent of their anxiety.' When Reagan was finally told, the news had a profound effect. He saw how the superpowers could blunder into a war through a combination of overblown rhetoric, muscle-flexing, misunderstandings, naïvety and accidents. Immediately he made overtures to Moscow to assure them that Able Archer really was an exercise, and he dispatched retired General Brent Scowcroft, a future National Security Advisor, for face-to-face diplomacy 'to assure that we have no intention to [attack the USSR]'.[21] The tension eased slightly, the Soviets stood down from maximum alert, but relations remained deeply sour. In December, the Soviets walked out of talks in Geneva on missile reductions, which were in any case meandering along with no prospect of success and had only been continuing for show. Andropov remained angry, frustrated and bellicose in the few months remaining to him.

The episode radically changed Reagan, who confided in his diary: 'Three years has taught me something surprising about the Russians. Many people at the top of the Soviet hierarchy were genuinely afraid of America and Americans. Perhaps this shouldn't have surprised me, but it did.' The realisation turned him from a harsh Cold Warrior into a far more emollient statesman.[22]

NINE

AMERICA'S LEADING DOVE

Washington DC, November 1983

AMERICANS DEEPLY MISUNDERSTOOD the man they elected twice as President in the 1980s. Even some of his close advisers did not realise until late into his presidency that Ronald Reagan was a closet nuclear disarmer, a radical heretic. He ceased to believe in the theories of nuclear deterrence which most of the hawkish people around him uttered with such grim certainty. Reagan was an optimist, a dreamer. In private, he called the idea of Mutually Assured Destruction, the conventional wisdom on which the defence of both superpowers and their allies rested, 'irresponsible, totally abhorrent . . . a suicide pact'. He was convinced that he could rid the world of weapons of mass destruction. In public – even to some of his aides – he dared not say it. He was the darling of the right and his supporters would not have understood him. In domestic affairs he acted as a conservative. On the world stage, though he crafted his rhetoric to sound bellicose, he became America's leading dove. His great contribution to the world was not as the fire-breathing anti-Communist and Cold Warrior that so many of his most zealous admirers portrayed him. It was Reagan the negotiator, the dealmaker, the visionary man of peace who was successful.

At sixty-eight, Reagan was one of the oldest men to achieve supreme office in the US. He was a man who famously did not read a great deal, or deeply. But, equally famously, he was easy to underestimate. He learned a vast amount about the Soviet Union towards the end of his first term though, typically, he wore his learning lightly. He still spoke in simple terms, often in anecdotes and old jokes. But it is clear from his private correspondence and recently declassified papers that while his folksy charm, sense of humour, sunny disposition and immense calm were genuine, his simple, straightforward demeanour was not. He was far more complex, clever and calculating than he seemed. In his first term, Reagan oversaw an immense American arms build-up, in line with his belligerent 1980 campaign rhetoric about 'peace through strength'. But the massive increase in defence spending was not all the new President's doing. His predecessor, Jimmy Carter, had ordered much of it in response to the Soviet invasion of Afghanistan. The new range of Cruise and Pershing missiles in Europe had been approved by the Carter administration. Yet in the first four years of Reagan's presidency, the Americans built and deployed at least 700 new nuclear missiles and placed scores of thousands of additional men and women under arms. Reagan's budget director, David Stockman, said defence spending reached US$ 1.46 trillion and 'they were screaming with delight throughout the military industrial complex'. Reagan was not a details President so he never questioned a cent of the extra expenditure until later. In his first term he spent nearly as much on defence as Presidents Nixon, Ford and Carter combined and more than the cost of both the Korean and Vietnam wars.[1]

After the Able Archer 83 exercise Reagan began a profound re-examination of his entire strategy towards the Soviet Union. A key moment was a week after the drill when he met the ultra-hawkish Defense Secretary Weinberger and the Joint Chiefs of Staff Chairman General John Vessey in the 'situation room' at the White House to review the exercise. Unusually for him, Reagan was deeply gloomy afterwards. He realised, as he said later, that 'there were some people in the Pentagon who actually thought a nuclear war was winnable. I thought they were crazy.' Reagan knew that he would run for re-election the following year and was sure he would beat whatever candidate the Democrats chose to oppose him. He now believed that the harsh rhetoric and his tough line against the Soviets were producing few results. They were not making the Russians more responsive and reasonable. They had led to increased paranoia and a more aggressive response. 'The impact of Reagan's hard-line policy on the internal debates in the Kremlin . . . was exactly the opposite of the one intended by Washington,' Anatoli Dobrynin said. 'It strengthened those in the [leadership] and the security apparatus who had been pressing for a mirror image of Reagan's policy.'[2]

Reagan wanted to talk with the Russians leaders, but he had two problems. The first, as he quipped once, was 'that they kept dying on me'. The second was that highly influential members of his own administration were firmly set against any negotiations with the Soviets. Reagan had to contend with warfare in his own team that was almost as bitter as the Cold War conflict in the world outside the White House. Caspar Weinberger and a group of his brightest and most ideological Pentagon officials, such as Richard Perle, Paul Wolfowitz and Donald Rumsfeld, continually tried to persuade the President that the Soviets were not serious about talks. Reagan played one group of advisers against another, led by Secretary of State George Shultz, who favoured making renewed contacts with Moscow.

Reagan was veering much closer towards the latter group – 'some advisors in the Pentagon strongly opposed my ideas on arms control . . . including my hope for eventually eliminating all nuclear weapons,' he admitted. But he did not wish to antagonise his 'base' supporters.[3] He appointed as his chief adviser on the Soviet Union a donnish diplomat, Jack Matlock, whose first task was to write twenty-five highly detailed and long briefing documents about Russian history, US / Soviet relations since World War Two and contemporary lifestyles and culture in the USSR. Reagan took the trouble to read them carefully and reached the conclusion that the time had definitely come to make new overtures to the Kremlin. 'Many in his administration . . . doubted that the Soviet leaders would negotiate in good faith, but Reagan was an optimist. For all his distaste for the Soviet Union he believed that it could change if subjected to . . . his personal negotiating skill.'[4]

Andropov died on 9 February 1984 and his successor was not a surprise. The geriatrics in the Kremlin were not yet ready to skip a generation and choose a younger man of vigour and energy. They selected one of their own, a man who would not threaten their retirement perks and privileges. Konstantin Chernenko – 'a walking mummy', according to one of his own foreign policy aides – was seventy-three. He suffered from severe asthma and lived on tranquillisers. He had been Brezhnev's crony and everyone knew he would be a stopgap leader. But he proved to be an embarrassment, the personification of the decay in the Soviet Union and its empire. Whereas Andropov, whatever his flaws, had clearly been a man of intelligence, Chernenko was just as clearly not. A CIA briefing paper described him as 'a weak sister', which was a kind observation compared to some of the comments from people who worked for him, bright young apparatchiks who in private could barely conceal contempt for their boss.[5]

Reagan knew that what was happening did not bode well. One of the first things Chernenko did was to readmit Vyacheslav Molotov, for long Stalin's deputy, into the Communist Party. Molotov was now ninety-three and had been 'purged' in the brief period of Khrushchev's anti-Stalin campaign after 1956. Now there was a barely hidden nostalgia among some of the aged magnates in the Kremlin for the 1940s and 1950s when the Soviet Union was still a fortress country isolated from the rest of the world. Chernenko considered changing the name of Volgograd back to Stalingrad, though he was persuaded otherwise. Nevertheless, President Reagan tried to start talks going with the new boss in the Kremlin. Two days after Chernenko was elected General Secretary of the Soviet Communist Party Reagan wrote to him. 'The US firmly intends to defend our interests and those of our allies, but we do not seek to challenge the security of the Soviet Union and its people,' he said. He received a brusque reply merely thanking him for his letter. Reagan continued to try and remained in closer contact with Konstantin Chernenko than some of his advisers realised. In reply to a letter from the Russian leader in March Reagan said: 'It was your hope that history would reveal us as leaders known to be good, kind and wise. Nothing is more important to me and we should take steps to bring this about.' On 16 April he wrote in his own hand a note: 'I have reflected at some length on the tragedy and scale of Soviet losses in warfare ... Surely those losses, which are beyond description, must affect your thinking today. I want you to know that neither I nor the American people hold any offensive intention towards you or the Soviet people. Our constant and urgent purpose must be ... a lasting reduction of tensions between us. I pledge to you my profound commitment towards that end.'[6]

Reagan was getting nowhere with his overtures to the Soviet Union and he was now sidetracked by his re-election campaign. Yet he was thinking deeply about the arms race and his commitment to nuclear disarmament was growing – dangerously so as far as the hardliners in his own administration were concerned. During the 1980 election Reagan and his campaign manager, Stuart Spencer, had a revealing conversation on the flight from Los Angeles to Detroit that took them to the Republican National Convention where Reagan would be nominated as presidential candidate.

> Spencer asked, 'Why are you doing this, Ron? Why do you want to be President?'
>
> Reagan replied instantly without a moment's hesitation, 'To end the Cold War.'
>
> Spencer asked, 'And how are you going to do it?'

Reagan said: 'I'm not sure, but there has got to be a way. And it's time.'

Reagan's Deputy White House Chief of Staff, Michael Deaver, a close confidant, knew early on Reagan's anti-nuclear views: Reagan, he said, 'believed he was the guy who could get the Soviets to the table and end the nuclear arms race. He was running for President because he believed he was destined to do away with nuclear weapons.'[7] Matlock went further. He suspected that if there was a war, Reagan would not retaliate and press the nuclear button. 'I think deep down he doubted that even if the United States were struck that he could bring himself to strike another country with nuclear weapons. He would never even hint that, but I sensed it . . . He said "how can you tell me, the President of the US, that the only way I can defend my people is by threatening other people [with destruction] and maybe civilisation itself. That is unacceptable."'[8]

Reagan had become excited by a scheme that American scientists from his own state, in California, had dreamed up to place a system of lasers and early-warning detection equipment in space to act as a shield against ballistic missiles. The idea was that, theoretically, missiles could be spotted and destroyed by laser rays the moment they left the earth's lower atmosphere. Reagan wanted to put the theory into practice and approved enormous expenditure on research into his favoured Strategic Defense Initiative or Star Wars project. He was totally convinced that if it worked – and he had faith that American know-how could make it work – it would render nuclear weapons redundant and ultimately result in the end of missile arsenals everywhere. He thought it was the ultimate defensive system that could rid humanity of the fear of nuclear obliteration. He genuinely could not understand how the Russians perceived it differently, as a dangerous and threatening new weapon in space aimed at them. He thought that if he could talk to the Soviets and offer to share the Star Wars technology with them, he could persuade them to change their minds. But first he needed a negotiating partner in the Kremlin prepared to deal with him. For that he had to wait.

TEN

A PYRRHIC VICTORY

Warsaw, Saturday 3 December 1983

LECH WAŁĘSA SPENT only a few days after the martial law declaration under guard in Warsaw. Then he was dispatched 500 kilometres from the capital – and almost as far from Gdańsk – to a remote hunting lodge in Arłamówo, in eastern Poland near the border with Ukraine. The house had once belonged to the former Communist Party leader Edward Gierek. Wałęsa was kept under strict house arrest, but treated relatively well. He was allowed weekly access to a priest and occasional conjugal visits from his wife, but he was a gregarious man and he was cut off from conversation. He was provided with enormous meals and as many cigarettes as he could manage, but took very little exercise. He emerged after eleven months a great deal heavier, paler, a little greyer and more sombre. He went back to Danuta and his children and returned to work at the Lenin Shipyard, where he became the most celebrated electrician in the world. He waited patiently, convinced that at some point the regime would have to negotiate with him and with Solidarity.

During the 'period of war' generals tried to cut Poland off from the rest of the world – and at the same time to 'modernise the nation'. They found the two impossible to reconcile. The country was run by a Council of National Salvation, known in Poland by the acronym WRONA (meaning Crow). It consisted entirely of soldiers, presided over by Jaruzelski. Around 10,000 people were arrested and detained in jails or in forty-nine hastily built internment camps. Millions of state employees, from train drivers to librarians, were forced to sign pledges of loyalty to the state – or rather, loyalty to the military junta now in power. Phone lines were cut and the use of telex machines was banned. Scores of newspapers were closed down, the secret police seized 370 'illegal' printing presses and 1,200 other pieces of equipment that could be used for samizdat publishing such as photocopying machines. The television news continued to be read by men in uniforms. Yet still martial law was half-hearted, restrained. There was none of the brutality following the crackdown after the 1956 Hungarian Uprising. People were not deported en masse or executed.

Wałęsa was constantly harassed. But Solidarity was allowed to exist underground, in a bizarre way that suggested uncertainty within the junta, an awareness they could not return in the 1980s to the barbaric measures of earlier times. There were diehards in the upper ranks of the Communist Party, known as the Cement Group, who wanted a far tougher war against the people, but Jaruzelski seldom took them seriously. Wałęsa was investigated for petty tax irregularities, he was routinely detained by the SB for short periods of a few hours and a barrage of propaganda was directed at him in the official media characterising him as 'the self-appointed American Ambassador to Poland'. But he remained firm. When the stick did not work, the regime tried the carrot. He was repeatedly promised substantial sums of money if he emigrated. He refused. In April 1983 he caused a sensation when – supposedly under twenty-four-hour surveillance – he managed to attend a secret three-day-long meeting with the leaders of 'underground' Solidarity. The secret police knew nothing about it. He always managed to maintain contact with members of the illegal organisation.

Around this time Wałęsa suggested that he might be willing to be conciliatory if he were granted a TV interview. The generals were delighted and imagined they could use it as a propaganda coup. But when the cameras and microphones arrived, Wałęsa used them for an eloquent denunciation of martial law and the regime. The interview was so clearly hostile to Jaruzelski that it could not be aired on state TV, even though the Communist Party's propaganda team tried to doctor it for public consumption. The government issued instructions that the tape be destroyed. But a copy of the soundtrack came the way of the sound recordist Wojciech Harasiewicz, a Solidarity supporter, who passed it on to the ABC News Warsaw correspondent David Ensor. It was played frequently on the Polish section of Radio Free Europe, and the BBC World Service – and bootlegged tapes were made and passed on throughout the country. It was a spectacular mistake by the military regime, which reacted with grim predictability. Harasiewicz was arrested and jailed.

However irritated the military were with Wałęsa, the generals could make no serious moves against him. He was too well known, especially after he won the Nobel Peace Prize in December 1983. He dared not go to Stockholm to receive the award, for he feared the junta would not allow him back into Poland. So Danuta went in his stead and read his acceptance speech on his behalf. Mrs Wałęsa was no longer the shy, retiring, nervous woman she had been when she married. Though she was in her husband's shadow, she was not awed by him – or by anybody else, as an extraordinary tape made by the Polish secret service makes clear. Never a Communist, she became vigorously and increasingly opposed to the regime over time. Their home in Pilotów Street, Gdańsk, was bugged, as all the family knew. When, on one occasion, SB officers arrived to pick up Wałęsa for interrogation, as they routinely did several times a year, he was out. Danuta opened the front door and this was the exchange that followed:

CAPTAIN MAREK ROGOWSKI: Where's Wałęsa?

DANUTA WAŁĘSA: So walk around the place. Feel at home. Mr Wałęsa! Militia here to see you. Hey, you [to another young policeman poking his nose around the rooms]. My husband will be here in a moment.

CAPTAIN ROGOWSKI: Let me in. I haven't come to see you.

DANUTA: Just wait . . . What do you think you're doing? You're behaving like a thug. What do you mean you have orders? To break into a person's place and start recording things?

CAPTAIN ROGOWSKI: Keep your hands off, Mrs Wałęsa. Stop pushing me.

LECH WAŁĘSA: (returning home) I'm on sick leave and not supposed to go out . . . You can't take a sick man by force.

CAPTAIN ROGOWSKI: Yes we will.

DANUTA: So four bulls have come to take my husband away. You're a thug. Oh, look at that one . . . he looks almost normal . . . Take your gun out and shoot, what do you have to lose? Swines, cannibals. Yes, keep on recording. I'll smash this ashtray over your heads, you blockheads.

CAPTAIN ROGOWSKI: I warn you that offending a policeman on duty . . .

DANUTA: I'm a citizen just like you. But I can't come into your place and record you . . .

LECH WAŁĘSA: Calm down, darling. There may be trouble.

DANUTA: You cops are running around like cats with sick bladders.

LECH WAŁĘSA: This is simply an assault on my home.

DANUTA: Those shits . . . You can't frighten me though.

CAPTAIN ROGOWSKI: I will ask our doctor to examine Mr Wałęsa.[1]

The effort and expense that for many years went into keeping tabs on Lech Wałęsa was extraordinary. He calculated once, some time later, after seeing documents about the surveillance operation mounted against him, that the cost of a limited three-week operation – recording and transcribing 170 hours of conversations, paying for twenty-one eight-hour days – could have financed a month's work of the entire welding unit at the Lenin Shipyard. And that did not cover payment for the night shift, nor the translators' wages, nor the cost of the cars and police van outside his home.[2]

Martial law was lifted in July 1983, but many of the regulations remained in place, principally the ban on Solidarity and on demonstrations. The war of attrition went on for a further three years. Few of the Solidarity leaders who managed to escape on the night martial law was declared stayed out of jail permanently. It was a cloak-and-dagger existence for some of them, said the inspiring young underground Solidarity leader in Warsaw, Zbigniew Bujak. 'I never stayed at any place for longer than a month – usually for a lot less,' he said. 'Each of us was designated a flat, but we never worked in the same place . . . we never met each other in the flats where we were living.' For some of the martial law period it looked as though Solidarity would disappear, said Bujak – but it was their job to make sure it survived.

There were rules of engagement, though. The violence from the regime was restrained. Though there were hotheads in Solidarity who had weapons, they were never used. Bujak said that when he discovered that one extreme radical group was stockpiling some rifles he found out where they were, raided the weapons cache, loaded them on to a van and threw the guns into the River Vistula near Warsaw. Some figures in the regime 'wanted to provoke us towards terrorism . . . but we were not interested in street confrontations . . . if we went down that road, we knew we would lose'. Bogdan Borusewicz, who ran the Gdańsk underground, said he was shot at twice in the martial law period, but that was exceptional. On the whole the police did not use their weapons. 'They were serious about catching us and arresting us but there was an unwritten agreement. Generally they didn't shoot at us and we didn't shoot at them . . . We did not step over certain limits . . . and they didn't keep us in prison too long.'[3]

The regime continually tried to create splits amongst the opposition, sometimes subtly, more often with the heavy-handed crudity expected of a military dictatorship. The historian and journalist Adam Michnik was jailed soon after martial law was declared. In December 1983 the Polish Security Minister, General Czesław Kiszczak, summoned Michnik's girlfriend Basia Labuda to his office. He asked her to convince Michnik to go abroad. 'I had the choice of spending Christmas on the Riviera or staying in jail for a few more years,' he said. 'From a corner in my cell I wrote to him "I know that in my place you would have chosen the Riviera. But that's the difference between us. You are pigs. We are not. I love Poland, even from my cell. I have no intention of leaving Poland. So don't count on it." '[4]

Pope John Paul met President Reagan in the Vatican on 7 June 1982. Despite agreeing on the evils of communism, the two were not ideological soulmates. The President, for a start, was a born-again evangelical of a thoroughly American kind. The Pope disapproved of rampant market capitalism and materialism almost as much as he did of Godless socialism, though his many supporters in the West rarely tended to read his homilies on that subject. Yet the Pope and the President joined forces in support of Solidarity. They agreed to share intelligence on Poland and at first most of it came from the Vatican. The Pope himself and the Polish clergy in Rome maintained good contacts in the country and passed on vital information to Washington. Reagan's CIA Director, William Casey, was an ardent Cold Warrior, a confusing mixture of brilliant thinker and uncouth eccentric who had learned his craft as an Office of Strategic Services operative in World War Two, before the CIA had come into being. He was a voracious reader, but had a strange habit while immersed in a book, or an interesting conversation, of picking his teeth and his fingernails with the same paperclip.* He believed passionately in renewing the

* Casey was firmly convinced that the KGB was behind the assassination attempt on Pope John Paul in May 1981. Though his deputy, Bob Gates, conducted an exhaustive inquiry that started from the premise that the Soviets were responsible and all that was needed was to find the proof, no evidence has been found linking the KGB with the crime. In fact, the best evidence suggested the Soviets were not involved. That did not deter Casey, though, who believed to his dying day that the KGB tried to murder the Pope through a bungling amateur assassin from Turkey, Mehmet Ali Ağca.

psychological, cultural and propaganda wars with the Soviets which had been a been a major part of the superpower struggle in the 1950s and 1960s. Poland, he thought, would be a vital front in that war. Casey, ebullient and unpredictable, was also a devout Catholic. He met regularly in Washington with Archbishop Pio Laghi, the Apostolic Representative in the US, and in the Vatican with Cardinal Agostino Casaroli, the Curia official in charge of foreign affairs, to plan how Solidarity could be provided with material support.[5]

Initially it was the Carter administration that began helping Solidarity. Carter's Polish-born National Security Advisor Zbigniew Brzezinski was a firm supporter of the union and had helped to raise substantial funds for it privately. But in public the US government was wary: Solidarity's cause would not be helped if it became known that the American government was aiding the movement, Brzezinski argued, and potentially it could be dangerous for the US to be seen interfering in Polish affairs. Small amounts of American money went towards launching a Solidarity-backed magazine, *Kultura*, and there was plenty of moral support. At first the Reagan administration was equally cautious and pledged no substantial funds, even immediately after martial law was declared. But a year later the Americans changed their minds and the CIA began funnelling large amounts of money, printing and broadcasting equipment, as well as hundreds of photocopying machines to Poland 'for the purposes of waging underground political warfare' according to Deputy CIA Director Robert Gates. It was channelled through the American trade union organisation, the AFL-CIO, via its European director Irving Brown, who had worked closely with American intelligence since the earliest Marshall Plan days.

Casey 'insisted that deniability was very important for Solidarity' as well as for the US, said Gates, so elaborate ruses to protect CIA involvement from scrutiny were worked out. The AFL-CIO handed money over to the Institute of Religious Workers, a Catholic organisation with close links to the Curia. Then the Vatican Bank, along with the Banco Ambrosiano, set up shell companies in the Bahamas and Panama in a paper trail that ended in accounts set up by the Solidarity-in-exile office in Brussels run by Jerzy Milewski. A soft-spoken physicist and Solidarity thinker, he had been in the West when General Jaruzelski launched his military coup. A charming, mild-mannered intellectual, he never imagined he would ever spend his days as a bagman for laundered money from an espionage agency, however noble the cause.

He organised aid shipments to Poland, through Sweden, hidden amongst consignments of charity donations from the Catholic Church and otherwise legitimate cargo. The Prime Minister Olof Palme – a Solidarity sympathiser – had assured Reagan that Swedish Customs would turn a blind eye to exports destined for Gdańsk.

Did the Polish regime know about the CIA/Vatican aid? General Władisław Pożoga, head of Polish counter-intelligence during martial law, insists, boastfully, that it did. 'We had infiltrated the [Solidarity] underground with precision,' he claimed. They had spies in Solidarity's Brussels office and had agents in Sweden. His boss, the Security Minister Kiszczak, agreed. 'Because of our agents . . . we kept track of the huge flow of printing materials being smuggled in,' he said. 'We could intercept messages sent to, amongst others, Lech Wałęsa . . . We broke the codes and thanks to a spy in Milewski's office all computer-coded intelligence set on . . . disks was read by the secret police.' They let all the equipment go through and allowed the contacts to continue as a way of 'keeping tabs on the Underground', he insisted.

If the generals knew the extent of the material entering the country it turned into a costly mistake to allow it through unhindered. Printing machines, books and all the communications equipment it was receiving helped to keep the flame of Solidarity alive, during dark days which could easily have seen the movement destroyed. In particular, the Americans sent a clever device, developed by the CIA, which could interrupt television signals. It transmitted a unique beam which over-rode the conventional signal broadcast by state TV. The normal screen would be obscured while a prerecorded screen appeared with the Solidarity logo accompanied by a message saying the movement lived and resistance could triumph. The transmissions were aired at peak viewing periods – at half-time in soccer matches, for example. The device had limited and localised effect – only for a couple of kilometres and for a few minutes. But the broadcasts had a profound psychological impact. They showed that Solidarity was still in a position to confound and embarrass the regime. Viewers were asked to 'make a sign' if they had seen the transmissions by switching their house lights on and off, creating spectacular lighting effects during Polish evenings. The CIA continued to supply Solidarity regularly until the end of 1988, with a brief hiatus in 1983 after the SB arrested and expelled an American businessman James Howard, who they claimed was a CIA agent they had picked up at a meeting with Solidarity activists in Warsaw. Altogether over about six years the CIA sent Solidarity, with the Vatican's assistance, more than US$ 50 million.[6]

At around four in the afternoon of 31 October 1984 the body of a badly battered man was fished out of a reservoir near the small town of Włocławek 120 kilometres east of Warsaw. Though he was barely identifiable, bloated and disfigured, the police frogmen who lifted him from the icy water knew whom they had found. It was the remains of a thirty-seven-year-old Catholic priest, Father Jerzy Popiełuszko. For the last ten days rumours about the pastor's disappearance had spread throughout the country. He was the most popular man in Poland – more so even than Lech Wałęsa because he wore a cassock and dog collar. Now the suspicion was that he was dead – and well before his body had been discovered, the received wisdom was that his death was a murder and the assassin had been the Communist regime.

Wałęsa called Popiełuszko 'Solidarity's unofficial chaplain' and the government branded him officially a 'provocateur'. His electric sermons at St Stanisław Kostka in Warsaw attracted regular congregations of 40,000, sometimes more on high days and holidays. He held them in the square outside the church, but people spilled on to adjoining streets to hear him. Each Sunday he spoke of 'the tears and injuries and blood of workers'. His sermons were beautifully crafted, elegantly expressed and unashamedly political. There were many troublesome priests in Poland, but in the regime's eyes Popiełuszko was without a doubt the most problematic of them all, the most eloquent and the most able to rouse the public. Apart from his gifts of rhetoric and the power of his faith, it was well known that he also stored substantial amounts of cash for the use of underground Solidarity groups in Warsaw. On the evening of 15 October three SB officers hijacked his car as he was returning to the capital from a visit to Gdańsk and abducted him. They carried him from the road to a remote wood. The plan had been to beat the priest and to scare him, not to kill him. But they botched the job. They hit him on the head with a wooden stake and he died. The SB officers panicked and threw him into the Vistula. The public reacted with fury and the government tried to respond swiftly. Communist regimes did not habitually deliver up to justice over-zealous secret policemen. So it was a milestone when the three men who killed Father Popiełuszko and the officer who ordered the abduction were immediately arrested, tried and given long prison sentences.* No conclusive evidence exists to prove that others higher up the chain of command were involved; the deed seems to have been the work of rogue elements in the SB. But the public did not believe it. The conviction spread that there was a cover-up to protect more senior figures.[7]

The Popiełuszko murder brought to the surface tensions and splits inside the Polish opposition and the Church. There were extraordinary scenes at the priest's funeral on Saturday 3 November at St Stanisław Kostka. An estimated 200,000 grieving congregants attended. The Primate, Cardinal Glemp, delivered a moving eulogy about Popiełuszko's 'sacrifice', but privately he was furious that even in death the priest had tried to thwart him. The fifty-five-year-old Cardinal was instinctively pragmatic, a man of compromise. He did not see Popiełuszko as a martyr, but as trouble. At the time of the priest's death, Glemp was trying to have him transferred from Warsaw, where he was highly visible, to a backwater parish somewhere quiet. Glemp thought that openly political priests threatened the unity of the Church and weakened its bargaining position with the Communists. Often he sided with the regime. He continued to assert that martial law was better than the alternative, which he believed was a Soviet invasion. In one important matter Jaruzelski and Glemp shared a common goal. Both wanted another visit from the Pope – the General because it would legitimise his rule and show that Poland looked like a 'normal' country, and the Cardinal because he thought it would strengthen the Church and his own position as Primate.

The Pope would agree to go only if the country was peaceful. For both Glemp and the regime, that meant that the Church should try to distance itself from the underground activities of Solidarity. Glemp disciplined 'wayward' priests, as he called them, and ordered them to keep politics out of their sermons. He summoned 300 of them to Warsaw where he issued a stern warning. 'I do not see any chances for the political victory of Solidarity,' he said. 'After the military victory of the authorities we can expect an attack on the Church. It is therefore the duty of priests to prepare for this . . . by concentrating on religious

* The three lower-ranking officers directly involved in the murder, Lieutenant Leszek Pękala, Captain Grzegorz Piotrowski and Lieutenant Waldemar Chmielewski, were originally sentenced to twenty-five years in jail, but three years later their sentences were reduced to between six and ten years. The senior officer who ordered them to commit the crime, Colonel Adam Pietruszka, received a twenty-five-year sentence, reduced in 1987 to ten years. Efforts were twice made in the 1990s to prosecute more senior commanders, but both trials collapsed when the prosecution produced insufficient evidence.

work. Priests should steer clear of politics.' He said the Polish Church was in danger of abandoning its spiritual mission for a political one and if that continued it would lose. 'Some priests are behaving like journalists,' he said angrily.[8]

The Pope returned to Poland in June 1983, to restore hope to a demoralised nation, as he put it. Part of an agreement the Vatican made with Jaruzelski was that martial law would be lifted if the trip went ahead, and the regime kept its word a month later. The visit lacked the joy and emotion of four years earlier. The crowds were again huge, but more restrained. There were few scenes of ecstasy. Again, as before, the Pope was careful to avoid overtly political statements but when, at a mass before a million people in his beloved Kraków, he spoke of 'the terrible injustices of history' and declared that Poles had been 'called to victory', his audience knew what he meant.

After the Pope returned to Rome, Glemp continued to compromise – and became increasingly unpopular. When he was appointed Primate, the Polish Security chief Czesław Kiszczak sent a secret minute to the KGB in Moscow saying Glemp's elevation was a great relief to the Warsaw regime: 'The new primate . . . is not as anti-Soviet as his predecessor. Wyszyński enjoyed immense authority; his word was law. He was the object of a personality cult . . . Glemp is a different kind of man and there are undoubtedly possibilities of exerting influence on him.' He was right. Glemp's breach with Solidarity came out into the open after he told a Brazilian journalist in 1984 that Wałęsa had lost control of the movement because Solidarity had 'become a sack into which everything was thrown, all the opposition, Marxists, Trotskyists and then all the careerists and Party members'. He won a few concessions – the regime allowed 900 new churches to be built and Glemp was given permission to appear at Christmas and Easter on TV. But in large and small things he caved in under pressure. A new word entered the Polish language that translated as 'Glempic' and was a term meaning sanctimonious waffle.[9]

'Let's not mythologise the role of the Church,' Michnik said soon after Popiełuszko's murder. 'Its support for the opposition was . . . by no means absolute. The Church may have been anti-Communist but it did not believe that communism was about to collapse. On the contrary, [it thought] communism was going to survive and this required judicious adaptation on the part of the Church. I don't blame the bishops . . . It was quite rational on their part. What I object to

... is the history of the Church presented as an unbroken wave of democratic opposition.'[10]

The generals were unable to run Poland any more efficiently than the Party apparatchiks could. They were given massive handouts by the Soviet Union to stabilise prices, which the Kremlin magnates admitted 'stretched us to the limit – yet they are still making more requests'. The military regime resorted to the same methods as its predecessors and touched Western bankers for further loans, stoking up greater problems for the future. Jaruzelski was beginning to see that Poland's plight was insoluble without abandoning Marxist theory. But he was not yet ready to do the unthinkable and find a way to share power with his opponents.

PART TWO

THE THAW

ELEVEN

THE NEW TSAR

Moscow, Sunday 10 March 1985

FOR THE THIRD TIME in less than three years the most powerful potentates in the Soviet Union met to anoint a new Red Tsar. Konstantin Chernenko finally gave up the ghost at 7.20 p.m. after a painful battle with pneumonia and emphysema. He had barely been seen for the last few weeks, except by the Kremlin doctors and his closest intimates. His death probably came as a relief to him and his family – and certainly to the USSR. Immediately, the Party elders left their country dachas, Moscow apartments and their own hospital beds to make a historic choice for the Soviet empire and for the cause of communism. Some of the eighteen men who began gathering at around 10 p.m. had been in power for so long they had worked in the same building for Stalin. Now they were greeted in the walnut-panelled room on the third floor of the ornate Senate – the room adjoining the Party leader's private office – by the youngest of their number, fifty-four-year-old Mikhail Sergeyevich Gorbachev.

Instinctively the Party elders would have preferred a candidate of their own vintage, a supposedly safe bet who would be no threat to their positions and perquisites. But even they had heard some of the jokes going round the city – 'The Congress has begun. Delegates are asked to stand. We will start as traditionally with the carrying-in of the General Secretary.' More importantly, there was not a plausible older man remaining who could do the job. Ustinov had died a few months earlier and Gromyko had made it clear he did not want the position. Gorbachev had been standing in for Chernenko ably and energetically when the leader was indisposed and he seemed the best-qualified candidate. But he had been the best man for the job just over a year ago when he was blocked by a group of diehards who were still in positions to thwart him if they wished. This time the ambitious younger man had a powerful ally. Though Gromyko did not want to be king, he did wish to be kingmaker. The two cut a deal, though they never met to make it.

The arrangements were handled by their emissaries. Gromyko's son Anatoli, himself a rising Party functionary, represented the Foreign Minister. Gorbachev's second was a close friend who was to become one of his key aides over the next few years, Alexander Yakovlev. Earlier that afternoon, when it became clear Chernenko had not long to live, the young Gromyko went to Yakovlev's office. 'So as not to beat about the bush, I'll explain what I have in mind,' he said. 'If it's not acceptable we'll consider it nothing more than my own personal proposal on my own initiative. My father is sure that only Gorbachev can lead the Party under the circumstances. He is ready to support that idea and take the initiative . . . At the same time he is fed up with working in the Ministry of Foreign Affairs and would like to change his job. He is thinking of the Supreme Soviet.' The meaning was clear. Gromyko would propose Gorbachev for the top job if the older man was given the largely ceremonial but grand-sounding post of President (technically Chairman of the Supreme Soviet). Gorbachev thought about the proposal briefly in his office and then told Yakovlev to take a message to Gromyko *fils*. 'Tell Andrei Andreyevich that it has always been pleasant working with him. I will be pleased to do so in whatever position we may hold in the future. And tell him I know how to keep my promises.'[1]

The rival candidate was another elderly man, Viktor Grishin, seventy-one, who had been Moscow Party chief for the past eighteen years. He was a throwback to the stagnation years – an embodiment of all that was wrong with the Brezhnev era, dull-witted, ponderous, lazy and mired in sleaze. It was well known that he was Chernenko's choice to succeed him, but his claims were seen off quickly. Over the last few hours, the head of the KGB, Viktor Chebrikov, had called several of the magnates and told them that at the meeting later he would be bringing a thick dossier detailing Grishin's involvement in massive graft in Moscow over several decades. There was also the question of some unsavoury family links that would not necessarily disqualify him as a national leader but were certainly embarrassing. These were connections with Lavrenti Beria, the thug who had enthusiastically murdered countless people in Stalin's purges and was himself discredited and killed in 1953. Beria's illegitimate daughter was married to Grishin's son.[2]

Gromyko and Gorbachev talked briefly before the other magnates sat down to start their deliberations.

'We have to unite our forces. This is a crucial moment,' Gorbachev said.

'It seems to me that everything is clear,' the older man replied.

Gorbachev responded: 'I am counting on the fact that you and I will co-operate.'

Then Gorbachev took the chair, as he had been doing in Chernenko's absence for the past months. The chief Kremlin physician, still Dr Chazov, delivered a formal report on the causes of Chernenko's death and then left the room. Gorbachev began: 'We first of all have to decide the question of who is to be General Secretary . . . I would ask comrades to express their views on this matter.' There was an established ritual at all such meetings of the Soviet leadership and, as always in the Kremlin, ritual was followed carefully. The unwritten rule since Lenin's death had been that nobody disagreed with the man who spoke first to propose a name as the new General Secretary. Andrei Gromyko began immediately. He had not finished half a sentence before it was clear who the next leader would be: 'I will speak frankly,' he said. 'When one thinks about a candidate . . . one thinks immediately, of course, about Mikhail Sergeyevich. That would in my opinion be the absolutely correct choice . . . When one looks into the future – and I will not hide the fact that for many of us that is hard to do – we must have a clear sense of the outlook. And that consists of the fact that we don't have the right to permit any damage to our unity.'

Gromyko halted. Nobody hinted at any objection so he continued.

> He has been doing much of the work already, and performing brilliantly. He has a deep and sharp mind, an ability to distinguish the primary from the secondary. An analytical mind . . . he's a man of principle and conviction. He'll uphold his views in the face of opposition and he won't hesitate to speak his mind for the Party . . . He's straightforward to people. If you're a true Communist, you'll leave satisfied, even though he might have said things that are not to your liking. But he can get along with different people when necessary . . . He does not see things in black and white. He can find an intermediate shade of grey in the interests of reaching a goal. For Gorbachev, maintaining a vigilant defence is a sacred duty. In our present situation, this is the holy of holies.

Gromyko concluded: 'He has a nice smile, but Comrades, Mikhail Sergeyevich has iron teeth.'[3]

The other established tradition was that, following a nominating speech, agreement had to be unanimous. Everyone was expected to speak and some of the unction of the occasion embarrassed Gorbachev, who sat with his head bowed, taking desultory notes and occasionally looking up with an uncomfortable smile. Prime Minister Nikolai Tikhonov, who was no friend of Gorbachev and had been influential in blocking his appointment the last time round, said: 'He is the first secretary who can understand economics,' which was not generous to Gorbachev's predecessors who, presumably, the Premier thought were incompetent. Nikolai Ryzhkov, who would soon be appointed Prime Minister in his place, explained, simply, the general view: 'We knew that if we chose an old man again, we would have a repeat of what we had for three years in a row – shaking hands with foreign leaders at a funeral.'[4]

At around three a.m. Gorbachev returned to his dacha in the country half an hour from Moscow. His wife, Raisa, was waiting up for him. Their habit every night, almost without fail, was to take a short walk together before going to bed – to relax and unwind but also, as Gorbachev said once, because it was only then that they could talk privately together without the KGB eavesdropping devices listening in to their every word. He told her the job was his and that he would take it. 'All those years ... it's been impossible to do anything important, on a large scale. It's like a brick wall. But life demands action. We can't go on living like this,' he said.[5]

The next day there was genuine excitement in Moscow. At 7 a.m. Soviet radio was broadcasting Chopin on all stations, which was the first indication that something significant had happened. No news was officially declared, but the gossip spread throughout the city that Chernenko had died. It was hardly a surprise. There was still no word for certain about the succession even in the Party bureaucracy, the *apparat*, until mid-afternoon when an announcement would be made at the marble-paved conference hall opposite the Kremlin on the other side of Red Square. Anatoli Chernyaev was in the audience that afternoon. He was a senior Party official who would later play a major part in government, a man desperate for change and reform in the Soviet Union. 'There was a mood of "waiting for Gorbachev" ever since Andropov died,' he confided to his diary. 'Under Brezhnev the country was already an embarrassment. Under Chernenko it became a shameful farce.'

Nearly a thousand people were crammed into the hall. Just before four p.m. the most senior magnates emerged on to the podium and sat under a ten-metre-high mosaic of Lenin in garish red and orange. Andrei Gromyko walked up to a lectern on the stage. He paid tributes to the 'dear departed Comrade Chernenko' and then hesitated briefly before declaring that the leadership had 'unanimously recommended ... Mikhail Sergeyevich Gorbachev'. The hall erupted in applause. Almost everyone under seventy was smiling and cheering in genuine enthusiasm. 'The ovation went on in waves and didn't stop for a long time,' Chernyaev recorded. 'The uncertainty is over ... now it's time for Russia to have a real leader.'[6]

In Washington, Ronald Reagan's principal adviser on the USSR, Jack Matlock, shared some of the enthusiasm people felt in Moscow: 'Both at home and abroad everyone was tired of watching the Soviet empire floundering under infirm incompetents,' he said. 'Gorbachev was like a breath of fresh air. He walks, he talks, his suit fits ... so he dazzled the world.'[7]

It was extraordinary that Mikhail Gorbachev should have reached the pinnacle of power in the Soviet Union. On the whole, people of intellect and imagination were weeded out by a system that favoured toadies and the mediocre. Yet Gorbachev rose almost seamlessly and – a greater achievement still – he kept the better part of his character intact.

He was born on 2 March 1931 in Privolnoye, a tiny village in the fertile steppes north of the Caucasus mountains known as the Kuban. The word *privilnoye* means free (as in free and easy) and traditionally the people of the Kuban were famed for their independent spirit. They were Cossacks who, unlike the peasantry almost everywhere else in Russia, had never been serfs. Under the Tsars they were allowed to keep their freedom; in return they were expected to defend the southern border of the Russian empire from incursion by Muslim marauders. After the 1917 Revolution many Cossacks refused to accept Bolshevik rule and fought against the Red Army in the Civil War. Gorbachev's native village was dirt poor – a ramshackle collection of mud huts and outhouses set amidst vast open plains. His mother, Maria Panteleyevna, was a forceful, outspoken woman who domineered over the young Gorbachev's mild-mannered father, Sergei Andreyevich. It was the baby's maternal grandmother Vasilisa who insisted that the boy should be baptised, at a time when the Communists were suppressing the Orthodox Church.

His birth coincided almost exactly with Stalin's brutal drive to collectivise the land, part of the great dictator's vision of turning backward semi-feudal Russia into the modern, industrial Soviet Union. It was accompanied by appalling suffering throughout the country, but in few areas as terrible as in the north Caucasus, where an estimated one million people died from the famine of the 1930s. The 'harvest of sorrow', as it came to be called, was entirely a man-made disaster. Scores of thousands of better-off peasants, the derided *kulaks* who owned smallholdings, were driven off the land or killed. Hunger carried away the others. Gorbachev would later often recall the many ruined houses in his own village where entire families had died from starvation. In the area around Privolnoye a collective farm was established in the summer of 1931 and its first chairman, an important man in the neighbourhood, was Panteley Yefimovich Gopkolo, the new baby Mikhail Gorbachev's maternal grandfather. He was a strong supporter of socialised farming from conviction as well as from opportunism. When Gorbachev was three, in 1934, his paternal grandfather Andrei was accused of 'sabotaging the spring sowing plan'. He had refused to join the collective farm – the *kolkhoz* – and a kangaroo court sent him to Siberia to cut trees. He left behind 'a tormented family' that soon became destitute, Gorbachev said. 'Half the family died of starvation.'

He survived mainly due to the position held by his other grandfather. But in 1937, at the height of Stalin's Great Purge in which millions were murdered or sent to prison camps, Panteley Gopkolo was arrested in the middle of the night by the secret police, the NKVD, and, in the usual language of the time, charged with belonging to 'an underground right-Trotskyist counter-revolutionary organisation'. Gorbachev recalled later that his grandfather was jailed 'and interrogated for fourteen months . . . he confessed to things he had not done, and so on. Thank God he survived.' But home in Privolnoye had 'become a plague house' which nobody dared to visit for fear of being associated with an 'enemy of the people . . . even the neighbours' kids refused to have anything to do with me. This is something that remained with me for the rest of my life.' Gopkolo was released and around the time the Germans invaded Russia in 1941 he was rehabilitated. He served for nearly two further decades as chairman of the local collective farm. He insisted until the end of his days that 'Stalin had no idea what the NKVD is doing'. Gorbachev kept quiet until the 1990s about these skeletons in the family cupboard, as did so many ambitious people of his generation who had similar backgrounds. It would have done no good to his impeccable Party record. Gorbachev's father was drafted into the army at the start of the war on the eastern front. Gorbachev was only ten and he did not see his father again for more than five years. The nearest big town, Stavropol, was occupied by the Germans, but only for five months. Privolnoye was spared the destruction and barbarity visited on so much of Russia during the Great Patriotic War.

He harboured ambitions at an early age. It was at his own insistence that, aged less than fourteen, he went from the small village school to the bigger secondary school in Krasnogvardeiskoye (Red Guard Town) ten miles away. He walked there each Monday morning, stayed during the week with an elderly couple from whom he rented a room, and walked back on Friday afternoon. At the weekends he worked in the fields with his mother. He shone at school academically, and, as important for his future, politically. The Party spotted his talent and clutched him in an embrace. The Party made him – and he was a true believer, even after the Soviet Communist Party ceased to exist. His main pastime outside school and political work was the stage. He loved acting and was good at it. For a fleeting moment, he thought of a theatrical career. His schoolfriends remember that from a young age he was a natural leader and was highly popular. They recall also that he was remarkably self-assured and confident. Even from adolescence he had a manner that told others he always knew he was right. 'I remember him correcting teachers in history class,' his sweetheart at secondary school, Yulia Karagodina, said. 'Once he was so angry at one teacher he said "Do you want to keep your teaching certificate?" He was the sort who felt he was right and could prove it to anyone.' How his teachers liked this priggish and pompous part of him we do not know. But, with the support of the Party, he was sent from a tiny, second-rate provincial school to Moscow State University, by far the most select in the country, to study law.

His dissertation for entry to the university was on the subject 'Stalin is our battle glory, Stalin is the Flight of our youth'. In school holidays he worked on the land and in the summer before he started university he performed two months of arduous back-breaking work in the fields bringing in the harvest, for which he was given an important state honour, the Order of the Red Banner of Labour. But he was not a star when in 1950 he arrived in Moscow. At first he was treated like a country bumpkin. Most of the students were children of the Soviet nomenklatura, more sophisticated and better-connected than he. He worked hard on smoothing out his rougher edges. He was one of the most active members of the Communist Youth organisation, the Komsomol, where his political views, according to his best friend at university, the Czech foreign exchange student Zdeněk Mlynář, were strictly orthodox – 'He was a straight Stalinist, like everyone else at the time.'

In 1953, at a ballroom dancing class early in his third year at the university, Gorbachev met Raisa Maximova Titorenko, a petite, pretty, dark-haired philosophy student a year younger than he was. She was a clever, cultivated and chic young woman – as convinced a Marxist and politically active as himself. For the young Gorbachev it was love at first sight, though she told friends later that it took her a little longer. They were married the next year and remained a devoted couple until she died in 1999. Her influence on him, and on the future of the USSR, was to become immense.

Gorbachev was sent back to his own province at Stavropol, where he was fast-tracked by the Party and destined for high positions. While Raisa taught Marxism at the polytechnic and worked on a PhD thesis on conditions among the peasantry in the collective farms of the Kuban, Gorbachev was rising through the Party ranks at unprecedented speed. One great influence on his career was the 'secret speech' in February 1956 by Nikita Khrushchev, who exposed the monstrous crimes of Stalin. It shook the world of Communists such as Gorbachev who, despite their family backgrounds and personal experience, had regarded Stalin as almost a god-like being. Khrushchev attempted to introduce a range of reforms to revive Russia's already creaking industry and agriculture but encountered so much resistance that he gave up. The couple learned as much from two long holidays in Western Europe during the mid-1960s – the first a 3,000-mile motoring tour around France and the second a Party-sponsored trip to Italy. In the Soviet Union at the time, for a low-to-middle-ranking official and his lecturer wife to be allowed opportunities to travel so freely showed total faith in his loyalty.

In 1967, aged just thirty-five, Gorbachev was promoted to be Party boss of the Stavropol region – effectively ruler of nearly three million people, with a direct line to the top men in the Kremlin. It was still a thousand miles from 'the Centre', as Moscow was always called by Party men, but here Gorbachev was a prince in his own domain. Apart from his youth, vigour and efficiency, he had earned a reputation as an incorruptible official in a bureaucracy that was a byword for sleaze and graft.

He must have been insufferably bored surrounded by second- and third-rate bureaucrats in the provinces, but life in Stavropol had benefits and opportunities. The area was regularly visited by many of the senior and sickly men from the Kremlin for its curative waters. The most exclusive spas and clinics for top Party officials were in his region – and Gorbachev made it his business to get to know his celebrity visitors. Among his gifts was an ability to charm and impress older and more powerful men. Two frequent visitors to the Stavropol spas became Gorbachev's chief mentors – Yuri Andropov and Mikhail Suslov. Word of the younger man's talents, his energy and above all his *Partinost* (a uniquely Communist word with no precise definition but meaning 'Party spirit') spread around Moscow. Gorbachev helped it on its way. He said later that 'In those years we all licked Brezhnev's ass, all of us.'

Sycophancy is a vital ingredient of success in all bureaucracies, but never was it as important as during the latter years of the USSR. There are some grotesque examples of Gorbachev ingratiating himself with his superiors in the Kremlin. In May 1978 he wrote a review of a turgid, almost unreadable book produced by Brezhnev's ghostwriters. Only those with hearts of stone could fail to snigger: 'L.I. Brezhnev has revealed a talent for leadership of the Leninist type,' Gorbachev gushed:

> His titanic daily work is directed towards strengthening the might of our country, raising the well-being of the workers and strengthening the peace and security of nations ... in the pages of Comrade Brezhnev's remarkable book, *Little Land*, ... the legendary heroes of the battles of the North Caucasus are portrayed in letters of gold ... In the number of its pages, *Little Land* is not very long, but in the depth of its ideological content, in the breadth of the author's opinions, it has become a great event in public life. It has evoked a warm echo in the hearts of Soviet people ... Communists and all the workers of Stavropol are boundlessly grateful to Leonid Ilyich Brezhnev for this truly Party-spirited literary work ...

Both Andropov and Suslov made sure that Brezhnev was shown the article and had an opportunity to meet its author. Less than six months later Gorbachev was summoned to Moscow to take on one of the top jobs in the Kremlin. He was put in charge of Soviet agriculture, following the sudden death of the powerful magnate Fyodor Kulakov, who had also been a patron of Gorbachev. Gorbachev was now at the centre of power in Moscow on the top leadership rung – nearly a decade younger than any of his colleagues. Raisa was eased into a prestigious academic job as a senior philosophy lecturer at her alma mater, Moscow State University.[8]

The ambitious men around Gorbachev could all see that he was clever, sharp and able, but nobody knew what he was thinking. As Anatoli Sobchak, who was a rising apparatchik at the same time, said:

> Gorbachev could tell us much we do not know about how a man feels, doomed to daily renunciation of his own will in favour of that of his superiors, compelled to daily self-abasement for the sake of career. To me the greatest mystery is how Gorbachev managed to retain his individuality, the ability to shape his own opinion and set it against the opinion of others. Evidently it was to preserve his own self that he developed his almost impenetrable mask. He learned to conceal his disdain for those he must have despised, to speak with them in his own language.[9]

Andropov groomed his favourite protégé for the top job, though he suspected that Gorbachev would be considered too young to be chosen immediately after him. But he gave him more responsibility and experience and helped to ensure that when the next vacancy occurred, Gorbachev would be the logical choice. In the brief Chernenko interregnum he was doing much of the day-to-day work running the country. But he needed to raise his profile on the domestic and international stage in order to place the seal on his succession, which he felt sure would not be long. He wanted to organise a visible foreign trip that would get him talked about – and would help to answer some of the criticism from Soviet officials who were worried that as the heir apparent in the Kremlin he had little experience of foreign affairs. He wanted to visit Washington. But that was impossible with the chill in Soviet/US relations, so he angled for a visit to America's closest ally, Britain, in an attempt to charm an ideological enemy every bit as fervent as Ronald Reagan: the Iron Lady, Margaret Thatcher.

She was as keen on receiving him as he was to go. 'We wanted to get an idea of what the next generation of Soviet leaders might be like and this was a great opportunity,' said Charles Powell, Thatcher's foreign policy adviser. 'We did not know for sure at that stage that Gorbachev would certainly be the man, but it was looking like it. The visit was extraordinary. You could tell from the first moment between Thatcher and Gorbachev that they were very interested in each other

... there was real chemistry between them.' He was willing to talk – at great length – about any subject and though he did not say anything new or particularly significant about the state of the world, it was the way he said it that counted. Thatcher famously declared, 'I like Mr Gorbachev. We can do business together' and his two-day visit to London in November 1984 marked the beginning of Gorbachev's seduction of the Western media. He was clearly a novel kind of Soviet politician, personable, amusing, approachable, rather than grim-faced and lugubrious like the figures the West had come to know. Raisa, elegant, stylishly dressed and visibly his consort, was entirely different from the traditional frumpy Kremlin wife usually kept carefully in the background.[10]

Gorbachev had a few weeks earlier impressed the French President, François Mitterrand, who was visiting Moscow, for his cleverness and agile mind, but also for his sense of humour and wit, not normally associated with Russian officials. Gorbachev arrived a little late to a meeting at the Kremlin attended by Mitterrand and the French Senator Claude Estier, who was accompanying the French leader. 'Gorbachev bustled in, sat down at the table and apologised for being late,' Estier recalled. 'He said he had been trying to sort out a problem in the Soviet agricultural sector. I asked him when the problem had arisen and he quipped in a flash: In 1917.'[11]

But the Kremlin potentates had not chosen the new supreme leader for his repartee. They believed he was a Party man and thought that with his relative youth and energy he would defend with vigour the interests of the Soviet empire. That was what he promised to do in his brief acceptance remarks after he was anointed: 'There is no need to change policy,' he said. 'The existing course is the true, the correct and genuinely Leninist one ... the most important thing is to keep our relations strong with the rest of the great socialist camp.' His colleagues were prepared for some modest reforms. They were not expecting years of revolutionary change. Mikhail Gorbachev was a Communist through and through. He did not seem then like the man who would do more than anybody else to destroy communism.

Four days after his accession, Gorbachev presided over his predecessor's traditionally lavish funeral in Red Square and hosted a magnificent banquet in the vast, marble St George's Hall in the Kremlin. That was the first glimpse most world leaders had of the new Soviet Tsar. He met some of the more important dignitaries in private, including a session of about an hour and a half with the American Vice President, George Bush, and Secretary of State George Shultz. Often, people who met Gorbachev came away thinking about him whatever they wanted to believe. This was a valuable gift for a politician to possess. A fine example was the contrasting cables President Reagan read the next morning from his emissaries at the Moscow funeral. Shultz was enthusiastic and gushing with hope about the new man in the Kremlin: 'In Gorbachev we have an entirely different kind of leader in the Soviet Union,' he wrote. 'Gorbachev was quick, fresh, engaging and wide-ranging. I came away genuinely impressed with his quality of thought, the intensity and the intellectual energy of this new man on the scene.' Bush was more cautious. He described Gorbachev as 'an impressive ideas salesman' but doubted whether there would be any significant changes in the Soviet Union:

> He will package the Soviet line better for Western consumption, much more effectively than any of his predecessors. He has a disarming smile, warm eyes and an engaging way of making an unpleasant point . . . and then bouncing back to establish real communication with his interlocutors. He can be very firm. For example, when I raised the human rights question with him . . . he came back with the same rhetorical excesses we have heard before – 'within your borders you repress human rights' (referring to African Americans). But along with this he would say the following . . . 'we'll be prepared to think it over . . . let's discuss it'.[12]

In the days following his succession, Gorbachev had spoken on the phone to each of the Communist leaders in Eastern Europe. They had all rung Moscow to pledge fealty, as to an overlord. Now, immediately after the funeral, he met them in a group and told them he wanted 'relations on an equal footing with them . . . [with] more respect for their independence and sovereignty. I told them they should take more responsibility for the situation in their own countries.' Gorbachev declared that he 'had the feeling that they were not taking it altogether seriously'. He should not have been surprised. As General Jaruzelski said: 'Brezhnev used to use very similar words. It didn't mean very much at the time.'[13]

TWELVE

THE SWORD AND SHIELD

East Berlin, April 1985

EVERY TUESDAY AFTERNOON at three o'clock the two most powerful men in East Germany met in an ornate office on the second floor of the Communist Party headquarters in Werderscher Markt, central Berlin. Party boss, Erich Honecker, and his secret police chief, Erich Mielke, talked usually for about an hour and a half in private. There was always just one subject on the agenda: the security of the state, interpreted by these two ageing Bolsheviks as the security of the Party, officially called the Socialist Unity Party (Sozialistische Einheitspartei Deutschlands, the SED).

In the spring of 1985 Honecker approved an ambitious, if Orwellian, plan to start collating computerised files and reports on every citizen in the country – around sixteen and a half million people. The dour Honecker, now seventy-three, had by then already been the supreme leader in East Germany for fourteen years. He was highly enthusiastic about a computerised snooping system. It chimed with his view of East Germany as a go-ahead country, progressive, on the cutting edge of modernity. Mielke, seventy-seven, a squat, bull-necked man seldom without a sneer on his face, was more sceptical. He did not altogether like the idea, conceived by young and keen juniors at the Ministerium für Staatssicherheit, the Stasi, which he had run almost as a personal fiefdom for more than a quarter of a century. Mielke believed in card indexes and paper files. He said they were preferable to computers, not least when there was a power cut – an important consideration under 'actually existing socialism', which was the politically correct way East Germans described the condition of their state.

Under Mielke the Stasi held a staggering number of files. The sheer volume was barely conceivable. By the late 1980s they took up 125 miles of shelf space, each mile containing seventeen million sheets of paper weighing fifty tons. Every country in the Soviet empire had a secret police force closely linked in a symbiotic partnership with the KGB. None was as thorough or had as high a reputation for well-oiled efficiency as the Stasi. Most East Germans called it by its euphemism, The Firm. 'Even when it wasn't watching you or listening to you, we thought it might be,' recalls Dr Matthias Mueller, who grew up in East Berlin in the 1970s. 'We imagined it knew everything. That was its mystique, its power and its reach.'[1]

It did not know everything. But it knew a lot. The Stasi was one of the single biggest employers in a country where there was no official unemployment and the staffing levels of some enterprises were enormous. In the middle of 1975 the Stasi had 59,478 full-time paid staff. A decade later there were 105,000, not counting the part- time informers of various levels of activity. There were about 15,000 full-timers in the hideous Normannenstrasse headquarters, a group of several heavily fortified buildings in the Lichtenberg district of East Berlin. More than half a million 'active informers' were recruited by the Stasi over the years. At the height of the Third Reich it is estimated that there was a Gestapo agent for every 2,000 citizens. In the mid-1980s there was a Stasi officer or regular informer for every sixty-three. The opening-up of East Germany to the West from the 1970s was welcomed by Honecker and his henchmen. Ending the GDR's isolation was considered a triumph for the supreme leader's diplomacy. It reduced Honecker's paranoia on the international stage, the sense that the world did not regard East Germany as a legitimate country. But in many ways it meant that internal surveillance was perceived by the Party as even more important.

When citizens retreated into their private lives the Stasi pursued them. Those who for whatever reason became the agency's targets were never alone. The Stasi corrupted their relationships and undermined trust within families. A top-secret directive from the highest levels close to Erich Mielke made clear in stark terms what was expected. Agents, it decreed, 'should seek the disintegration of opponents by means of systematically discrediting reputations ... the systematic organisation of professional and social failure to undermine self-confidence ... the creation of doubts ... sowing mistrust and mutual suspicion ... determined exploitation of personal weaknesses'.

Officers performed tasks that ranged from the banal to the utterly chilling. They seemed to think of everything. Even the *smells* of individuals were collected. At every police station and Stasi interrogation room in the country the chairs had an extra adhesive layer of foam on the seat. These collected the odours of everyone brought in for questioning. They were preserved in jars and used to assist tracker dogs in pursuit of their quarry. A mere handful of people were captured this way. But nothing was too much effort for state security, which was given four billion Marks a year to spend – not much below 5 per cent of the country's budget.

Gone were the days, by the 1980s, when people were locked up for long periods, physically tortured and left to rot in camps. But there was twenty-four-hour surveillance of thousands of people. Most of the information painstakingly recorded in every detail in the tonnage of the Stasi's files was mind-numbingly boring and irrelevant. The writer Lutz Rathenow, who was working on a guidebook of Berlin, was followed for months. His secret service minders rarely got anything more significant than this:

> Rathenow then crossed the street and ordered a sausage at a stand. The following conversation took place.
>
> RATHENOW: A sausage, please.
>
> VENDOR: With or without a roll?
>
> RATHENOW: With, please.
>
> VENDOR: And mustard?
>
> RATHENOW: Yes, please.
>
> Further exchanges did not take place.

The Stasi produced 40,000 pages of reports on Wolf Biermann before he was exiled to West Germany. Most were entirely unhelpful in protecting the state from subversion; Biermann was a notorious womaniser, but he would never say anything of political significance at his home because he knew eavesdropping equipment was placed in every room. 'W.B. had sexual relations with a woman. Afterwards he asked her if she was hungry ... she replied that she would like a drink of cognac. She is Eva Hagen. Then it was quiet inside.'[2]

Ulrike Poppe was one of a very few political activists in the GDR. She belonged to a peace group and an environmental group that was looking at pollution levels in Berlin. Her husband Gerd was a highly regarded physicist. 'We had a microphone in our apartment,' Ms Poppe said. 'It was not a small device – a big one connected to a cable that led to another apartment two floors below where the receiver must have been. There was a video camera installed in the building opposite us, which was trained on our window. Every private word we said, every dispute about who had to do the dishes, every argument with the children was listened to and noted down. Everyone who entered the house was videotaped.'[3]

They were harassed and targeted by The Firm. They lost their jobs. Stasi agents did their best to break up the Poppes' marriage and turn their son Jonas against them. A Stasi report explained how they could achieve their objective:

> To encourage UP in her ... intention to separate from her husband ... [we should] suggest that if she were to drop all her public activities and stop co-operating with the enemy she might be able to embark on a programme of advanced study ... She should be encouraged to believe that if she separates from her husband she will be financially secure ... The travel ban [against her] could be eased. To exacerbate the marriage crisis, contact person 'Harold' will be introduced to Mrs Poppe with the aim of establishing an intimate relationship ... Gerd Poppe must be prevented from improving his professional and social prospects. Through a campaign of 'anonymous' letters he is to be discriminated against in the workplace ... The headmistress of School 15 in Prenzlauer Berg is to exert a positive influence over Jonas Poppe. The success of a socialist education will demonstrate, within their own family, the uselessness of their hostile actions.

Poppe, once a leading figure at a scientific research institute, found a job as a swimming pool attendant.[4]

The most unsettling was perhaps the case of Vera Lengsfeld. Her father had been a Stasi officer from its inception after the war. Throughout her youth she was a loyal and obedient nomenklatura child, but later she rebelled. She became a member of the Communist Party but was expelled in 1982 when she became a Christian convert. She joined a peace group linked to the Lutheran Church, which began to protest against nuclear missiles based in Europe – including the presence in the GDR of Soviet missiles. She was constantly watched, jailed for brief periods and was fired from her job as a teacher at a Berlin social research academy. Sixty Stasi officers were on permanent assignment to keep tabs on her and report on her every move. The busiest of them turned out to be her husband, the mathematician Knud Wollenberger, father of her two sons, who to all intents and purposes appeared to be a loving companion and a doting parent. He reported to his Stasi handler under the codename 'Daniel'. He passed on every detail of her life, their intimate moments and pillow talk, her every headache, shopping trip, bad mood, emotional vulnerability and telephone call. Wollenberger met, courted and married her on orders from the Stasi. 'The marriage was false from the start,' she said. 'Our home life, everything . . . was a lie.' It was 'unimaginable' that a man could marry a woman just to spy on her and 'still more incomprehensible that he could father children in the process'.[5]

When she found out 'it was as if one had died for a moment and then returned to life . . . the surprising thing was that the reports were written as if about a stranger, not a wife . . . To him I was an enemy of the State and he had done everything, to fight me, the enemy.' He said that he had been a loyal citizen of the GDR and when the Stasi asked him to help them, 'I felt I couldn't say no'. He said that when he went to work from home it was 'like going through a mirror and being in a totally different world'.*[6]

Many thousands of East Germans felt they could not refuse what the Stasi asked of them. Of course the fattest files were on writers, artists, journalists and people married to foreigners – including from Eastern bloc countries. But they were interested in performers of all kinds – sportsmen and -women who went abroad for international competitions, which were extremely important for the rulers' prestige. Stasi officers seemed obsessively interested – probably because most of them were men – in the Miss GDR beauty contests. All the competitors were routinely spied on. The extent to which people were willing to denounce their neighbours is unnerving. There are many reports from informers with acquaintances whose daughters were seen wearing a cross on a chain around their necks, or whose sons cut their hair in a style that 'seemed to be punk'. As time went on the regime began to be seriously worried by rebellious youth and, like the neighbouring Czechs, began mounting campaigns against rock music. Informers reported on contacts who they had observed, or suspected, had received mail from *Drüben* – 'over there' (meaning West Germany).

* Vera Lengsfeld became a Christian Democrat politician after the reunification of Germany and old habits died hard with her. As a Member of Parliament she was frequently rebellious and critical of the CDU leadership under Chancellor Angela Merkel. For a while Knud Wollenberger made a name for himself on chat shows and he published a slim volume of poetry. Nature enacted a painful retribution on him: he was afflicted with a rare form of Parkinson's disease that left him semi-blind and crippled.

Mielke had been an intelligence agent for more than fifty years. A street thug who had fought for the Communists against the Nazis in the 1920s, the Soviets spirited him out of Germany to Moscow in 1931 after he had murdered two policemen and loudly boasted of the achievement one night in a Berlin bar. He became a full-time KGB officer. In the Spanish Civil War he earned medals not, as a former colleague said, 'for fighting the fascists, but for killing Trotskyites and anarchists'. Immediately after the Russians liberated Berlin, he was sent to help establish a 'sword and shield' for the Party in East Germany. Mielke was convinced that he ran the most efficient spying organisation in the Communist world and he had set opinions about intelligence work. The most effective spies, he maintained, were simply those who had the most contact with the public. The Stasi cultivated tram conductors, cleaning women, doctors and nurses. Teachers, for example, were particularly good at identifying children whose families watched Western television – those people who Mielke said 'emigrated to another country at eight o'clock in the evening'. It was permitted to watch Western broadcasts from the late 1970s. In fact the regime tolerated it as a form of nightly political amnesia. But nonetheless the Stasi wanted to know about these watching habits. Informers did not receive much payment – approximately 400 East Marks, around 10 per cent of the average wage. Most did not do it for the money, but from a desire for approval, the hope of better job prospects or a place for a relative's son or daughter at a better university. As the Stasi became a state within the state, spies spied on other spies. And Mielke kept extensive files on all his fellow Communist oligarchs in the GDR – including his long-time colleague Erich Honecker, who the Stasi chief knew had plenty of secrets to conceal.[7]

One writer described the Stasi as a state of mind. It is a powerful idea to describe the condition of life in a police state. But Berliners had no need for metaphor. They had the Wall. It was the concrete symbol that East Germans – East Europeans – were imprisoned in an arbitrarily divided country. The Wall separated families, destroyed dreams and almost extinguished hopes. The Wall turned Berlin into an unreal city where major through routes suddenly became dead ends, solely because of politics. If you tried to leave the wrong way you could die – 119 people were killed trying to jump it, climb it, tunnel under it or fly over it. The first obstacle was a three-metre-high concrete wall – the 'hinterland fence'. Then a two-metre-high 'signal fence' of barbed wire and steel mesh which triggered an alarm if touched and, along some stretches, activated floodlights. Anyone who made it through those defences had to cover ground full of hidden devices such as steel bars in the earth covered with metal spikes. Escapees by now would almost certainly have been spotted by guards from observation towers positioned – at the Berlin section of the border – every two hundred metres or so. The next barrier was the so-called 'death strip', a six-metre area covered with sand (along which footprints could easily be seen) and patrolled by Stasi-trained dogs. Finally came the three-and-a-half-metre-high Grenzwall 76 (named after the year it was fortified) which was topped by razor wire and a sewer pipe designed to stop anyone trying to climb from getting a good grip. There was no sense of logic to it. The Wall did not divide districts, but often sections of streets. It was the result, simply, of where Russian troops had reached on the day fighting ceased on 6 May 1945. At night on one side the streets were lit by eerie searchlights. It was a physical manifestation of a few people's fear and paranoia.

There had been, in effect, an open border in Germany after the two sides were officially divided in October 1949, when the GDR came into being. In Berlin, people could come and go as they pleased. Many lived on one side and worked on the other, using the U-Bahn metro system and S-Bahn overground rail network to travel around the city. They had to negotiate various checkpoints, where Eastern border guards would check travellers' papers. But they were allowed to pass unhindered. Over time increasing numbers were leaving the East as they saw what was happening. The regime was becoming more authoritarian, particularly after June 1953 when a strike in a few factories turned into anti-government riots that were suppressed by Soviet tanks. The East was fast becoming relatively poorer, more regimented, greyer, duller, less free compared to West Germany. As the Cold War became icier, people voted with their feet – the only way they were allowed to vote. By 1961 the exodus was reaching crisis proportions. From 1955 around 20,000 people a month were leaving and heading to West Germany, where they were granted instant citizenship. The Federal Republic did not recognise the existence of the GDR. Now about 30,000 people a week were trying to emigrate and the austere Stalinist in charge of the East German regime, Walter Ulbricht, decided something had to be done. At first the Soviets were firmly against the idea of sealing the borders, and particularly opposed to the plan to build a Wall. They were worried about how the West would react. But Ulbricht finally convinced his masters in Moscow that it was necessary for the very existence of the state – and he was almost certainly right. More than three million people had fled the GDR over the last dozen years, over a sixth of the population. Half were under twenty-five, well educated, the brightest and best in the nation.

When Khrushchev assured himself that the US would do no more than complain about the construction of a Wall, he reluctantly gave his approval. Ulbricht put his protégé and right-hand man, Erich Honecker, in charge of the highly secret Operation Rose. It was the younger man who coined the phrase 'Anti-fascist protection barrier' to describe the Wall and from then on, in public at least, he never called it anything else. It was planned with the utmost secrecy – even half the East German leadership was not told the details. Building began, suddenly, overnight, on the weekend of 12–13 August 1961 and proceeded with supreme efficiency. In central Berlin, for several hundred metres around Checkpoint Charlie, the barrier which divided the Soviet and American sectors of the city, workers toiled around the clock and the job was finished within three days. The logic of Communist rule had been established with a powerful and ugly symbol – and the career of Erich Honecker was inextricably linked to its concrete foundations.

Erich Honecker, said a one-time comrade and former colleague in the East German leadership, Wolfgang Leonhard,

> had the main characteristic ... essential for success as a young functionary: absolute average intelligence. In a Communist Party on the Stalinist model, you have to have a good memory and an ability to absorb reams of resolutions and turn them into directives, so you need a basic intelligence. You can't be plain dumb, as was required under the Nazis, because the ideology is much more complicated. But you can't be too intelligent, because people of above average intelligence have a tendency to challenge the arcana and spot the flaws ... which can make them disobedient. When the system is in crisis the bright people come to the fore: Kádár in Hungary, Dubček in Czechoslovakia, Gorbachev ... But during normal times, it is the average who rule: the Ulbrichts, the Honeckers. The system demands them.[8]

The central fact of Honecker's life was the ten years he spent in a Nazi prison. That formed him as much as his childhood in the Saarland, the border area with France, where, the fourth child of six, he had a hard upbringing. His coal-miner father, Wilhelm – himself a militant leftist – was out of work much of the time and the family was often near to starvation. He was saved by the Young Spartacists, the youth wing of the Communist Party, which took him under its wing, gave him a cause to believe in and in 1930, when Honecker was eighteen, sent him to Moscow for further education at the Lenin School. Five years later he was ordered back to Germany undercover to set up an office in Berlin and act as an aide to the head of the Young Communists, Bruno Baum. His first mission ended in lamentable failure and Honecker was shown up as anything but a hero. Though he stated later as a Party chieftain after the war that these 'were days of fortitude' and he never flinched from his Communist ideals, the facts tell a different story. He was arrested in a farcical manner. Soon after he arrived in Berlin he arranged to meet a courier from Moscow who was to hand over some money and confidential documents. He realised after the meeting that he was being followed, panicked, and ran away leaving the documents and incriminating evidence behind. He was picked up by the police the next day. Under interrogation, he gave them detailed information about the Communist underground in Berlin, including the names of leaders like Baum, who was jailed, later went to Auschwitz, but survived to play a leading part in the Ulbricht regime in East Germany. The Russian courier, Sarah Fodorova, suffered ghastly torture but gave nothing away.

The decade in Brandenburg Prison turned an already hard man into granite. After the war his record was forgiven by the Soviets – many activists had done far worse things. He made himself useful to Ulbricht, whom Stalin installed as the satrap in his German fiefdom. Ulbricht liked Honecker's energy and he was groomed by the leader as his eventual successor. He was head of the Communist Youth wing until he was into his forties, then rose through the Party machine. When Ulbricht was removed – partly with the help of Honecker and other officials wielding an axe – he slithered into the leader's chair, with the approval of Moscow.

A stern, unsmiling and unbending man with a cold, stand-offish demeanour, he liked the company of women. In matters of sex Honecker was not the pillar of Bolshevik rectitude expected of a high-ranking and high-flying Party apparatchik. He was married three times, though his official biography is curiously vague about his wives. His first marriage, to Lottie Grunel immediately after the war, was never mentioned in the Party CV at all – possibly because she was politically suspect as the daughter of a family of Jehovah's Witnesses. She had a mental breakdown and died in 1946. He was coy about the dates of his second marriage, to Edith Baumann, which he remarked once happened 'around 1948, as far as I remember'. He did not say when he was divorced. His third wife was the politically ambitious, shrill Margot Feist, who became a top Party functionary in her own right. The Education Minister for many years, she was as stern as he was and known throughout the country, even by those who worked for her, as The Witch or The Lilac Dragon.[9]

Several senior Party chiefs knew of Honecker's philanderings. 'He had quite a taste for blonde girls in blue uniforms,' the long-serving Berlin Party chief, Günter Schabowski, revealed. The uniforms were those of the Communist Youth movement. The spy chief Markus Wolf, who ran East Germany's foreign intelligence service, said that not long before Honecker became supreme leader 'I once received a report from a puzzled employee . . . who had seen Erich Honecker . . . slipping surreptitiously through the back streets of Berlin after dismissing his driver at dusk. It was clear to me that Honecker must have been visiting a secret girlfriend . . . Once I joked to this effect with Erich Mielke [his boss] saying "well, we hardly have to keep that on the files" and I made to throw away the report. "No, no," came the reply. "Let me have it. You never know." It joined other unflattering details of Honecker's life in [Mielke's] red boxes.'[10]

East Germany seemed like the success story of the socialist bloc. There were no food queues and almost no absolute poverty in the mid-1980s. It was an ordered society of reliable workers, living in dreary but functional box-like apartment blocks. Its cradle-to-grave welfare provisions were the envy of the rest of the Soviet empire. There seemed to be little open dissent. The Stasi had eradicated it. From an early age it was instilled into East Germans that they must conform and not stand out in any way that might attract attention. The country seemed to be riding high – especially in sport. The regime spent vast sums on glory at the athletics track, skating rink, ski-jumping slope and swimming pool. In the 1980 Olympic Games the GDR won forty-seven gold medals compared to Britain's five and France's six. In the 1984 Winter Olympics, East Germany won nine golds, more than any other nation, beating both the USA and the USSR. Honecker regarded these victories as highly significant. The regime was satisfied that this sporting prowess gave the Communist state legitimacy it might otherwise have lacked. There were other important achievements. The standard of education was as high as anywhere in Europe. If anything, the workforce was over-qualified for the menial tasks most people were expected to perform. In 1984 the World Bank reported that the GDR was the world's twelfth most successful economy and the following year the CIA declared in a top-secret memorandum to President Reagan that East Germany's GNP was fast approaching the Federal Republic's.

But it was all a mirage based on a series of elaborate lies. The country was in a terminal crisis forced by foreign debt. Honecker and a few of the very top leadership knew, but continued borrowing and spending regardless, in a state of absolute denial. They wanted to keep the public content with consumer goods and social benefits; they spent twice as much as most of their East European allies on defence and 'security' – including the Stasi – and they seemed oblivious of the consequences. One of the Party's top finance experts, Günter Ehrensperger, was looking at the growing debt problem and went to Honecker to warn of a potentially serious crisis. At that point foreign debt was increasing tenfold in six years. 'I was summoned to him again that same evening,' he said. 'Honecker told me I was immediately to cease working on such calculations and studies. I was to receive no further material . . . and I was to have all the statistical bases in the department destroyed.' Manfred Uschner, former chief aide to Hermann Axen, a member of the top leadership, said that figures were kept highly confidential, only seen by a few of the elite. When some numbers did come 'they were presented in an almost unreadable format . . . on purpose'. Quickly all the documents were gathered up and shredded. 'We had to strain ourselves, and in great haste, to see the magnitude of our indebtedness. Then it became clear to us: the GDR was totally bankrupt and there was no way it could get out of the . . . fatal circle of indebtedness, renewed indebtedness, new credits and the growing burden of interest payments.'[11]

In 1983, the country reached a point when it could barely meet the payments. It was bailed out through the good offices of an unlikely figure: the right-wing Minister-President of Bavaria, Franz Josef Strauss, who had been West Germany's aggressive Defence Minister when the Berlin Wall was built. For decades Strauss had been vilified by the GDR regime as an ultra-reactionary warmonger who was trying to obtain a West German nuclear bomb. Honecker himself described him as 'a militarist who would not stop at marching through the Brandenburg Gate to recapture Berlin'. Now Strauss acted as a go-between to help arrange a US$ 1 billion credit from a consortium of West German banks so that the GDR could make ends meet. On this occasion Honecker agreed to pay a political as well as a financial price. Part of the deal, which the FRG undertook to keep confidential, was an agreement by the GDR to let 35,000 East Germans emigrate to the West. Strauss was presented as an honoured guest at Honecker's beloved hunting lodge in Thuringia, Werbellinsee.

The negotiator on the Eastern side was one of the most curious figures to emerge from Soviet-style communism. Alexander Schalck-Golodkowski was a spiv on an epic scale who ran an alternative and highly secret 'other' economy on behalf of the East Berlin regime for which it did not have to account. Golodkowski, born in 1932 to Russian immigrants in Berlin, was adopted when he was eight by a German family called Schalck – hence his double-barrelled name. He started work for the Ministry of Trade in a low-grade post. But he was spotted early as a creative accounting talent and also as a discreet, politically reliable and highly sophisticated young man. He was the brains behind the Bereich Kommerzielle Koordinierung (Bureau of Commercial Co-ordination), known as Ko-Ko. It was charged with earning foreign currency outside the normal planning system, and Schalck-Golodkowski was given extraordinary freedom of manoeuvre. It started as a way for the East German elite to fund their elaborate lifestyles and buy Western goods unavailable to all but a few of their compatriots. It soon became the method by which the GDR tried to plug the gaps in the myriad failures in its economy. Towards the mid-1980s, East Germany entirely depended on Ko-Ko to raise enough convertible currency to remain solvent from week to week. As Manfred Seidel, one of the men who signed Ko-Ko's cheques, said, it was the organisation's task 'to employ all available means to create foreign currency for the GDR. To that end, no legal restrictions were to be taken into account. That was the case at home and abroad.'[12]

Ko-Ko's work was technically supervised by the Stasi, where Golodkowski was given the rank of General. But only three other men knew the main details of his dubious transactions: Honecker, Mielke and the GDR's industry and finance chief, Günter Mittag. A huge, bulky, cheerful and gregarious man, Golodkowski operated as an entrepreneurial freebooter, with enormous success. He set up 2,000 fictitious accounts and hundreds of fraudulent front companies in East and

West for stock-market deals, gold and precious gem transactions and commercial speculations of all kinds. Golodkowski ensured that the elite always had plenty of cash in hard currency at their disposal. Honecker had an account, number 0628, at the Deutsche Handelsbank in East Berlin, which always had to contain at least one hundred million Marks. But he did not always use it entirely for himself. One year he sent forty million Marks' worth of grain to help the Sandinistas in Nicaragua. Another, a shortage of apples and bananas in the GDR produced discontent outside food stores among consumers fed up with the limited choice of fresh food available. Honecker wrote a personal cheque for two million Marks for the importation of fruit.

Some sources of Ko-Ko's funds were cruel and criminal. Golodkowski 'persuaded' the curators of certain museums and galleries to reclassify some of their treasures as 'not worth keeping'. They were then sold in the West. More than 600 pictures from the Dresden collection went missing in the 1980s. The Stasi confiscated some paintings and ceramics known to be owned by individuals, which were then sold in the West. The owners were handed huge and fictitious tax bills they did not owe – and told to hand over a painting or valuable antique in lieu of the tax demand.

The East's relationship with Franz Josef Strauss continued, typically with a bizarre business venture. Golodkowski met Strauss to negotiate a deal involving the brothers März, who ran a huge meat company in Bavaria. They bought mass deliveries of cheap pork and beef from the East, which never went through any books in either the East or the West. Payments were made by the millionaire butchers in hard currency which the head of Ko-Ko took home personally in a briefcase.

Golodkowksi's conscience remained relatively clear. East Germany could not have continued in the style to which it became accustomed, without him – or someone like him. 'It was only my job. I had to get Honecker his tailored suits,' he said.

THIRTEEN

LENIN'S APOSTLE

Moscow, Thursday 4 April 1985

WITHIN DAYS OF HIS ACCESSION, Mikhail Gorbachev showed himself to be a new kind of Kremlin leader. His first high-profile campaign, launched three weeks after he took office, was a dramatic drive against a besetting Russian vice: booze. It was a noble cause, worth fighting for, and he went ahead with optimism, vigour, passion, a measure of priggishness and – at the start – clever political salesmanship. The campaign had far-reaching consequences, unforeseen by him, that precipitated a crisis almost as serious as the one he tried to solve. It was typical of the way he was to govern for the next six and a half years.

Russia's appalling drink problem has been a national disease for centuries, as Pushkin, Dostoyevsky and Tolstoy testified. It was probably worse than ever in the late twentieth century, though there are no accurate figures about vodka consumption during serfdom. Now in the late Soviet era there were forty million officially recognised alcoholics in a population of around 270 million. That figure was sure to have been an underestimate. The ascetic Yuri Andropov had made a token effort to reduce alcoholism, but the task defeated him. On the whole, the Communists over the decades had done little to address the issue, even though it was the workers and the poor who suffered the most. Successive regimes reckoned, as the Tsars did, that a nation anaesthetised by alcohol was likely to be politically compliant. In 1984 more than nine million drunks had been picked up off the Soviet Union's streets. The premature deaths, absenteeism, crime, poverty, ruined families and misery caused by alcohol were to be seen everywhere.

The new man in the Kremlin was determined to do something about them. Gorbachev summoned a group of key Party power-brokers on 4 April 1985 and simply announced what he had decided, leaving little room for argument. It fell short of outright prohibition, but not by

Kiss of life and death. The Soviet Union's leader, Leonid Brezhnev (left), and East Germany's Communist Party Secretary, Erich Honecker, in a clinch much parodied by caricaturists, at the thirtieth anniversary celebrations of the founding of the GDR in October 1979.

Working-class hero. Unemployed electrician Lech Wałęsa leading the August 1980 strike in Gdańsk that launched the Solidarity trade union's challenge to the Communists.

The Czechoslovak rock band The Plastic People of the Universe had not intended to spark a revolution, said its chief lyricist Milan Hlavasa. 'We just loved rock and roll and wanted to be famous,' he claimed. The imprisonment of some band members in 1976 inspired the formation of the dissident group Charter 77.

The most powerful intellectual voice behind Charter 77 was the playwright and pholosopher Václav Havel. He was in and out of police stations and jail so often over the next decade that – just in case he was arrested – he kept a suitcase permanently packed with prison essentials.

When the Chernobyl nuclear reactor in Ukraine exploded in April 1986, it was 'a very Soviet disaster'. A mixture of faulty equipment, human error, bureaucratic bungling and suffocating secrecy were among the causes. The Kremlin dealt with it in a traditional way, with lies and deceit.

The Soviet Union's Vietnam. The Red Army was bogged down in Afghanistan for more than nine years in a war that ended in a humiliation for the world's second superpower. Groups of Mujahideen guerrillas – The Army of God – like those from the Yakub Khan clan (*below*), defeated the Soviets with the help of plentiful American weapons.

The three men who negotiated the end of the Cold War: Ronald Reagan, George Bush and Mikhail Gorbachev (with the Soviet leader's interpreter Pavel Palazchenko).

Lech Wałęsa and the Polish communist leader, General Wojciech Jaruselski. The General had tried hard-line tactics to defeat Solidarity. His decision in early 1989 to make a deal with Wałęsa led to Round Table talks which were copied elsewhere in the Warsaw Pact states later in 1989.

Lieutenant-General Boris Gromov, the last commander of Soviet forces in Afghanistan and the last Russian soldier to leave, crossing the Friendship Bridge between the two countries into the Soviet town of Termez, where thousands of Russians were flown to a military base to greet their returning loved ones.

Mikhail Gorbachev, in typically forthright and declamatory mood. A 'Party man' through and through, his aim was to save communism. He did more than anyone to kill it.

Hungary opened its frontier with Austria on 1 May 1989, when border guards began cutting down the wire fence that had comprised the Iron Curtain.

On 19 August 1989 hundreds of East German refugees stormed a gate at Hungary's frontier with Austria – and border guards stood by and let them. It began a massive exodus of East Germans, who had found a way of getting around the Berlin Wall.

Surprising even himself, in June 1989 Lech Wałęsa won an overwhelming victory in the first genuinely free elections held in a Warsaw Pact state since the 1940s. Two months later the Communist regime in Poland fell and Solidarity formed a government.

US Secretary of State, James Baker, and the Soviet Foreign Minister, Eduard Shevardnadze. A business relationship that began at a working summit in Jackson Hole, Baker's ranch in Wyoming, became a longstanding and warm friendship.

much. He trebled the price of vodka. Beer and wine production was reduced by nearly three-quarters. A faint note of caution was expressed by Vladimir Dementsev, the Finance Minister, who warned that income to the state would be reduced and the proposal would leave a black hole in the national budget. He came prepared with figures – it would cost four billion roubles that year and fifteen billion within five years. Gorbachev barely let him finish: 'What you've said is nothing new. We know there's no money to cover it. But you're not proposing anything other than to keep people drunk. Do you propose to build Communism on vodka?'

That was the end of the debate. The measures went through and Gorbachev pursued his course with determination – but to disaster. There were huge queues outside the liquor stores and a thriving black market in vodka was created overnight. The biggest problem was home-distilling of various types of hooch. Sugar disappeared from the shops and had to be rationed. The financial black hole Dementsev warned of was even deeper than he had projected. The death rate shot up from consumption of poisonous home brews. Historic vineyards, mostly in Georgia, were destroyed and never recovered. After three years Gorbachev admitted he had made a mistake and abandoned the alcohol campaign, but the damage had been done.[1]

The launch of the alcohol campaign was less of a shock to the old-timers who had been in comfortable office for so long than another initiative Gorbachev proposed at that same meeting. He must have had in mind the years of toadying and sycophancy he had endured in the Brezhnev years when he made a second announcement, apparently casually, but which was carefully pre-planned. As he was gathering up his papers to return to his private office in the adjoining room, he said: 'I ask Comrades to wait a minute. I would like to exchange opinions on ... the need to struggle systematically against ostentation, arrogance, vainglory and bootlicking.' He went on to say that he hoped at the highest levels of the Party there would be fewer high-flown banquets, fewer medals displayed on chests and altogether more modesty. The others – some wearing honours proudly even at the meeting – left the room looking aghast.

Gorbachev was the first Soviet leader who went on regular public walkabouts to meet the people and be publicly seen. He was good at pressing the flesh, better there than at larger formal gatherings where often he was inclined to be verbose and retreat into dreary, unintelligible Marxist-Leninist speak. In front of huge applauding crowds, his personality shone through; he appeared relaxed, warm, amusing, considerate, thoroughly decent. He was admired by the public and his appearances were 'events'. It was noticed that his wife was nearly always with him, often touching him or holding his hand – normal for a Western leader, but unprecedented in the USSR. People were as intrigued by him as they were inspired.

It was at a walkabout in Leningrad in May, a couple of months after he took power, that two terms forever identified with the Gorbachev era first entered the lexicon. *Perestroika* and *glasnost* became buzzwords throughout the world. In Russian they have specific definitions. When Gorbachev used them they meant whatever he chose them to mean. Gorbachev never wanted to abandon communism. He thought it was his destiny to save communism and purify it. In its early days perestroika – 'restructuring' – meant a process of fairly modest reforms to improve workplace discipline. He launched a rush of energetic measures to allow enterprises to show more initiative and made some minor economic changes in distributing goods around the country. He removed a raft of Brezhnev cronies and bureaucrats who had shown themselves over many years to be incompetent. The KGB moved against a powerful network of corrupt magnates in the Central Asian republics and Gorbachev shook up the Party apparat in Ukraine and other regions. He made some halting steps to introduce a little more democracy into the system. He wanted to reorganise electoral lists – though still in a one-party state – so that people could choose *which* Communists would be elected for certain positions. But none of this was revolutionary. He had no intention of abandoning central planning, introducing a market economy, or abandoning the Communists' monopoly of power. He wanted to 'restructure' everything, but without touching the foundations.

Gorbachev believed in socialism and was convinced that Lenin had outlined the true path, but the project had gone wrong when Stalin deviated from it and 'misrepresented' it. That was a powerful illusion he and many Communist true believers shared. Perestroika, Gorbachev thought, would return to Lenin's ideals. Gorbachev often talked of Lenin, whom he spoke of reverentially as a 'special genius'. There was no cynicism involved. Sergei Tarasenko, a highly experienced and shrewd Foreign Ministry official, said that most apparatchiks throughout the Soviet empire merely paid lip service to the teachings. 'It was politically correct to have Lenin in your library. If you had to . . . write a speech you were keen to find a Lenin quote . . . so you turned to the index.' Hardly anyone any longer believed the teachings, but Gorbachev did. When he quoted Lenin, as he frequently did, it was because he thought the founder of the Soviet Union had a special relevance to his own situation seventy years on.[2]

Glasnost – 'openness' – was also a movable feast, subject to interpretation. He began cautiously, grew far bolder later and the consequences were a transformation in the way the Soviets and the East Europeans saw themselves. Gorbachev believed that if people knew more about the way the Soviet Union worked – or was not working – they would *choose* to make it operate better. He said that there should be 'no black spots' in Soviet history, confident that if the public knew the truth they would understand the achievements of socialism as well as the mistakes and appreciate their rulers. It was typically optimistic, some would say naïve, but at least it was based on the moral principle that the public had a right to know. This *was* revolutionary, in a state that had been run for decades by a governing class paranoid about secrecy. The Party controlled information and employed thousands of censors to make sure nothing it did not authorise was printed or broadcast. Under Gorbachev they were still employed, but they had increasingly less to do.

Soon after taking office Gorbachev was telling groups of journalists that they should feel free to expose corruption in high places, the failures in the system, and be open about some of the horrors in Soviet history. Slowly, cautiously, they began taking him at his word and in the Gorbachev period there was some brilliant campaigning journalism which for the first time in the Soviet Union went beyond Party propaganda and revealed a more accurate picture of the state of the nation. It was not a wholly free press, if such a thing exists anywhere. The state owned nearly all of the media, not to mention the production of newsprint, all big printing presses and the paper distribution network. Communist Party chieftains could still hire and fire editors – or even journalists lower down the chain. But it was freer than at any other time in Soviet history. Newspapers and magazines contained lively debate, an unprecedented irreverence towards powerful institutions and readers were at last provided with information they wanted to know.

Circulation rocketed. The most extraordinary success story was Vladimir Starkov's weekly, *Argumenti y Facti*. It started life in 1979 as an arcane publication for statisticians and economists, with a circulation of around 10,000. Transformed into a popular, though intelligent, paper, telling stories about the lives of ordinary people in Soviet factories and housing estates, at the high point of the glasnost reforms of the 1980s it sold thirty-three million copies. Interesting new television programmes started to be broadcast. There was still a lot of dry propaganda material but some fresh and challenging shows aimed at a young audience were being screened – for example the weekly *Vzglyad* (*Spark*), which ran well-made investigative items about such previously taboo subjects as AIDS, destitute street kids living rough in Moscow, the plight of Afghan War veterans or the untold riches (by Soviet standards at the time) earned by hard-currency call girls working in Moscow hotels. The Soviets stopped jamming foreign radio stations like the BBC World Service and Deutsche Welle.[3]

Hundreds of previously banned books by some of Russia's most gifted writers were published in the USSR for the first time. Alexander Solzhenitsyn's work had been available only in samizdat or in foreign translation, read by a handful of intellectuals in Moscow and Leningrad and by Party bosses. Gorbachev and his wife were avid readers of 'underground' literature most Soviet citizens were not allowed to see. Now Solzhenitsyn's books came out by official publishers in huge print runs and were bought voraciously by a highly literate public starved of honest literature for so long. Boris Pasternak's *Doctor Zhivago* appeared legally in the Soviet Union – about twenty years after David Lean's film version received its world premiere. The biggest popular sensation of the glasnost years was the publication of Anatoli Rybakov's *Children of the Arbat*, the epic novel of Soviet life under Stalin. The decision to publish or not went all the way up to Gorbachev, who gave his approval.

There was a renaissance in Soviet film, which in the early days of the USSR had earned a deservedly high reputation, but which had produced little of note for decades. The release of Tengiz Abuladze's extraordinary anti-Stalinist allegory *Repentance*, set in Georgia in the 1930s, caused a sensation, but was handled carefully. The movie had contemporary themes and the Kremlin reformers did not want to provoke a reaction from conservatives in the Party, who were terrified by the very notion of glasnost. *Repentance* was not 'officially' released, but shown to 'invited audiences'. Soon the producers of the film had issued so many 'invitations' that more than twenty-five million people had seen it. Vitali Korotich, editor-in-chief of the news magazine *Ogonyok* (*The Flame*), was a major beneficiary of the Soviet Union's new journalism. He was given encouragement from the top and was told that his reporters could write what they wanted. He thought that

Gorbachev was only half-sincere about glasnost. '[Gorbachev] had in mind giving an old trollop a sponge bath and putting clean clothes on her, assuming this would restore her virginity,' he said. Yet the transformations 'openness' produced were so radical that, whether or not the leader or his advisers had predicted any of the consequences, they became unstoppable.[4]

Gorbachev wanted to make a mark on the world stage immediately. He believed the first imperative of the Soviet Union should be to avoid a further slide into confrontation with the West. He told his aides repeatedly that 'domestic and foreign policies are totally interconnected' – that none of the reforms he hoped to make at home were possible without 'a more advantageous international environment'. Disarmament talks with the US had run into the sands. He wanted to restart them. Among his first decisions, less than a month after taking office, was to halt the deployment of further SS-20 medium-range nuclear missiles in Europe. For a mixture of personal, political and moral reasons he tried hard to earn a reputation as a 'peacemaker'. But his main problem was the way the Soviet Union was perceived abroad. The diplomat Sergei Tarasenko explained:

> We had amassed such a negative legacy ... that we had to free ourselves from that. The first thing we had to do was change the country's image. We had to become a 'normal' country. We could no longer play the role of a rogue state. In all respects we were up against a brick wall ... In world public opinion we were on the level of barbarians. We were feared, but at the same time no one respected us ... We were 'the evil empire'. We had to get out of the corner we had been driven into in respect of human rights, freedom to emigrate, Afghanistan and so on. But all we could do was snap at people. There were demonstrations against our Foreign Minister, Gromyko, everywhere. Few people read *Pravda*, but everyone read the *New York Times*. The people who read *Pravda* were Fidel Castro ... and the World Peace Council, whose services we paid for.[5]

Gorbachev abandoned the old dogmas about the Soviet Union's place in the world. When he talked about 'new thinking' he meant it. He blamed his predecessors for isolating the USSR from the outside world, where it had to return if the country was to modernise itself and compete with the West. He was always urging 'new thinking' on his aides, a phrase he used in conversation far more often than either the words perestroika or glasnost. Many apparatchiks had become so used to hearing meaningless slogans from their leaders and to the launch of insincere campaigns which would soon be dropped, that they assumed this was mere rhetoric and propaganda. But they were wrong. When some of the diehards realised Gorbachev was in earnest, they were shocked. From the first, Gorbachev had to be careful not to push the conservatives around him – many of the people who chose him for his job – too far. The veteran head of the Party's international section, Boris Ponomarev, a highly influential man in Kremlin circles and among the ruling Parties in the satellite states, was heard to grumble: 'What is this new thinking? Let the Americans change their thinking instead . . . Are we now against force, which is the only language imperialism understands?' But he would not dare to say so publicly to the leader, who, once selected, had almost dictatorial powers if he chose to use them. 'Foreigners have a hard time understanding to what extent the post of General Secretary was influential in the Soviet mentality,' said Anatoli Gromyko, son of the former Foreign Minister. 'You see, to object to [the top leader] or even worse to debate his opinions in public – at that time I don't think anyone would dare to do that.' Valeri Boldin, Gorbachev's confidential secretary, who saw him every day and went with him everywhere,* said that foreign affairs were the prerogative of the leader and a small group of trusted intimates. '*Nobody* dared venture into the sphere of international relations unless invited or instructed by him to work on a given subject.'[6]

Gorbachev relied on a core of intimates and political soulmates. By far the cleverest and most talented was Alexander Yakovlev, the intellectual inspiration behind Perestroika and a behind-the-scenes fixer in the Kremlin bureaucracy of subtle skills. Born in 1923, Yakovlev was almost a decade older than Gorbachev. His most formative experience was the Great Patriotic War, in which he served as a lieutenant in the marines. Half his friends were killed and he survived only because four of his comrades sacrificed their own lives to rescue his bullet-ridden body from the battlefield. He was left semi-crippled for life.

Yakovlev rose through the ranks of the nomenklatura performing

* Boldin was among several of Gorbachev's key aides who ultimately betrayed him. He took part in the (failed) coup against Gorbachev in August 1991 when a group of lacklustre conservative diehards tried to seize power in Moscow while the leader was on holiday at his seaside villa in the Crimea. One of Gorbachev's weaknesses was that he was not always a good picker of aides and advisers – a factor which, as time went on, became a serious problem for him.

sensitive political tasks with distinction. He seemed like a Party man, if an unusually bright and interesting one, but he started to have doubts. The first came in February 1956 when he sat through Khrushchev's 'secret speech' and heard for the first time details of Stalin's crimes. They were fuelled when he went to Prague in the days after the Red Army invaded Czechoslovakia in 1968. He was acting head of the Communist Party's propaganda department. While he trotted out the line that the Russians were saving the Czechs from American imperialism and fascism, he did not believe a word of it. He said later that crushing the Prague Spring was 'a sign that the system was doomed'.

Yakovlev was one of the very few members of the Soviet leadership with any significant experience of the West. In 1958 he had been an exchange student at Columbia University. He hated his year in New York. He admired American technological know-how and enterprise, but loathed being harangued about the superiority of the Western way of life. He repeatedly told the story of how in a Manhattan shop he was once asked to take off his hat to show that it was true that Russians did not have horns. The future godfather of perestroika wrote vitriolic anti-American articles in the Soviet press containing observations such as this: 'American monopolistic monsters believe that their domination of the world would offer the best solutions to the problems of international politics. They consider war a peerless catalyst to achieve this goal . . . The weapons makers and the brass hats have formed an alliance with death . . . postwar American leaders have always behaved like fighting cocks with nuclear talons, straining to fight Communism and the Soviet Union.'[7]

A rising star in the Party, Yakovlev landed himself in serious trouble in 1972 for writing an article criticising anti-Semitism and Russian nationalism. As 'punishment' he was dispatched to an out-of-the-way posting as Soviet Ambassador to Canada. In this comfortable exile, where he remained for more than a decade, he started to rethink his entire world view and, in the strictest secrecy, to write a critique of Marxism-Leninism, which he began saying in private was 'a philosophy concerned only about the idler, not the worker'.

In 1983 Gorbachev, then in charge of Soviet agriculture, was on a ten-day official visit to Canada and Yakovlev was given the job of looking after him. They toured around Canada in a small plane, stopping off in out-of-the-way towns and villages, and became firm friends. Soon they talked honestly with each other about the state of the Soviet

Union and found that their views were remarkably similar. Yakovlev describes how at one stop the pair had a two-hour walk in cornfields. 'I took advantage of the circumstances and told him what I really thought. He did the same.' Within a few weeks of their meeting, Gorbachev brought him back to Moscow as head of the influential think-tank, the Institute for World Economy and International Relations. When Gorbachev became General Secretary Yakovlev was made head of the leader's brains trust and a key member of the new team in the Kremlin. Yakovlev had effectively abandoned communism – though not yet the Party – and became a social democrat. He always urged Gorbachev to 'take that extra step' towards radical reform. He produced proposals for far-reaching democratic changes aimed at abolishing the one-party state and introducing the beginnings of a market economy. Gorbachev was not ready to go as far – but he listened to Yakovlev's ideas, and his tactical acumen, with great care. One of Yakovlev's regular refrains was to refer to the satellite states as 'parasite socialism' and he urged the leader to make an urgent reappraisal of their importance to the Soviet Union.[8]

The greatest influence on Gorbachev, though, was his wife. Jack Matlock, when American Ambassador to Moscow, was told by a senior official in the Kremlin – obviously expecting the story to get back to Washington – that 'he was unable to make decisions without her advice'. Many of Gorbachev's aides say the same. Raisa was a clever woman, and did not mind the world knowing it. She was a novelty to Kremlin officials, who did not at first understand how to react to her. There was no formal role for a Soviet leader's wife, but as Boldin, who dealt with her every day – sometimes many times a day – and disliked her intensely, said: 'She became the First Lady of the Soviet Union quickly, or at least in less time than it took Gorbachev to feel that he had truly established himself as leader of the Party and the State.'[9]

When the couple arrived in Moscow from Stavropol – their only child, Irina, was already in her twenties and had left home – Raisa immersed herself in the world of think-tanks, discussion groups and conferences. She loved being in the intellectual centre of the country, but she was careful about too obviously involving herself in politics. That changed when her husband was chosen as leader. While Kremlin wives had earlier confined themselves to running a household, Raisa was a true feminist and wanted to be treated as a serious person. That was the way Gorbachev regarded her. Almost everyone else around him was male and middle-aged. Many of them resented the fact that

Gorbachev listened to her. Aides gossiped amongst themselves about how bossy she was, how Gorbachev would defer to her. As Boldin put it, 'with his rather mild character and his inability to stand his ground, Gorbachev often found himself under his wife's influence . . . she was a political figure in her own right, who asserted herself'. The couple continued their tradition of taking a walk every evening and some officials were furious, not just with her 'lordly manner' but with the extra workload the habit imposed on them. 'He often phoned at a very late hour to issue instructions on unexpected matters that had occurred after his evening walk with Raisa,' Boldin said. 'His wife's attitude played a decisive role in Gorbachev's fate – and of that of the Party and the entire country.'[10]

FOURTEEN

SILENT MEMORIES

Budapest, Saturday 18 January 1986

THE SOVIETS SAW one part of their empire as a laboratory testing-ground for some of the reforms proposed by the new thinkers around Gorbachev. Hungary was often hailed, in the West at any rate, as 'the merriest barracks in the camp'. From the outside it seemed more easy-going, welcoming and a lot less dreary than elsewhere in the socialist bloc. Travel restrictions had been relaxed in the 1970s, though it was so expensive for Hungarians to visit anywhere outside the COMECON states that limited numbers enjoyed the freedom. Yet knowing it was possible to leave, unlike in neighbouring Czechoslovakia or Romania, made a big psychological difference. Nobody by the mid-1980s was scared for political reasons of talking openly to foreign visitors, about almost anything. Budapest was the first capital city in a Communist country to get a Hilton hotel, typically a modern eyesore commanding beautiful views over the Danube, built above the ruins of an ancient monastery. It was the first to receive a pilgrimage from the American evangelist Billy Graham, who thought it such fertile territory, and with such fine cuisine, that he returned three times in the 1980s. It was the first to receive, in February 1984, a visit from Margaret Thatcher, who was allowed to extol the virtues of consumer capitalism on state-controlled television. Around the same time she was in Budapest, the Hungarians entertained another important visitor, one of their colonial masters from Russia. Mikhail Gorbachev, then in charge of Soviet agriculture, toured Hungary for three weeks 'studying the achievements and the results of our reforms', said Miklós Németh, one of the officials who showed him around. 'He said then that . . . he saw a lot in the Hungarian example that he would like to see in the Soviet Union.'[1]

From the Soviet perspective Hungary appeared to be a positive signpost towards sensibly managed transformation. 'It wasn't a basket case like Poland,' one of Gorbachev's advisers said. 'It was stable, prosperous and didn't look like it was going to blow up at any moment.' But Hungary, and especially Budapest, displayed surface gloss that tried to hide deep-rooted problems and national neuroses. A visitor from the West, who in the mid-1980s strolled with a local down Budapest's principal shopping street, Vaci utca, would have been surprised by the Hungarian's reaction. First there would have been a measure of pride – even, for example, that some of the shops were filled with a few luxurious Western items that were unobtainable in Prague, Warsaw or Berlin, let alone in Moscow or Bucharest. Then, most likely, would follow the complaints, similar to those that were heard elsewhere in the socialist bloc: housing was so scarce that divorced couples were forced to live together for months and years before they could find somewhere else; young couples waited seven years or more to find a home. Women had a tough time under communism – in Hungary as in all the countries of 'actually existing socialism'. There was supposed to be full employment, so practically all women worked. But on average in Hungary in the 1980s women were paid 30 per cent less than men for doing the same jobs – on the factory floor or the office. Then they had another job. On the whole East European countries were traditional male-dominated societies where men performed few domestic tasks and women ran the home.

The regime was proud of 'gulyás communism', as the country's successful and talented spin doctors called it. Hungary had begun experimenting with a New Economic Mechanism in 1968, but it did not take off until the early 1970s. It conducted the most liberal and decentralised foreign trade policy of any COMECON country. Collective farms were given substantial amounts of freedom to run themselves. Farmers were encouraged to set up their own plots of land on the side and take the produce they grew to local markets. Predictably, given the freedom, within a few years almost as much was grown on these small privately farmed plots as in all the big co-operatives. A few of the monopolies were broken up. Factory managers were given more autonomy and told to make profits – previously considered a dirty word – rather than simply meet arbitrarily set production targets. Some commodity prices were linked to world markets and no longer to the unrealistically fixed prices in the Five Year Plans. Some privately owned shops and small business were permitted – restaurants, clothing stores, service suppliers like electricians.

The predictable result was an explosion in the size of a second, 'black' economy outside the state that was never officially acknowledged. This was not only tolerated but encouraged by the regime. Naturally, the black economy operated much more efficiently than the official one. In the mid-1980s around 80,000 artisans working privately were meeting nearly two-thirds of the demands for all kinds of services from plumbing to lap-dancing. The economists behind the NEM said that without these reforms the entire Communist system would disintegrate into poverty – 'reproducing shortage', as the best-known of them, János Kornai, said. The NEM had many admirers in the West. More circumspectly, it had growing support in countries like East Germany and Czechoslovakia, whose regimes had turned their faces against reforms. As Honecker maintained: 'Capitalism and communism were as different and incompatible as fire and water.' The GDR, he said, 'was not going to be a field for experimentation'.

One big problem faced the NEM: it did not work. Hungarian prosperity was an illusion, as all the moonlighting builders, taxi drivers, electricians and cooks desperately doing their second and third jobs to make ends meet knew well from personal experience. 'Every time visiting journalists or academics came here telling us what a success story Hungary was, we would try to explain the truth patiently and their eyes would glaze over,' Sándor Zsindely, a research chemist at an institute in Budapest during the 1980s, said. 'It was not the story they wanted to hear. They thought we were just miserable Central Europeans who enjoyed our melancholy.'[2] The reforms failed because they ended in the worst of both worlds. Hungary had the constraints of communism without the benefits of capitalism. The Party was still not prepared to surrender the commanding heights of the economy, because that risked losing power politically. Hungary was forced to adopt the same methods of staying afloat as its neighbours: borrowing on a huge scale. By the mid-1980s it had foreign debts of around US$ 18.5 billion – more than US$200 for each Hungarian, not far short of the average person's annual income. The country had the highest per capita debt in Europe.

On the morning of 8 February 1986 a group of around 400 people took a walk near the village of Nagymáros in one of the most picturesque parts of Hungary. It was a freezing cold day, but this was a popular route taken at all times of the year to see the glorious Danube Bend where, fifteen kilometres north of Budapest, the majestic river sweeps through a narrow valley in the Carpathian Basin. The views here are stunning but these hikers were not there that day to see one of the natural wonders of Europe. They were there to protest against a joint plan by the Hungarian and Czech governments that would forever destroy the beauty of this bucolic spot. Soon after ten a.m. the marchers reached a quiet glade on the riverbank that was cordoned off by wire. This was where work was scheduled to begin on a huge new hydro-electric dam – a great feat of engineering, the two governments explained, one of those gigantic projects with which the Communists proposed to serve humanity by taming nature.

As they approached the cordon the demonstrators saw they were not alone. Dozens of riot police confronted them wielding plastic shields and truncheons. János Várgha, the leader of the group, a bearded, forty-three-year-old former biologist turned science journalist, remonstrated with the officer in charge that this was 'a peaceful nature walk, we are doing nothing against the law, nothing political'. But this was ignored. The police were under orders to break up the demonstration. They fired tear gas grenades and beat up around thirty of the protesters. When Várgha returned to Budapest he heard that he had lost his job on the magazine *Buvar.*

But if the regime thought it had silenced protest against the US$ 3 billion Nagymáros dam project, it was forced to think again. Várgha's Danube Circle gained publicity around the world. In Hungary it attracted overwhelming support even from people who did not care about the environment and thought – as the majority in the West did during the 1980s – that the Greens were kooks. Within weeks more than 10,000 people signed a petition calling for the two regimes to halt the project. This was an extraordinary number in a country where, for thirty years, since the revolution against the Soviets, people had been careful not to push at the limits under which they were constrained by 'gulyás communism'.

The idea of damming the Danube had first been suggested in Stalin's time. It fitted with the big Soviet dreams of turning small agricultural countries into 'nations of iron and steel'. The plan was dropped in the 1950s but resurrected in the 1970s and the two governments signed an agreement to go ahead with the project in 1979. It involved building an enormous and complex system of dams, reservoirs and canals along a 200-kilometre stretch of the Danube that runs through Slovakia and Hungary. The Danube is a relatively slow-moving river at this point, but that did not deter the Planners. Twice a day water would be dammed at Gabčikovo, a plant on the Czechoslovak side, creating a swell in the river. Water would also be diverted into a twenty-kilometre-long canal on the Czech side, leading to a second dam at Nagymáros, on the Hungarian side, where there would be a huge energy-creating turbine. The main attraction for the two Communist governments was that most of the cost would be met by the Austrian government, which insisted on taking 60 per cent of the energy. It was a deeply cynical move from the Austrians, who a couple of years earlier had planned a dam further upstream at Hainburg, but were stopped from proceeding by their own environmental campaigners. The two Communist regimes imagined they would benefit from hard currency, even though their own energy supplies would be increased only moderately – in Hungary's case by just 5 per cent.[3]

In Czechoslovakia objectors to the scheme were suppressed. The moment the Husák regime heard of the formation of any protest groups it closed them down and jailed their leaders. In Hungary, at first, objections were permitted. The Party was careful to burnish its liberal image for Western consumption and did not immediately see that an environmental protest would become a political threat. It allowed objectors to argue publicly in the state-owned press that the scheme would have serious consequences. Várgha formed the Danube Circle in 1984 after he began to write a series of articles about the potential ecological impact of the scheme. He discovered that 150,000 hectares of land would be flooded, including riverbanks, the wetland habitats of 200 species of animals, and prime agricultural fields. The beautiful, medieval town of Visegrád would be destroyed, wonderful scenery would be marred by huge and hideous power plants and the shipping industry along the river would be severely dislocated. At first the Danube Circle remained a small group that received more attention outside than inside Hungary. But when details of the Austrian deal emerged in late 1985, and now three governments seemed determined to press ahead with the scheme despite the protests, support grew fast. Here, at last, was a popular issue that could galvanise Hungarians. 'This could unite people,' the dissident activist Miklós Haraszti said. 'We could say look, these are real concrete issues about the environment, about health, the land. It wasn't about largely theoretical things like civil rights, human freedoms and so on.'[4]

Dissident opposition groups in Hungary had been allowed increasing freedom since the mid-1960s, but were tiny and had little influence. They operated in a climate not so much of fear but of officially encouraged amnesia. The Communists ruled, as in Czechoslovakia, on 'silent memories of a stolen past', as one of the underground writers put it.

For three decades the country had been led by a clever, subtle and masterly political tactician, János Kádár. He was the only East European Communist who merited an 'ism' after his name. Kádárism depended on people appearing to forget about the trauma of 1956 and particularly Kádár's own less than heroic role in those dramatic events. Hungarians had to accept the basic tenets of socialism – even if they did not believe any of them – and they had to accept colonial status with 75,000 Soviet troops stationed in the country. In return Kádár would provide material benefits, peace, stability and as little visible interference from the Russians as he could negotiate from Moscow.

Dissidents were permitted to operate – within carefully circumscribed limits. Intellectuals in the centre of Budapest were allowed to produce samizdat publications and hold meetings. They were watched, of course, by the secret police. But that was not a particularly onerous job. Haraszti estimated that in the mid-1980s there were probably no more than a thousand regular opposition activists in the entire country. The main groups published two magazines, *Beszélö* (*Speaker*) and *Hírmondó* (*Messenger*), but there were dozens of smaller ones. Every Monday night a 'samizdat boutique' was held at the Budapest apartment of the architect László Rajk. The various publications would be laid out on a long table. The 'customers', whose names would never be taken, would say which magazine they wanted, and Rajk's team of 'copiers' would produce the texts in time for them to be collected the following week. It was a remarkably efficient system.

Every now and then a writer or activist would be picked up by the police and interrogated, but on the whole the dissidents were left alone as long as they stayed in the capital and talked amongst themselves or within the Communist Party, where a reform wing was starting to grow. If they began stirring up labourers on the land or industrial workers they were stopped. The last political prisoner was Haraszti in 1973, who took a job in a factory for six months and wrote a compelling book, *A Worker in a Worker's State*, about the dreadful conditions in Hungarian industry, and its woeful inefficiency. He was jailed for eight months after the book was circulated in samizdat. The social contract between Kádár and his cowed people worked – up to a point. Over time he became a popular and widely admired figure. But the deal was now disintegrating.

János Kádár was still in his mid-seventies a good-looking man, tall, sandy-haired, with an ascetic manner. He was born János Czermanik, illegitimate, on 25 May 1912 in the port town of Fiume, now Rijeka in Croatia. His mother was a Slovak servant girl and his father, a private soldier in the Austro-Hungarian army, abandoned them both at his birth. He always remembered his tough childhood. He left school at fourteen and trained as an apprentice toolmaker. He drifted into the Communist Party in his early teens, when it was a banned organisation under the authoritarian rule of Admiral Miklós Horthy. He found a faith he never lost. As an underground Party organiser, he was jailed in 1937 for nearly three years. During the war, he ran the Communist underground, under the pseudonym Kádár (meaning a cooper, or barrel-maker) which he kept for the rest of his life. When the Communists took over Hungary, he rose through the Party ranks as an able apparatchik. The ruler Stalin placed in charge of Hungary, Mátyás Rákosi, ran at that time, in the early 1950s, the most brutal regime in the Soviet imperium. Kádár was always careful to give little away about his opinions. He had a dry sense of humour but was too circumspect to show it often in public. An apparently cheerful man with a frank look, it was during the purge years, when Communists turned on each other, that Kádár displayed the shiftiness and untrustworthiness that lay in his character. He betrayed his best friend, László Rajk, in a macabre and chilling manner.* He was then forced to witness Rajk's execution in 1949. A couple of years later it was Kádár's turn to be a victim. Arrested on bogus treason charges, he spent three years in jail.

In 1956 Kádár was initially on the side of the revolution. He became Communist Party boss, but a few days later turned coat. When the Russians dispatched tanks to crush the Uprising with overwhelming force, he was installed as head of the puppet Soviet regime. At first his methods were brutal. Around 300 so-called 'rebels and counter-revolutionaries' were executed. Kádár ensured that the political leader of the revolution, his rival Imre Nagy, was hanged – initially against the wishes of Moscow. For years he was the most hated man in Hungary. But over time and in stages he relaxed his iron grip. He declared often from the early 1960s that 'those who are not against us are with us', and he tried to gain as much independence as he could from Moscow. He developed the brand of communism that eventually attracted the interest of reformers such as Gorbachev, though the

* Godfather to Rajk's then seven-year-old son, Kádár, in order to save his own life, was forced to visit his friend in jail and try to extract a confession of treason out of him. The interview was secretly taped and a transcript published towards the end of 1990. It makes gruesome reading, but is instructive of life in a totalitarian police state.

'merry barracks' had the highest suicide rate in Europe. Kádár hardly ever talked about the tragedy of 1956 and his social contract with Hungarians depended entirely on the people keeping their silence too. It was the one big taboo subject for dissidents and Party reformers. Kádár became crustier as he grew older and more forgetful.

As the economic news worsened he tried to row back from the reforms he had inspired and led. He tried to crack down on the Danube Circle, though when he realised how popular the group had become he shied away from a serious confrontation. He declared in private that he had little time for Gorbachev – 'an upstart'. He was beginning to look like an old-fashioned Stalinist and the young, ambitious Communist Party apparatchiks around him were beginning to say more and more openly that Comrade Kádár had hung around too long.[5]

FIFTEEN

'WE CANNOT WIN'

Moscow, January 1986

TWO MONTHS AFTER Mikhail Gorbachev took power he handed one of the cleverest generals on the Soviet high command a highly secret and sensitive task. Anatoli Zaitsev, a tall, lean, dark-haired forty-four-year-old, was ordered to Kabul to produce an honest answer to the question: can the Soviet Union win the Afghanistan War? Zaitsev was a highly skilled military planner and though he had seen some action in the Afghan War, he was not responsible for the debacle the Russians faced on their south-eastern border. Zaitsev returned to Moscow with, essentially, a one-word answer: no. He concluded that the only way the war could end on Soviet terms was hermetically to seal Afghanistan's borders with Pakistan and Iran, to prevent shipments of arms to the Mujahideen and keep the guerrillas trapped inside the country. That was impossible without sending hundreds of thousands of additional soldiers into a conflict that had already dragged on for five and a half years and had by now cost the lives of around 7,500 Soviet soldiers.[1]

Gorbachev had already decided that the war must be ended. The Zaitsev report simply furnished him with an additional argument against the few diehard militarists around the Kremlin who still believed in the mission. 'The question was not whether to pull out, but *how*,' one of Gorbachev's closest aides, Andrei Grachev, said. 'It had become obvious (to most of the leadership) that we could not go on paying such a heavy price – in casualties, expenditure and isolation on the international scene.' Gorbachev frequently fumed to his associates in private 'This can't be delayed. We can't let the Brezhnev /Andropov war become the Gorbachev war.' Yet he continued to delay. Fearing resistance at home from his conservative critics, he could find no way to secure peace with honour – or without what he saw as humiliation.[2]

Andropov had realised the Afghan invasion had been a mistake soon after he had so forcefully recommended that it go ahead. During his short tenure at the top in the USSR, he tried to negotiate a deal with the Pakistani President, Zia-ul-Haq. The Soviets would withdraw, he offered, if the Pakistanis ended their support for the Islamic guerrillas – 'the terrorists of the Mujahideen' he called them. But as he approached death the talks came to nothing. Now Gorbachev was determined to seek a way out. In mid-October 1985 he summoned the Afghan Communist leader, Babrak Karmal, secretly to Moscow and gave him a stern warning: 'By next summer, 1986, you will have to figure out how to defend your cause on your own,' he said. 'We will help you, but only with arms, no longer with troops.'

The Soviets had become disappointed with Karmal soon after they had installed him as head of the Afghan regime. Gorbachev had been sent numerous KGB reports saying he was weak, capricious and indecisive. Gorbachev often used to say 'Karmal walks like a pretzel' – a Russo / Yiddish phrase meaning someone is drunk. Inside Afghanistan, the Communists controlled the capital and the other cities, but even with Soviet armies helping them, large areas of the remote and mountainous land were in the hands of the rebels. Gorbachev now lectured Karmal on how to run a largely Muslim country: 'If you want to survive you'll have to broaden the base of the regime. Forget socialism. Make a deal with the truly influential forces in the country, including the Mujahideen commanders. You'll have to revive Islam, respect traditions, and try to show the people some tangible benefits from the revolution.'[3]

Two days later Gorbachev met his fellow Kremlin magnates and came straight to the point: 'It is time to take a decision on Afghanistan,' he said. 'With or without Karmal's consent we take a firm line on the matter of our rapid withdrawal.' He came well prepared. Gorbachev began reading from a series of emotional letters he had received from mothers of dead and wounded soldiers. 'They ask: "International duty? in whose name?" Do the Afghan people want it? Is it worth the lives of our boys, who don't even know why they were sent there. What are they defending?' Gorbachev got his way. Not a single voice now seemed in favour of Soviet troops remaining in Afghanistan. Yet pulling out became an agonisingly slow process.[4]

A key ally and friend became Gorbachev's creative partner in radical changes to the Soviet empire. In July 1985, Andrei Gromyko, for so long the stern face of Soviet diplomacy, was kicked upstairs to the powerless post of President. Gorbachev confounded the entire Soviet political class when he named a successor: Eduard Shevardnadze. It shocked the new Foreign Minister, too, who could scarcely believe what he was being told when Gorbachev ordered him to take the job. 'But I am not Russian and have absolutely no experience in foreign affairs,' he said hesitantly. Gorbachev waved all the doubts aside: 'As to your nationality, it's true you're a Georgian, but above all you're a Soviet man,' he said. 'No experience? Perhaps in this case it's a good thing. Our foreign policy is in need of a fresh approach, it needs courage, dynamism and innovation.' Gorbachev was not always a great picker of advisers, aides or colleagues to trust. But Shevardnadze was an inspired choice. They had known and liked each other for many years, but, more important, they agreed on the essentials. Neither had been a party to the decision to invade Afghanistan. They had been junior members of the Kremlin leadership at the time and were not informed about it until the day after the troops had arrived in Kabul. At their meeting when Shevardnadze accepted his new post both of them used the same word to describe the war almost simultaneously – 'criminal'.[5]

Shevardnadze, like Gorbachev, often used to say war formed him. He was thirteen when the Germans invaded the USSR and one of his brothers was killed in the first days of fighting. One of his other two brothers was almost immediately sent to replace him and stayed on the front for the duration. His father, a teacher, survived Stalin's Great Purge, but only just. He had been a Menshevik around the time of the 1917 revolution, and joined the Bolsheviks only during the Civil War. He was arrested in 1937, on the usual suspicion of 'deviationism', but by chance was recognised amidst the other prisoners by a NKVD officer who had been a pupil, and he was released. Shevardnadze, from Mamati, a remote village about 150 miles west of Tbilisi, used Georgian as his native tongue and always spoke Russian with a strong accent. He became a Party member in 1948 and was a zealot. 'Communism was my religion,' he said, and it brought him material rewards. He joined the apparat, and swiftly rose through the ranks in posts involving internal security. As, successively, police chief in Georgia and then Interior Minister, he had close links with the intelligence service – 'the organs' as the forces of repression were called. In 1951 he married a petite, beautiful and glamorous young woman, Nanuli Tsargareishvili. During the purges she had seen her father, a general noted for his bravery, arrested in the middle of the night. He was taken away and shot. She recalled how for a long period afterwards she cried herself to sleep. Later she remembered weeping genuine tears when Stalin died, for she too became a committed Communist.[6]

During the 'stagnation' years the Georgian Communist Party was one of the most corrupt in the Union. In 1972 the Party chief in the Republic, Vasily Mzhavanadze, was removed in a well-publicised bribes scandal and Shevardnadze replaced him, with orders to clean up the mess. He was highly respected as a man of integrity and stories abound of how he campaigned hard against the endemic Caucasian diseases of crime and graft. He once called for his colleagues in the Georgian leadership to vote at a Party gathering with their left hands. When they raised their hands he noted how many were wearing fancy and expensive Western watches, which at that time must have been dubiously acquired. Dressed in peasant clothes, he once took off north from Tbilisi and headed towards Moscow in a battered old car whose boot was stuffed full of tomatoes. Rules had recently been introduced in Georgia that no vegetables should be exported from there. As he drove, he counted the number of policemen he bribed when he was stopped, so the story went, and then purged the Georgian police.

He was relatively liberal, but could act in traditional Soviet ways. He had scores of dissidents arrested and jailed during the crackdown on human rights campaigners in the 1970s, including the distinguished scientist and writer Zviad Gamsakhurdia. When required, he could outdo Gorbachev as a crawler to those higher up the chain of command, once praising Brezhnev in a speech for his 'breadth of vision, humanity, uncompromising class position, loyalty, principles and skill at penetrating into the soul of his interlocutor'. Georgia, he said, 'would always be loyal to its Russian brother . . . They call Georgia a sunny land. But for us . . . the real sun rises not in the East, but in the North, in Russia, the sun of Leninist ideas.'[7]

He was promoted to a ministerial job in Moscow in 1976, a couple of years before Gorbachev, but continued in relatively obscure posts. He had met Gorbachev often when they were both regional Party bosses, but they became close family friends as they worked together in Moscow. They were discreet and careful Party men but it became clear as they talked that they both saw the flaws in the system which, Shevardnadze said, could 'reduce a person to a cog who could be crushed with impunity'. They agreed on the kind of domestic reforms needed and the only way they could be introduced. 'Gorbachev said to me there are two roads we can take', according to Shevardnadze. 'Either we tighten our belts very tightly and reduce consumption, which the people will no longer tolerate – or we can try to defuse international tension and overcome the disagreements between East and West – and . . . free up the gigantic sums we spend on arms.' They met privately twice a week for long sessions and at several formal government and Party meetings. For many years it was an exceptionally close bond, unusual in Soviet politics.[8]

Shevardnadze was a fast learner with an extraordinary memory, his closest aide, Sergei Tarasenko, said. He had to be. Within three weeks of his appointment he had a scheduled meeting in Helsinki with the US Secretary of State, George Shultz – a highly experienced foreign affairs expert – when he made no bones about his ignorance of the details of arms limitations talks and other technicalities. Shultz was impressed by the Georgian's honesty and candour. In a memo to President Reagan immediately afterwards he wrote: 'The contrast between him and Gromyko was breathtaking. He could smile, engage, converse. He could persuade and be persuaded.'[9]

To the wider public, Shevardnadze presented a change almost immediately, with his handsome, warm face, his avuncular-looking white hair, cheerful demeanour and his fondness for a joke and a chat. He had first-rate public relations skills, said Tarasenko:

> He was the first Soviet minister who began to speak with protesters [against the USSR] . . . As soon as he saw placards like 'Russians out of Afghanistan' he would get out of his car, speak with them, invite their representatives to the Embassy and spend a few hours with them. As a result . . . demonstrations against it more or less stopped. In the course of half a year he removed antipathy against us. Before that none of our leaders had been so open or, for the most part, so honest. They would . . . evade questions. Gromyko used to say things like 'That's a provocation. I refuse to answer that question.' But Shevardnadze would answer the question, discuss it. He . . . [held] an intelligent conversation with people.' It was a deliberate tactic he and Gorbachev discussed at great length 'to eradicate the image of the USSR as an enemy'.

There were immediate changes in the way the Kremlin ran its empire. When previous Russian leaders told their underlings in the colonies that they would be given more independence and control of their affairs, they had not meant it. Shevardnadze and Gorbachev did. The practice since Stalin's day was that when any of the satellites considered anything, however minor, with international implications, they would ask the advice of officials in Moscow before acting. 'Our people would then prepare an answer – think about this further, say, or scrap the idea,' Tarasenko said. 'Soon after he became Foreign Minister Shevardnadze was asked for such advice and he replied he had none to give. Those were sovereign states and . . . they could do what they deemed necessary. He got quite emotional about it and said "this practice should stop".'[10]

Ronald Reagan found the Soviet negotiating partner he was looking for. Gorbachev was anxious to meet him as soon as it could be arranged. He was confident that he could outsmart the American and Reagan was convinced he could outcharm the Russian. They fixed on a summit in Geneva in November 1985 – the first of four held over the next three years that transformed the postwar world. Nothing of major substance was concluded at that Swiss meeting – no agreements were signed or grand statements were made. But it forged a unique round of personal diplomacy that ultimately – and speedily – brought the Cold War to an end. It was a curious bond, as Reagan perceptively pointed out to Gorbachev at the last of their one-on-one sessions at the Château Fleur d'Eau summit on the shore of Lac Léman: 'I bet the hardliners in both our countries are bleeding as we shake hands,' he said. Reagan from that point speeded up the process he had already started of distancing himself from his erstwhile conservative supporters in the US. Gorbachev began a series of bruising battles with the reactionaries in the Kremlin, as he described them, who longed to take the Soviet Union backwards to isolation, and with his powerful military. Gorbachev initially thought little of Reagan's intellect. 'I felt I had encountered a caveman,' he told aides. 'He said things that can't be called anything but trite. He was so loaded with stereotypes that it was difficult for him to accept reason. Whenever I brought up specifics, the President immediately let Shultz take over. And when we had our "fireside chats" as the President called them, Reagan had prepared texts.' Later he grew to admire and respect him. From the first Reagan liked Gorbachev, who was so different from the leader he had expected to encounter from the 'evil empire', but he kept asking himself whether the Russian could be trusted and was sincere about changing the Soviet Union. He decided he had no choice but to do business with him.[11]

One major sticking point led to a shouting match in Geneva, despite the warm atmosphere during most of their five hours of private talks.

Reagan was absolutely committed to the Star Wars project. The Soviets feared it would lead to a new arms race in space, which they would lose. Reagan maintained that SDI was a defensive system. Gorbachev repeatedly responded that from the Russian point of view it was seen as offensive: if the Americans had a shield that worked, what was to stop them launching an attack on the Soviet Union, knowing they were safe from retaliation? Star Wars 'would destabilise everything', he remarked. 'We would have to build up in order to pierce your shield.' Reagan said that would be entirely unnecessary: 'You have to believe that this is so important for the world that we will give you the technology as we develop it.' Gorbachev laughed and replied bluntly: 'Surely you realise I can't believe that, since you won't even give us the technology for milking machines on our farms.'[12]

An impasse on Star Wars continued throughout the Reagan presidency, though that did not prevent a wide range of arms agreements later that eased tensions between the superpowers. Gorbachev was receiving conflicting advice on space weapons. His military men were telling him that Star Wars was a dangerous new threat. His best scientists insisted that the American scheme was a 'fantasy' that could not work. The leading physicist Yevgeni Velikhov, Vice Chairman of the Soviet Academy of Sciences, and Roald Sagdeyev, head of the Soviet space programme, assured Gorbachev that a shield could not be developed that was 100 per cent reliable and could not be penetrated. They told him the Soviets could develop an equally effective system to counter the SDI, using missiles that were in space for only a few moments, which, as Gorbachev said, 'would cost ten per cent of Star Wars'. The question remains: if he believed that, why were the Soviets so obdurately opposed to the project? Gorbachev's aides say the reason was political rather than strategic. The more the Americans spent on developing Star Wars technology, the greater pressure he faced from his own military to compete. The harder it then became for Gorbachev to reduce his vast arms budget and redirect money towards domestic spending to save socialism in the USSR.[13]

Another sceptic of Reagan's Star Wars vision was far closer to the President ideologically. His great friend and fellow conservative Margaret Thatcher had grave doubts that a protective shield was technically possible, and more serious concerns about its principal aim. She believed that nuclear weapons had kept the peace for four decades. The defence of both superpowers rested on the theory of deterrence, she argued. It had maintained stability, which could be severely disrupted by dreams of a protective shield. She often tried to argue Reagan out of his belief in the project in her usual forthright fashion, but in vain. Reagan told his National Security Advisor, Robert McFarlane, that he had been 'handbagged' and dispatched him to London to persuade 'Margaret at least to lower the level of criticism ... She gave me the same lecture she had given [him] and seeing I was getting nowhere I interjected during a pause: "Prime Minister, President Reagan believes that there is at least US$ 300 million a year that ought to be subcontracted to British companies which would support SDI." ... There was a long pause and she finally said "there might be something in this after all".'[14]

SIXTEEN

'LET THEM HATE'

Bucharest, Sunday 26 January 1986

IN THE ROMANIA of Nicolae Ceauşescu, 26 January was the most important day of the calendar. Celebrating Christmas was, naturally, banned and Liberation Day, which marked the end of World War Two, was a muted celebration. May Day was a big event, with huge parades throughout the major cities. But the dictator's birthday was turned by the regime into a vast commemoration of the life and achievements of one man. It was the last day of the year that most Romanians felt in festive mood – their Great and Wise Leader had brought the nation to penury. But to look miserable on such a day might be considered politically unreliable, so people brushed up their happy faces. Life in Romania in the late years of Ceauşescu's rule had become, as an old comrade who once shared a prison cell with him said, 'a permanent ceremonial enacted by the entire country in front of a single spectator'.[1]

On 26 January 1986 the *Conducător* turned sixty-eight, though on all the many millions of posters and photographs displayed ubiquitously throughout the country he did not look a day over forty-two. The court poets surpassed themselves on the front pages of all the newspapers. 'I feel bound to praise you and kiss your temple,' wrote Dumitru Brandescu. The leader's favourite versifier, Adrian Păunescu, oozed something slicker:

> This is no flattery as we portray him. We love him for his struggle and his humanity. We love him, because this country is free under the Sun. One's soul has the urge to shower him with eulogies.[2]

The newspaper *Luceafărul* said this was 'a crucial date in Romanian history by which the nation, glorifying its chosen ones, glorifies itself'. Elsewhere, in all the other special editions, there appeared many of the usual descriptions of the deified leader:

The Giant of the Carpathians
The Source of Our Light
The Treasure of Wisdom and Charisma
The Zodiac
Our Tall Standard
The Great Architect
The Living Fire
The New Morning Star
The Celestial Body

Even Mao Zedong or Stalin might have cringed at some of this nonsense. But Nicolae Ceauşescu and his wife Elena, who enjoyed flattery even more than he did, had no sense of humour or of the ridiculous. They believed the gush written about them and surrounded themselves with fawning toadies and courtiers.

A few weeks before his birthday the Creator of this Epoch of Unprecedented Renewal, as the Communist Party newspaper *Scînteia* called Ceauşescu, announced a further round of food rationing. Always conscious of their own waistlines, he and Elena were not gluttons. He had been diagnosed with diabetes in the mid-1970s and required insulin injections to control his blood-sugar levels. They accused Romanians of being too fat and created a Rational Nourishment Commission that ordered a 'scientific' diet: 114 eggs a year, 20 kilos of 'fruit and grapes', 54.88 kilos of meat, 14.8 kilos of potatoes, 114.5 kilos of flour. In theory it was not a bad diet. But in practice supplies fell far short of these targets. By the mid-1980s simply obtaining enough to eat required a major effort for almost every family in Romania. At the end of 1985 rationing of bread, milk, eggs, meat and vegetables became stricter and the queues longer. Romania is one of the most fertile lands in Europe and there ought to be abundant food produced. So there was. But Ceauşescu's eccentric economic policy forced deliberate destitution on his people. The leader was determined to be entirely free of foreign debt, as a way, so he thought, of ensuring independence.

Considering the burden Western credits were placing elsewhere in Eastern Europe, reducing the levels of borrowing was no bad thing. But the Great Leader's way of doing it was disastrous. In 1982 he announced that he would pay off all foreign loans by 1990. In order to do so, he squeezed Romanians. More than three-quarters of the nation's food production was sold abroad. Energy was rationed strictly so that it could be sold to Italy and West Germany. Romanians were allowed to use only a single forty-watt bulb per room, when electricity worked at all. Electrical heating was permitted for only two hours a day, fuelling few homes but the often repeated, grim joke: 'In Romania what is colder than cold water? Hot water.' In bad winters many elderly people died in their own apartments from hypothermia, which was not entirely unknown among the poor in Western Europe. A common Romanian phenomenon was the number of younger people found asphyxiated by gas in their own homes. This was not through suicide but because they had left gas cookers lit to keep warm and they had fallen asleep. The supply had been cut, then restored later while they were still sleeping.

Few streets were lit at night. Even the broad boulevards of Bucharest – once known as the Paris of the Balkans – were deserted and dark after dusk. The last screening of movies in cinemas was at five p.m. Bucharest had been famed for its café culture and nightlife. Now there were no bars or cafés and just a handful of restaurants frequented by Party bureaucrats and their families or hotels where the few foreign visitors permitted into the country stayed. Ceauşescu had a plan to reduce oil consumption. One of the announcements he made soon after his sixty-eighth birthday, in the spring of 1986, was to launch a programme of breeding horses so that petrol-guzzling transport could be replaced. On farms which in the 1960s and 1970s used tractors, the harvests were in the 1980s being gathered by scythes and sickles. The leader was taking Romania back to the previous century – or the one before that. In order to maximise production, of natural resources like oil and gas and from the land, he instituted a rota system forcing people to work on Sundays and public holidays, much like the *corveé* in France before 1789.

The country lived in fear and by rumour on a scale unlike anywhere else behind the Iron Curtain. Ceauşescu openly admired Stalin, whose funeral he had attended and at which he was seen to weep. Romania was the most brutal police state in the Eastern bloc, but run in an uniquely Romanian way. The Stasi in East Germany was designed to keep order, though it used some terrifying methods to destroy its victims. The Securitate was built to inspire fear. Liviu Turcu was a senior officer in the organisation until he defected in the 1980s and knew from the inside how it operated. 'Imagine a huge apparatus spreading rumours, fear and terror, an atmosphere in which people felt that if they try to do the most insignificant thing identified as an act of opposition to Ceauşescu, they will disappear,' he said. 'It was psychological terror that paralysed the Romanian population and the most outstanding piece of disinformation was the rumour, deliberately spread by the Securitate itself, that one out of every four Romanians was a Securitate informer.' The Securitate had such deep roots within the population and had sown such mistrust, that it is possible there were that many. True or not, people were unwilling to put it to the test. The number of agents or informers was not the important thing. The Securitate spread word of its ubiquity and infallibility through innuendo, bluff and double bluff. The public believed it and submitted. 'They – the spooks – did not have to keep a watch on people if everybody *thought* they were being watched,' said Alex Serban, a teacher in a small town outside Bucharest during much of the 1980s. 'That was one of the most sinister things.'[3]

For a Romanian to talk to foreigners was not technically illegal. But any conversation had to be reported to the police within twenty-four hours. The inevitable interrogation and harassment afterwards discouraged most people from meeting visitors. There was no Charter 77, Solidarity, KOR or Danube Circle in Romania. A few dissident writers existed, but hardly any opposition groups were formed. One was founded in the mid-1980s with the simple name The Anti-Totalitarian Forum. It consisted of three families. Its leader, Viorel Hancu, explained: 'If we had taken anyone else in we would have exposed the group to infiltration by the Securitate.'[4]

Ceauşescu dealt with industrial unrest in a robust manner. Miners in the Jiu mining valley went on strike in 1977 for better wages and working conditions. At first the leader was emollient, negotiated and agreed to the miners' demands. A few weeks after the workers had gone back to work, he had the strike leaders rounded up, executed some and jailed the rest. The following year the wage increase was rescinded. A decade later workers at the Red Star tractor factory in Braşov, northern Romania, struck. Ceauşescu used precisely the same tactic. He was not a man learned in the classics, but he would often quote the Emperor Caligula to his aides: 'Better to be feared than loved.' He removed favourites at a stroke. Ion Iliescu was a rising Communist Party official, fast-tracked for the highest positions. A Minister for Youth in his early thirties, he became head of Party propaganda in his early forties. He was a regular dinner companion with the Ceauşescus and often played chess with the leader, wisely permitting him to win. When in 1971 Ceauşescu heard Iliescu being talked of as heir apparent, he exiled the younger man to minor posts in the provinces. Later, he was allowed back to Bucharest, but put in charge of a publishing company producing technical manuals.

Nobody knew how many political prisoners there were; the number was never collated, though statistics on practically everything else in the country were. Nor was anybody entirely sure what constituted a political crime. It depended on the Conducător's whim. In 1982, for no obvious reason, he suddenly began a campaign against yoga. A young Bucharest medical student, returning from an exercise class, was beaten up by the Securitate and told to stop practising yoga. She obeyed – after realising that four secret policemen continued to follow her twenty-four hours a day. It had the desired effect. Once it became known that studying yoga was considered a political act the art all but disappeared from Romania.

People could not find consolation in religion. Ceauşescu corrupted the churches, though he had plenty of willing accomplices among priests and rabbis. The Orthodox bishops and the Protestant leaders such as Gyula Nagy and László Papp among the Hungarian minority in Transylvania were deeply compromised by their close relationship with the security services. Like the East Germans, the Romanians encouraged a human cargo of political exiles. Ceauşescu could not exact the same price as Erich Honecker managed – Romania got around US$ 10,000 for each German 'sold' to the Federal Republic and Jew to Israel. Ceauşescu once explained to Ion Pacepa, his counter-intelligence chief who defected to the US, that 'oil, Jews and Germans are our most important exports'. Leaders of the German minority, the Szeklers, and Moses Rosen, the Chief Rabbi, were complicit in this trade and in other dealings with the regime.

Almost no samizdat publishing existed in Romania. There were only a handful of photocopiers in the entire country, mostly in Party or government offices. Under a law introduced in March 1983 every typewriter had to be registered with the police and an example of the typeface from every machine in Romania was kept on record so it could be traced. The decree establishing the law sums up much of life in Ceauşescu's Romania:

> The renting or lending of a typewriter is forbidden. Every owner of a typewriter must have for it an authorisation from the militia, which can be issued only after a request has been made. All private persons who have a typewriter must, in the next few days, seek to be issued with such an authorisation. Such a request, in writing, must be sent

> to the municipal militia, or the town or community militia, wherever the applicant happens to reside, and the following details must be supplied: first and second names of the applicant; names of his parents; place and date of birth; address; profession; place of work; type and design of the typewriter; how it was obtained (purchase, gift, inheritance); and for what purpose it is being used. If the application is granted, the applicant will receive an authorisation for the typewriter within 60 days. On a specified date, the owner of the typewriter must report with the machine to the militia office in order to provide an example of his typing. A similar example has to be provided every year, specifically during the first two months of the year, as well as after every repair to the typewriter. If the application is refused, the applicant can lodge an appeal within 60 days, with his local militia. If the appeal is dismissed, the typewriter must be sold within 10 days (with a bill of sale) or given as a gift, to any person possessing the necessary authorisation. Anyone wishing to buy a typewriter must first of all apply for an authorisation. Anyone who inherits a typewriter or receives one as a gift must apply for an authorisation at once. Defective typewriters which can no longer be repaired must be sent to a collection point for such material, but only after the typewriter's keys, numbers and signs, have been surrendered to the militia. If the owner of a typewriter should change his address, he should report to the militia within five days.[5]

Isolated writers criticising the regime occasionally spoke out bravely. Doina Cornea, a specialist in French literature at the University of Cluj, in north-western Romania, spent years under house arrest. She said the Ceauşescu regime was 'crushing people's innermost being, humiliating their aspirations and legitimate claims, humbling their consciences and compelling them under pressure of terror to accept the lies as truth and truth as a lie.' The lies were big and small – even about the weather forecast. In Romania the temperature never officially dropped below 10°C, even when there was ice and snow on the ground, because the law said that heating in public buildings had to be turned on when it did.

In every office with more than a few hundred employees there was a full- or part-time official liaison person to deal with the Securitate – as well as the unofficial informers willing to spy on their colleagues. Sensitive trades had several intelligence agents. For example, on the state-owned TV station the Securitate had an entire 'protocol department' whose task was to ensure that Nicolae Ceauşescu always appeared in the best possible light. Film editors were watched carefully by the secret police. 'All of Ceauşescu's involuntary pauses, hesitations, stutters and grimaces had to be removed before anything could be shown,' one senior executive on television news said. 'It was hours of extra work The discarded snippets of film were collected by the Securitate and destroyed lest they fell into the wrong hands.' TV producer Nick Melinescu once fell foul of the guidelines, with serious consequences. 'On one occasion there was a picture that was a few seconds too long in which Ceauşescu did everything wrong. He scratched, blinked, stuttered and it was all left in. All hell broke loose . . . I was blamed and as a result I was banned . . . my salary was cut for three months. It was bad, one of the worst things that could happen.' Elena was equally careful about her Mother of the Nation image: 'There was a huge list of dos and don'ts when recording her images. First and foremost, she was never supposed to be shown in profile because she had a huge nose – and she wasn't a beautiful woman anyway.' The propaganda department of the Party had issued instructions that Ceauşescu's small-to-medium size (five feet five inches) should never be emphasised on film. When state guests taller than he were in his company they had to be filmed in such a way that the difference in height was minimised – the French President Valéry Giscard d'Estaing towered over the Romanian leader. They were never shown standing together. All newspapers employed one sub-editor who had a vital job: to check that there was never a spelling error in any mention of Nicolae Ceauşescu's name.[6]

The future despot of Romania was born in the small village of Scorniceşti in German-occupied Wallachia, southern Romania. His mother, Alexandra, and father, Nicolae Andruță, were middling-income peasant farmers, who would have been better-off if he had not drunk away the fortunes of his wife and seven children. He named three of his sons Nicolae, allegedly because he was on such an alcohol-induced bender when he went to the nearest town to register the births that it was the only boy's name he could remember. The young Ceauşescu's school record was poor, though even his teachers at elementary school realised he had a shrewd intelligence, as well as an almost uncontrollable temper. His formal education ended at fourteen when he went to live with one of his married elder sisters in Bucharest. He became an apprentice shoemaker and was radicalised partly by his socialist brother-in-law and partly by the life offered by the leftist underground. As one contemporary said: 'He was more attracted by the violence than the ideology . . . he was keen to be where the action on the streets was.'

Romania in the 1930s limped along from crisis to crisis in the corrupt and decadent reign of King Carol II, who was involved in various dubious financial dealings and had a love life resembling a soap opera. His affair with the divorcee Magda Lupescu filled the gossip pages not only in the Romanian press but also in much of Europe's. It was his flirtation with fascism that became more serious for his country's future. Under him the notorious Iron Guard gained enormous influence in public life and the young Ceauşescu became a political street brawler against the thugs on the Right. He was first arrested before he was sixteen, in 1933, and was in and out of jail for the next dozen years. Communist Party membership was illegal and Ceauşescu received an education from the Marxist intellectuals who were in prison with him. Among other things he was taught to control his stammer, though when he was nervous, tired or stressed that returned in later years. While he learned at their feet, he proved highly useful to them running errands, scrounging extra food and finding ways to communicate with the outside world.

Out of jail in 1938, at a Communist Youth League meeting, he met and fell in love at first sight with a very attractive, dark-haired girl whom her friends called 'Pasarica' (meaning little bird). She was Elena Petrescu, a year older than he and with a similar peasant background. A prudish man, Ceauşescu never looked at another woman in a sexual way in his entire life. She was more experienced and confident in the ways of love and before they were married she had a number of affairs. He was back in jail before they could pursue their relationship further, but soon after he was released from the harsh Târgu Jiu prison at the end of the war they met again and soon married.

The Soviets installed a puppet government in their Romanian domain and Stalin placed a cold, clever and calculating political tactician, the highly experienced Gheorghe Gheorghiu-Dej, in charge of the new Communist regime. Ceauşescu had been in prison with Gheorghiu-Dej and admired his brains and ruthlessness. The older man began to use Ceauşescu as a fixer who, in those days, had some natural political and diplomatic skills as well as an ability to apply bully tactics to get his way. He was put in charge of creating a Communist army and later rose through the ranks of the Party. He would often do the leader's dirty work for him, such as conducting the various purges and witch hunts characteristic of Soviet-style communism. He navigated the often precarious world of Balkan politics with greater dexterity than the cleverer, wittier and more sophisticated intellectuals around him. After Gheorghiu-Dej died – in severe pain from cancer in 1965 – Ceauşescu was not the obvious choice to succeed him. While older rivals intrigued and destroyed each other, he emerged as a compromise candidate.

Initially he presented a liberal image. He lifted censorship slightly, encouraged a measure of private enterprise and seemed in his first few years a breath of fresh air. Often he sounded more like a nationalist leader than a hardline Communist. But a radical change came over him after he went on a long state visit to North Korea and China at the end of 1971. He was massively impressed by Kim Il-Sung and Mao Zedong's personal style of rule, the cult status they enjoyed, the vast rallies in Peking and Pyongyang with hundreds of thousands of people waving pictures of the leader and treating him like a living god. He felt he deserved similar adoration in Bucharest, where he was convinced people loved him, but ought to show it more than they did. He returned tougher and pursued relentlessly Stalinist ways. He turned the screw against the traditional Romanian enemy, the large Hungarian minority living in Transylvania. New laws were introduced barring them from teaching Hungarian in schools and maintaining cultural centres. He spent massively increased sums on the Securitate. Selectively, he had opponents murdered or jailed and he turned Romania into the most desperately miserable and destitute part of Eastern Europe.[7]

While Ceauşescu grew increasingly hated at home, he was fêted abroad. He was the West's favourite Communist, even as he brutalised his own people. The reason was simple. He steered as independent a path as he could from the Soviet Union and in the Cold War that was all that mattered. His predecessor Gheorghiu-Dej had played the nationalist card and it had worked for him. He had negotiated a deal that removed Soviet troops from Romanian soil, and though Romania remained a loyal member of the Warsaw Pact, it occasionally spoke with a voice of its own. Ceauşescu followed in these footsteps. Just before Warsaw Pact troops invaded Czechoslovakia in 1968 he turned up in Prague offering support to Alexander Dubček. He refused to let Romanian troops take part in the invasion and spoke regularly against the Soviet Union interfering in the affairs of other socialist countries.

He wanted Romania's economy to be less dependent on Russia's and made overtures to the West for improved relations.

The leaders of the free world formed a queue to ingratiate themselves with this Communist who dared to challenge Moscow. They did not imagine they could detach Romania far from Moscow's embrace, but they believed that if they encouraged Ceauşescu to show yet further independence, they could cause the Soviets considerable embarrassment. So he was awarded medals and honours and invited on lavish state visits to Western capitals. He went to Paris and stayed at the Elysée. The French President, Giscard d'Estaing, warned his next hosts, in London, about the tendency of the Romanian entourage to pilfer lighters, ashtrays and ornaments of all kinds and he suggested that anything the British wanted to preserve should either be hidden or bolted to the floor.

When the Ceauşescus stayed at Buckingham Palace in June 1978 Queen Elizabeth II was amused when she was told that early in the morning the Romanian President and his aides held a meeting out in the garden because they assumed all the bedrooms in the Palace were bugged. At a formal reception she said: 'We in Great Britain are impressed with the resolute stand you have taken for . . . independence. Consequently, Romania holds a distinct position and plays a significant part in world affairs. Your personality, Mr President, as a statesman of world-wide repute, experience and influence is widely acknowledged.' Margaret Thatcher was not to be outdone. She said she was 'impressed by the personality of President Ceauşescu . . . and was left with particular impressions of him as leader of . . . a country willing to develop her co-operation with other nations'.[8] He was given an honorary knighthood and several other medals.

Elena's craving for honours was even more desperate than his. Though her education was patchy – she had been thrown out of school aged fourteen – eventually she took a chemistry degree. She wanted to be taken seriously as a scientist. Her husband had made her head of the ICEHCM, Romania's most distinguished chemical research laboratory, even though she was not qualified even to work there as a junior, let alone be in charge of it. When the London visit was planned, her aides sent feelers out to obtain an honorary FRS, the highest award in British science. She was rejected. Oxford and Cambridge were approached for honorary degrees but turned her down. She did receive a fellowship from the Royal Institute of Chemistry and an honorary degree from the Polytechnic of Central London. At the award ceremony Sir Richard Norman, President of the Institute, praised her contribution 'to macromolecular experimental chemistry, especially in the field of the stereospecific polymerisation of ijisoprene on the stabilisation of synthetic rubbers and on copolymerisation'. Mircea Corciovei, the leading Romanian chemist who had actually done most of the research for the work under her name, was philosophical. 'We were told: no paper can be written or published, no conference lecture delivered without Elena Ceauşescu's name appearing in first place. We never saw her, we never heard from her, at any time during our research or afterwards. She never even acknowledged our existence. We were producing papers with words which we knew she could not pronounce let alone understand.'[9]

Ceauşescu was the subject of fawning biographies, not only in Romania but in Western Europe. A hagiography published in Britain in 1983 was prefaced with a no-holds-barred 'interview' by publisher, former MP – and subsequently disgraced newspaper tycoon – Robert Maxwell in which one of his first questions was: 'Dear Mr President, you have been holding the highest political and state offices in Romania for almost eighteen years, a fact for which we warmly congratulate you. What has – in your opinion – made you so popular with Romanians?'[10]

In the US he was equally showered with honours and praise. President Gerald Ford said: 'President Ceauşescu's influence in the international arena . . . is outstanding.' Jimmy Carter asserted: 'His prestige has gone beyond the boundaries of Romania and Europe . . . The whole world appreciates him and regards him with admiration.' Even his eccentric behaviour did not make the Americans stop to think. On a three-day visit to the US in 1979 he walked out of a dinner given in his honour in New Orleans because he took umbrage when a cardinal on the same table said grace before the meal. On his last afternoon in America he had a meeting with the Mayor of New York, Edward Koch. Outside the Manhattan hotel where the Ceauşescu entourage were staying there was a small demonstration by a group of Hungarian exiles. Halfway through the meeting, Koch said: 'Mr President, down there some friends of mine were demonstrating against you, and they tell me you don't give freedom of religion and cultural freedom to your Hungarians living in Transylvania. Is that right?' Ceauşescu was incandescent with rage. He turned to the US diplomatic official accompanying him on the visit and demanded: 'What does the State Department have to say about this? How dare he talk to me like that?' He was told that whatever policies the Federal government may have, the

Mayor of New York was allowed his say. The Conducător became further incensed. He gave orders that the party should immediately head back to Bucharest. There was a slight hiccough in that plan, though. Elena was in Cartier's, where she was being given a personalised tour, and insisted on staying for a further three and a half hours. They flew home at the time their itinerary said they would. Four years later George Bush, then Vice President, went to Bucharest and announced at the end of several hours of talks with Ceauşescu that 'he was one of the good Communists'.[11]

Romanians, with typical gallows wit, called it socialism in one family. Ceauşescu filled the top posts in the country and the ruling Party with his siblings, nephews, nieces and in-laws. An elder brother, Nicolae Andruta, was a Lieutenant-General and key link-man in the Interior Ministry and security service. Another brother, Ilie, was Deputy Defence Minister, who along with yet another brother, Marian, ran a highly secret arms business: they sold Soviet-made rocket and electronic communications systems to the Americans, who in return provided Romania with Western weaponry, which it then passed on to the Soviets. Another brother, Florea, was the leader's eyes and ears in the Party newspaper, as an editor on *Scînteia*. His favourite brother-in law, Gheorghe Petrescu, was a Deputy Prime Minister. Brothers-in-law Ilie Verdeţ and Manea Mănescu had top Party posts. His favourite niece, Maria, was made head of Romania's Red Cross organisation. But his closest adviser was always Elena, who was given increasing power. By the early 1980s she was placed in charge of the country when he was away on tours abroad. Romania never was a shared dictatorship – Elena was number two – but she became more shrewish, adopted grander airs and he grew ever more reliant on her. She frequently said in other people's hearing: 'I am the only person you can truly trust.' There were signs that he could be scared of her rages. 'He was afraid of her, I am sure of that,' said the Party historian Ion Ardeleanu, who knew them both well. 'If he was late for a meal, or a meeting with her he would look at his watch and start sweating and stammering.'[12]

They were unfortunate with their children. The eldest, Valentin, was adopted as a baby in 1948 and tried from an early age to keep a calculated distance from his parents. He was a physicist, fairly distinguished, who obtained a good degree from Imperial College in London. His parents disapproved of his marriage to Iordana Borilă, partly because she was Jewish but, worse, because she was the daughter of one of Ceauşescu's rivals during the power struggle inside the Party in the 1960s. Petre Borilă had a romantic past as a fighter in the Spanish Civil War, while Ceauşescu was languishing in a series of jails. Valentin and his wife lived in a modest two-room apartment in an unfashionable part of Bucharest, like average Romanians, and had all their nomenklatura privileges withdrawn. He worked quietly in the Institute of Physics. The marriage did not last, but Valentin was never forgiven. He kept out of politics, though he did once say of his compatriots, 'Absolute power corrupts absolutely, but submission corrupts too'.

Their natural daughter, Zoia, born in 1950, tried rebellion too, but her story was sadder. She was a bright mathematician and, while a student at Bucharest University, had her eyes opened to the conditions for most people in Romania. She became appalled. In 1974 she attempted to run away with a boyfriend. The long reach of the Securitate tracked her down.* After that, as Zoia told friends, she was trapped.

There was a bizarre twist to the fury and revenge of the First Couple. They blamed Bucharest's Mathematical Institute, where Zoia was studying for a PhD. The Ceauşescus were convinced it was encouraging a 'bohemian mentality' in their only daughter, so they simply closed the Institute down, dispersing the staff elsewhere. Uncharacteristically, they allowed some of the Institute's best minds to leave the country. Maths was one of the few scientific specialities where Romanians were conducting high-level work. All that disappeared, as more than 100 leading mathematicians fled to the West. Zoia returned to the family fold, reluctantly, and on occasion tried to talk to her parents about the food queues and the general misery in the country, 'but they would never listen to me', she said. She became a lonely and reclusive character and turned to drink.

* The Ceauşescus closely monitored, and interfered with, their children's relationships. For a brief period in the 1970s Zoia dated Petre Roman, son of a leading Communist official, a glamorous and well-connected scholar who later became Romania's first post-Communist Prime Minister after the Revolution. Elena, in particular, did not approve of the liaison. She rang Petre's father, Walter Roman, and demanded the couple put a stop to their relationship. 'One Jew in the family is enough,' she told him – a reference to her brother's wife, who was Jewish. She and Roman *père* dispatched the young man abroad to study and the romance fizzled out. She organised a match for her favourite son, Nicu, with a woman she did approve of, Poliana Cristecu. Marriage was the last thing the rakish Ceauşescu son wanted. The wedding ceremony was performed by the Mayor of Bucharest and attended by family and a few leading Party chieftains. Immediately afterwards, as the couple signed the marriage register, he turned to his new bride and said: 'Now, go live with my mother . . . she should sleep with you because *she* chose you.'

The crown prince was Nicu, another natural son, born in 1951. He was far less serious than his siblings and seemed to care for little in his early years other than to enjoy the privileges that went with his birth. He was a playboy who in his youth whored his way around Bucharest and foreign capitals, enjoyed driving fast cars, and like his sister developed a serious drink problem. But he was the Ceauşescus' favourite and they lavished attention on him. He calmed down his habits as he grew older, though he continued to drink heavily, a weakness that eventually killed him. He was given political duties and handed an entire province of northern Romania to run. He was being groomed by his doting parents to take over as head, so they hoped, of a ruling Communist dynasty.*[13]

Women suffered the most in People's Romania. In 1986, to coincide with his birthday, Ceauşescu announced a new law forbidding abortion to women under forty-five. For the past twenty years the ban had applied to all women under forty, but the law was toughened up because the old one was not working, the leader thought. The Ceauşescus had a dream of increasing Romania's population from twenty-three million to thirty million. He launched the campaign in 1966 with a decree that made pregnancy a state policy. In the mid-1980s he said: 'The foetus is the property of the entire society. Anyone who avoids having children is a deserter who abandons the laws of national continuity.' Romania was the only country in the socialist bloc with laws against abortion, which throughout Eastern Europe was widely used as the main form of birth control. In Romania contraception was banned, there was no sex education in schools, and the minimum marriage age for girls was reduced to fifteen.

At first the birth rate soared, but after about three years it began to drop sharply and Ceauşescu resorted to barbaric forms of coercion. Women were forced to undergo compulsory medical examinations every one to three months. They were rounded up from their work-

* Zoia Ceauşescu was jailed for eight months after the revolution but could not find any kind of job after she was released. Her home was confiscated and she spent her last years living in the spare room of friends. She died of lung cancer in 2006. Nicu served two and a half years in prison. Occasionally he was quoted in the Romanian press justifying his parents' actions, before he died from cirrhosis of the liver in 1996. Valentin is alive at the time of writing; he was often critical of his parents after the revolution and was in jail for nine months before all charges against him were dropped. He was involved in a long legal argument with the post-Communist Romanian authorities in which he claimed they confiscated property that rightfully belonged to the Ceauşescu family, whatever his parents had done while in power. He lost.

places and taken to clinics by armed squads of officials – dubbed the menstrual police. There, usually in the presence of a Securitate officer, they were examined for signs of pregnancy, or for evidence that they may have had pregnancies terminated. A pregnant woman who failed to give birth at the proper time could expect to be summoned by the police for questioning. Women who miscarried were suspected of having arranged an abortion. Doctors were punished in districts where the birth rates declined, so naturally they resorted to fiddling the figures. 'If a child died in our district, we lost 10 to 25 per cent of our salaries, but it wasn't our fault,' said a Bucharest doctor, Geta Stănescu.*

Predictably, abortions were driven underground. The death rate from terminations was higher than anywhere else in Europe. Back-street abortions were performed in terrible conditions. Bucharest Municipal Hospital dealt with around 3,000 failed abortions every year, including about 200 women who needed major surgery. Many other women were too frightened to go to hospital. More than a thousand women died in Bucharest every year from bungled terminations. Illegal abortions usually cost between two and four months' average wages. If they went wrong, fear often prevented women from seeking medical help. 'Usually women were so terrified to come to the hospital that by the time we saw them it was too late,' said the Municipal Hospital's Dr Alexander Anca. 'Often they died at home.' As conditions worsened in the 1980s and the country was driven to destitution, infant mortality grew rapidly – to twenty-five deaths per 1,000 live births, more than three times the European average. Tragically, the other increase was in the opening of state orphanages, filled in the mid-1980s with around 100,000 abandoned children whom families did not want or could not cope with. Privately, among trusted intimates, people would often refer to Bucharest as 'Paranopolis'. But the hungrier Romanians became, while they froze in winter, the louder they were expected to sing the praises of the man who was inflicting the misery on them.[14]

* Women who had five or six children were awarded a Maternity medal; for seven to nine children they received the Order of Maternal Glory and for ten or more children they joined the ranks of Heroine Mother. On the other hand, harsh financial penalties were imposed if you failed to procreate for your country. Couples who remained childless beyond the age of twenty-five faced higher tax bills.

SEVENTEEN

CHERNOBYL: NUCLEAR DISASTER

Pripyat, Ukraine, Saturday 26 April 1986

FOR THREE DAYS engineers had been conducting a supposedly routine experiment on Reactor Number 4 at the Chernobyl nuclear power plant around 140 kilometres north of Kiev. They were trying to establish whether the reactor could operate under electricity produced by its own turbines. It should not have been complicated or in any way dangerous. The procedure was regularly performed on the scores of similar water-cooled RBMK reactors which the Soviets had built since the 1950s. But the engineers had made a series of errors and were lax in monitoring how the experiment was progressing. Nobody spotted that they had allowed the power in the reactor to fall to a critically low level. The mistake was finally noticed late the previous afternoon. Scientists at the plant considered cancelling the procedure and trying again at some future date. There was no urgency about the experiment. But the Deputy Director of the plant, Anatoli Dyatlov, felt assured that all the earlier mistakes had been corrected and he decided to proceed as scheduled.

Just after 1 a.m., engineers noticed that again power had fallen, dangerously low to 1 per cent of its normal level. This meant that the pumps which were supposed to circulate the water to cool the reactor core were no longer working. The third of a kilogram of nuclear fuel in 1,661 pressurised steel rods was overheating wildly. The engineers tried to push the emergency shutdown button, but it was too late. At 1.23 a.m. a tremendous blast ripped through the domed roof of the reactor hall, spewing red-hot splinters of nuclear fuel, chunks of cement and steel upwards into the night sky. It was a radioactive release ten times more powerful than the Hiroshima atom bomb. Four seconds later another huge explosion demolished two of Reactor 4's walls and started a fire that shot flames and tiny particles of highly radioactive graphite 1,200 metres into the air. A radioactive cloud immediately headed north-west with the wind. About five minutes later, the first of the engineers who tried to control the reaction were sent on a desperate errand without any protective clothing or breathing equipment in a vain attempt to shut down the reactor manually. Two workers who were in the reactor room during the blast suffered excruciating burns. They were taken to the plant's first aid unit, which had been closed down some years earlier. Managers had thought it would never be needed, so smoothly had the plant been operating. For many hours nobody at Chernobyl had any idea how much radioactivity had been released. The Geiger counters they used inside the building were designed to measure low radiation levels. They were off the gauge. The more powerful machines to measure high atmospheric levels had been locked away in a safe, on the basis that they would never be necessary.

Local firefighters were at the scene within ten minutes, but without any special equipment. Military firemen were called up as reinforcements and arrived around half an hour later. Between them, they got the fire in the radiator hall under control by 3.30 a.m., but the reactor itself was still burning and belching radioactive dust. Chernobyl's Director, Viktor Bryukhanov, reported at dawn to his superiors in Moscow that there had been some minor problems but that Reactor Number 4 was still working and that radiation levels at the plant 'were within normal levels'. It was a lie. Bryukhanov had not reached his position by telling his bosses news they did not want to hear.

A high-flying bureaucrat, originally trained as an engineer though not in nuclear power, he was first appointed director of a nuclear plant at just thirty-five years old. It was astonishingly young in the Soviet system to have risen so fast. But he had always managed to meet his targets laid down in the Plan, which pleased his superiors – and his workers, who received extra bonuses. If he had to cut a few corners, so be it. By the time errors were uncovered he would probably be elsewhere, in a better job. There had been a minor accident in one of the plant's other reactors four years earlier; Bryukhanov had managed to hush up any information about the incident and repair the damage before Moscow knew of it.

His first concern was to protect himself – not so much from radiation poisoning. He did not at first believe the problem was particularly serious. He wanted to shield himself from blame, in the manner that Soviet bureaucrats habitually did. One of his most senior engineers, Anatoli Sitnikov, told him that he believed the reactor had been destroyed. Bryukhanov did not believe him. Sitnikov went to look for himself and received a fatal dose of radiation. He told the Director what he had seen with his own eyes. Bryukhanov told him he was exaggerating. The Director did take some action, though: soon after that conversation with Sitnikov – who was already amongst the walking dead and knew it – the Director ordered that all the non-essential telephone lines around Chernobyl should be cut, so that 'unauthorised' information to the public could be kept minimal.[1]

The military were the first outsiders to hear about the disaster. Their instinct for secrecy was even more powerful than that of a mid-level Communist Party official. The absurd attempt to cover up the Chernobyl explosion – even when the rest of the world knew of it – was partly because in the Soviet Union all nuclear matters, civil or military, were in effect controlled by the armed forces. Army Chief of Staff Marshal Sergei Akhromeyev was told at around 2.20 a.m., though details were sketchy. He did not know the extent of the damage at Chernobyl, or that a plume of radioactive poison was spreading outside Soviet borders. The Soviet Prime Minister, Nikolai Ryzhkov, was informed just after 6 a.m. and he immediately called Gorbachev. Both were misled; they had been assured that the fires were out, and that there had not been a significant radiation leak. They were told that nine people at the plant were seriously ill and twenty-five military had moderate injuries, but the recommendation of the army and the Energy Ministry was not to evacuate anybody from the area. That would cause panic.

Over the next few hours, the military became aware of the scale of the disaster. The reactor was still red-hot and on Sunday morning scientific experts decided that the only way of cooling it was to try smothering the reactor from the air with sand from a nearby quarry. It was a difficult and dangerous procedure, requiring courage and precision from pilots. A squadron of MiG-8 'workhorse' helicopters were selected for the task. The heat and radiation levels were enormously high and pilots had to find a fast route to the crater, drop bags of sand at a carefully calculated spot and then manoeuvre away from the heat, all within seconds. They made ninety-three of these 'bombing runs', without protective clothing. One of the pilots remembered later that they stuffed lead plates under their seats and joked to each other, 'If you want to be a dad, cover your balls up with lead.' Joking did not prevent some of them developing cancers in later life.

Officials in Moscow knew the reactor core was still burning. Gorbachev had sent a commission headed by the Prime Minister to take on-the-spot control and provide honest reports back to the Kremlin. They arrived late on Saturday afternoon. On Sunday morning, more than a day and a half after the explosions, the local authorities finally decided that it was time to evacuate Pripyat, the dormitory town of around 45,000 people just three kilometres from the Chernobyl plant. It was, by Soviet standards, a well-built industrial town, in a lovely setting that had not been entirely spoilt by the sight of the reactor domes, or the slight humming sound that the plant emitted. Pripyat was clean, the apartment blocks were solid and there were excellent recreational facilities for inhabitants, most of whom worked at Chernobyl. The surrounding countryside was beautiful woodland, pine trees beside a meandering river. It was a fine and warm spring weekend. From the edge of town, a favourite place for walks, people could see the damage to the power plant and the emergency services hard at work. But they had been told throughout the Saturday that there was no danger, that radiation levels were barely higher than normal, and there was nothing to worry about. So they took advantage of the warm weather. They took country walks. Children played outside. Sixteen couples were married. It was a normal spring day.

By mid-morning on the Sunday the inhabitants were told to leave in a hurry, most of them expecting that it would be safe to return in a few days. They left most of their belongings behind. By 1.30 p.m. all of them had left and Pripyat looked like a ghost town, its only inhabitants the domestic pets left to fend for themselves. They either died or turned wild. The evacuation was too late. If people had been moved earlier they might have been saved from long exposure to high levels of radiation. Or if within a few hours they had received iodine they might have been spared the tumours to the thyroid gland from which thousands of Pripyat residents suffered later. Many hundreds died from cancers and leukaemia within three years – many more within a decade.[2]

By Sunday afternoon the rest of the world was beginning to know about Chernobyl. A radioactive cloud blew north-west, dusting eastern Poland, the Baltic and Scandinavia. By Sunday afternoon in Helsinki a laboratory reported that it was seeing radiation levels of six times higher than normal background. By dawn on Monday 28 April the Studsvik energy laboratory on the Baltic coast in Sweden and the

Forsmark nuclear power plant around eighty kilometres north of Stockholm recorded radiation levels 150 times higher than background. Initially it was thought that the contamination might have come from a missile test or a nuclear weapon that had accidentally blown up in its launch silo. But soon the Swedes discovered that the cloud must have come from a power plant – nuclear weapons and nuclear energy produce distinct kinds of fission material. Calculating wind direction and velocity, Sweden officially announced that there must have been a large explosion at a Soviet nuclear power plant that was spreading radiation across northern Europe. It was the front-page story throughout the world for the next several days.

The Soviets had said nothing. They did not inform governments of the countries that were being contaminated, or their own people in Ukraine, Russia or Byelorussia. They did not tell the comrades in the 'socialist commonwealth'. This was not the first nuclear disaster in Soviet history. Unknown to the rest of the world and the Soviet public, there had been at least one accident at a weapons-testing site and thirteen serious power-reactor accidents since the Soviet Union had become a nuclear nation in the late 1940s. In the earlier accident at Chernobyl Number 1 reactor in 1982 the central fuel assembly had ruptured and relatively low levels of radiation had leaked out. In 1975 the core of the Leningrad plant, an RBMK reactor similar to the four at Chernobyl, partly melted down, spewing radiation into the atmosphere. But the wind carried the radioactive cloud over Siberia. In 1985, fourteen workers at the Balakovo plant on the Volga River near Samara were killed when jetting steam of 500°C burst through the reactor hall when they were restarting the core following routine maintenance.[3]

Always the Soviet Union's reaction had been to keep silent, or if asked any questions to deny that any accident had happened. The instinct on this occasion was to follow the traditional pattern. This was the first major test of Mikhail Gorbachev's policy of glasnost – and he flunked it badly. On Sunday, the day after the explosion, the newspaper *Izvestia* was told not to mention the accident. Gorbachev did not give the gagging order directly, but he knew it had been issued and he did not overturn the instruction. By Monday morning the world's media was jamming the phone lines to the USSR with official inquiries. The Soviet government was still saying nothing. At 11 a.m. the senior magnates met in the Kremlin for the first time since the disaster. The military still proposed staying silent and issuing denials, arguing that

Chernobyl should be treated like a state secret. There was a long debate about the accident. Most of it concerned how much information to release. Amazingly, Shevardnadze had not heard anything about the accident until early that morning, more than forty-eight hours after the explosions. Soon world leaders and foreign embassies would be protesting about Soviet behaviour. But such was the culture of secrecy, that nobody thought to tell the Foreign Minister that he would soon be required to handle a diplomatic crisis.

At first, only Shevardnadze and Yakovlev suggested saying anything about Chernobyl. Shevardnadze quoted a speech Gorbachev had given about 'openness' just a few days earlier in which he said: 'We categorically oppose those who call for releasing public information in doses. There can never be too much truth.' Shevardnadze's comment did not raise even the slightest ironic eyebrow. Then he said it was impossible to deny Chernobyl. 'It's an affront to common sense, it's absurd. How can you conceal something that can't be hidden? How could people [here] complain that we are washing our dirty linen in public, when it is radioactive and had slipped out in spite of us?' Gorbachev was convinced. 'We must issue an announcement as soon as possible. We must not delay,' he said. But the military and the conservative bureaucracy were unhappy. For hours nothing happened and then late in the afternoon all that appeared was a bland announcement: 'From the Council of Ministers of the USSR. An accident has occurred at the Chernobyl nuclear power station. One of the four atomic reactors has been damaged. Measures are being taken to eliminate the consequences of the accident. Victims are being helped. A Government commission has been created.'[4]

It was a next-to-useless statement that raised far more questions than it answered. Predictably, as the world's media was getting so little officially from Moscow, and no Western journalists were allowed anywhere near the disaster site, some stories were becoming increasingly lurid. Reports told of thousands of deaths from the explosion and vast numbers more from radiation poisoning in Ukraine. Some in the Soviet leadership seemed more concerned with the press coverage in the West than the radiation cloud. The KGB chief Viktor Chebrikov thought there was a plot to 'smear' the USSR and he proposed to use traditional methods to deal with it. He reported to Gorbachev on Tuesday 30 April, four days after the disaster: 'Measures are being taken ... to control the behaviour of foreign diplomats and correspondents, limiting their opportunities to collect information about ... Chernobyl and to break up their efforts to use it for mounting an anti-Soviet campaign in the West.'

That Tuesday *Pravda* was allowed to report on the disaster for the first time, but the story was carefully censored and brief. It claimed that 'eighteen people are in a serious condition'. On the same day a secret report to Kremlin officials said that 1,882 people were treated in hospital and that 204 people (sixty-four of them children) were suffering from high levels of radiation poisoning. The Soviets were losing the propaganda war. The aftermath of the Chernobyl disaster was not Gorbachev's finest hour. He did not go there to meet and greet victims, or to show that he was in charge. He did not ensure that his policy of openness was followed. Rather, he conspired to keep the truth from the public and the outside world. He did not say anything about it until eighteen days after the accident – and then he gave a lacklustre performance. He spoke of a 'great misfortune that has befallen us', but misled the public about the casualty figures and about efforts to control the damage. When he spoke on TV on 18 May the reactor core was still burning and would do so for another three weeks. He did not mention that as he lambasted the West, with old-fashioned Cold War rhetoric, for attempting 'to defame the Soviet Union . . . with a wanton anti-Soviet campaign . . . and a mountain of lies'. This did not sound like 'new thinking'.

Chernobyl had a profound effect on Gorbachev. It was a devastating blow to the public's trust in him, and to his trust in those who worked for him. It was a tragic reminder of how badly the Soviet system functioned, and spurred him on to try reforming it with renewed vigour. He handled the crisis poorly, but he was determined to learn from it. He had been lied to by complacent officials who were protecting their own backs. Three key managers at Chernobyl were tried and sent to jail for periods of up to ten years for their misjudgements, errors and deceptions on that fatal night: the Director of the plant, Bryukhanov, his deputy, Dyatlov and the chief engineer Nikolai Fomin. But the entire system was to blame, as Gorbachev well knew: the plant had been rushed into service too quickly under pressure to fulfil the Plan; safety regulations had been abandoned; the reactors had a defective design. A concrete and steel containment structure around the reactor, such as American, West European and Japanese plants possessed, would almost certainly have confined the explosion. But Soviet reactors were not built with them. They were too expensive and took too long to construct. Chernobyl was a failure of the Soviet way of doing things. Nevertheless, he needed to blame some more individuals. He was seething against the scientific establishment and the nuclear chieftains who were refusing to accept any of the responsibility, and officials in the Energy and Planning ministries whom he thought incompetent. Nine weeks after the explosion, on Monday 3 July 1986, he summoned a group of about twenty of them for a dressing-down. He did not mince his words:

> For thirty years you told us that everything was perfectly safe. You assumed we would look up to you as gods. That's the reason why all this happened, why it ended in disaster. There was nobody controlling the ministries and scientific centres. Everything was kept secret ... Even decisions about where to build nuclear power stations were not taken by the leadership. The system is plagued by servility, bootlicking, secrecy, favouritism, clannish management. And there are no signs that you have drawn the necessary conclusions. In fact it seems as though you are trying to cover up everything ... We are going to put an end to all this. We have suffered great losses, and not only economic ones. There have been human victims and there will be more. We have been damaged politically. All our work has suffered. Our science and technology has been compromised by what has happened ... From now on, what we do will be visible to our people and to the world. We need full information.

He said the scientists, and the military, would require some independent control and they would have to learn to explain themselves.[5]

Chernobyl turned Gorbachev into a far more passionate nuclear disarmer. From now on a constant refrain was how nuclear war would be 'infinitely worse than a thousand Chernobyls'. He redoubled efforts to reach arms limitations deals with the Americans. 'Its effect was the single biggest event on the Soviet leadership since the Cuban Missile Crisis,' one of Gorbachev's aides said. For the first time the most secret, most sacrosanct, impenetrable part of the Soviet system – its nuclear programme – became the target of criticism.

It had a deep personal impact on Gorbachev, too. There were officials around Reagan who doubted whether he would push the nuclear button under any circumstances. There were soldiers in the Soviet Union who knew Gorbachev would not, and some of them had contempt for him as a result. Shortly after the Chernobyl disaster

Gorbachev was taking part in a simulated war games exercise in the Kremlin bunker. It came to the point when a Soviet response was required to a supposed American attack. As he told one of his officials later, 'From a central control panel came the signal: missiles are flying towards our country, make a decision. Several minutes passed. Information pours in. I have to give the command for a strike of retaliation. I said "No. I will not press the button even for training purposes."'[6]

EIGHTEEN

ETHNIC CLEANSING

Sofia, June 1987

THEY USED TO COME at the dead of night. Bulgarian armoured vehicles would circle a village, the bright glare of searchlights and the shouts of soldiers would wake peacefully sleeping people from their beds, and then the terror would start. Militiamen, as witnesses recorded later, would burst into every home occupied by ethnic Turks. Guns at the ready, they would thrust a piece of paper in front of the man of the house. It was a form on which he was ordered to write a new Slavic name for himself and the rest of his family to replace the Muslim names they were born with. If the men refused or visibly hesitated they were beaten. In many cases they were made to watch as their wives or daughters were raped. If they still refused – for Islamic names are considered holy – they were taken away to prison camps or simply murdered on the spot. This was all necessary, as the Bulgarian Prime Minister Georgi Atanasov said in private to other Communist Party chiefs in Sofia, 'in order to finish with the Turkish question, by flame and by sword, once and for all'.[1]

Most Bulgarians were not aware there *was* a 'Turkish question'. Ethnic Turks comprised about 900,000 people, 10 per cent of Bulgaria's population, concentrated in two main areas in the north-east and the far south of the country. They were descendants of the Ottomans who had ruled Bulgaria for centuries, though now they were a powerless minority. They had lived at peace with their neighbours for many generations on good agricultural land where they had been industrious and efficient farmers. Though Islamic in some customs, few practised any religion. They were well educated and seemed an integrated part of Bulgarian society. 'It was hard to tell who was an ethnic Turk and who wasn't, except by name,' said Ionni Pojarleff, a physicist who lived in Sofia but for years had a country home in one of the so-called Turkish villages. 'We were all oppressed together. But then from the mid-1980s the regime went for the Turks – and that changed everything.'[2]

It was a brutal campaign launched by the Bulgarian dictator in a cynical attempt to take the minds of his subjects from the grim and decaying condition of the country. Todor Zhivkov had held power since 1954. While he seemed on the surface still to have an iron grip and he was as feared by the people as ever, there were signs in the mid-1980s that he was starting to ail. Bulgaria, like neighbouring Romania, had never been a democracy. It had gained independence only in the 1870s and was run along the lines of an ancient Eastern-style despotism as much as a Communist one. Zhivkov's rule was absolute and personal, like that of a pasha or occidental potentate. Though he was not a monster on the scale of Ceauşescu, he could be vicious. There were harsh camps in his Balkan gulag, such as the notorious two at Skravena and Belene, where thousands of political prisoners had been sent until the mid-1960s. Zhivkov had murdered hundreds of opponents and possessed a loyal secret police force, the Sigmost, as his sharp sword and hefty shield.

Before he became the supreme leader he was in charge of the Party's private army, the People's Militia, and had organised the purges in the late 1940s against 'deviationists'. He knew how to use brute force. But he never sought to be a living god. He just wanted to stay in power, where he could continue to embezzle money on a grand scale which he could stash away in Switzerland, and tour the country at his leisure staying at the two dozen well-appointed mansions that he had appropriated for his family's use. A short, squat, pug-faced figure, he could be 'Uncle Tosho', with some folksy charm when he chose to display it, who spoke the language of common Bulgarians. But as his long-time Foreign Minister, Petar Mladenov, used to say in private, 'Zhivkov is morbid, suspicious and maniacally ambitious.'[3]

He had emerged as an orthodox Stalinist, but for three decades he tacked and trimmed when that was required. It was when he felt threatened that he played the nationalist card and began the barbaric forced assimilation of the Turks. Earlier, in the 1970s, the regime had compelled Bulgaria's 100,000 or so Slavic Muslims – known as Pomaks – to change their Islamic names. That had been accompanied by relatively little trouble or overt opposition. Though around 500 Pomaks were jailed for refusing to comply with the law, there had been limited violence. In 1985, Zhivkov banned education in Turkish, closed down Islamic cultural centres and said he was 'encouraging' the Turks to change their names. Hundreds of thousands had done so by the middle of 1987 when the campaign was said to be completed. A Zhivkov aide said it had been 'entirely voluntary because a spontaneous groundswell of pride in Bulgaria swept throughout the country'. Away from the capital, and any publicity, the truth about the assimilation campaign emerged later. The militia had conducted their night raids on hundreds of villages, nearly 1,000 ethnic Turks had been killed and more than 25,000 imprisoned.[4]

While Turkish villages were being despoiled, major building works were proceeding apace in another part of rural Bulgaria. Pravets, around 120 kilometres east of Sofia, was being turned into a 'model village' of some 4,200 inhabitants. One of the few motorways in the country linked it directly with the capital. Some light industrial plants were established there for the first time. New equipment was provided for the collective farm and for a few private plots where individuals were – exceptionally in Bulgaria – allowed to work on their own land. Many homes were rebuilt, including the once-modest house where Todor Zhivkov was born on 7 September 1911. It was opened as a museum eulogising the heroic role played by the leader in Bulgaria's struggle for socialism, his sacrifice as a partisan fighter during the war and his inspirational leadership of the country over the decades. Zhivkov, a printer in the state-owned stationery office for most of his early life, had in fact been a minor functionary in the Communist underground in the 1930s, and never took part in any partisan action during the resistance against the Nazis. He became a leading figure in the Communist movement only after the war when he was the much-loathed head of the Sofia police.

Nationalism was a double-edged sword for the dictators in the satellite regimes. It was hard for a Communist leader who had been placed in his position by the Soviet Union to wield it effectively for long. The public would remain silent from fear, but in private people would ask inconvenient questions about the country's colonial status as part of the Soviet empire. In Bulgaria's case there were further complications. Bulgaria had long and close cultural ties with Russia. The Tsars had liberated the Bulgarians from Ottoman rule and the two countries were traditional allies. The languages were similar. They both used the Cyrillic alphabet. Historically they had both been Orthodox in religion. After World War Two, Bulgaria seemed the most slavish of all the satellite states. Its first Communist leader, Georgi Dimitrov, was born

Bulgarian but had been exiled for nearly two decades. He was an astute Bolshevik activist who became world-famous after he was accused (wrongly) by the Nazis of starting the Reichstag fire. He lived in the USSR for many years as the feared head of the Comintern. He was a Soviet citizen when Stalin sent him back to Sofia to turn Bulgaria into a Communist state along Soviet lines.

After Dimitrov died in 1949 a vicious power struggle ensued in Sofia. Zhivkov was selected, with Moscow's backing, as the Bulgarian leader in 1955. When Zhivkov took power he outdid any of the other socialist leaders in obsequious greasing to whomever held power in the Kremlin. The joke often went around Sofia that when Khrushchev (later it was attributed to Brezhnev) met Zhivkov he asked, 'Todor, do you smoke?'. The reply came quick as a flash: 'Why, should I?' It was no joke when in 1972 Zhivkov approached Brezhnev and requested that Bulgaria should be allowed to join the Soviet Union as the sixteenth republic. Brezhnev wisely turned the idea down.[5]

Zhivkov had remained in power for three decades by the straightforward expedient of doing whatever Moscow requested of him. But now his relationship with the Soviet Union was cooling. The main reason, though not the only one, was financial. The Soviets gave the Bulgarians, along with the other COMECON countries, a giant subsidy in the form of cheap oil. Bulgaria immediately turned round and sold it to the West at world market prices and pocketed the difference in hard currency. When the Soviets found out about the scam they were furious. The Bulgarians, like most of the other satellite states, were heavily indebted to the West – by more than US$ 10 billion in the mid-1980s. The Bulgarians used their debt levels as an excuse, which infuriated the Soviets further. When oil prices were high and rising, the Bulgarian wheeze was an annoyance. The Soviets were themselves receiving high revenues. But after oil prices started to collapse in the mid-1980s the Soviet Union lost almost half of its foreign earnings. It began heading towards economic catastrophe and Moscow's resentment of Bulgaria mounted. Officials in the Kremlin never forgave Zhivkov, least of all Mikhail Gorbachev, who said it was 'entirely unacceptable that Soviet citizens should make sacrifices this way to help Comrade Zhivkov'.[6]

To Gorbachev, the Bulgarian dictator was one of what the Soviet leader's aides called a 'gang of four' hardline men, hangovers from a different era, who refused to move with the times and embrace the 'new thinking' that would save communism. The Soviet leader linked him with Honecker, Husák and Ceauşescu. He was losing patience with them. Gorbachev was an enigma to Zhivkov, now in his mid-seventies and long corrupted by power and lavish living. Initially Zhivkov did what he had always done and imitated the top man in Moscow. He welcomed perestroika and glasnost. He spoke admiringly of Gorbachev and came up with his own reform plans, grandiloquently called 'Keynotes of the Conception about the Further Construction of Socialism in Bulgaria'. The proposals went further than the Soviet Union's, particularly about liberalising trade and introducing private enterprise. But he did not mean any of it. His big mistake was that he did not think Gorbachev believed any of the reform ideas either. He imagined it would be enough simply to make sweeping statements, agree with the Soviet leader whenever he was asked an opinion, but in reality do nothing. When he realised Gorbachev was serious he tried to distance himself from the Soviets. But it was too late.

Domestically, he was beginning to face the kind of opposition he had never encountered before. It was still muted, but he now had to find new ways of dealing with dissent. Zhivkov had been adept at cultivating and flattering the intelligentsia to keep them on his side. Occasionally he would revert to the brutal methods of the past, but on the whole, as the essayist and historian Maria Todorova said, 'he was successful at corrupting and dividing . . . us while not creating martyrs'. That mixture of bribery and intimidation had worked for a long time. No longer. There was still no samizdat publishing in Bulgaria, but for the first time dissidents ceased their isolation. They began to hold meetings, if not to form even semi-official groups. They did not dare, yet, to talk about dismantling communism, let alone attack the supreme leader. That was too dangerous. But they discussed forming independent trade unions like Solidarity and, particularly, they talked about the environment. A beautiful old border town on the Danube in the north of the country, Ruse, was being destroyed by pollution from Giurgiu, a chemical plant in Romania that was spewing poison into the air. Scores of people from the town and nearby villages were suffering from severe lung disease. The historic monastery at Rila in the south-west of the country, one of Bulgaria's most important tourist destinations, was threatened by a scheme to dam two tributary rivers of the Danube for a hydroelectricity plant. The Traika plain, near the border with Greece, once had the best agricultural land in Bulgaria. For the last decade it was being polluted by a ferrous metal plant. Bulgarian cities were clogged with air pollution seventeen times the

European average. Protest was beginning to grow under a loose organisation calling itself Ecoglasnost.[7]

Zhivkov was not seriously worried about a few environmental campaigners, though he detested the idea of a free trade union that might stir up the workers. He still held all the levers of power in his hands. He and a few cronies of his own age retreated further into their own world, in Uncle Tosho's case increasingly fuelled by alcohol. When, in the late 1980s, a French journalist, Sylvie Kaufmann, went to interview him the appointment was fixed for 10 a.m. Zhivkov began by offering his interviewer a brandy. She refused, having just finished breakfast. He drank several. During their talk he was often incoherent. 'It was embarrassing,' she said. 'When he meant to say Gorbachev he would instead say Brezhnev. The translator would try to correct him but he said Brezhnev again anyway.'[8]

NINETEEN

HUMBLED IN RED SQUARE

Moscow, Thursday 28 May 1987

ON A WARM SPRING EVENING, almost shirt-sleeve temperature, everything seemed calm, still and normal in Red Square. An amateur artist had set up an easel at one of the traditional positions to capture rays of sunlight on the onion domes of St Basil's Cathedral. A few tourists were milling around the entrance to Lenin's mausoleum. Others were investigating the windows of the GUM department store to see if anything new or interesting had arrived recently to buy. But, as usual in the Russia of those days, it had not. What was unusual, shortly after six o'clock, was a faint buzzing sound above downtown Moscow and the sight of a small, low-flying, light propeller plane. No private aircraft existed in the Soviet Union, so its presence was a mystery. The white plane disappeared from view for a short while. Then, suddenly, it reappeared on the ground. Its wheels were heard on the cobblestones outside the Spassky Gate leading to the Kremlin and it came to a halt almost in the middle of Red Square.

The painter thought it was some sort of aeronautical display or sports event, as this was Border Guards Day, a minor national holiday. Some foreign visitors became excited as they imagined it might be Mikhail Gorbachev's plane. His office was only about 300 metres away. A few security men stood about, looking bemused but doing nothing. The aircraft's engine switched off, the propeller blades stopped turning and out stepped a slim, intense, dark-haired young man wearing spectacles and a red aviator's suit. He announced himself as Matthias Rust, a nineteen-year-old bank clerk from Hamburg, who had come to the Soviet capital on a 'mission of peace'. A friendly crowd gathered around him and he signed autographs, munching bread that well-wishers had thrust into his hands. Looking earnest, he explained that he had brought with him a twenty-two-page plan to abolish all weapons and to end the Cold War. He said he wanted to meet the Soviet leader to discuss it. After about three-quarters of an hour of total confusion he was finally taken away by police.[1]

The brave and bizarre adventure of Matthias Rust had begun a fortnight earlier. On 13 May he rented from his flying club outside Hamburg a Cessna 172-B, one of the smallest commercial planes on the market, and headed first across the Baltic to Norway. He stayed there a few days and then flew to Finland. Just after 1 p.m. on 28 May he took off from Helsinki's Malmi Airport, telling Finnish air traffic control that he was heading for Stockholm. Immediately after his final contact with them he turned east. Helsinki controllers tried to reach him to tell him he was off his course to Sweden, but he had switched off his radio. Soviet military radar spotted him at 14.29 as soon as he crossed into their air space on the Finland/Estonia border, flying at around 1,800 feet. They assigned his plane a 'contact' number – 8255 – used by suspected enemy planes. But then a series of confusing accidents, mistakes and misjudgements led to one of the most humiliating embarrassments for the Soviet military since World War Two.[2]

A MiG-23 interceptor jet was sent to investigate Rust's plane as soon as it was picked up by Russian air defence. The pilot reported that it was a 'light sports plane flying just below the clouds'. That did not seem very likely to the air force command, but since the Korean Flight 007 disaster of four years previously Soviet air defences were expressly forbidden from acting aggressively towards any civilian aircraft. As Rust flew further east towards Moscow, two other interceptors were sent to track the plane, but they lost sight of his Cessna amid the low clouds. When radar picked Rust up again, his plane was mistaken for a weather balloon. Then he was 'lost' for a second time, and tracked again a quarter of an hour later when senior officers of the national air defence system decided the Cessna was 'a formation of birds . . . we concluded that it was geese'. For the last crucial twenty minutes before Rust reached Moscow, the capital's central air defence district was closed down while routine maintenance work was carried out on some radar equipment, so he was not picked up at all.*[3] 'My plan was to land

* Rust was sentenced to four years in jail but served eighteen months in a KGB cell separated from other prisoners. He was treated relatively well, considering the embarrassment he had caused. Anatoly Chernyaev records in his diary that the kid-glove way his case was dealt with showed the transformations in the Soviet Union. 'Not so long ago he would just have been taken away, shot and never been heard of again,' he said. Rust returned to West Germany but never settled down. He took odd jobs in the financial sector and drifted in and out of prison on various criminal charges ranging from theft and fraud to sexual assault on a nun.

in Red Square,' he said. 'But there were too many people there and I thought I'd cause casualties. I had thought about landing in the Kremlin but there wasn't enough space. I circled Red Square three times looking for somewhere to land. It had to be somewhere very public.' He finally set down on Vasilevsky Spusk, adjoining the Kremlin walls, and he taxied around 300 metres before coming to a halt. He had flown more than 600 kilometres over Soviet territory and was permitted to land, unchallenged, at the seat of Soviet power.[4]

The Soviet leader was not in Moscow when Matthias Rust's plane landed. Gorbachev was in Berlin at a Warsaw Pact summit, and was already in a bad mood when he heard the embarrassing news. He had just endured several hours in the company of Erich Honecker, Gustáv Husák and other old Stalinist throwbacks of East European socialism who depressed and bored him. The Chief of the Soviet General Staff, Marshal Sergei Akhromeyev, had not been told anything about the Rust fiasco until the young German was already in an interrogation cell and facing questions from the KGB. Akhromeyev had fought on the Leningrad front during the war and was a highly bemedalled Hero of the Soviet Union. But he was dreading telling Gorbachev of the extraordinary events in Moscow that evening. The leader exploded in fury. All his entourage knew that Gorbachev frequently used colourfully foul language in private. This was an occasion the expletives flowed freely. 'It's a national shame . . . as bad as Chernobyl,' he raged. The old soldier could only agree. Gorbachev told aides that he suspected the military leadership – which disagreed with him on arms control and reducing defence budgets – had deliberately let the plane land in Red Square as a way of embarrassing him politically. He said they would not be allowed to get away with a trick like that. 'They have disgraced the country . . . humiliated our people. Well, so what, let everybody see where power lies in this country. It lies with the political leadership . . . We will put an end to this hysterical chatter about the military being in opposition to Gorbachev.'[5]

He cut short his time in Berlin and returned to Moscow, where the next day he summoned the military top brass for a dressing-down, in front of all the other Kremlin potentates. Gorbachev was brutal. He addressed General Pyotr Lushev, the army commander responsible for Moscow's defence: 'This went on for two and a half hours, while the offending plane was in the zone of the Sixth Army . . . was this reported to you?' Lushev replied: 'No. I knew when the plane landed in Moscow.'

Gorbachev responded with biting sarcasm: 'I suppose the traffic cops told you?' He spoke for more than an hour, accusing the Defence Ministry of 'complete hopelessness ... laxness, professional inadequacy' and senior generals of attempting to sabotage his reforms. Looking at the Defence Minister, Marshal Sergei Sokolov, he said: 'Under the circumstances, if I were you, I'd resign at once.' Sokolov, who had commanded the Soviet troops which invaded Afghanistan, stood erect, saluted, and resigned on the spot. He was replaced immediately by General Dmitri Yazov, a congenial and hearty figure with a reputation as a 'yes man', who leapfrogged over a number of more senior and apparently better-qualified candidates. Alexander Koldunov, the commander of Soviet air defence, a former World War Two fighter ace, was not allowed to resign or retire. He was summarily dismissed for 'negligence'. Gorbachev concluded: 'An event has occurred that surpasses everything that has happened before in terms of its political consequences ... We are talking about the people's loss of faith in the army, for whose sake people have made many sacrifices ... for a long time. A blow has also been struck against the political leadership of the country, against its authority.'[6]

Akhromeyev survived, as did Lushev, but more than 150 officers were removed, some of them court-martialled, for their part in the Rust affair. Most, though, were soldiers who had been identified as opponents of perestroika. Humiliating it may have been but, ever an opportunist, Gorbachev used the incident to crush the military. Within a year, the entire top echelon of the Soviet Defence Ministry, the General Staff, the Warsaw Pact commanders and all the military district commanders had been changed. 'Even during Stalin's bloody purge of the Red Army in 1937–8, the percentage of change in top-level posts was not as high,' one military observer pointed out. Gorbachev became ever more contemptuous of the army chiefs. Often from now on at meetings he would sneer ironically and make comments to anyone around him in a uniform such as: 'So, Comrade General, whom do we plan to invade today then?' The military bitterly resented such treatment. In the short term it appeared as though he had scored a victory over them. But they found ways to wound him in return.[7]

TWENTY

THE GANG OF FOUR

Moscow, June 1987

THE DICTATORS OF Eastern and Central Europe took a long time to realise they were on their own. Even when they were clearly told that the Russians would no longer defend communism and the Soviet empire in the traditional way, with tanks and troops, they remained in a state of denial. Men like Honecker, Zhivkov and Husák were accustomed to taking orders from Moscow and showing obedience. Ceauşescu was more independent-minded, but was trapped in the ideological orthodoxies of the 1950s. They had been permitted a certain limited degree of autonomy. Generally, the bigger the satellite country, the greater freedom of manoeuvre it was allowed. This had increased over the years, but ultimately all the East European leaders had accepted their colonial status and had tried to avoid offending their feudal masters. They had no legitimacy in their own countries, a fact they had always well understood. They had been placed in power by Soviet force, against the wishes of their people, and could continue in their positions only with the support of the USSR. They served at the Kremlin's pleasure.

But now the mood in Moscow was changing. When Mikhail Gorbachev assumed power and warned the satellite leaders that they must 'assume greater responsibility' for their own countries, they did not at first take him seriously. They saw it as a ritual declaration, which the new man in charge was making for form's sake. Over the decades, other Soviet leaders had said similar things but then, soon, the orders from above would follow, and the daily interference on a whole range of matters, great and small. Now the number of instructions from the Soviets had declined to a trickle and the whole mechanism of empire was breaking down. Soviet advisers, who had wielded enormous power and influence in every government department and Party secretariat from Berlin to Sofia, were ordered by Moscow to stay on the sidelines.

Their advice tended to be 'Well, comrades ... you can do what you think best'. It confused and unnerved the dependent Gang of Four to be on such unfamiliar terrain.

Gorbachev had little experience of Eastern Europe when he assumed supreme power. He had travelled around the satellite countries on short visits when he was in charge of Soviet agriculture, but had not thought in any depth about the relationship between the USSR and its European colonies. One of his best friends from Moscow University days was the Czech 'reform Communist' Zdeněk Mlynář, a leading figure in the Prague Spring. But he had been purged after the Soviet invasion in 1968 and exiled himself to Vienna. Years later Gorbachev said that the Soviet Union's 'biggest mistake was when we did what we did in 1968 against the democratic reforms in Prague ... if all these countries had, then, embarked on roads to reform their societies, it would have led to different results'. There is little evidence that he thought so at the time. Certainly he did not utter such heretical opinions within Party circles when he was climbing the greasy pole towards leadership. When he took charge in the Kremlin, he regarded the Soviets' imperial possessions as stable. Poland was traditionally difficult to control but General Jaruzelski had, it appeared, imposed peace and order there. Romania went its own way, but was fundamentally loyal. 'Elsewhere the tranquillity suggested that at least in the near future there would be no surprises,' Gorbachev's aide, Andrei Grachev, said. 'Having received the formal expressions of fealty [from the satellite leaders], Gorbachev ceased to think about Eastern Europe.'[1]

After about a year and a half, he began to consider the matter anew, heavily influenced by Shevardnadze and Yakovlev, who firmly believed the Soviets should relax their grip yet further in the 'outer empire'. Gorbachev was now convinced that the satellite states were a burden on the Soviet Union that the country could no longer afford to carry. 'In order to buy loyalty and political reliability – and guarantee minimum internal stability – the Soviet Union was subsidising a standard of living in the East European countries largely superior to that of the majority of the Soviet population,' Grachev said. The costs had risen. Each time there was a political crisis in one of the satellites, it had to be smoothed over afterwards with extra cash. Gorbachev was told that it was costing about US$ 10 billion a year in security to keep the East European countries 'stable'. Some economists advised him that the drain on the Soviet economy from additional financial subsidies was a further US$ 30 billion above that. He was shocked when he was presented with these figures and became determined that from henceforth the 'socialist brothers' would pay their way. In November 1986 he summoned the rulers of the satellite countries to Moscow for a summit that convulsed the socialist world.[2]

He announced a revolution in the rules of exchange between the colonies and Moscow that had lasted since Stalin's time. The system had depended on a flow of raw materials from the Soviet Union to the satellites, in return for manufactured goods moving in the other direction. Now Gorbachev declared that 'trade must be built on a mutually beneficial basis and under real market conditions'. He meant that they would have to pay world prices for their imports – and the Soviet Union would have more choice about whether or not to buy the low-quality manufactured goods that were produced in Poznań, Leipzig or Bratislava. He made it entirely clear, too, that there was no way the USSR would guarantee the loans from Western banks that the East Europeans had racked up over the past years. Not all of his listeners immediately grasped the enormity of the implications. Overnight, the Soviets had transformed the socialist empire – or 'killed it', as an East German official at the talks recognised. 'It was the economic equivalent of withdrawing Soviet troops from Eastern Europe,' said one of the other apparatchiks who had heard the announcement.[3]

Gradually, the consequences began to sink in and the other leaders were appalled. They could no longer look forward to lives of relative ease, protected by guaranteed credits from Moscow and the flow of cheap oil and gas from the East. At the same time, Gorbachev gave them all a long lecture on the changes he was making in the Soviet Union, on perestroika and glasnost. The Gang of Four looked increasingly uncomfortable as they listened. He imagined that his example would encourage a wave of imitators to appear on the scene in the satellite states. He hoped to see a number of 'little Gorbachevs' in Eastern Europe, all pursuing reforms in step with his own, because its elites had become so used to following the Soviet Union. 'The inertia of paternalism had made itself felt for a long time,' Gorbachev said. 'In the socialist countries . . . the traditions of dependency and obedience to the leader, the desire to agree with "big brother" on nearly every step, so as not to call down the wrath of the Kremlin had . . . deep roots.' Above all, he was convinced that, given the choice, people in the socialist commonwealth would choose to remain in the familiar system, within the Soviet orbit. It was a naïve assumption from a man still so committed to his beliefs that he seemed to forget that communism had been imposed on the satellites by his predecessors, at the point of bayonets. He did not believe he was taking any major risks by loosening the Soviet grip.[4]

Gorbachev 'despised' most of the East European leaders, except Jaruzelski whom he liked and Kádár whom he respected, according to Valeri Musatov, deputy head of the Soviet Communist Party's powerful international department. He had utter contempt for the obsequious Zhivkov and thought Honecker and Husák were tiresome bores. 'They're reactionary leftovers, relics from Brezhnev times,' he often said privately. With slightly more circumspection, he said later: 'It was not yet senility, but the weariness of leaders who were ... seventy and who had been at the helm for two or three decades was quite obvious.' He had a particular loathing for Ceauşescu, whom he called 'the Romanian führer'. Gorbachev said: 'Anyone could see his delusions of grandeur ... [Romania] was wholly subordinate to its ruler's great power ambitions and was coming to look more and more like a horse being whipped and driven by a cruel rider. I have encountered many ambitious people in my life ... It is hard to imagine a major politician without his share of vanity. In this sense, though, Ceauşescu was in a class of his own.'[5]

He was unenthusiastic about visits anywhere in the socialist bloc and several of his aides said it was always a troublesome business getting an itinerary together as Gorbachev would drag his heels about agreeing whom he would see and whom he would not. When he did go, he would remain polite, but wanted to make sure that the public wherever he went knew that he was encouraging the leaders to reform. But he did so by tacking and weaving. He did not always make his intentions clear. Touring Czechoslovakia in April 1987, he was careful to avoid saying that the Russian invasion in 1968 had been wrong. That disappointed the dissident underground. But as his entourage was leaving Prague, his spokesman was asked by a Western reporter what Mr Gorbachev thought was the difference between the Prague Spring reforms of Alexander Dubček and the current Soviet ideas of perestroika and glasnost. 'Nineteen years,' came the reply. That gave a huge fillip to the opposition and was a blow to the regime.

Gorbachev preferred visits to the more glamorous capitals of the West, where he quickly became a political superstar. Invariably he was greeted by tremendous cheering crowds of people keen to catch a glimpse of a Russian leader who could smile, talk without reading from prepared notes, and looked distinctly like a human being. There was a good political reason for turning his attention to the West. He needed to lower international tension, so that he could cut military spending and then address the pressing issues at home. But many people who worked closely with him agree that his stunning personal success abroad – the 'Gorbymania' that continued for his first years in power – went to his head. No other Soviet leader had cut such a dash or behaved like a Western politician. The press and television in America and Europe treated him like a celebrity. They covered his appearance, his manner and his gestures, if not his speeches, which were often of inordinate length and contained much waffle. For a while the Western press fell in love with his wife. Journalists wrote endlessly about her wardrobe, her make-up, her hairstylist. She adored the attention. He enjoyed meeting world leaders, foreign ambassadors and Western journalists, while he was bored to distraction when he saw Party functionaries from Warsaw or Berlin. He cultivated his image and understood how to manipulate the media in the West. He could be verbose, but he realised the value of a good soundbite. He, or rather his chief spokesman and public relations adviser, the tall, dark-haired, easy-going and witty former Ambassador to Portugal, Gennadí Gerasimov, coined a phrase to describe Gorbachev's policy regarding the Soviet Union's satellite states. The Brezhnev Doctrine, he said, was dead. Now the Soviets proceeded on the Sinatra Doctrine. 'You know the song "My Way". Well . . . these countries – they can all do it Their Way.'

TWENTY-ONE

GORBACHEV'S VIETNAM

Washington DC, Tuesday 19 April 1988

AT CIA HEADQUARTERS in Langley, Virginia, there was a group of senior officials known as 'the Bleeders'. They took the name from Mikhail Gorbachev's term for the Afghanistan war, which they knew he used often – 'our bleeding wound'. Their objective was to keep the Soviet forces tied up in the Afghan mountains for as long and expensively as they could. Officially, the Americans declared that they wanted the Soviets to leave Afghanistan. At the Reykjavik summit in autumn 1986, President Reagan had pleaded with his Russian counterpart to withdraw Soviet troops. Dramatically, in Iceland the two said they had come close to a bold and visionary agreement abolishing all nuclear weapons. Reagan's insistence on pursuing the Star Wars project put paid to that idea, though it has since become clear there were so many other stumbling blocks that no such deal was ever a real option. Still, from then on Gorbachev ceased calling the Americans 'that gang' or Reagan 'a caveman' and the pair grew to trust each other more.

Not, however, on Afghanistan. From a trickle, the flow of American arms delivered to the Mujahideen via Pakistan became a flood. 'It was a war fought with our gold, but their blood,' the CIA's officer in charge of dealing with the guerrillas, Frank Anderson, said. From the end of 1986 onwards the holy warriors were sent highly sophisticated, up-to-date equipment, such as Stinger ground-to-air missiles, that changed the nature of the conflict. The Russians could no longer conduct low-level bombing runs on Mujahideen bases or strafe Afghan villages without serious risk of losing planes and pilots. Inside the Company 'the Bleeders' had won the argument, enthusiastically supported by CIA Director Casey, and, after he died in May 1987 following a sudden and harrowing illness, by his deputy, Robert Gates. 'Here's the beauty of the Afghanistan operation,' Casey mused shortly before his death. 'Usually it looks like the big bad Americans are beating up on the natives. Afghanistan is just the reverse. The Russians are beating up on the little guys. We didn't make it our war. The Mujahideen have all the motive they need. All we have to do is give them help – more and more of it.'[1]

They were not aware how desperate the Soviets were to find a way out of the quagmire. But the CIA had always been lamentably ill-informed about Soviet intentions in Afghanistan. Repeatedly in the months leading up to the Soviet invasion the Agency said the Russians would not send in troops. On Monday 17 December 1979 the then CIA Director, Admiral Stansfield Turner, confidently told President Carter that although there was movement of Soviet troops close to the border, 'we do not see this as a crash build-up' and there was nothing significant to be concerned about. Two days after that the President's National Intelligence Daily – his brief that supposedly told him everything important about foreign issues – had predicted that 'the pace of Soviet deployments does not suggest ... urgent contingency'. Three days later, scores of thousands of Soviet troops crossed the border and began to take control of the country.[2]

The agony of Soviet withdrawal from Afghanistan was long-drawn-out. A new leader in 1985 could have simply pulled out the troops and declared a 'victory' for international socialism, or, more honestly, withdrawn the armies, accepted the debacle and blamed it on his predecessors. Gorbachev would have earned widespread plaudits throughout the world if he had done so within weeks or months of taking office. But he lacked the will or the courage. Even his greatest admirers knew he was making a fateful error. Yakovlev, and Gorbachev's chief foreign policy adviser, Anatoli Chernyaev, continually told him that ending the Afghanistan War should be the top priority. But Gorbachev vacillated and hesitated, unwilling to confront the Kremlin conservatives, the KGB and the military. 'It was our Vietnam,' said Chernyaev. 'But worse. It was a huge weight ... on his reforms and greatly restricted his freedom of manoeuvre.'[3]

Babrak Karmal, whom the Soviets had installed as Afghan leader when they invaded in 1979, was removed in May 1986. He was replaced by Mohammed Najibullah, a handsome and intelligent thirty-nine-year-old doctor from one of the wealthiest aristocratic Pashtun families in Afghanistan, who had been the ruling Party's ruthless security chief for several years. Though 'Najib' was sober most of the time, unlike Karmal, he was as ineffective as his predecessor at attracting support for Kabul's Communist regime or waging war against the guerrillas.

Repeatedly, Gorbachev said he had made a definite decision to withdraw the troops. 'We have been fighting in Afghanistan for six years now,' he told his Kremlin colleagues on 13 November 1986. 'If we don't start changing our approach we'll be there another twenty or thirty years. We have not learned how to wage war there. We had a clearly defined goal – to get a friendly and neutral regime in Afghanistan. We don't need socialism there, do we? We must end this process as quickly as we can – to finish everything, pull out the troops in one, maximum two years.' The last of the old guard who made the decision to invade in the first place, Andrei Gromyko, was still an influential figure among the Moscow power-brokers. He had changed his mind about the war: 'We underestimated the difficulties when we . . . agreed to give the Afghans military support,' he said. 'It is necessary now to actively pursue a political settlement. The people will feel relieved if we go down this route.'

Now the army accepted that the war was unwinnable. Marshal Sergei Akhromeyev, head of the armed forces, was a contradictory figure. For years he had revered as his patron the long-serving Defence Minister Ustinov. Akhromeyev was a passionate Communist and invariably in favour of increasing military spending to counter 'imperialist expansion'. But he held heretical views about the Soviet Union continuing to waste money on propping up regimes in Third World troublespots like Ethiopia, Angola and Nicaragua. A tall but stooping, bespectacled figure, sixty-three years old, he looked more like a Russian intellectual than a soldier. He had played a key role in planning the invasion of Afghanistan in 1979, as he had been ordered to do, despite many doubts. Summoned into Gorbachev's presence, he now said it was not possible to win the war. 'There is no piece of land in Afghanistan that has not been occupied by a Soviet soldier at one time,' he said. 'Nevertheless, most of the territory remains in the hands of the rebels. We control Kabul and the provincial centres. But we cannot control political authority on the territory that we seize. We have lost the struggle for the Afghan people. Only a minority of the population supports the government.' Soviet soldiers were not to blame, he insisted. They had fought bravely in adverse conditions. But to occupy towns and villages temporarily had little value in such a vast land where the Mujahideen could disappear into the hills, wait for the Soviets to leave, and then return. Winning was an 'impossible mission.

We can maintain the situation as it exists now. But under such conditions the war will continue for a long time.'[4]

Despite all his intentions, Gorbachev continued to procrastinate, and raise doubts. No definitive orders were given for Soviet forces to retreat for more than a year after the decisions were made to withdraw. The Kremlin chieftains continued to deliberate. For a superpower to admit defeat is a bitter pill. 'The situation is not simple. We're in ... but how to get out racks one's brains,' Gorbachev despaired at one point:

> We could leave quickly, not thinking about anything else ... But we can't act that way. Our friends in India would be concerned ... and in Africa. They think this would be a blow to the authority of the Soviet Union ... And they will tell us that imperialism will go on the offensive if we leave Afghanistan. How will we justify ourselves to our people if, soon after we leave, there's a real slaughter and the establishment of a base hostile to the Soviet Union? The domestic aspect is important too. A million of our soldiers have been in Afghanistan. And all in vain, it turns out ... They will say: you've forgotten about the sacrifices and the authority of the country. It provokes a bitter taste. They will ask: what did those people die for?[5]

Talks in Geneva under the auspices of the United Nations to end the war started at the beginning of 1987. They progressed at a snail's pace. The Soviets wanted to ensure that a government 'friendly' to them remained in charge in Kabul. Shevardnadze continually pleaded with the Americans to halt their arms shipments to the Mujahideen, but in vain. The Americans wanted to keep the Soviets fighting so they could extract the highest possible price from the USSR. It is arguable that the US prolonged the war unnecessarily by making it difficult for the Soviets to pull out of a Cold War battleground. 'American arms supplies only dragged out the war,' said Alexander Yakovlev, the principal thinker behind perestroika. 'Gorbachev, Shevardnadze and I were ... convinced that we did not need Afghanistan and had no business being there. We would have lost the war anyway. We should have learned from the British that Afghanistan is a country that cannot be conquered. But the struggle between the two political systems drove us and the Americans to do stupid things.'[6]

The argument of 'the Bleeders' was simple: they did not believe that the Soviets were serious about withdrawing. When Shultz reported at a meeting of Reagan's advisers that Shevardnadze had told him the Russians would definitely pull out – 'and I believe him' – the CIA Director Robert Gates was contemptuous. 'Well I don't believe it,' he said. 'I don't see they have any real intention of pulling out.' He offered Shultz a US $10 bet that the Russians would be staying put in Afghanistan 'for the foreseeable future'.[7] Finally, in April 1988, the Soviets produced a timetable for their departure. They would start removing formations from the 109,000 troops stationed in Afghanistan on 15 May. All the soldiers would be out by 15 February the following year. Gorbachev remained furious that the Americans 'are not going to help us'. But eventually he saw that there was little reason from Washington's perspective why they should. 'We're going to pull out whatever the Americans do,' he told his fellow magnates in the Kremlin. 'It would have been better with an agreement, but the primary concern is that our boys are still dying there. Not to mention the billions it is costing us each year.' It took him three years to reach a final decision, and it would be nearly another year before the last Soviet soldier was out. But he was insistent that somehow it had to be spun correctly. 'We must say that our people have not given their lives in vain.'[8]

TWENTY-TWO

OLD MEN'S TALES

Bonn, Monday 7 September 1987

IT WAS THE PROUDEST MOMENT of Erich Honecker's life. At around 11 a.m. his Ilyushin jet touched down at the airport in Bonn after a fifty-five-minute flight from Berlin. He walked down the steps on to the tarmac, shook hands with the dignitaries who greeted him, and inspected the guard of honour. Then the East German national anthem was played, the German Democratic Republic's flag with its Communist emblem was ceremoniously hoisted, and the usually earnest visage of the GDR's ruler softened into a broad, satisfied smile. He beamed bonhomie. He was the first East German leader to be received in the Federal Republic and at last his country was getting the international status it most desired. 'It was his crowning achievement, as he saw it,' Günter Schabowski, the Berlin Communist Party chief, one of the most powerful oligarchs in the GDR, said. 'His main concern was that East Germany should be recognised. But the most important thing, more important than recognition by the rest of the world, was recognition by West Germany ... it was a declaration of East Germany's right to exist, its unassailability.'

Honecker remained in the best of humours throughout his five-day tour. Even when Helmut Kohl, an immense man who towered over him, raised the supposedly taboo subject of German reunification in a speech widely broadcast in the East, Honecker kept his cheerful countenance. He said nothing in public about the Berlin Wall, or the borders question, and simply adopted the formula he invariably used when asked: 'The two systems, socialism and capitalism, are like fire and water.' In private, he categorically denied that he had issued East German border guards orders to 'shoot to kill' people who tried to escape to the West. He smiled as he told Kohl that this 'simply is not so. We enforce the regulations on the border ... as you do.'[1]

He made an emotional visit to his birthplace in the Saarland, and to the nearby town of Trier, where Karl Marx was born and raised. His hosts were less delighted with the trip. As Dorothee Wilms, the Minister in charge of relations between the two Germanies, said: 'It was bitter for us . . . Kohl said it was one of the most galling points of his political life. But we had to do it – to achieve further improvements for our fellow Germans.' The historic tour had nearly not taken place. For many years, despite numerous requests from Honecker, the Soviets would not allow him to go because East/West relations were so poor. Honecker, it appeared, shared at least one discomfort with his people: he could not travel to West Germany. But Gorbachev finally relented, as one of his principal aims was to forge close ties with the West. His new favourite soundbite in Western capitals was to speak of 'our common European home'.[2]

When Honecker returned to Berlin, he might have rested on his laurels and enjoyed his triumph. Instead, he set to work with renewed confidence, convinced that his cause was right and that age had not diminished his abilities physically or mentally. He had always been a fitness fanatic. He had built a gym which he used every day at his mansion in Wandlitz, the suburb twenty-five kilometres north of Berlin reserved entirely for the top two dozen or so Party oligarchs. The leader would not listen to talk of economic or liberal reforms. Quite the reverse. He retreated into Stalinist certainties. He had spent a lifetime subservient to Moscow and the Soviet Communist Party. Now, for the first time in his life, he began to be critical of the Kremlin leadership and he grew contemptuous of Gorbachev. He told confidants: 'If Gorbachev goes on like this, socialism will be dead in two years.' Though he was one of the few people who knew the parlous state of the GDR's economy, he behaved as though the country was the success story of the Soviet bloc. Soon after his West German visit, Honecker was in the Soviet Union and accompanied Gorbachev on a trip to the industrial town of Sverdlovsk (now, as before the 1917 Revolution, Yekaterinburg, where the last Tsar and his family had been executed). He lectured the Russian leader about where the perestroika project was heading: 'Look, here in the shops people have nothing to buy, not even toilet paper,' he told Gorbachev. 'That is the result of the reforms. We don't need them in the GDR.' He told the East German counter-intelligence chief Markus Wolf clearly, 'I will never allow here what is happening in the Soviet Union. Never.'[3]

There were a few younger voices within the Berlin leadership who favoured some modest measures to liberalise control of the media. Their views were ignored. Honecker and his fellow oligarchs – whose average age at the time was sixty-nine – decided to stamp hard on dissent. Censorship was tightened. One of Honecker's chief henchmen, Joachim Hermann, was in charge of propaganda, an important role in the People's Democracies. He had formerly been editor of the main Party organ, *Neues Deutschland*. He had a phone on his desk linked directly to red telephones by the editors of every newspaper, radio station and TV newsroom in the country. Hermann's office would be in touch at least once a day with each of these media. Their instructions would follow a daily meeting between Hermann and Honecker, who would frequently pass the proofs of the first two pages in the main papers such as *Neues Deutschland*, change layouts he did not like and even crop pictures. It did not appear strange to any of the regime's functionaries or to the GDR's journalists that the leader of the country would find time to proof-read the morning newspaper. As Schabowski, himself a one-time *ND* editor, explained about journalists under 'actually existing socialism': 'Their role was [to be] apologists for the authorities. Their overriding function was not the provision of information, but propaganda and indoctrination. There was much direct falsification of facts, but that was not the case at all times and in all situations. The socialist media's most devastating effect was the way it … ignored reality.'[4]

Just because glasnost was prevailing in Moscow did not mean it would apply in Berlin. Chief Party ideologist Kurt Hager made that plain: 'Just because your neighbour changes the wallpaper in his home does not mean you have to redecorate yours,' he said. Some Soviet newspapers and periodicals were banned in East Germany – for example, the magazine *Sputnik* – because Honecker reckoned their support for Gorbachev-style reforms was subversive. He would not allow Party spokesmen in public speeches to utter the words perestroika or glasnost. In January 1988 Honecker laid on a large shoot at his hunting lodge in Thuringia for the diplomatic circuit. It was an annual event and usually a formal occasion. At one point he took the Soviet Ambassador, Vyacheslav Kochemasov, aside for a word in private. According to the Ambassador he said:

> I want to tell you that from now on we are not going to use the word perestroika and I want you to understand why and then you are welcome to tell everyone who needs to hear it in the Soviet Union.

> Perestroika is a step back from Leninism and we . . . are categorically opposed to this kind of revisionism in the way we interpret Soviet history. We are against blackening and undermining the achievements of the Soviet people. There are some matters we can't agree with. One can't say that Stalin was as bad as Hitler, as your journal *New Times* did recently. That is why we will not allow the translation of that into German . . . We are against destroying everything that millions of people, including those in the GDR, have believed in over many years.[5]

Censorship of books became more heavy-handed and suspect writers and artists were kept under increasingly tight surveillance. The Stasi doubled the number of agents watching the novelist Stefan Heym, who had fled to the US in the Nazi years and who out of conviction chose to return to the East rather than West after the war. Occasionally, on cold days, he would take cups of coffee out to them on a tray. His concern for their welfare ceased after he discovered that his cleaner was an agent paid to inform on him and was stealing his manuscripts so that the Stasi could photocopy them. Writers had been used to an elaborate system of censorship in East Germany. Like elsewhere in the Eastern bloc, nothing could be published without the regime's permission. The state owned the country's seventy-eight publishing houses. But in the GDR literature became part of the Plan. Some writers could do fabulously well, as their royalties depended on how many copies of a work were produced, not on the numbers sold. Favoured authors would be awarded enormous print runs for their often turgid works. Bizarrely, writers whose works were banned in the East were often permitted to publish them in the West – as long as they paid three-quarters of the royalties and advances to the state. The government decided how many books would be published years ahead, and which ones. This did not improve the topicality of the books produced. But worse, the East German system under which each writer before publication was assigned a 'helper', something between an editor and a mentor – and often a Stasi agent – who would 'assist' the work through to the printing press. The structure encouraged an insidious form of self-censorship described by the poet and novelist Günter Kunert:

> As authors we were always trying to be ahead of the censor, to second-guess his instinct about what was 'in' and what was 'off'. That means

> we put ourselves in the position of the censor ... After a couple of decades of doing this, we got so used to this second opinion lurking in our own heads that we considered it our own. We believed we were writing in freedom, and under our own influence, but we weren't. That was the most odious aspect of the system – it allowed us to believe we were free and we wanted to believe [it] too. So we played along with our own oppression.

Amongst the words the censors now found problematic were 'Soviet', 'glasnost', 'reform' and 'environment'.[6]

Honecker made an agreement with the West Germans when he was in Bonn which had far-reaching implications. Soon his aides and the Stasi began to realise it was a mistake. Since the Berlin Wall was built, almost nobody except the people most highly vetted by the security forces, or the prisoners sold to the Federal Republic for profit, was allowed to travel to the West, even on short visits. Now, for the first time, Honecker relaxed the rules and allowed older people who had close relatives in West Germany to see their families. It was a slow and laborious process getting the visas authorised, but it was possible and soon it caused the regime serious problems. Now there were two classes of East Germans: those who could leave, even temporarily, and those who could not. Talk of travelling 'over there' became the subject of most East German dinner tables and the dreams of millions of people were focused on leaving their country.

Early in the morning of 8 December 1987, the Czech police and officers from the StB security service began ringing Kampa Park, the charming little open space in central Prague directly below Charles Bridge. For the last five years on this date there had been rallies attended by thousands of young people to commemorate the death of John Lennon. Apart from football matches, they had been the largest public gatherings in Czechoslovakia since the Prague Spring. They had attracted more than five thousand people. The last two of the events, organised by the John Lennon Peace Club, had begun as festivals where the late musician's songs were played. They turned rowdy later, though, and were broken up by riot police who had beaten some of the fans and made scores of arrests. This year the regime had considered banning the rally. But the Lennonists, as they called themselves, had become well known in the West, so the government let it go ahead, ordering the group to ensure that it would not become a political demonstration.

The Communists reckoned they knew how to counter groups of young people whom they regarded as hippies, malcontents and assorted pacifists with a devotion to a dead pop star.

By early in the afternoon about 1,500 people had gathered in Kampa Park and Beatles music was being played on the loudspeaker system, as well as a few forbidden songs by the Czech composer Karel Kryl. Some people were dancing, despite the bitterly chill wind. The police took no action. A few were even seen singing along with the Lennon tunes. Then one of the organisers of the rally, Ota Veverka, a writer, musician and an original signatory of the 1977 Charter, stood on a platform to speak. He read out, as he put it, 'a petition against nuclear weapons, against the "fraternal army" temporarily stationed in our country (though temporary . . . doesn't seem to end), and against other measures that I don't like. And I guess the rest of us don't like them either.' He was quickly surrounded by knots of people eager to see the petition. The police took this as their cue. They arrested Veverka and about a dozen other activists, beat up a few more and declared the rally over.[7]

It was not strange that the most vocal protest in Czechoslovakia came from disaffected youth and was expressed through rock music. A decade earlier The Plastic People of the Universe had been the catalyst for disaffection. Samizdat literature was read by a handful of intellectuals in Prague and Bratislava. In ten years of underground activity, and with relatively wide coverage in the Western media, Charter 77 had gained small numbers of new supporters. By the end of 1988 only around a thousand people were brave enough to attach their names to the document and attract the attention of the StB. The Chartists held a demonstration in Wenceslas Square two days after the John Lennon rally in Kampa Park. It was attended by around 200 people. Compared with Poland, where the Church had become almost an independent state within the State, or even East Germany, where a few Lutheran pastors had begun in halting fashion to voice opposition, Czechoslovakia was an irreligious society. This was partly historic. Church attendance had been falling off since the Enlightenment. Partly it was because the Czech regime since the war had been successful at suppressing, harassing and corrupting established religion.

The majority Catholic Church was viciously persecuted in the 1950s. Parishes simply ceased to exist. More than 10,000 priests and monks were thrown into labour camps and many were never seen again. The

Catholics allowed the Party to dictate who could be a priest. Those who preached sermons which the authorities disliked were sacked. The Vatican in the late 1970s named Father Miloslav Vlk as Bishop of Hradec Králové, a traditionally important centre of pilgrimage eighty kilometres east of Prague. The regime vetoed him because in his parish he had attracted too many young people to the Church. For good measure they withdrew his licence to preach and he was reduced to finding work as a milkman. The clergy in the Protestant churches were riddled with police collaborators and agents. Religion played little part in life in the Czech lands, though slightly more in overwhelmingly Catholic Slovakia. But even there the Church seemed crushed. With neither a political nor a religious voice, young people especially found a way to express their discontent through music.

After twenty years of 'normalisation', Czechs learned to be afraid. There was plenty to be scared about. The human rights activist Jiří Wolf served three and a half years in jail for Charter 77 activities. Almost immediately after he was released he wrote a letter to the Austrian Embassy in Prague about poor prison conditions in Czechoslovakia. He was arrested again, charged with subversion and sentenced to a further six years. Typically, Czechs resorted to black humour in response. Protests against the harsh jail term recalled a joke in *The Good Soldier Švejk*: 'I never imagined they'd sentence an innocent man to ten years ... sentencing an innocent man to five years, that I've heard of, but *ten*? That's a bit much.'[8]

Joking apart, Czechs heeded the warnings and generally they were obedient. As Havel – who proudly boasted that he was a Lennonist – pointed out, two decades of forgetting had created apathy and hypocrisy:

> The number of people who sincerely believe everything that the official propaganda says ... is smaller than it has ever been. But the number of hypocrites rises steadily; up to a point that every citizen is, in fact, forced to be one ... Seldom ... has a social system offered scope so openly and so brazenly to people willing to support anything so long as it brings them some advantage; to unprincipled and spineless men prepared to do anything in their craving for power and personal gain; to born lackeys ... It is not surprising that so many public and influential positions are occupied, more than ever before, by notorious careerists, opportunists, charlatans, and men of dubious records; in short, by typical collaborators.[9]

The placemen in the regime were still relatively unconcerned by the John Lennon Club, and the other similar groups with names like the Jazz Section and The Society for a Merrier Present. But they were worried that Gustáv Husák was starting to lose his grip. A group of hardliners had long been plotting to oust him as Party leader on the grounds, they said, that seventy-five-year-old Husák was showing a fatal weakness against opposition. Rumours were spread that he was beginning to favour the bottle too much and was exhausted. They made their move soon after the Kampa Park rally and the Charter 77 demonstration that followed. Husák made no effort to keep his job. He admitted he was tired and went with grace. On 17 December he was 'promoted' to the largely ceremonial post of State President.

When Czechs learned who his successor was they were aghast. Miloš Jakeš was a slightly younger version (he was sixty-five) of Husák in his Stalinist prime. A dark-haired, pasty-faced, burly former electrician, he had been among the hardliners who hated the reforms of the Prague Spring, had requested the Kremlin to send troops to invade his country, and had been responsible for humiliating Dubček. He had been the witchfinder-general in charge of the purges after 1968. He performed the task with relish. Around half a million Communists were thrown out of the Party; thousands of academics, teachers, civil servants and journalists were sacked. He personally supervised many of the interviews in which people were required to sign loyalty pledges to the State and to the Party. If he suspected hesitation, he ensured the sceptic lost his or her job. He was a poor public speaker, mumbling and bumbling through laboured speeches full of jargon. Some officials who worked for him held his intellectual capacities in contempt. A widespread joke in Communist Party circles in Prague was that 'Jakeš would fail a lie detector test if he began a sentence with the words I think.'

The men around him who engineered his succession were brighter, but also in their mid-sixties and implicated in the brutal suppression of the dreams of 1968. Prime Minister Lubomír Štrougal was a known thug, with close links to the KGB. Vasil Bil'ak, a crucial Party powerbroker for the last twenty-five years, firmly believed that Gorbachev-style 'restructuring' was a betrayal of communism. The US Senator John Glenn, who led an American delegation to Prague, asked him why the Czechs would not emulate the Soviet reforms. He replied: 'You Americans used to accuse us of being Soviet puppets, of slavishly following the Soviet model. Now you accuse us of not following the

Soviet model closely enough.' Ideology chief Jan Fojtík warned that Party members would face expulsion if they raised the issue of the Soviet invasion: 'I am sure we can establish a dialogue with reasonable people,' he said. 'But there can be no dialogue with those who set out to destroy our society.'[10]

The Soviets wanted to be rid of Husák, but were stunned by the rise of Jakeš, who they knew was no friend of their new thinking. But Gorbachev's team did nothing to prevent it – proof, an adviser of the Soviet leader said, that he had lost interest in his East European empire.

The sharks who circled around János Kádár in Budapest six months after Husák was dethroned were altogether different. They were a younger generation from the Party elite, impatient that the old man was keeping them from power – and they believed that communism was doomed. Unlike Poland, where revolution came from below, from the workers' movement Solidarity, in Hungary change came from the top. The retreat from communism was led by Communists. Kádár had dominated Hungary for three decades, but he was starting to lose the grudging respect he had earned even from many of his opponents. Gulyás communism had been daring and original in its time. But its defects were now clear for all to see.

Kádár had been an authoritarian figure, though he was a relatively benign despot by Cold War standards. He lived modestly with his wife Mária, and had not been corrupted by gracious country homes full of servants, foreign bank accounts and Savile Row suits. He had never let a personality cult develop around himself. It was hard to find a picture of him in Budapest, and the Party newspaper *Népszabadság* (*A Free People*) seldom carried photographs of him. But he was visibly decaying and started to look like an old Stalinist, which in reality he had never been. He was forgetful, repeating himself at meetings and losing his thread in long rambling monologues. Some among those who worked for him felt embarrassed for him and wished he would voluntarily stand down. At night he could barely sleep, racked by guilt, said some of his friends, by his role in the brutal crackdown after 1956, and particularly his decision to hang his then rival, Imre Nagy. He was not so senile that he was unable to see his reform vision was failing. His answer was to return to the orthodox and familiar path – at least on economic policies. He feared that Gorbachev was making serious mistakes and would drive communism to its grave. In the summer of 1987, a group of economists and Communist theoreticians presented him with a package of deeper reforms. He vetoed the ideas and expelled from the Party the advisers who dared to suggest them.

Younger men thought the only way they could save their own positions was by removing Kádár. A majority of Party members were behind them. But bringing down an institution was a hazardous and difficult process. The logical replacement was the Prime Minister, Károly Grósz, a middle-of-the-road technocrat aged fifty-seven, a Party man through and through. A short, wiry man, he was usually cautious and pragmatic, but he could be ruthless. His chief accomplice – though they were to fall out spectacularly soon – was chief spokesman for the reform wing of the Party, Imre Pozsgay, an ebullient, jolly, fat and brash charmer who even then was telling Western journalists that in a few years' time he thought that Hungary would be 'like Austria – or perhaps Sweden'. This was a heretical belief at the time. But even though the Party rank and file agreed that it was time for Kádár to go, the assassins needed help and a nudge from abroad.[11]

Grósz had regarded Kádár as a father figure for many years, but he told him early in 1988 that it was time for him to retire because of his age, 'in the interests of the Party.' Kádár was not prepared to listen. Grósz then dispatched an intermediary to Moscow, Gyula Thürmer, the Hungarian Party's leading specialist on the Soviet Union. Thürmer had a short interview with Gorbachev. Though he respected Kádár as an elder statesman of communism, the Soviet leader thought it was now time for him to go and he wished to encourage the reformers in Budapest. But Gorbachev did not want to be seen to interfere. Gone were the days, he continually said, when the Soviet Union should pick and choose who were the leaders of other countries. He told Thürmer, diplomatically, that Kádár was a distinguished man 'who should know what he should do in such a historic situation'. He added that 'this is an entirely unofficial suggestion'. When Thürmer returned to Budapest, Kádár asked him what the Russians had said to him and he reported the exact words Gorbachev used. 'He heard my words without comment,' said Thürmer.

The Soviet President, Gromyko, visited Budapest at the end of February. Kádár told him that he planned to stay in power until 1990. When Gorbachev's advisers heard that they began to warn him of 'grave risks of serious . . . convulsions' in Hungary if Kádár clung on to power. The Soviet Communist Party's chief ideologist, Vadim Medvedev, told Gorbachev that Kádár should be persuaded to go and Grósz supported as a replacement, but it must all be done 'within the accepted norms of the relations between the two parties'. The Soviet Prime Minister, Nikolai Ryzhkov, passed through Budapest in April. Kádár asked him what he should do about his future and Ryzhkov replied point-blank, 'You should retire.' Kádár replied balefully: 'You too say that?' Grósz, exasperated, went public in April and spoke of 'the biological laws' that affected elderly leaders. Late in the evening of 2 May Kádár summoned Grósz to his office and said he was willing to retire. Yet he continually delayed. He did not step down without direct Soviet involvement. The KGB's Deputy Chairman, Vladimir Kryuchkov, arranged it. He had been a diplomat/intelligence officer in Hungary during the 1956 Rebellion and knew the Hungarian leader from those painful and violent days. He worked out a deal that gave Kádár a newly created figurehead position – Party President – if he went graciously. Even then Kádár tried to cling on. At a Party meeting on 20 May, in a giant trade union building in central Budapest, he made a long rambling statement justifying his actions. He was heard in silence. Grósz took over from him as Party leader that evening. At the end Kádár stayed in the hall, talking to nobody, waiting for his wife to drive him home. It was a pathetic finale to an extraordinary and dramatic career.[12]

The West German government played a significant role in the removal of Kádár. During Grósz's manoeuvres, Horst Teltschik, Chancellor Helmut Kohl's foreign policy adviser, told the coup plotters that if they succeeded in removing Kádár and began economic reforms 'then the West German government would support this programme ... with financial credits ... We kept our word ... in the shape of a billion Deutschmark credit.' Why should the West German government help to topple a long-serving Hungarian leader? 'What we were doing was to support policies of reform, wherever they began to develop, but obviously ... we were hoping that this would increase pressure on East Germany.' It was claimed in return that the new leaders in Budapest passed on Warsaw Pact secrets to Bonn – in effect turning Hungary into a spying organisation for the West. But this has always been denied and though the suspicion may remain, there is no evidence to prove one of the most fascinating conspiracy theories about the fall of communism.[13]

The money went straight into paying interest on the other outstanding foreign loans, explained Miklós Németh, the forty-year-old economist who took over from Grósz as Prime Minister. Németh had realised earlier that 'in a nutshell, everything had gone wrong with communism. We were close to an abyss at this point, close to total crisis. The killing of the socialist bloc, of the Communist system, began at the moment the Western banks and financial institutions gave loans to countries like Hungary. At that point we were on a hook.' A shrewd, intelligent, intense-looking and quietly spoken man, Németh was appointed as a Communist Prime Minister. 'But I knew that under the one-party system there was no way to make life better, to make reforms work,' he said. 'If you wanted to achieve basic reforms you had to make major changes not just in the economy, but politically as well. It meant overthrowing the Communist system.'[14]

TWENTY-THREE

ENDGAME IN POLAND

Warsaw, Wednesday 31 August 1988

STRIKERS WERE ON THE PICKET LINES in Poland – again. There was an air of familiarity about the wave of industrial protest that had swept across the country since the early summer. Poland had been here often in the past dozen years. But this time the sense of crisis and chaos were overwhelming and the regime ran out of options to deal with them. The government had tried all the usual methods of rule: bribery, coercion and finally a civil war against its own people. None had worked. The country was in a state of economic, political and moral collapse. The regime, still largely run by military men though martial law had been lifted long ago, embarked on something new: serious talks with Solidarity. When the Interior Minister and former spy chief General Czesław Kiszczak met Lech Wałęsa on a searingly hot day in central Warsaw and offered to 'discuss everything' with him, it began a direct process of negotiations that led to the collapse of East European communism.

Martial law offered temporary relief, but no solutions. It enfeebled the Communist Party, which according to a senior official had 'used up all its strength and imagination in the battle against Solidarity in 1980–82'. The Party had fatally lost confidence in itself. More than half of its three million members had left in the past five years. An internal Party in 1986 showed that nearly a third admitted to attending Catholic mass regularly, while a further 20 per cent went to church but would not admit to it. Membership now was made up of older people and those who had joined principally in order to keep their jobs. Barely any young people were joining. They could sense that it was no longer as advantageous to be a Party member as it was: the nomenklatura system was breaking down.

In an attempt to break the logjam, Jaruzelski took a huge tactical gamble, and lost. The previous November – after consultations with

Gorbachev – he hastily called a referendum designed to win support for a package of perestroika-style reforms. He tried to present himself anew as a liberal, though he represented, as Adam Michnik said, 'not so much Communism with a human face, as Communism with some of its teeth knocked out'. The referendum asked strange, detailed questions about how much voters thought prices should increase – and whether 'you approve of the government's economic reforms, even if it means two or three years of sacrifice?' Then it asked vague questions: 'Do you favour the Polish model of profound democratisation?' The General's advisers assured him the plebiscite was a clever way to put the opposition on the spot. If Solidarity urged a Yes vote, the union was co-opted as a partner of the regime. If it came out against, it could be portrayed as being against reform. But the referendum proved to be a spectacular mistake. The turnout was 67 per cent, and of those 66 per cent voted Yes. That was still a defeat for the regime, though. Jaruzelski himself had added a provision in the rules to ensure that 51 per cent of registered voters had to approve the measures – a suicidal amendment. Adding up the abstentions, the General had 'won' 44 per cent of the vote. The referendum was meant to show that the government was as democratic as Solidarity. Instead, Jaruzelski appeared like a loser.

A bad loser, too. Another of Poland's periodic financial crises hit the country soon after the referendum debacle, prompted as usual by foreign debt. Poland was close to defaulting on loans, again a familiar position for the country. But this was worse than before. Now inflation was running at more than 50 per cent and rising fast. Living standards were deteriorating badly. There were severe shortages of basic necessities: milk, most medicines, cotton wool, sanitary pads, most cuts of meat, bread, fresh vegetables, mineral water. This was a time, said Michnik, 'that the fondest dream was to find a roll of lavatory paper'.[1]

It was worst for the women, as they had to do most of the queuing. Alina Pieńkowska was a nurse at the Lenin Shipyard, a Solidarity activist from the first days of the 1980 strikes and married to a trade union organiser who had been one of the leaders of the Solidarity underground in the martial law years. 'It was a struggle to get basic things like washing powder,' she said;

> That was almost impossible . . . I had to wash my hair with egg yolks because there was no shampoo. Getting hold of things required a lot of time and patience . . . A working woman just didn't have enough

> time (in the day). If you wanted to live at a certain level, with work and standing in queues, you had practically no time for anything else. One of the worst things was that family ties, contact with my child, was getting so small . . . One could not satisfy the needs of growing teenagers. There was not enough protein and things that were essential for a developing child . . . After I paid for the kindergarten and rent there was hardly anything left. If we didn't have information about life elsewhere, that would have been different. But we were conscious of the way [other] people lived.[2]

In April 1988 Jaruzelski did what all his Communist predecessors in Poland had done. He raised prices – by 40 per cent on most foods. Within weeks much of the country was at a standstill. The first strike, on 1 May, started in the bus and tram depot in the north-west city of Bydgoszcz, where workers demanded a 60 per cent pay rise. They spread rapidly. At the Lenin Steelworks in Nowa Huta, the giant sprawling plant near Kraków, 15,000 men downed tools and demanded a 50 per cent wage increase. Security forces stormed the factory and detained around a dozen workers, as well as the Solidarity adviser Jacek Kuroń. Strikes closed sixteen coal mines and the shipyard in Szczecin. Stoppages were being planned throughout the country's transport network and at the Gdańsk plants.

The unrest revived Solidarity, which came through a period in the doldrums. Membership was less than half the nine million or so that it had been at the height of the union's first flowering in 1980–81. Martial law and the following years of stagnation dashed people's hopes and led to widespread apathy. Solidarity's influence waned. The gnome-like features of Jerzy Urban, the face of Polish communism as press spokesman for Jaruzelski, was often to be heard calling Solidarity 'a non-existent organisation' and Lech Wałęsa 'the former head of a former trade union' or 'a private citizen'. Archbishop Glemp had told Vice President Bush, who visited Warsaw on a whistle-stop tour towards the end of 1987, that 'Solidarity is a closed chapter in Polish history'.[3]

The regime had tried hard to discredit Wałęsa. The secret police resorted to crude forgery at least twice. It released a film, *Money*, purporting to show him at a birthday meal with his brother Stanisław at which they are heard talking about how much cash the Solidarity leader was receiving personally from the West. It was a bungled exercise, as were so many of the SB's operations. The dialogue had been made by splicing together some of Wałęsa's statements and meshing them with misleading extracts from a stolen tape they had of him meeting other Solidarity figures. The voice was not Wałęsa's, but that of an actor imitating him. It was a libellous fabrication and so obviously a fake that it was entirely counter-productive. Jaruzelski told the Soviet Ambassador, Aristov, that the SB was assembling new material, including some pornographic pictures of Wałęsa in a compromising position, that the General said would expose the Solidarity leader as a 'scheming, grubby individual with gigantic ambitions'. That never saw the light of day, as it did not exist.[4]

Rumours began to circulate that Wałęsa was an SB informer who had betrayed around a dozen Solidarity activists to the authorities during the martial law years. His opponents inside the union, with whom he had fallen out over the years, were spreading these stories with alacrity. It is true that in the early 1970s Wałęsa had been 'in contact' with the secret police, as the SB files state. The documents name him BOLEK and apparently implicate him in links with the intelligence services. He signed a few 'interrogation protocols', but these appear to have been routine statements he made when he had been picked up for questioning. They show little else. This was the period before he was Solidarity leader, when he was a relatively unimportant figure. The SB was notorious for exaggerating its competence, often boasting it had recruited informers when all it had done was to ask a suspect a few questions. Like all espionage agencies, it had a vested interest in claiming successes it may not have earned. KGB and Polish security files do not prove anything against Wałęsa. One Soviet document claims that when he was detained under martial law the SB had tried to intimidate him by 'reminding him that they had paid him money and recorded information from him'. This may be the only reference to money passing hands in thousands of pages on him in Polish and Russian secret police files. It is more than likely to be part of the various plans to smear him. Wałęsa always denied that he ever betrayed anyone to the SB and there is no evidence that he ever did – least of all while he was detained, when his brave resistance to the military regime infuriated the junta.[5]

The strikes continued throughout the summer and Wałęsa put himself at the head of them. He was convinced now that this would be the final showdown with the Communists, but winning would be a laborious process. 'I knew that the Communist system was finished,' he said. 'The problem was what would be the best way to get rid of it.' He repeatedly pleaded for talks with the regime to form 'an anti-crisis front'. General Jaruzelski always thought of himself as a realist. It was a conversation he had with Gorbachev that finally convinced him that it was time to face the fact that the government needed Solidarity. Some Communist reformers had been saying so for some time. His Foreign Minister, Marian Orzechowski, said: 'Martial law could work only once . . . The army and the police cannot be mobilised against society again.' The new Prime Minister, Mieczysław Rakowski, said that 'in practice we have recognised the opposition as a lasting element in the country's political map', and it was time formally to accept the realities. Still, the General delayed.

On 12 July Gorbachev visited Warsaw and was given a rapturous reception by, mainly, Solidarity supporters. Jaruzelski told the Soviet leader that he was considering legalising Solidarity and negotiating with Wałęsa. Gorbachev asked what he was waiting for and urged him on. Jaruzelski knew that the Soviets would do nothing to save him if his political skin was in danger and he had to look out for himself. The strikes had brought the country to a virtual halt. Poland was almost ungovernable. He had managed to obtain a loan of half a billion dollars from the Soviets to stave off immediate bankruptcy, but he realised that no money would be forthcoming from the West unless he could find a way to cut a deal with Solidarity.[6]

On 26 August Jaruzelski contacted Wałęsa and proposed a 'Round Table discussion' to end the impasse facing Poland, but he left it up to his Interior Minister to work out the details. Kiszczak was a curious figure, a dapper sixty-three-year-old career intelligence officer who had much good humour and charm for a man of his profession. He established a curious relationship, almost a friendship, with the opposition even though he was their sworn enemy, the man who had presented the harsh face of military rule. He was one of the chief sponsors of the Round Table talks and did much to ensure their success, while simultaneously spying on the opposition. When he met Wałęsa, he said Solidarity could be legalised, and that a wide range of democratic reforms could be introduced, if the union leader would get the striking workers to return to their jobs. Wałęsa knew how high the stakes were. He calculated that he had to accept the offer, though breaking a strike yet again could risk undermining his authority within Solidarity. Many of his closest advisers warned him that he was making the biggest mistake of his life by entering into the talks. Bronisław Geremek, one of the canniest members of Solidarity's leadership, understood the regime's tactic. 'What they meant to do was to corrupt Solidarity, divide us, compromise us,' he said. Wałęsa persuaded him and the other doubters that there was no alternative. He understood the risks, he said, 'but better a round table than a square cell'. There was no way of winning without talking, he added. A crucial factor was that the Pope supported the talks, as did the Church in Poland, which was one of the chief sponsors of the Round Table.[7]

But even the talks about talks were heavy going. Wałęsa told Kiszczak that there had to be a timetable for the legalisation of Solidarity. The police chief said that was impossible. At the end there might or might not be a legal union, depending on how the negotiations went. Wałęsa accepted the deal. For the next few days he toured the country, using all his skill and energy to persuade the workers that negotiating with the regime was the only way to secure what they wanted. He assured the workers that he could be trusted not to sell them out. Reluctantly, most of the membership went along with him.

Jaruzelski had problems of his own. His advisers – particularly Rakowski – outlined a cynical strategy that they assured the General would preserve real power for the Party, while appearing to grant major concessions to Solidarity. The opposition would be given a few ministerial posts in a new 'unity' government. Solidarity would share responsibility for the crisis – and the blame if things went wrong. The West would be impressed by Poland's move towards liberalism and offer new loans. Jaruzelski was convinced, and declared that 'it was worth the risk'. Many in the high ranks of the Party were deeply sceptical. The 'cement group' of diehards were certain that to share power would ultimately be to lose it and they were scared of giving up their perks and privileges. 'Many of us were afraid that [if we accept Solidarity] now . . . we would not be able to put the genie back in the bottle,' said Stanisław Ciosek, a former Polish Ambassador to Moscow. 'The Party was much better able to understand and trust the Catholic Church, another strong and centralised structure, than an unbridled Solidarity.'[8]

Some were scared of losing their lives if the 'counter-revolutionaries and reactionaries' took over the country. They demanded, and got, more time to consider such a momentous decision that one of them said 'will be the beginning of the end for us'. The General had a battle on his hands persuading his comrades to accept his leadership.

TWENTY-FOUR

PRESIDENT BUSH TAKES CHARGE

Washington DC, Tuesday 8 November 1988

THE OVERWHELMING ELECTION VICTORY of George H.W. Bush in the US presidential election was hardly a surprise. He had been a well-known figure even before he became Ronald Reagan's Vice President eight years earlier. He rode on the coat-tails of one of the most popular Presidents in American history and he had faced a lacklustre Democratic opponent, Michael Dukakis, who mounted a poor campaign. Despite the Iran-Contra scandal that engulfed Reagan during his last term, he remained a hugely admired, a loved, figure at home. He had succeeded in his main aim of making America feel good about itself. And now he could claim, reasonably, that he had played a leading role in reducing Cold War tensions. Bush was widely respected, if not much liked. He was a fit-looking sixty-four at his election, tall with a loping stride and a patrician air. While Reagan was warm and approachable, Bush could appear cold and distant. He had been training himself for the top job in American politics for decades. He was the son of a Senator, a Washington insider, though he had moved to Texas in his twenties to make his fortune in the oil business. Earlier, he had been a decorated fighter pilot in World War Two. Bush had served administrations of both colours, as Ambassador to China, Director of the CIA, Ambassador to the UN and finally as Vice President. He was vastly experienced, particularly in foreign affairs.

Bush had never been a favourite of the conservative wing of the Republican Party. He was a moderate, a traditionalist, who did not wear his religion on his sleeve. He was not a romantic, like Reagan, who he said privately had become 'too sentimental about the Soviets'. He was prosaic and pragmatic. Bush was no hawkish neo-conservative like the ideologues who had surrounded Reagan in his first term, men he described as 'marginal intellectual thugs'. But he was a conventional man, who believed that nuclear weapons had kept the peace for forty years. He thought that disarmers like Reagan were reckless dreamers who could wreck the global superpower balance. He was sceptical about the agreement signed in Washington DC the previous year which Reagan thought was one of the high points of his presidency. The Intermediate Nuclear Forces Treaty was the first time an entire range of nuclear weapons was abolished. In public Bush supported the deal, under which hundreds of European-based, land-launched missiles from both sides were destroyed. But he expressed some doubts in private. He was not convinced that the Soviets were prepared to cede their East European empire and he thought that all their talk of the 'Sinatra Doctrine' was mere public relations spin. He was contemptuous of the 'theatre' that the Reagan/Gorbachev roadshow, as he put it, had become. One scene he watched on television when Reagan visited Moscow earlier in the year angered him. The President was on a walkabout around Red Square. Gorbachev suddenly picked up a small boy and asked him to 'shake hands with Grandfather Reagan'. A reporter asked the President if he still thought the Soviet Union was the Evil Empire and he smiled. 'No, I was talking about another time, another era.' From that point on Bush deliberately began to sound more sceptical about the Soviet Union and during the election campaign he declared many times 'that the Cold War is not over'.[1]

Bush had known many CIA operatives for years even before he became Director of the Agency under President Ford. He took what the CIA said seriously. Reagan, on the other hand, believed what the Agency said when he wanted to believe it. He had made up his mind that Gorbachev was a man who could be trusted, who genuinely wanted radical changes in the Soviet empire. He thought Gorbachev needed enthusiastic encouragement. His top intelligence agents were giving him different advice. The CIA's deputy head, Robert Gates, had for many years been one of the Agency's leading analysts on the Soviet Union. He was extremely dubious about Gorbachev's motives and prospects and regularly advised Reagan not to make agreements with him. On 24 November 1987, a fortnight before the INF Treaty was signed, he wrote a top-secret memo to Reagan:

> There is general agreement among the Soviet leaders on the need to modernise their economy – not so much for its own sake or to make Soviet citizens more prosperous, but to strengthen the USSR at home, to further their own personal power and to permit the further consolidation and expansion of Soviet power abroad. There clearly are

great changes underway . . . in Soviet diplomacy. Yet it is hard to detect fundamental changes, currently or in prospect, in the way the Soviets govern at home or in their principal objectives abroad . . . The Party certainly will retain its monopoly of power . . . A major purpose of economic modernisation – as in Russia in the days of Peter the Great – remains the further increase in Soviet military power and political influence. Westerners for centuries have hoped repeatedly that Russian economic modernisation and political reform – even revolution – signalled an end to despotism and the beginning of Westernisation. Repeatedly since 1917 the West has hoped that domestic changes in the USSR would lead to changes in Communist coercive rule at home and aggressiveness abroad. These hopes have been dashed time and again . . .[2]

Just two months before the election, in September 1988, the CIA confidently ruled out any substantial changes in the satellite states. In a confidential report on the future of the Warsaw Pact states, presented to Reagan, it said:

There is no reason to doubt [Gorbachev's] willingness to intervene to preserve Communist Party rule and decisive Soviet influence in the region. For Gorbachev, as for his predecessors, the importance of Eastern Europe can hardly be exaggerated. It serves as a buffer zone, military and ideological, between the USSR and the West, a base for projecting Soviet power and influence throughout Europe and a conduit for Western trade and technology. It is a key external pillar of the Soviet system itself . . . There is no reason to doubt ultimate Soviet willingness to employ armed force to maintain Party rule and preserve the Soviet position in the region . . . Gorbachev's vision of a 'Common European Home' of growing intra European co-operation implies a degree of national autonomy far beyond what he or any other Soviet leader would countenance . . . Moscow would find it increasingly difficult to promote this line in the West without introducing new divisions in Eastern Europe as well. The Berlin Wall will stay . . .[3]

Reagan dismissed most of the CIA's scepticism. As an old Cold Warrior he understood whence it came. Gates said later that there could have been only one explanation for 'the Gipper' to ignore the CIA's advice: he was beginning to go senile. 'As his second term wore on we would hear [his old stories] told over and over again with no point at all,' Gates said. 'I thought he was still on top of the issues, at least the important ones, but a quality I believed was ... magical was waning day by day.' Talking to him by 1987, said Gates, 'I had the sense that he could not have recalled my name five minutes later.'[4]

Bush appointed equally moderate and pragmatic people to senior posts in his administration. His Secretary of State was a close friend from Texas and Republican politics, the subtle and sharp-witted scion of an old-established Houston law firm, James Baker III. He was a fair-haired, loose-limbed fifty-eight-year-old who had served as Reagan's Chief of Staff in the first term and Treasury Secretary in the second, before he ran Bush's presidential campaign. In the previous administration he earned a reputation in Washington as a tough negotiator and consummate deal-maker. His first words of advice to the new President Bush were 'to avoid rashness ... The biggest mistakes, particularly at the beginning of an administration, were frequently those of commission, not omission.' The new National Security Advisor, General Brent Scowcroft, had been an air force commander and Henry Kissinger's deputy on the National Security Council in the Nixon presidency. He was a far more hawkish figure who advised Bush to be careful before he invested any further in Mikhail Gorbachev. 'When the leaders in the Kremlin selected Gorbachev ... clearly they did not think they were selecting someone who would overturn the system, but one who would get it back on track,' he said. 'The character of the chief sponsors of his rise through the ranks seemed to confirm their choice. Were they all wrong? ... I didn't think so.'[5]

In contrast and for balance he listened to other voices who were more enthusiastic about doing business with the Soviets. Jack Matlock was Ambassador to Moscow and a brilliant young academic from Stanford, Condoleezza Rice, was appointed, aged just thirty-four, as his NSC adviser on the Soviet Union and Eastern Europe.

TWENTY-FIVE

TRIUMPH IN MANHATTAN

New York City, Wednesday 7 December 1988

IN TIMES SQUARE the lights blazed the message WELCOME COMRADE GENERAL SECRETARY GORBACHEV. Below the words, in garish red, flashed the hammer and sickle emblem. Throughout Manhattan, the Mecca of world capitalism, the streets were lined with New Yorkers waving the flag of the Soviet Union waiting to catch a glimpse of the forty-seven-car motorcade accompanying the world's most prominent Communist. Thousands of people were chanting 'Gorby, Gorby'. Hundreds of placards were visible through the crowds reading 'Blessed is the Peacemaker'. On Wall Street, optimism was expressed in the traditional way. The markets experienced a surge. Inside his Zil limousine Gorbachev, as he confessed, was feeling mixed emotions. Part of him was exhilarated. He was too intelligent to miss the irony of the ecstatic greeting he had received in the US. Yet he revelled in the cheering crowds and on this occasion he was convinced that he deserved their adulation. He had that morning achieved one of his greatest triumphs.

In a dramatic speech to the United Nations, he abandoned much of the ideology that had defined the Soviet Union over the past seven decades. The concept of 'class struggle' – the basis of Marxist understanding of history – was dead, the Soviet leader announced, now replaced by 'universal human values'. These would include the civil rights and individual freedoms which he admitted had sometimes been denied by Moscow. The Cold War that had consumed the energies of the superpowers for forty years was over: 'We are witnessing the emergence of a new historic reality – a turning away from super-armaments to the principle of reasonable defence sufficiency.' He renounced the use of force to settle international problems. He talked of general principles, and then he announced the nitty-gritty. As a token of Soviet sincerity, he said, the Red Army would unilaterally be reduced by half a million men. He announced that 50,000 troops and 5,000 tanks would soon be taken out of the Soviet armies stationed in East Germany, Czechoslovakia and Hungary. He said that the people of Eastern Europe would be allowed to choose their own destiny. 'Everyone must have the freedom to choose. There must be no exceptions.' He spoke for just over an hour – brief by his standards – but it had been an exceptional performance. For a few seconds there was silence. Then, slowly, his audience of presidents, prime ministers and ambassadors rose to applaud in a standing ovation. Long-serving UN hands said they had never seen such an emotional reception given at the General Assembly to anybody.[1]

Gorbachev could not bask in the glory for long. While he was being driven from the UN building on the East River to a lunch on Governors Island with President Reagan and President Elect Bush, he received an urgent phone call from the Kremlin. The Russian Prime Minister, Nikolai Ryzhkov, told him of a devastating earthquake that had struck Armenia a short while earlier that morning measuring 6.9 on the Richter scale. Details were still sketchy, Ryzhkov said, but many thousands had almost certainly died. At first Gorbachev stuck to his itinerary. When he met Reagan a few minutes later, the President offered American aid for Armenia. Gorbachev thought for a moment and then, in a historic about-face for a Soviet leader, accepted with gratitude. It was the first time since Hitler invaded the USSR that the Russians had sought foreign help. Gorbachev had intended to stay in the US for another day and then go to London for a visit that would include talks with Margaret Thatcher, with whom he had built up a close, if argumentative, relationship. But throughout the day he was being updated with further grim news about the devastation in Armenia. Early that evening he decided to cut short his tour and return to the Soviet Union. He flew straight from the bright lights and the applause of New York to the human misery of Leninakan and Spitak, the two Armenian towns almost entirely destroyed by the earthquake. 'In my entire life I've never seen one thousandth of the suffering I've seen here,' he said, soon after he arrived and witnessed the devastation.[2]

The relief effort was a tragic fiasco. It showed the Soviet Union to be a Third World state rather than a true superpower – 'Upper Volta with nukes', as the former West German Chancellor Helmut Schmidt pithily described it. A mixture of incompetence, corruption and poverty led to needless loss of life and misery. Troops reached the spot fairly quickly, but with so little heavy equipment which could lift rubble there was a limited amount they could do. They patrolled the hills, weapons at the ready, as though they were expecting an invasion instead of reacting to a natural disaster. Some tents arrived for survivors, but nowhere near enough for the half a million or so made homeless by the earthquake. There was not enough transport to reach the rural areas badly affected in a cold winter. Few doctors and nurses were sent to the scene for several days, and pitiful quantities of medicines. The civil defence authorities were simply unable to cope. It quickly became clear why the scale of the disaster was so enormous. Virtually none of the buildings in the stricken towns were able to withstand even a modest earthquake. It turned out that the steel rods that should have been used to reinforce the concrete had been stolen and sold on the black market. Government and Party officials knew, but allowed apartment blocks, hospitals and schools to be built anyway, aware of how flimsy they could be in an area of the Caucasus well known as a potential earthquake risk. Most of the 25,000 people who died were buried under rubble. It was, as a Kremlin official observed later, 'a very Soviet disaster'.[3]

Even the radical decision to accept outside aid backfired. Gorbachev and the Kremlin leaders might have been keen to see British, American, West German and French assistance. But the bureaucrats in remote Armenia did not know how to deal with these foreigners, who included Vice President Bush's younger son Jeb, speedily dispatched on a goodwill mission from the US. Aid workers encountered endless red tape before they could enter the afflicted area. One aspect of Gorbachev's reforms was working, though: glasnost. The quake was covered as no domestic disaster had been before by Soviet television and newspapers. On prime-time TV Ryzhkov, co-ordinating relief work, was shown berating Soviet Foreign Ministry officials for not giving foreign volunteers enough help. 'Some of the foreign groups are leaving now with heavy hearts,' the Prime Minister said. 'Not because of what they have seen, but because of the treatment they received here.' Aid worth millions of dollars sent from abroad – and from Moscow – never got further than the airport in the Armenian capital, Yerevan. There, much of it was stolen and found its way to the black market.

While Gorbachev was enjoying celebrity status throughout the rest of the world, his popularity was plummeting at home. A *New York Times* editorial soon after his triumphant UN speech asked readers: 'Imagine that an alien spaceship approached earth and sent the message "Take me to your leader?" Who would that be? Without doubt Mikhail Sergeyevich Gorbachev.' Yet in the Soviet Union, his appearances now were at best treated with indifference or at worst, as in Armenia following the earthquake, with downright hostility. 'We promised things would get better, but they were getting worse,' Yakovlev admitted after the first years of 'restructuring'. Living standards were falling rapidly. The sharp drop in oil prices and in revenues from alcohol was having a devastating effect on the economy. The Soviet Union was much more free, but much more chaotic. Gorbachev found it increasingly hard to carry his reforms through the country, and especially within the Soviet Communist Party. Even some of his enthusiastic supporters saw a weakness in Gorbachev's style and his 'project'. It was high on inspiring rhetoric, but low on practical details. 'Gorbachev never thought through a plan,' said Anatoli Dobrynin, who liked and greatly admired his boss but was often exasperated by him. 'You can't just stand on the Kremlin porch and declare that from tomorrow we are starting a market economy. Gorbachev never had a programme. He jumped from one idea he liked to another. One day he "reforms" one thing and the next day he jumps to something else.'[4]

Another great admirer who worked for Gorbachev over many years said his entire method of governing was 'to bob and weave'. He was unable to chart a clear course and stick with it for any length of time. Often he would declare a radical new policy but then wait too long before implementing it. An obvious example was the withdrawal from Afghanistan. But he was similarly hesitant elsewhere. He failed to start any meaningful economic reforms when he had the chance, according to his aide Anatoli Chernyaev. Then he became engulfed in such economic crisis that it became impractical to try. One reason is that he had little understanding of how a market economy operated. Gorbachev once told the American Secretary of State, James Baker, that it was dangerous to decontrol prices because 'it will take money out of people's pockets'. Baker, who had been US Treasury Secretary, replied with a simple free-market argument: precisely the opposite should happen in the long run, he said. Letting prices float to their market level will stimulate production and growth and put more money into people's pocket. Gorbachev did not seem to grasp the concept.[5]

Some of the influential Communist oligarchs who had chosen him began to regret it. Gromyko had done more than anyone else to ease

Gorbachev into office. For the past year he had been telling Party officials that he had made a 'mistake' and called the team around Gorbachev 'the Martians' for failing to understand the world most people inhabited and for their ignorance of realpolitik. 'I wonder how puzzled the US and other Nato countries must be ... It is a mystery for them why Gorbachev and his friends ... cannot comprehend how to use pressure for defending state interests.'[6]

He overcame a series of bruising encounters with Party traditionalists. A month before Gorbachev's United States trip, the Party leaders discussed restoring Russian citizenship to the writer Alexander Solzhenitsyn, who was living in exile in Massachusetts. The KGB boss, Viktor Chebrikov, was adamantly against the idea. He advised Gorbachev: 'We must leave in force the decree stripping the citizenship of a traitor to the Motherland.' Gorbachev replied: 'Yes, Solzhenitsyn is a staunch and irreconcilable enemy of the regime. But highly principled. And in a law-governed state, we won't prosecute people for their convictions. As for "treason" there's really no substance to the charge. And in general, all the procedural norms were violated in this case, there wasn't even a trial ... so this proposal won't do.' Chebrikov growled: 'But he did betray ...' and left the sentence unfinished. Gorbachev just cleared his throat, expressing annoyance. But it was two years before he signed the decree restoring the writer's citizenship.[7]

Two weeks before Gorbachev's UN speech, he faced a major clash with the military over the troop cuts he was planning to announce in New York. The Defence Minister, Yazov, and most of the generals were adamantly opposed. It would show weakness, they argued, and the troops were needed to protect the empire. Gorbachev harangued them:

> Why do we need such a big army? The truth is that we need quality, not quantity. Why do we spend two and a half times more on defence than the United States? No country in the world – except the underdeveloped ones, whom we flood with arms without ever being paid back – spends more per capita on the military ... Do we want to continue to be like Angola? ... [The military] still gets the scientific and technical talent, the best financial support, always provided without questions ... Why do we need an army of six million people? What are we doing? Knocking our best young talent out of the intellectual pool. Who are we going to implement reforms with?

He bludgeoned his will through and defence cuts were made, albeit slowly. But he faced growing resistance as it became clearer to many people that his domestic policies were not showing the intended results.[8]

Consistently, Gorbachev and Shevardnadze battled with the chief spokesman for the Kremlin conservatives, Yegor Ligachev, a grey and uninspired apparatchik a decade older than Gorbachev, who was number two in the Soviet leadership. Initially Ligachev had supported the anti-corruption campaigns and helped to ease some of the incompetent Communist barons from the provinces. But within a couple of years he began complaining that Gorbachev wanted to 'destroy' the socialist order and began to manoeuvre against him. Ligachev was demoted from his position in early 1988, but he continued to be a powerful figure in the leadership. He warned Gorbachev that he risked 'the demolition' of the Soviet bloc. 'Arguably, we will muddle through and will survive,' he said. 'But there are socialist countries, the world Communist movement, what do we do about them? Would we risk breaking up this powerful support that has existed side by side [with us] . . . We should think not only about the past but about the future.' Gorbachev ridiculed him and others he saw as 'panic-mongers who feared the destruction of what was built up by Stalin'. Shevardnadze made an outburst that appalled Ligachev and the rest of the Party old guard. 'As far as the Communist and working class movement today is concerned, there isn't much to rescue,' he declared. 'Take for instance Bulgaria, and the old leadership in Poland, take the current position in the GDR, and in Romania. Is this socialism?'[9]

Gorbachev never thought through a consistent policy on the satellite states. He did not want the burden of empire, but it is clear that he never clearly calculated the consequences of retreating. He regarded Soviet relations with the bigger Western countries as much more important than the old 'fraternal ties' with the socialist commonwealth. It was clear when he met Helmut Kohl for the first time, in October 1988, that Gorbachev saw the summit as far more significant – and more congenial – than his frosty meetings with Honecker. West Germany counted substantially more in Soviet policy-making than East Germany. As domestic considerations began to overwhelm him, he left others to handle mundane matters to do with Eastern and Central Europe. He had long ago ruled out in his own mind using force to maintain Soviet control over the satellites. He had said it many times – not least to the dictators who relied on Soviet troops to keep them in power. Most of his advisers agreed with him. As one of his most knowledgeable experts on Eastern Europe, Georgi Shakhnazarov, told him, the best way of maintaining influence in the region was 'to use the force of example, not the example of force'.[10]

Yakovlev and Shevardnadze now managed to persuade a reluctant bureaucracy to set non-intervention down as an absolute principle of Soviet foreign policy. For more than forty years, maintaining its European empire had been a Soviet priority. Now a highly secret Soviet Foreign Ministry policy declaration on the future of Eastern Europe said that the satellite states were not worth keeping:

> The allies are displaying an attempt to get more from the Warsaw Pact, mainly from the Soviet Union, than they contribute to it and showing independence to the detriment of common interests. At the same time it seems improbable that in the foreseeable future any of the allied countries will raise the question of leaving the Warsaw Pact. The Western powers do not wish confrontation with us on account of Eastern Europe. In the event of worsening crises ... in individual countries they will most likely deploy restraint and not intervene in [their] internal affairs, least of all militarily, counting on their patience being rewarded in time. We ought to keep in mind that our friends have recently received the impression that, in conditions of intensive dialogue between the USSR and the US, our relations with the socialist countries have become secondary for us ... We should proceed from the fact that the use of military force on our part in relations with the socialist countries ... is completely excluded even in the most extreme situation (except in cases of external aggression against our allies). Military intervention would not prevent but worsen the social and political crises, cause mass outbreaks of protest even as far as armed resistance and lead in the final account to the opposite effect, the reinforcement of anti-Sovietism. It would seriously undermine the authority of the Soviet Union, would worsen our relations with the Western powers ... and would lead to the isolation of the Soviet Union. If the situation worsens in one or other of the socialist countries, we should refrain ... from giving public support to repressive actions of the authorities.[11]

Gorbachev did not believe that the satellite states would rush to independence. It was his greatest miscalculation. He thought that when he visited Berlin or Prague, greeted by large crowds cheering

'Gorby, Gorby' and waving placards reading 'Perestroika', that the people supported his style of reform communism. He was convinced they would choose to stay allied to the Soviet Union. He did not realise that he had been wrong until after the Soviet Union ceased to exist. Gorbachev failed to see that the demonstrators were hiding behind him as a way of protesting against their own rulers. But occasionally the thought that they might want their freedom had occurred to him. As he told aides at the end of 1988: 'The people of these countries will ask "what about the Soviet Union . . . what kind of leash will it use to keep our countries in?" They simply do not know that if they pulled this leash harder, it would break.'[12]

PART THREE

REVOLUTION

TWENTY-SIX

THE WAR OF WORDS

Budapest, Sunday 1 January 1989

MILITARY INTELLIGENCE OFFICERS in both the superpowers were growing increasingly worried about unprecedented troop movements along the 100-kilometre border between Hungary and Romania. It seemed barely conceivable that there could be a war between two countries allied together in the Warsaw Pact. Yet the signs were ominous. The Romanians had for many weeks been building a fortified wire fence on their side of the frontier. This was a second Iron Curtain, mainly to keep people imprisoned inside Romania. But when newly mobilised and heavily armed divisions of soldiers began appearing in the area, tension mounted. The Hungarians responded. The new Communist Party leader in Budapest, Károly Grósz, who had been in power for little more than six months, moved a crack regiment that had been deployed on the Austrian border to confront the Romanians. It was more than a symbolic gesture to indicate that Hungary now saw itself facing westwards. It was a response to genuine fear that Romania's dictator might launch an invasion.

The Russians were worried. Within their empire it was theoretically impossible that 'fraternal allies in the socialist commonwealth' should be in conflict. In former days even minor disagreements between the satellite states were not supposed to be aired in public, while comrades displayed a traditional show of unity under the benign 'leading role' of the Soviet Union. Communists, so the theorists said, had progressed beyond the stage of 'bourgeois nationalism' which had led to two world wars. But the Soviets had lost their sense of imperial mission. They no longer possessed the power to control all events in their domains, particularly events in Romania.

The Hungarians and Romanians were historic enemies. The main dispute between them was over the beautiful, mountainous, wooded region of Transylvania, with some of the most fertile farming land in

Europe. Transylvania had been part of Hungary for centuries, until the end of World War One when it was awarded to Romania under the Trianon Treaty. The loss was grievously felt by a defeated Hungary, where there remained small groups of nationalists who believed they had a natural right to the region. About a million and a half Hungarian speakers, who culturally looked towards Budapest, formed a substantial minority inside Romania. Ceauşescu had been mistreating them for a decade and a half. He banned the teaching of Hungarian in Transylvanian schools. He tried to suppress the Hungarian Reformed Church. He closed down Hungarian cultural centres in Transylvanian towns, and the Hungarian consulate in the main city in the region, Cluj. Ultimately, his vision was to destroy the Hungarians as an identifiable community within Romania.

Around a third of Hungarians possessed relations in Transylvania. Ceauşescu tried to sever the links between them. Romanians were not allowed to visit Hungary, and he tried to stop Hungarians crossing into Transylvania. As conditions worsened in Romania throughout the 1980s, Hungarians were barred from sending food parcels to ease the plight of their relatives and friends in Transylvania. Ceauşescu thought most of the reform ideas that came from Budapest were subversive. He banned the Hungarian newspapers from Romania, even the principal Communist Party organs. He had already banned the Soviet press, after his aides had shown him flattering references in some Russian papers to perestroika and glasnost.

In Transylvania, Ceauşescu's latest idea to reorder civilisation was perceived as the most dangerous threat yet to the Hungarian minority's way of life. The dictator called his grand vision for the Romanian countryside 'systemisation'. He planned to raze to the ground 8,000 of Romania's 13,000 villages and replace them with 500 vast agro-industrial centres. The agricultural workers – nobody was to be called a peasant any longer – would live in the same kind of vast concrete blocks in which the urban proletariat were housed. Ceauşescu imagined this was a progressive step to bring the benefits of Communist planning to ramshackle and poverty-ridden parts of the countryside without roads, electricity in some places, and plumbing. But no doubt he thought it would also be easier to keep an eye on the 'agricultural workers' in vast apartment blocks than in traditional villages dotted throughout Romania. By 1988 only three villages were destroyed, all close to Bucharest and near to already existing big collective farms. But the rumour was that the systemisation programme was to start – in Transylvania – soon and would be directed at Hungarian villages. The rumour alone caused an exodus of people to risk their lives and livelihoods in an effort to leave Romania. Over the years a trickle of Transylvanians had managed to cross into Hungary to begin new lives. Now, more than 25,000 went within a few weeks. Scores died in the attempt and thousands were arrested on their way to the border.

The refugees sparked a crisis in Hungary. In the past, the Kádár regime had frequently complained to the Romanians about their treatment of the Hungarian minority. Although an agreement between the two countries signed twenty years earlier stated that 'illegal' refugees should be returned to Romania, the Hungarians in fact had sent none back to the tender mercies of the Securitate. The few refugees who managed to reach Hungary were made welcome and provided with accommodation by the authorities. Now the larger numbers created a dilemma. They were looked after by relatives, friends, churches and charitable groups. The Hungarian people were generous. But the public was outraged that the government appeared to be doing little to help the new arrivals and had approved only small amounts of money to provide for them. Legally their status was unclear. They seemed to be in limbo, while Ceauşescu was demanding that they should be handed back to Romania. The Hungarians suggested that independent intermediaries go to Transylvania to look at conditions there, but Ceauşescu said he would refuse to let them enter the country.

This was another issue, like the Danube dam, that galvanised Hungarians. It was even more powerfully emotional than an environmental cause, as it touched a still-raw nationalist nerve. At first the government did not sense danger. The Communists thought that anti-Romanian protests could turn out to be a release valve that might reduce some of the pressure against them. One of the most prominent of the Communist reformers, Imre Pozsgay, placed himself at the forefront of the campaign against Ceauşescu, whose 'incomprehensible and idiotic political posturing is an injury to European civilisation and a crime against humanity'.[1]

In the spring and summer of 1988, a series of huge demonstrations were held in Budapest and other big towns. They began with demands that the government should provide assistance for the Transylvanian refugees but they quickly turned into anti-Communist rallies. 'Of course we went because we cared about the Hungarians in Transylvania, but mainly we went because we hated the Communists,'

Sándor Zsindely, whose family looked after several of the refugees, said. 'These demonstrations were the only way to show it.'[2]

The coup against Kádár was intended to buy time for the reformers in the Party. They believed that if the old man went, the public would think the *ancien régime* had gone and would warm to his successors. They were mistaken. The biggest of the demonstrations, on 28 June, was held six weeks after Kádár was ousted. More than 90,000 people marched on the streets of Budapest, a city of around one and a half million people. Pressure increased on Grósz, from outside and inside the country. Ceauşescu summoned the new Hungarian leader to a conference at Arad, a small town just inside Romania, to discuss the refugees. Grósz accepted, against the advice of his close aides, leading Communist Party officials and most voices in the growing opposition, who wondered what the Hungarians could possibly gain from the encounter. They met at the end of August and Ceauşescu seemed on his best behaviour. He was affable, and though he made none of the firm commitments Grósz wanted, on reopening the Cluj consulate for example, Ceauşescu assured him he would guarantee civil rights to the Hungarian minority and ensure that Hungarian was taught in Transylvanian schools. Grósz went back to Budapest convinced that he had a deal with the Romanian dictator. But he had been ambushed. As soon as Ceauşescu returned from Arad he bitterly denounced 'Hungary's intolerable interference in Romanian affairs'. The Romanian Party newspaper, *Scînteia*, declared that Hungary 'was now making demands that not even the fascist Admiral Horthy dared to make in the 1930s'.[3]

Leading figures in his own party accused Grósz of naïvety for accepting Ceauşescu's assurances and showing weakness. He never recovered his authority and was forced into making excessive concessions he had not intended to make. A new company law was announced that had far-reaching implications for communism, though the financial consequences were not seen for some time. In effect, central planning was abolished. Private share ownership was allowed for the first time; no limits were placed on the size of private firms; joint stock companies could be formed; foreign firms were allowed to buy entire Hungarian companies. A whole range of new tax incentives were introduced. 'We have entered uncharted waters,' Reszö Nyers, one of the economists who produced the plan, declared.[4]

The war of words with Romania grew increasingly bitter. In November diplomats were withdrawn from both sides. Ceauşescu demanded the return of the refugees. Hungary responded by granting the refugees asylum and signing the 1951 UN Convention on Refugees. It was a first – none of the Soviet bloc countries had signed the document before. It was intended to give the Hungarians a legal cover for refusing to send the Transylvanians back, as the agreement between the two countries stipulated. The Party's lawyers advised the government that the UN treaty superseded any agreement signed by countries within the Warsaw Pact. Ceauşescu warned that if it came to an armed conflict, 'Romania has the capability to build nuclear weapons'. It was a dubious claim, but Grósz could not be entirely certain it was a bluff. He had been surprised a few months earlier to discover that the Soviets had based nuclear weapons in his own country. Even as Prime Minister nobody had told him that. In Hungary it was a secret known only by the Communist Party chief, the Defence Minister and two army generals.

As the new year started, Ceauşescu was reinforcing the border fence yet further and sounding more bellicose. The Romanian army was three times the size of Hungary's. If it came to an armed conflict the outcome was unclear. The latest reports from Moscow were calmer and suggested that the Romanian Conducător was merely sabre-rattling and the row between the neighbouring states would blow over, but Grósz was not celebrating. He had been a Communist loyalist all his life and he was beginning to realise how quickly changes were about to take place. That day the Party paper, *Népszabadság*, had removed its 'Workers of the World Unite' emblem from its front page. In ten days' time, on 11 January, under his leadership and against all his instincts, Hungary would become the first country in the socialist bloc to allow the formation of rival parties to the Communists.

It was a historic moment, as faithful old comrades were telling Grósz this new year, that made him the gravedigger of communism. For a brief moment he considered taking drastic action. He ordered his most trusted aides to make a contingency plan to declare martial law in Hungary, in case of war with Romania or total economic collapse. It could also be the only way to keep the Party in power. He discussed the idea with few people in Hungary, but according to his foreign policy adviser, Gyula Thürmer, Grósz sought the advice of General Jaruzelski, who firmly warned him against the plan. It had done little good in Poland. 'We won that battle, but the war was lost,' the General said. He advised Grósz to stick to the route of making a deal with the opposition. Grósz resigned himself to his likely fate of being one of the shortest-lived leaders in Communist history.[5]

TWENTY-SEVEN

HAVEL IN JAIL

Prague, Monday 16 January 1989

THE CZECH COMRADES were less gloomy about their prospects. They could see no reason to surrender power. They were bracing themselves for some opposition on the streets at the start of the year, and were making the usual preparations to handle it. The regular police, the militia and the secret service, the StB, were placed on high alert throughout the Czech capital and were warned by the Interior Ministry that they might have to deal with 'the enemy ... rowdy elements, hooligans and counter-revolutionaries'.[1]

The regime knew that plans had been laid by Charter 77 and other groups to commemorate the suicide of Jan Palach. Twenty years ago this day, the Prague Economics School student stood on the steps outside the Czechoslovak National Theatre in Wenceslas Square. At precisely 4 p.m. he reached for a bottle inside the plastic bag he was carrying, poured petrol over himself and set his coat alight with a match. Three days later, with 85 per cent of his body covered by burns, he died, in agony, at a Prague hospital. Aged twenty, he had left behind a note explaining that he could see no other way to protest at the Soviet invasion of Czechoslovakia five months earlier than to immolate himself. By a few brave voices since then he had been considered a martyr, but the regime regarded him as a non-person. His ashes had been removed from the cemetery outside Prague where they had originally been interred, replaced by the remains of an old-age pensioner entirely unconnected with the dead young man. Opposition groups announced they would mark the entire week from 15 to 21 January 1989 'Palach Week' and would organise a series of events to commemorate the anniversary of his death.

The name Jan Palach had barely been mentioned in the official media for two decades. Now the regime decided that it was time directly to confront his memory. On 12 January the Communist Party newspaper, *Rudé Právo* (*The Red Way*), described his suicide as 'a senseless, tragic act' and declared that all commemorative rallies or demonstrations would be banned. Two days later the paper went on the attack again: 'Dissidents who try to put at risk the lives of our youth will not be listened to,' it said. 'We shall not allow the republic to be threatened.' Most Czechs, unconcerned with politics, did not know until then that any protests had been organised for an anniversary that had generally been forgotten. Opposition at the time, as one dissident admitted, 'numbered a very few thousand throughout the country on the fringes, a few hundred at the centre, and fewer than a dozen in any position of leadership'. The unprecedented publicity ensured that there would be crowds turning up at the rallies, even if it was to see protesters being beaten up by the police.

It was a mistake to draw attention to Palach Week, as Communist leaders like the increasingly loathed Miloš Jakeš – usually nicknamed Dumpling Face because of his heavy build – confessed later. But it was intended to show where power resided in People's Czechoslovakia. In the past year the regime had sent contradictory signals to the opposition. Two months earlier Jakeš had allowed Alexander Dubček to receive an honorary degree from the University of Bologna. Over the past twenty years Dubček had maintained a discreet silence on politics, working for most of that period as a junior official in the Slovak Forestry Commission. In Italy he broke his silence for the first time, with a passionate defence of his own actions during the Prague Spring and spoke of the 'incomparable moral failure' of the Czech regime since then. The government said that it was only with reluctance that it allowed Dubček to return home. It made a firm decision then to crack down on dissent. On Human Rights Day, 10 December 1988, the Prague Party boss, Miroslav Štěpán, personally supervised police as they sprayed protesters in the centre of the city with water cannons. 'There will be no dialogue,' he declared.[2]

At the first of the Palach commemorative demonstrations on 15 January, around four and a half thousand people gathered in Wenceslas Square, far more than had shown themselves at an overtly political demonstration since 1968. It was an entirely peaceful protest. Riot police charged the demonstrators, arrested ninety-one people and beat up many more. There were protests from abroad, as expected, but it was the reaction of Czechs that surprised the dissident groups. In the past, most people, apathetic and 'in a death-like torpor' as a Charter 77 activist put it, would have left the scene to keep out of harm's way.

Now many uninvolved passers-by protested against the brutality of the police.

The next day a smaller group returned to Wenceslas Square to lay flowers at the spot where Palach had set fire to himself. Václav Havel was there and described what happened: 'I decided to stand on the sidewalk and observe the ceremony on the sidelines so that if the police intervened I would be able to deliver a report to friends and the foreign media,' he said. 'The police did intervene, but so clumsily that it aroused the interest of passers-by and immediately mushroomed into a large spontaneous demonstration. I watched the whole thing from a distance, fascinated, although I knew that sooner or later they could arrest me. And then I walked away from Wenceslas Square, to prepare my report. They arrested me on my way home.'

There were demonstrations for the next four days, all violently broken up by the police. More than five hundred people were arrested and half of them tried, mostly for hooliganism or disturbing the peace. Ota Veverka of the John Lennon Peace Club was sentenced to a year in jail. Charter 77 spokesman Alexander Vondra, who managed to lay three daffodil blossoms in honour of Palach before his arrest, received a suspended sentence and a fine of about one hundred dollars. Havel was charged with 'inciting public unrest and resisting the authorities in connection with a proscribed demonstration'. He was sent to jail for nine months. The protests from foreign governments and human rights groups abroad could safely be ignored. It was harder to dismiss the petitions calling for Havel's release at home, from people who would formerly have kept silent, like official writers' organisations and the Actors' Union. More than four thousand people signed the main petition, an unheard-of number for a protest of this kind in Czechoslovakia. 'The regime clearly had not been expecting this and did not know how to respond,' Havel said. 'It's not a problem to lock up individual dissidents, but locking up all the famous actors in the country? That was something they no longer dared to do.'

On this occasion the government gave Havel national publicity as a 'troublemaker' in an effort to discredit him. There were profiles in the press of the jailbird intellectual, emphasising his privileged upbringing and wealth. They did not have the effect intended. Most Czechs had never heard of him before. Now they knew who he was and he became established as a daring anti-Communist. 'I was a rather special prisoner,' he said. 'I was strictly isolated from the others and under strict surveillance, but nonetheless enjoying very circumspect treatment.

Compared with my previous stints in jail, this was almost like a holiday. Among other things I was in a cell with two handpicked communists who had been locked up for many years for economic crimes and were afraid to speak to me at all for fear of making their own situation worse.'[3]

The regime was satisfied that its show of strength had taught the opposition a lesson and dealt with Václav Havel. When, at a West German Embassy party, the ideology chief Jan Fojtik was asked about the playwright by an American official he was told: 'Havel's morally insignificant and has no popular appeal. Communism [here] will prevail.'[4]

TWENTY-EIGHT

THE ROUND TABLE

Warsaw, Monday 16 January 1989

AROUND THE SAME TIME that Václav Havel was arrested in Prague, General Jaruzelski was receiving the kind of rough treatment in Poland that he had not encountered for years. The General was unused to being insulted, least of all by stalwart Communists of a certain age who usually understood how to respect rank. But today a session of the Polish Communist Party began where veteran Party members harangued him for showing weakness against the enemy and for abandoning the cause of socialism. There was an unwritten rule within the Polish Communist Party that Jaruzelski would not receive the kind of personal criticism a civilian politician might face. Deference would be shown to him in public. That was ignored when the country's most senior Communists met at the vast, ugly white headquarters of the Polish United Workers' Party on the corner of New World Street and Jerusalem Avenue in the centre of Warsaw. Jaruzelski was determined to start talks with Solidarity and to reach a settlement that might ensure industrial peace in Polish factories. For the last three months Solidarity had been ready to begin negotiations. As Wałęsa said with Churchillian echoes, 'I'd be prepared to talk with the devil himself if it would do some good for Poland.' Now the General faced a showdown with Communists who wanted to block any deal with the opposition that would surrender Party power.[1]

Jaruzelski and the Prime Minister, Mieczysław Rakowski, tried to explain the power-sharing arrangement they had in mind. A majority of the Party leadership seemed doubtful. 'There was a lot of opposition,' said Dr Janusz Reykowski, a psychology professor in Warsaw and a prominent Communist who had been adviser to the Interior Ministry for twenty-five years. 'Many people in the Party thought that Solidarity was a group of foreign agents and adventurers.' The key issue was the legalisation of free trade unions. The General said that it was impossible to keep the economy stable without Solidarity, or maintain the kind of untrammelled power the Communists had possessed for decades. Then, speaking from martial law experience, he said the union could not be wiped out. 'We do not have a choice but to start these talks,' he said. The Prime Minister said there would be 'revolutionary upheaval if the Party clung on to outdated ideas'. Several times he repeated that 'we are not dreaming about giving up power . . . we are talking here about arranging to retain power'.[2]

By now well over half of the fast-dwindling membership of the Communist Party were over fifty years old. The leadership comprised nearly all men in their mid-sixties, loyalists whose best days had been those of 'socialist discipline' before Solidarity was born. As Jerzy Wiatr, a political scientist at Warsaw University and a leading figure in Polish communism, admitted: 'We could have succeeded in a confrontation with the intellectuals, but when [we] found ourselves in conflict with the workers, the whole mental house of cards began falling apart.' Many Party members did not understand Solidarity, a loose, apparently undisciplined force entirely alien to them.[3]

One of the main leaders of the Cement Group of Poland's Party diehards was Alfred Miodowicz, head of the official government-backed trade union movement, entirely an adjunct of the Communist Party. Usually a bluff, cheery, avuncular figure fond of chewing his pipe and of a quiet life, he was now in a sombre and disturbed mood. He had remembered what had happened to his organisation, the OPZZ, in the first year and four months of Solidarity's existence in 1980–81 when there had been competition between the two organisations. Solidarity had been triumphant, gaining almost ten million members, while his union and the Party were almost wiped out. Worse would happen if Solidarity was legalised, he said.

Miodowicz had a personal motive for wishing to scupper talks with Solidarity. At the end of November he had appeared in a live television debate against Lech Wałęsa. It was the first time most Poles had seen the Solidarity leader since 1981, and many people had forgotten what he looked like. Immediately, he seemed like a refreshing, encouraging and uplifting sight. Miodowicz was an experienced performer, accustomed to appearing on TV. But Wałęsa trounced him. While the Communist spoke in jargon and statistics, Wałęsa adopted his most bluff and charming 'man of the people' style. From the moment he said 'The West goes by car – and we're on a bike' the entire audience was on his side. Miodowicz had no reply, looking humiliated. Now he stared at Jaruzelski pointedly as he said that it was dangerous to hand more propaganda weapons to a popular opponent who had plenty of charisma.[4]

After more than ten hours of heated argument spread over two days, Jaruzelski finally insisted that a decision be made. He and his advisers knew the vote would be close. Some of his aides were convinced he would lose. He tried a risky new tactic. Suddenly, just before the vote was taken on legalising Solidarity, he threatened to resign if it went against him. 'I could see no other way than to blackmail them.' He persuaded the Interior Minister, General Kiszczak, his Defence Minister, General Florian Siwicki and Rakowski to resign too – 'together, we represent a real force,' he said. The General demanded an immediate vote of confidence in himself. If the Communists wanted to try governing in a constitutional crisis without the most powerful members of the regime, they would be welcome to try. The General won, overwhelmingly. The next day he announced that Round Table talks with Solidarity would begin on 6 February, at which he hoped a grand settlement of a long-running Polish crisis would be reached. It was the day the old Party died.[5]

The talks began at the elaborate white-fronted, neo-classical Radziwill Palace in Warsaw's Old Town on a blowy, grey and freezing morning. The Pope sent a message offering prayers for the success of the negotiators. Before they started he had explained to a visitor at the Vatican the dilemma that had to be solved in Poland: 'The Government has all the physical power but no influence, and the opposition has influence but no physical power.' The dissident Adam Michnik, a central figure in the negotiations, put it another way. Both sides were weak, and that is why they had to compromise. 'The authorities are too weak to trample on us. And we are too weak to topple them,' he said.[6]

There were in fact eight tables – and they were doughnut-shaped, with an empty space at the centre. From this day Round Tables – shaped to reduce friction between negotiators and suggesting equality – became the symbols of revolution in Eastern Europe. Over the next two months various teams of Solidarity activists would painstakingly negotiate a package of detailed agreements with the generals and Party officials in ninety-two sessions of talks. There were talks on working practices on the shop floor, safety in industrial plants, health and education. But all the main deals about future elections, guaranteeing rights for Solidarity and the future shape of a democratic

Poland, were made at five highly secret talks at a villa in Magdalenka, a small town twenty-five kilometres south-west of Warsaw, between Kiszczak and Wałęsa. The plush house, set amidst woods and protected by round-the-clock guards, was used as a recreation centre by the SB.

The fact that they were talking at all stunned even those Solidarity members who had worked hard towards bringing the negotiations about. When Adam Michnik arrived at the opening ceremony of the negotiations he had an uncomfortable moment. 'To get to the debate room one had to go upstairs and there was General Kiszczak welcoming the guests,' he said.

> I managed to hide in the bathroom so as not to be seen by anybody shaking hands with the former chief of police. I was afraid my wife would kick me out of the house. So I found a hiding place, waited for several minutes . . . but as I emerged Kiszczak was still there offering his hand to shake. Lights, camera, action. This was the way I lost my political virginity. Only two and a half years before I had been let out of prison, and there were my colleagues, friends from the Underground. I was aware that [something] historic was going on. The democratic opposition was finally taking a step over the threshold of legality.[7]

The public was awakened from apathy. Solidarity had secured an important concession before the Round Table talks began that the union would receive equal access to the official state media. Every night on television Poles could see the Solidarity leaders patiently explaining what had happened at that day's negotiations. Men like Geremek, Mazowiecki and Kuroń looked intelligent, decent and patriotic, not as the 'traitors' and 'hooligans' official propaganda had portrayed them. Geremek was the figure Solidarity fielded most often, a quiet, serious, polite and patient former professor of medieval history whose mild manner was surprisingly persuasive. He became a household name simply for stating straightforward, reasonable opinions shared by the overwhelming majority of people.

The Communists were equally surprised by the calibre of the opponents they were dealing with. Krzysztof Dubiński, the Interior Minister Kiszczak's private secretary, said: 'The authorities eventually saw that the people facing them were not enemies or foreign agents but normal people who were thinking in terms of the national interest.' In fact, the regime knew almost everything about the Solidarity negotiators. Kiszczak may have turned himself into a reform Communist, but he was still a secret policeman by nature and profession. He authorised an eavesdropping operation on all their phones and placed listening devices in all the rooms used by the Solidarity team and by the Church's observers at the talks.

TWENTY-NINE

SHOOT TO KILL

East Berlin, Sunday 5 February 1989

IT WAS A CLEAR but bitterly cold night, −3°C. Ice lay on the ground as two young East German men walked through the Treptow district of Berlin, laughing and joking with one another. Nobody looking at them could have guessed the desperate, bold and foolhardy deed they were about to perform. Chris Gueffroy was a twenty-year-old barman. In three months he was due to be conscripted into the army for compulsory two-year national service. He was not politically active, but he hated the idea of being ordered to join the armed forces. He used to watch a great deal of West German television, where he could learn about the outside world, and his dream was to travel. Above all he wanted to see America. His old friend, Christian Gaudian, had recently heard an extraordinary claim from an acquaintance who was a conscript with the border patrol in Thuringia. He was told that, secretly, the regime had abandoned the 'shoot to kill' policy under which guards were under strict instructions to fire on anybody who tried to cross the Berlin Wall illegally.

There was never any publicity given to 'wall-jumpers', as they were called. All news about them was kept out of the official media, although occasionally articles appeared about the twelve border guards who over the years had been killed in action performing their heroic duty towards the Fatherland. But everyone in East Germany knew that many had been shot trying to escape and some had succeeded in their attempts. Although the 'shoot to kill' policy was always denied publicly, everyone knew it existed. The two youngsters were aware that the last to die trying to cross the border illegally in Berlin was twenty-four-year-old Lutz Schmidt, who on 12 February 1987 attempted to crash a truck through the Wall at a spot near Schoenfeld Airport. He was shot through the heart by border guards. The official version in the local newspapers was that he had died 'in a tragic road accident'. But that had been two years ago. Since then the death penalty had been abolished in East Germany, Ronald Reagan had stood at the Brandenburg Gate eighteen months earlier and pleaded with the Soviets to 'tear down this wall' and just three weeks ago Erich Honecker had signed a Co-operation in Europe Treaty which stated that everybody 'possessed the unrestricted right to leave . . . and to return to their own country'. The two friends, Gueffroy and Gaudian, were convinced the rumour that they had heard was true. They decided to test the softer image East Germany was presenting to the world.

At around 11 p.m. they approached the Britz district canal, the border separating the East from the Neukölln neighbourhood of West Berlin. Nearby was a well-known area of allotments. The two friends broke into a garden hut and found a spiked hoe, which they tied to some strong rope and managed to turn into a makeshift grappling hook. Their plan was to use the hoe to haul themselves over the first barrier, a three-and-a-half-metre-high barred fence. They managed without much difficulty. On their way to the border Gueffroy had joked with Gaudian, saying 'Imagine, soon I'll be calling my mother from the Ku'damm [West Berlin's main shopping boulevard] saying "Hi, mum guess where I am?"' Gaudian thought that perhaps he would.

Five metres further on there was a second, lower fence, which they also managed to climb with relative ease. But this was wired and they set off a loud flashing alarm. The area was suddenly floodlit by searchlights. Border guards from the nearest watchtower were alerted and they fired warning shots. The two youngsters panicked and made a dash towards the third, and last, of the barriers before the border, a metal lattice fence. They ran into two guards who opened fire with automatic rifles. Gueffroy was hit in the chest by ten bullets and died instantly. Gaudian was hit on the foot and fell to the ground.

The pathologist's report recorded 'death due to natural causes'. Gueffroy's mother was not allowed to see his body. She objected to a cremation, but the authorities went ahead with one anyway. It was standard Stasi practice for such incidents, to remove for ever any possible evidence of bullet holes in a body. Usually only the close family attended a funeral. On this occasion there were more than 120 mourners who had heard of the incident. Gaudian was arrested and at Pankow District Court on 24 May he was sentenced to three years in jail for 'attempted illegal border crossing'. The two guards, Ingo Heinrich who fired the fatal shots, and his comrade in arms Andreas Kühnpast, were given awards and merit payments of 150 East Marks. Their superiors told them 'not to lose sleep over it . . . you did the right thing', though they were both posted to other duties.*

This time the regime could not hush up the murder, as usual. The official report said in its usual GDR-speak that the border guards 'carried through border-tactical activities and placed both violators under arrest'. But an enterprising reporter from the West German *Frankfurter Rundschau* newspaper was smuggled into the cremation and the story was given mass coverage on Western TV, watched by most East Germans. Honecker faced an international outcry. The Soviets sent a polite, but stern, protest, wondering if the death had been strictly necessary. Even Honecker realised that the time had passed when young people could be shot on the border with impunity.† Two months later he lifted the 'shoot to kill' instruction. But as it had never officially existed, and Honecker had a year and a half earlier looked the West German Chancellor Helmut Kohl in the face and sworn it did not exist, the decision to abandon it was a state secret. Chris Gueffroy was the last of 238 people to be shot seeking a route to freedom through the Berlin Wall. But he was not the last to die. On 8 March Winfried Freudenberg, a thirty-three-year-old worker in a chemical factory near Berlin, filled a home-made balloon with gas and flew over the border. He made it to the West Berlin suburb of Zehlendorf, but he did not live to taste freedom. His balloon crashed and he died instantly when he hit the earth.[1]

*Both were tried in the spring of 1992 and their defence was that 'at the time we were obeying the laws and commands of the German Democratic Republic'. Heinrich was sentenced to three and a half years in prison and Kühnpast was given a two-year suspended sentence in a trial which set the precedent in post-Communist reunited Germany that officials 'obeying orders' under the legal East Germany before November 1989 could be prosecuted. A few senior politicians were later convicted, as well as border guards and low-level officials.

† Documentary proof that the shoot-to-kill policy existed did not surface until 2004. In 1966 the then Defence Minister Heinz Hoffman put the order on paper: 'Anyone who does not respect our border will feel the bullet.' In 1974 the leadership toughened up the rules and issued a written instruction that border guard commanders should be punished if the number of successful escapes went up. Honecker stated: 'Firearms are to be ruthlessly used in the event of attempts to break through the border – and the comrades who have successfully used their firearms are to be commended.'

THIRTY

THE FRIENDSHIP BRIDGE

Termez, Afghanistan, Wednesday 15 February 1989

LIEUTENANT-GENERAL BORIS GROMOV had been given an unenviable task. A trim, handsome and dashing forty-five-year-old, he was the commander of Soviet forces in Afghanistan. His orders were to organise the Red Army's withdrawal after nearly ten years of futile war in the Afghan hills, but not to make it look like a defeat. Mikhail Gorbachev and the Soviet high command had repeatedly vowed that Soviet forces would not leave in disarray, as the Americans had done from Vietnam. They could recall the chaotic sight of American helicopters taking off from the roof of the US Embassy in Saigon and demanded that nothing of the kind should happen for the world to see in Kabul. Just a few days before the final troops withdrew, in conversation at the Kremlin with Shevardnadze, the Soviet leader had said that 'a defeatist position is not permissible. We must not appear before the world in our underpants, or even without any.'[1]

A retreat is the least satisfying military manoeuvre for a general to make and often the trickiest. Gromov executed the Soviet Union's final, painful withdrawal from Afghanistan with skill, efficiency and some panache. Under the terms of the Geneva Accords Russian tanks, artillery and soldiers had been on the move along the Salang Highway back to the USSR since the previous May. They were leaving by the same route the invasion force had come, crossing the brackish Amu Darya River over the Soviet-built wrought iron 'Friendship Bridge'. Gromov, like the 100,000 or so troops he commanded, was glad to be going home. The son of a celebrated Red Army officer who was killed crossing the Dnieper in World War Two, he had a meteoric career. He was a company commander by the age of twenty-four, a full Colonel before he was thirty-five, and a Major-General at thirty-nine. His birthday was 7 November, the holiest day in the Soviet calendar, as it celebrated the anniversary of the Bolshevik Revolution.

Like so many of the Soviet officer class, Gromov had been a deeply committed Communist. Then, gradually, doubts began to creep in, prompted principally by the Afghanistan conflict. He loathed Afghanistan, which he thought was a backward country undeserving of the benefits socialism could bring. He hated the unwinnable war his political masters had launched without thinking through the consequences. He was now on his third tour of duty there. The first had been in 1980 as a colonel, just after the invasion began. He had been commander of Soviet forces for the last two years. He had seen comrades fall and suffered personal tragedy when his beloved wife was killed in a plane crash in the Carpathian Mountains. He barely had any time to spend with his sons Maksim and Andrei, who were growing up without a parent while he was performing his duty in that pestilential place, Afghanistan.

Unheroic the task may be, but he was determined that there would be an orderly and dignified retreat. Above all he wanted to ensure as few deaths as he could of 'my boys'. Nearly 15,000 Soviet soldiers, mostly young conscripts, died in vain in a war that he had realised for many years held little strategic value for the Soviet Union and had nothing to do with furthering the cause of communism. More than 53,000 had been wounded. Publicly Gromov bristled at any suggestion that the Soviets had failed in Afghanistan. When troops began returning home last May he declared to journalists: 'The troop withdrawal is not a defeat. It is the completion of an internationalist mission ... None of our units, even the smallest one, has ever retreated. That is why there is no talk of a military defeat.'[2]

Privately, among his aides and select comrades in arms, he acknowledged the truth. That was why he wanted to reduce the number of casualties – at least on the Soviet side. He was still fighting a war, though. He had to protect the convoys of men and matériel heading home from attack by the guerrillas. He ordered Soviet special forces to destroy scores of villages along the main route back to the Soviet Union, along the Salang Highway to Termez. Hundreds of people died in the last few weeks of a conflict that cost more than a million Afghan lives and created more than three million refugees.

Four weeks before the withdrawal deadline, with long columns of Soviet hardware and troops heading towards the Friendship Bridge, Gromov received a message from the Mujahideen leader who controlled the high ground along most of the Soviets' line of retreat. Ahmad Shah Massoud offered a ceasefire: 'We have put up with the war and your presence here for ten years now,' he said. 'God willing, we will put up with you for a few more more days. But if you begin military action against us, we will give you a worthy response.' It had a limited effect. Fighting continued between the departing Soviets and other guerrilla groups until the bitter end. The weather took its toll. The convoys were held up by freezing conditions in the mountains. Snow blocked the highway for days at a time. An avalanche killed the last Soviet troops to die in Afghanistan.[3]

Gromov's detachment of the Soviet Fortieth Army, 500 troops from the 201st Reconnaissance Division, reached the Friendship Bridge early in the morning on the deadline day agreed in the Geneva Accords. The military mounted an elaborate show to keep up appearances on their side of the border. It was made to look more like a victory parade than the return of an exhausted and defeated army. The small town of Termez was bedecked with bunting and regimental flags. A military band played marching songs. A huge red banner at the point where the troops reached Soviet soil read: 'The Order of the Motherland has been Fulfilled'. Crowds of veterans' families were specially flown in and garlanded the troops with flowers. However it was dressed up, though, the retreat from Kabul was a humiliation for the Soviet Union. It was a point carefully considered by East Europeans who dreamed of soon seeing the Red Army leave their own lands.

The last Russian soldier to leave Afghanistan – defying normal military protocol – was Lieutenant-General Boris Vsevolodovich Gromov. He was a flamboyant man with a flair for the dramatic and for public relations opportunities. He had told his men, and reporters, in advance that he would not leave until he knew all his troops were safely in the USSR. His gesture caused trouble with his superiors. When the Minister of Defence, Marshal Dmitri Yazov, heard of Gromov's intentions he called the General and barked a complaint: 'Why are you leaving last, and not first, as a commander should?' Gromov replied: 'This was my own decision ... I consider that five and a half years' service in Afghanistan gives me the right to make a small breach of army traditions.' The Minister did not respond. At around 9 a.m. Gromov told his driver to go the last few hundred metres across the river ahead of him in another vehicle. He drove his own armoured personnel carrier to the bridge. There, he hopped out and calmly walked into Soviet territory. He turned round briefly, looking back into Afghanistan one final time before he was greeted by a Russian television crew and by his fourteen-year-old son Maksim clutching a fistful of carnations.[4]

It was not the end of the story of the USSR's tragic involvement in a land that has a long tradition of defeating foreign invaders. Najibullah knew that he could not survive long in power after the Soviet withdrawal. The Mujahideen controlled four-fifths of the country and were massing for a final assault. They were about to capture the country's second city, Jalalabad, and preparing to attack Kabul. Early in March, Najibullah bombarded Gorbachev with desperate pleas for help to buy some time. 'He was imploring us with demands . . . to launch air strikes from Soviet territory – or else in a few days everything would collapse,' said Chernyaev.

Shevardnadze, and Kryuchkov, who was now head of the KGB, supported the idea. It was a curious call by Shevardnadze, given his opposition to Soviet involvement in the war. But he had met Najibullah several times, including a few weeks earlier when he had assured him that the Soviets would not abandon him completely. He had already told Gorbachev in private that 'we must recognise we are leaving the country in a lamentable state . . . its towns and villages have been destroyed; the capital is starving'. Now he pleaded with him that they must back Najib and not break their word. 'It's the only way,' he said. 'Otherwise, it's treachery . . . We promised and if we don't we're deserting friends . . . what will the Third World say?' Gorbachev put his foot down and nearly lost his temper with his Foreign Minister: 'No. Absolutely not. I am definitely against all bombings or anything of the kind,' he said. 'While I am General Secretary I won't permit anyone to break the promise we made in front of the whole world [to withdraw]. Didn't we know what we are doing when we decided to withdraw our troops? There won't be any other answer than a refusal to drop any bombs.' Now the Soviets' long agony in Afghanistan was over.[5]

THIRTY-ONE

THE CURTAIN FALLS

The Kremlin, Friday 3 March 1989

THE HUNGARIAN PRIME MINISTER, Miklós Németh, was tense and worried as he entered Gorbachev's office soon after 10 a.m. He knew the Soviet leader reasonably well from Gorbachev's visits to Budapest. He liked and admired him enormously. Yet he was apprehensive about the reaction he would receive to the momentous news he was about to relay. The youthful-looking Németh told him that the Hungarians planned to tear down the 300 kilometres of barbed wire and electronic fences that comprised Hungary's border with Austria. 'It has outlived its usefulness and only serves to stop citizens of the GDR and Romania who try to escape illegally to the West,' he said. Gorbachev was entirely unfazed. For more than forty years the Iron Curtain had been the most powerful symbol of Soviet strength and of the extent of its European empire. It was the stark physical reminder of continuing ideological battles between East and West. Now a Hungarian Prime Minister was proposing, here in the Kremlin, to tear down this barrier that had been considered so vital to Soviet interests. Not so long ago his predecessors would have treated the Magyar as a colonial upstart and had him sent to the Lubyanka or running a saltworks. Gorbachev knew how significant this moment was. But he barely reacted. Still, Németh was cautious, expecting a further response. He said 'that of course we will have to talk to comrades' elsewhere in the Warsaw Pact. Gorbachev, as Németh later recalled, just looked distractedly at him and said: 'We have a strict regime on our borders, but we are also becoming more open.'[1]

In Hungary the Iron Curtain had been corroding for a long time and was now beginning to fall apart. In the 1950s and 1960s there had been minefields on the Eastern side. They were removed in the mid-1960s, leaving a wire with a low-tension current that was constantly going wrong and sending regular false alarms. As Gyula Kovács, head of the border guard command, said, the fence had become an embarrassment. His men spent a lot of their time chasing animals, but they had to make checks every time an alarm sounded. 'Usually an animal triggered it off,' Kovács said. 'But the soldiers in the response units would only know later and could tell only from footprints. Sometimes it was a hare, sometimes a pheasant or a deer. In one case it was a bear. We were surprised by that as [we thought] there were no bears in Hungary.'[2]

At the end of the previous year the Interior Minister, István Horváth, suggested to Németh that the fences be dismantled – for reasons partly symbolic, partly practical. 'It was costing millions to maintain . . . and for what?' he said. Hungarians had been allowed to travel freely for a number of years and by 1989 six million a year were going abroad, mainly to the West. More than twenty-five million tourists were entering Hungary. 'Every year we had between 200 and 250 cases of foreigners trying to cross illegally, while the maximum number of Hungarians is ten a year,' Horváth said. 'These were drunks, children with bad school reports and husbands sneaking away from their wives. With such a huge legal traffic, what was the point of catching this handful?'[3]

The economist Németh, who subsequently became a banker, knew it would cost upwards of US$ 50 million to revamp the fence and make it effective. It was money Hungary did not possess. 'I decided that we did not want to spend this money for this end,' he said. If Gorbachev had ordered the Hungarians to rebuild the fence, Németh would reluctantly have agreed to go along with it. He was amazed by Gorbachev's insouciance. He dropped what a year or so earlier would have been another bombshell. Németh predicted that, following the Hungarian government's decision a few weeks earlier to legalise all political parties, there would almost certainly be free elections in Hungary quite soon. The Hungarian Communists would offer Polish-type Round Table talks with the opposition, starting in June. How would the Soviets react? 'I don't know when we will have these elections,' Németh told him. 'But as you have 80,000 troops stationed in our country, and bearing in mind the experience of 1956 . . . would you repeat what you did then?' Gorbachev, looking intently at the Hungarian, replied in an instant: 'I don't agree with the multi-party system . . . or with the introduction of a multi-party system in Hungary. But that's not my responsibility. That is up to you. But you can be certain that there would be no instruction or order from us to crush it.'

The Soviet leader had an equally remarkable interview later the same day with the Hungarian Communist Party chief, Károly Grósz, who in private asked him to remove all nuclear weapons from Hungarian soil. These were the missiles that Grósz did not even know were based in his country until after he had succeeded Kádár as General Secretary. Gorbachev agreed at once. Grósz was surprised and tried to push further. 'To reinforce the Party's legitimacy with the people, and to distance us from the memories of 1956, I put it to you that all Soviet troops should leave Hungary.' Gorbachev said they would – and soon – but he wanted to try negotiating with the Americans first to obtain an agreement for troop reductions in Nato at the same time. But even if he did not get one, Soviet troops would withdraw from Hungary. 'It is not in the West's interest to have instability in Hungary. I am not concerned they will interfere. I will do everything that is compatible with . . . preserving stability.' As an earnest of Soviet intent, more than 500 tanks and 5,000 troops were withdrawn from Hungary within three weeks of their meeting. Grósz said later that he was dumbfounded. 'Every time I asked Gorbachev for something that I believed would be very . . . delicate from the standpoint of Soviet interests, he always said yes,' said Grósz. 'I came to the conclusion that he and Shevardnadze had in mind a plan to disengage the Soviet Union entirely from Eastern Europe.'[4]

Grósz was right. But it was not so much a carefully worked-out plan as a conviction that they would let the satellite states go the way they wished and the Soviet Union would live with the consequences. They wanted to withdraw troops gradually, though, for domestic reasons. At a private meeting just before the Hungarian delegation arrived, Gorbachev said that as far as he was concerned he was ready to remove all Russian forces from Eastern Europe. Shevardnadze said he agreed but saw the pitfalls. 'Once we start withdrawing troops, the howling will begin,' he said. 'They will say "what did we fight for? What did twenty-seven million of our soldiers die for in World War Two?" Are we going to renounce all that?'[5]

When the East German leaders heard that the Hungarians were dismantling the border, they instinctively felt the threat to themselves. The Iron Curtain was vital to them to keep their compatriots imprisoned. 'When the Hungarians opened the border, it was especially important because the socialist bloc as a whole took no part in the decision,' said Günter Schabowski, the East Berlin Party boss. 'It was threatening to the leadership [who] didn't want to believe it at first.' Honecker called his Defence Minister, Heinz Kessler, and demanded: 'OK, tell me, what have the Hungarians been up to? Do you know anything about it?' Did the Hungarians comprehend the consequences, he wanted to know. Kessler replied that he had been as surprised as Honecker. Kessler then called his opposite number in Budapest, Colonel-General Ferenc Kárpáti, and demanded an explanation. Kárpáti had been briefed by Németh, who told him to play for time and obfuscate if he was asked any direct questions from Berlin. 'If we start to explain the full situation we'll give ourselves away and get into even worse trouble.' Kárpáti prevaricated and told Kessler that he did not agree with the decision either, 'but don't get agitated, it was done entirely for financial reasons'. He assured him that the Hungarians would secure the border to make certain that East Germans could not get through. Honecker was not entirely convinced. He dispatched the GDR's Foreign Minister, Oskar Fischer, to Moscow to protest against Hungary's action. Shevardnadze gave a simple, curt answer that 'we can't do anything about it. This is a matter between the GDR and Hungary.'[6]

According to Schabowski, that was the moment that some of the Party bosses realised 'that we could not rely 100 per cent on Moscow. The opening of the border was the beginning of the end of the socialist bloc ... Some people in the GDR, myself included, thought that the GDR was not safe, because Moscow was no longer protecting it and who else could guarantee its existence?'[7]

Twelve days after the Hungarian delegation returned home from Moscow, a vast demonstration clogged the streets of central Budapest. The Fifteenth of March had for a century been an important traditional holiday. It was the anniversary of the start of the 1848 Hungarian Revolution against the Habsburg empire. That had been crushed by the armies of Tsar Nicholas I, which had gone to support the Austrians. Under the Communists any celebrations of the day were banned, as they could prompt anti-Russian protests. But an estimated 100,000 people marched through the Hungarian capital. Some demonstrated for environmental causes under the Danube Circle banner; some were demanding better treatment for the Transylvanian refugees; some were members of the newly formed political parties like the Democratic Forum or the Association of Free Democrats, which had existed as legal political parties for only a few weeks. On that morning the government had declared that 15 March would again be a national holiday, and that talks with the opposition would begin within a few weeks, leading to free elections within a year. At a vast gathering in Kossuth Square, in front of Hungary's extraordinary nineteenth-century Parliament building, the dissident philosopher János Kis, one of the main opposition thinkers of the past decades, said: 'History has pronounced its death sentence on the system called socialism.' That he could say it, without a policeman in sight, showed how complete was the surrender of Hungary's old regime.

THIRTY-TWO

THE CAUTIOUS AMERICAN

Washington DC, Saturday 1 April 1989

PRESIDENT BUSH WAS A cautious man. It was his greatest virtue according to his Secretary of State, James Baker, the crucial factor in the resolve he showed in the years when the Soviet empire was imploding. His chief adviser on Russia, the gifted, ambitious and determined Condoleezza Rice, has said that Bush's immense, reassuring calm was a vital factor in bringing about the end of the Cold War. His great contribution, as another American politician said, 'was what he didn't do, as well as what he did. He played it cool. He helped to grease the skids on which the Communists were slid from power. There was little Bush could have done to promote the revolutions of 1989 . . . There is much an American President could have done to derail [them].' For those who did not work for him, Bush's caution could be maddeningly frustrating.[1]

Bush decided he would take his time to decide how to deal with Gorbachev and the Soviet Union. Soon after he was elected to the White House, but before he was inaugurated, he sent a message to the Soviet leader via the former Secretary of State, Henry Kissinger, still an immensely influential man in the making of American foreign policy and diplomacy. Kissinger went to Moscow at the start of the year for a highly secret meeting with Gorbachev and his key adviser Alexander Yakovlev. He delivered a handwritten letter to Gorbachev in which the President promised to continue the progress made in Soviet/US relations under Reagan, but not immediately. He hoped Gorbachev would understand, he wrote, if the new administration took time for 'a pause' to consider various options. Gorbachev was not sure he did understand. He was expecting a seamless transition, that Bush would simply start where Reagan had left off. Though he learned to respect Reagan, Gorbachev was getting tired of hearing the same anecdotes repeated over and over again when they met. He wanted to deal with someone whose attention span and grasp of detail were equal to his own. He hoped Bush would be a brighter, younger version of Reagan and that America was too committed to their 'partnership of understanding', as he put it, to change course now.

Bush wanted to convince himself that Gorbachev was not 'too good to be true'. He ordered a thoroughgoing review of American policy on the Soviet Union and Eastern Europe. In his first weeks as President, he held a series of seminars at the White House and at weekends in his mansion at Kennebunkport, in Maine. They were delivered by a wide range of historians, economists, academics, journalists and staff from America's most influential foreign policy think-tanks. Most of them pointed to Afghanistan, the Polish talks, Hungary, all of the Soviet talk about the 'Sinatra Doctrine' to show how the world was being transformed. He took seriously the advice from Condoleezza Rice that even if Gorbachev was ousted, 'it would be hard for the Soviets to reverse . . . to put the genie back in the bottle'. Baker, though as cautious as the President was, thought 'there was no other show in town . . . and Gorbachev has a good show'.[2]

Yet for Bush there remained doubts. He well recalled their last conversation, at a reception on Governors Island in New York City, shortly after Gorbachev's triumphant UN speech. At one point during the lunch Reagan said that a recent poll showed that 85 per cent of Americans supported the new US relationship with Moscow. Gorbachev directed his response to Bush: 'I'm pleased to hear that. The name of the game is continuity.' Bush said, 'What assurances can you give me that I can pass on to American businessmen who want to invest in the Soviet Union that perestroika and glasnost will succeed?' Gorbachev shot back a curt reply that Bush thought petulant: 'Not even Jesus Christ knows the answer to that question.' Later, in more emollient mood, he told Bush:

> I know what people are telling you now – that you've won the election, you've got to go slow, you've got to be careful, you've got to review, that you can't trust us, that we're doing all this for show. You'll see soon enough that I'm *not* doing this for show, and I'm not doing this to undermine you or surprise you or take advantage of you. I'm engaged in real politics. I'm doing this because I need to. I'm doing this because there's a revolution taking place in my country. I started it. And they all applauded me when I started it in 1986, and now they

> don't like it so much. But it's going to be a revolution nonetheless . . . don't misread me.[3]

That left Bush uncertain. So did the sceptics who warned Bush about Soviet intentions. His National Security Advisor, Brent Scowcroft, thought Gorbachev was the 'clever bear' who followed the Brezhnev practice of pursuing expansionist goals while lulling the West into a false sense of security. Gorbachev was a threat precisely because he appeared so reassuring. 'Gorbachev's goal was to restore dynamism to the Socialist system and to revitalise the Soviet Union domestically and internationally to compete with the West,' Scowcroft said.

> Gorbachev is potentially more dangerous than his predecessors, each of whom, through some aggressive move, had saved the West from the dangers of its own wishful thinking about the Soviet Union before it was too late. Gorbachev was different. He wanted to kill us with kindness rather than bluster. He was saying things we wanted to hear, making numerous seductive proposals to seize and maintain the propaganda high ground in the battle for international public opinion . . . My fear was that Gorbachev could talk us into disarming without the Soviets doing anything fundamental to their own military structure and that, in a decade or so, we could face a more serious threat than ever before.[4]

Scowcroft was a highly experienced soldier, an acknowledged foreign affairs expert as well as a close friend of the President. Bush trusted him. Both of them were still receiving daily reports from the CIA about the strength of the USSR, including its economic power. These were helpful only up to a point. The CIA somehow missed the fact that its main enemy was dying and its empire was withering away, said Admiral William Crowe, Chairman of the Joint Chiefs of Staff under President Bush, later. 'They talked about the Soviet Union as though they never read the newspapers, much less developed clandestine intelligence,' he commented. Every intelligence agency, for its own bureaucratic as well as ideological reasons, has a vested interest in overstating the threat posed by an adversary. Often they tend to base their analyses on the 'better to be safe than sorry' principle.

Many operatives in Langley had a more accurate picture of the chaos and bankruptcy of the system. 'But even if we knew, we would never have been able to publish it,' said the CIA's chief Soviet analyst for two and a half decades, Douglas MacEachin. 'Had we done so, people would have been calling for my head.' Heretical views seldom reached the White House or the upper reaches of the National Security Council. So the CIA was constantly reporting that the economies of the Soviet Union and some of the satellite states were growing. 'They used simply to take what the Soviets officially announced, discount it a per cent and put it out,' Mark Palmer, Ambassador to Hungary and later a distinguished State Department Kremlinologist, said. 'And it was just wrong. Anybody who had spent time ... [there] in the towns and villages could look around and see that it was just crazy.'[5]

Unusually, on 1 April Robert Gates, the former CIA Director and now the Agency's main point man in the White House, went public with his doubts. He said in a speech in Brussels that neither Gorbachev nor 'his power structure were irrevocably committed to reform' and warned of 'prolonged turbulence' in the Soviet Union and its empire. He repeated his claim that Gorbachev was still committed to the dictatorship of the Communist Party, which remained untouched and untouchable. Soon afterwards another ardent Cold Warrior in the Bush administration questioned the point of further rapprochement with the Soviets. The new US Defense Secretary, Dick Cheney, appeared on a TV talk show. He speculated: 'If I had to guess today I would guess that Gorbachev will ultimately fail ... and [be] replaced by someone far more hostile to the West.' Both were told by the President to keep silent about their doubts in public. But the Soviets were seething.

Gorbachev's long-term objective was to reach further arms limitation agreements with America, massively reduce Soviet defence spending and obtain huge loans from the US to prop up the Soviet economy. He was prepared – if it came to the point – to dismantle the 'outer empire' to achieve these goals. But the lack of enthusiasm for him and his reforms that came from the US made things harder for him at home. He constantly had to watch his back in case the Kremlin conservatives and the Soviet military delivered blows against him. The Russian generals were deeply unhappy about some of the criticism they were now hearing from Washington. After he saw Cheney's television performance the Chief of the Soviet General Staff, General Mikhail Moiseyev, thundered: 'Are we sure we know what we are doing with these people? Haven't we made a mistake in believing that we can do business on a mutual basis with them?' He was further enraged at the beginning of April when the Pentagon leaked a story claiming – wrongly, as it turned out – that the Soviets had been sending long-range bombers to Libya. Even the patient and cheerful Shevardnadze was infuriated when, three days after Gates's Brussels speech, the US State Department made a claim – which turned out to be true – that the Soviets had been caught trying to place listening devices in the American Consulate in Leningrad. He said that the Americans were 'waging an old and disagreeable kind of campaign against us'. It was sounding like the Cold War language of a decade or more earlier.[6]

Gorbachev complained to his old sparring partner and one of his earliest supporters in the West, Margaret Thatcher. They met at the start of April when Gorbachev made a brief visit to the UK. He told her in private at 10 Downing Street that he was 'enraged' by Washington. Bush's 'pause' was an obstacle, he said. 'Why does it take so long for a President who was part of the previous administration to work out his own approach? You have several times vouched for President Bush,' he added. Had she not assured him that the new President would pick up where Reagan had left off? That was not happening. 'Instead . . . nothing except a lot of petty harassments. The whole situation is intolerable.' Thatcher advised him to be patient. 'I know George Bush and James Baker very well,' she replied. 'I do not see how they could . . . contradict President Reagan's course. Of course, Bush is a very different person. Reagan was an idealist . . . Bush is a more balanced person. He gives more attention to detail. But on the whole he will continue the Reagan line.'[7]

Gorbachev went away slightly mollified. He trusted Thatcher and he knew that everything he said would be passed on to Washington. As it was. Thatcher tended to agree with the Soviet leader. She had already, six weeks earlier, told Baker that she was 'worried by the apparent air of relaxation in Washington'. She advised the Americans: 'Don't let things linger. Don't let them lie fallow.' Now, immediately after Gorbachev left her office, she sent Bush a note telling him how angry Gorbachev had been – 'and with good reason'. She said the administration was taking an awfully long time to make its mind up.[8]

Bush had another reason to be hesitant. He had often said that personal relationships among leaders were vital. 'If a foreign leader knows the character and heartbeat of [another] there is apt to be less miscalculation on either side,' he wrote. He still had doubts about Gorbachev's character, dating from the Russian's visit to Washington in 1987 when the INF Treaty was signed. Bush felt that 'Gorbymania' had turned the Soviet leader's head. He had seen it for himself, he told Scowcroft. 'We were to go from the Soviet Embassy to the White House in the same motorcade and he was running a little late, although it didn't seem to concern him,' Bush said. 'He impulsively asked me ... to get in the same limousine with him. As we drove along, the crowds were enormous ... At one point, I told him I wished he had time to stop and speak to people, and that he would be well received. A minute later the limo screeched to a halt ... Secret service agents from both the Soviet Union and the US rushed to get into position as he plunged into a surprised and responsive crowd ... shaking hands and greeting them in Russian ... it was like adrenaline to him. He got back in the car visibly uplifted.'[9]

Bush was envious of Gorbachev's popularity – he seldom saw adoring crowds like that at his own appearances. But there was a larger point. Gorbachev's skill at public relations, his headline-grabbing initiatives, put pressure on him to match the Russian for rhetoric. 'I'll be damned if Gorbachev should dominate world public opinion forever,' Bush wrote with frustration in a private letter to an old friend of his, the Aga Khan.[10]

After many revisions – because the President did not think the document imaginative enough – Condoleezza Rice was finally given the job of producing the Bush administration's policy on the Soviet Union and Central Europe. The top-secret National Intelligence Estimate 11–4–89 was far better written and much more positive about reforms in the USSR. 'The Soviet Union's use of military power as a lever abroad is likely to reduce further,' it said. 'The process Gorbachev has set in motion ... is likely to lead to lasting changes in Soviet behaviour.' Its final conclusion, though, was typical Bush. The Soviet empire would probably crumble on its own. America did not have to do anything to hasten the process. He decided, with due caution, to wait and see.[11]

THIRTY-THREE

THE LOYAL OPPOSITION

Warsaw, Tuesday 4 April 1989

IN POLAND THE FORMER JAILERS had been talking with their former prisoners for nearly two months. At last a historic deal was struck between Lech Wałęsa and General Jaruzelski which paved the way for the first democratic elections in the Soviet bloc for nearly forty-five years. It was hard and often painful going and at the end neither side left the Round Table entirely satisfied. But both the Solidarity leader and the Communist Party boss knew they could sell the agreement to their sceptical followers.

The deal did not seem like a surrender by the regime. It legalised Solidarity and recognised the union as an official opposition. This was a victory for the union. But after weeks of haggling the best Wałęsa's team of negotiators were offered was a semi-free election, which on the face of it seemed gerrymandered to ensure that the Communist Party could not lose. Thirty-five per cent of the seats in the Lower House, the Sejm, would be contested freely. The rest would be reserved for the Communists and their allies. The 100 seats in the Upper House, the Senate, would all be elected freely, but the arithmetic suggested that there was no way that Solidarity could win outright. The arrangement was based on the elections that had just been held nine days earlier in the Soviet Union, which had allowed opposition candidates to stand for the first time. That, too, was fixed to guarantee a Communist victory in a Gorbachev-designed Congress of People's Deputies, though it saw the election of a sizeable group of former dissidents including Andrei Sakharov. Wałęsa particularly disliked the part of the deal that established a presidency, specially created with Jaruzelski in mind, who had control of the army and the police. He told Kiszczak that 'there has to be a more democratic President. A presidency as you suggest would probably end up as a President for life and you could probably only get rid of him by execution . . . We don't want to end up in a corner worse than Stalinism.' Yet he eventually agreed, convinced that an imperfect deal was better than no deal. He shrewdly saw further than his advisers the historic possibilities that it could offer Solidarity.[1]

The Communist chieftains never imagined that they would lose power. 'We do not see that as possibly on the horizon,' Prime Minister Rakowski told the General. 'We will create a position where we share power with the opposition . . . it would be a ten- to fifteen-year process.' Jaruzelski was willing to go along with the agreement, though some high-ranking officials counselled caution. Professor Wiatr, the Warsaw University politics professor and influential Party figure, warned: 'They massively underestimated the calibre of the opposition. They became victims of their own wishful thinking.'[2]

Wałęsa agreed about the timetable. He was telling supporters that Solidarity would be sharing power 'at the end of the century'. Bronisław Geremek said that the aim of the Party bosses was to preserve their position. At the negotiating table 'they used to say, flatly, that they had the power. We could only answer, yes, but don't forget we are the people and that is why you have come to find us . . . We insisted we would accept limited elections this time, but never again.'[3]

Some Solidarity activists, the radicals, accused Wałęsa of selling out. Anna Walentynowycz, whose sacking from the Lenin Shipyard nine years earlier was the spark for the Solidarity revolution, was a marginalised figure now. But many listened to her when she begged the union not to sign an agreement. 'Up until the Round Table Communism was a dying corpse,' she said. A deal with the regime now would bring it back to life. Wałęsa pointed out that the Party was still in control of the army and the police, the Russians could invade if they believed their empire was under threat and Poland was surrounded by Communist countries. He repeatedly insisted that Solidarity had to be 'realistic'.[4]

The deal was finally agreed with a shake of the hands between Wałęsa and Kiszczak at Magdalenka. A bishop blessed the agreement 'in the name of the Father, the Son and the Holy Ghost'. The Communist secret policeman, a devout atheist and cynic all his life, looked bemused and simply shrugged his shoulders.

THIRTY-FOUR

THE DICTATOR PAYS HIS DEBTS

Bucharest, Wednesday 12 April 1989

THE DICTATOR HAD LET IT BE KNOWN that he would be making an important announcement. Romanians were weary of their duty to pay attention to the leader's grand statements of intent. They invariably went on for an exceedingly long time, were drearily read out in meaningless Marxist-Leninist jargon, and spelled bad news. Nevertheless, if it happened to coincide with the two hours a day that power was switched on in their neighbourhoods, people with TVs watched their sets. This time it really was important – and in a country now so inured to grinding hardship, exceptionally bad news. Ceauşescu announced triumphantly that all of Romania's foreign debt had been cleared, seven months ahead of schedule. Today, the statement said, was a great day for national independence.

Briefly, some Romanians may have imagined that at last the regime might stock the shelves with food that had been sold to Western Europe to repay the debts. They were wrong. All the exports would continue in the interests of sovereignty so that Romania would remain independent. The tight rationing of meat, eggs, milk, flour, sugar – almost all foodstuffs – would stay in place. Some, according to the statement, might even become stricter in coming months. All the restrictions on using energy would continue. In the ugly and crumbling apartment blocks where most of the people lived, the past winter had been bitterly cold. Hundreds of old people had been found in their beds, wrapped in overcoats but dead from hypothermia. Queues for bread were getting longer; fresh vegetables were almost impossible to find. Now Romanians were told there would be no improvement to living standards. They realised they would never benefit from the sacrifices that they had been forced to make for so many years. 'That was the most miserable time of all,' teacher Alex Serban said. 'And we had to put up with being told we were in a Golden Age. Our hatred of

Ceauşescu was a national obsession, and hatred of ourselves too for just accepting what he had done to the country as an unalterable fact of life.'[1]

The Ceauşescus turned Romania's back on the outside world, and the world ignored Romania. The country was less significant to the West than it had been. The changes in Poland and Hungary, the Soviet Union's warmer relationship with the US, had made Romania irrelevant to the West's strategic interests. Ceauşescu was no longer welcome in Western capitals and foreign leaders no longer sang his praises. But he was seldom criticised either. Romania was a closed country. The regime rarely permitted Western journalists to visit and little reliable information came out. There were hardly any protests of any kind against the dictatorship, but occasionally they happened and merited brief paragraphs in Western news reports. A few weeks before the announcement about foreign debt, on 2 March the forty-seven-year-old painter Liviu Babeş died after setting himself alight in front of a group of Western tourists in Braşov, drawing attention to the abuses of the regime. He carried a placard reading 'Romania = Auschwitz'.

Romanians are passionate about football and twice matches were a catalyst for rare anti-Ceauşescu demonstrations. There were scuffles between the police and a few fans at a local derby between the two big Bucharest teams, Steaua and Dinamo, the previous June. It began as the kind of hooliganism common at soccer matches, but turned into a small anti-government protest. The crowd was quickly dispersed. Several demonstrators were beaten up and arrested. A few months later there was a riot in the centre of Cluj after Romania beat Denmark in a World Cup qualifying match. Wild cheers of joy turned into shouts of 'Down With Ceauşescu' – words hardly ever heard in Romania.

The previous March six veteran Communists, who had all in the past held prominent positions in the regime, wrote an open letter to the Party complaining that Ceauşescu was 'betraying socialism'. They were all aged men in their seventies, but they still carried weight as 'loyal Party members' as they put it. Two had been former prime ministers, including Gheorghe Apostol, who had originally proposed Ceauşescu as Romanian Communist Party boss. Now they complained about the dictator's human rights abuses and said that Ceauşescu was taking Romania to the brink of disaster. This 'Letter of the Six' found its way to Radio Free Europe and Voice of America, where it was covered 'as a statement from Romania's National Salvation Front'. It had been delivered to the foreign media by Silviu Brucan, one of the most fascinating, if sinister, of all the Romanian Communists.

Born Saul Bruckner in 1916, he changed his name in his teens – in Romania between the wars it did not help ambitious young men to sound Jewish. He was a gifted and witty journalist, for decades a stern Stalinist. He had close ties to the KGB. When the Communists took power after the war, Brucan became editor of the Party newspaper *Scînteia*. His wife, the frightening but highly clever Alexandra Sidorovici, was a public prosecutor at the People's Tribunals which sent thousands of people to their deaths on bogus charges during successive purges. Brucan rose to become Romanian Ambassador to the US and to the UN. Then he returned to Bucharest as head of Romanian Television. He was a fawning associate of the Ceauşescus for years, but they never entirely trusted him. He began, privately, to be critical of the dictator in the late 1970s and then, more publicly, from 1987. He gave an interview to the BBC World Service criticising the regime. Brucan had to be punished for his 'treachery', but Ceauşescu was careful about how it was done. Brucan was an inveterate schemer and he managed to keep friends in the Kremlin, in the Lubyanka, in Washington and New York from his seven years in the United States, and also in the high reaches of the Securitate at home.

Ceauşescu had a 100-page file on him detailing every personal foible, every domestic quarrel with his family or conversation he had with journalists from the BBC and the *International Herald Tribune*. He was kept under strict surveillance, but he was so well connected that he was handled with kid gloves. Brucan and the other signatories of the notorious Letter of the Six were placed under house arrest. But he was evicted from the comfortable villa where he had lived for years in the smartest district of Bucharest, among all the top officials, and moved to a run-down shack with no running water in the remote countryside. He was given a brand-new passport and encouraged to use it, in the hope that he would leave the country and not return. He did leave – on visits to the Soviet Union and to the US – but he kept going back to Romania.[2]

Ceauşescu was not worried about football hooligans, or even the tiny number of dissident intellectuals with access to the foreign media. He was scared that the Soviet Union would try to topple him in a coup. All his food was now tasted by two people well before it reached him or Elena. His fears doubled after Gorbachev's disastrous visit to Bucharest in the summer of 1987. Gorbachev had not wanted to go, and it showed throughout the two and a half days he was there. On the first night the two men had a shouting match at a private dinner while the wives maintained a sullen silence, barely even looking at each other. At one point Ceauşescu ordered that all the doors and windows be shut so that nobody, not even the bodyguards, should hear what the argument was about. Gorbachev was trying to persuade Ceauşescu to relax his Stalinist grip and embrace perestroika. 'You are running a dictatorship here ... you must open yourselves up to the world,' he said. Ceauşescu insisted that Gorbachev was destroying communism and the whole edifice would crumble if the Soviets continued along their dangerous road.

The next day Gorbachev was shown around the Unirii market in central Bucharest, the city's biggest. Run-down of late, it had been recently refurbished for the Soviet leader's visit and specially stocked with all kinds of produce most Romanians had not seen for a long time. The shelves were overflowing with fresh fruit, vegetables and meat. As the limousines of the two leaders were leaving, a riot erupted, in Ceauşescu's view. Bystanders broke through the police perimeter and stoned the store, trying to force their way inside before waiting trucks took the food away for sale at the shops used by Party chieftains and Securitate officers. Gorbachev did not see it, but his aides told him what had happened later. Just before he left Romania Gorbachev made a speech calling for the removal throughout Eastern Europe 'of all those who cannot keep up with the times ... who have tarnished themselves with dishonesty, lack of principle and nepotism, and who, in the pursuit of profit, have sacrificed the moral image proper for a Party member'. He criticised Romania's treatment of its Hungarian minority. Ceauşescu, standing close to the Soviet leader on the podium, was visibly seething with rage. He was convinced from then on that the Soviet Union was waiting for the right moment to overthrow him.[3]

Much of the Ceauşescus' time was spent in the late 1980s on a new grand project for the capital that would prove their greatness. He and Elena were obsessed with a plan for a building that would leave their mark on history for ever as benefactors of their nation. The People's Palace, they decided, would be the biggest building in the world. Even Hitler and Albert Speer in their plans for rebuilding Berlin did not promise anything so gigantic. Stalin's wedding cake-style palaces of culture, copies of which he generously donated after the war to most of the capital cities in his new domains, were positively puny by comparison. The destruction it unleashed on Bucharest was monumental.

The Ceauşescus decreed that the whitewashed front of the 200-metre-wide, 100-metre-high structure should face a broad 'Victory of Socialism Avenue' that had to be at least as long as the Champs-Élysées in Paris. The project would require two ancient districts of Bucharest famed for their charm to be bulldozed. Arsenal Hill was a beauty spot from which the entire city could be seen. Uranus was an old, mainly residential area of gracious houses, many of them with lovely gardens, a monastery and several churches, chestnut trees, schools, shops and tramlines. Both would be entirely destroyed, replaced by the Palace and huge concrete apartment blocks along the newly created Avenue. It vandalised nearly a sixth of the city, in order to create a building that would bring all the state and Party offices on to one site, as well as living space and a nuclear bunker for the Ceauşescus. The architect was Anna Petrescu,* a young woman barely out of college, who in 1978 won an open competition at which the only judges were the President and the First Lady.

It was six years before work began, but then the Ceauşescus became more directly involved. Soon Ms Petrescu regretted that she had won the competition. The Ceauşescus meddled constantly. They would visit the site two or three times a week. Every Saturday morning they spent at least two hours there. No item of decoration or furniture was considered too small for their personal consideration. They decided everything, from the size of the lights and fountains along Victory of Socialism Avenue to the shape of the door handles and the patterns of the inlay on Elena's cherry-wood desk. By the middle of 1989 the People's Palace was close to completion. The cost was originally estimated to be five hundred million lei, but new demands by the Ceauşescus kept increasing the final bill. The project was delayed for months because they could not decide whether to opt for Doric or Ionic columns (after several changes of mind they went for Doric). Then the Ceauşescus, almost as an afterthought, decided to add on two extra storeys to the building, for office space. It took several months for a tunnel to be dug for a small underground railway for the First Couple's personal use, linking the Palace with downtown Bucharest. Eventually the cost rose twelvefold to around six billion lei. Dark jokes aside, there was a shortage of almost everything in Romania during 1989. While his people were freezing and queuing for bread, each year the President was spending almost the entire national welfare budget of the country on his new Palace.

* On this occasion, although the name sounds familiar, this Petrescu was not a relation of Ceauşescu.

THIRTY-FIVE

A STOLEN ELECTION

East Berlin, Sunday 7 May 1989

IT WAS POLLING DAY in the East German municipal elections and everything seemed to be running as normal. The results were not exactly close. When they were announced, late in the evening, the National Front list of officially approved candidates – the Communists and their sibling parties – won 98.6 per cent of the vote. In some districts the governing regime for the last forty years proved even more popular: in Erfurt, it polled 99.6 per cent and in Magdeburg an impressive 99.97 per cent, though in Dresden it took a mere 97.5 per cent. The results were in line with previous local elections, marginally better than the corresponding votes four years earlier. The Communist oligarchs, considering events from their Wandlitz villas, pronounced themselves satisfied. An editorial in the party organ *Neues Deutschland* declared: 'The people of the GDR are determined to continue ... with success on the road towards a developed socialist society and to strengthen the socialist fatherland. There exists a relationship of solid confidence and close unity between Party and People ... The results are a step towards the further perfection of our democracy.'

The man in charge of the electoral commission, fifty-two-year-old Egon Krenz, heir apparent to Erich Honecker and the Party's trouble-shooter-in-chief, seemed content as he declared that the poll had been conducted entirely in the proper manner. Krenz, who had been a Communist apparatchik throughout his working life, had unfortunate large and protruding teeth and generally went by the nickname 'Horse Face' throughout East Germany, even in Party circles. Speaking in the style most of his listeners were accustomed to hearing from him, he said: 'The results ... are an impressive declaration of support for the politics of peace and socialism of the Party of the working class.'[1]

Voting in East German elections was a different process to exercising the franchise in a Western-style democracy. In an East German polling station voters appeared before a board of two or three electoral commission officials, presented their ID papers and were issued with a ballot paper. To vote for an approved candidate from the official slate was straightforward: you simply folded the paper and placed it into the box near the entrance to the polling station. To vote another way was daunting and required courage. You had to walk across the room to mark a ballot paper in a secret voting booth where at least one, often two, 'Vopos', Volkspolizei or People's Police, stood. These voters' names were carefully noted down and the consequences could be serious for their entire families. They faced the sack or demotion at work. Students could be thrown out of university. They would definitely be kept under close surveillance by the Stasi.

East Germans had been used to this electoral process for four decades. Generally, they conformed obediently, or did not take the business seriously. But at this election there was a difference. More people than before had taken the risk and bravely voted against the regime. On this occasion a sizeable number of people knew for sure that the results were fixed. For the first time, in a few score polling stations, the votes were monitored. A quietly-spoken forty-six-year-old Lutheran pastor from Berlin Friedrichshain, Father Rainer Eppelmann, and a few other priests had asked the government if Church groups could exercise the right laid down in the GDR constitution for the public to watch the casting of votes. They were joined by activists from a few fledgling peace groups and environmental organisations which were tolerated, though barely, by the regime. The government agreed. It was a bad mistake.[2]

The monitors saw as soon as the first results were announced that the election was a fraud. The figures they produced of the numbers who voted against the official candidates differed widely from the official claims. Overall, they said that between 9 and 10 per cent voted No. Among young people and students the figure was much higher – spectacularly so in some places. At the School of Fine Arts in Berlin, 105 students voted against the official candidates and 102 voted for. Nevertheless the official tally recorded 98.5 per cent in favour. In Dresden, Party boss Hans Modrow knew that four times the officially published number voted against the approved list, but he declared the doctored figures as a matter of routine.

Honecker and his henchmen realised quickly they should not have permitted the monitors anywhere near the polling booths. For several days West German television was full of well-informed coverage of how the election had been rigged. Often it repeated the point that in the Soviet Union a few weeks earlier there had been a free election of sorts – at least the counting appeared to have been fair. In Poland there would be an election a month ahead in which a real opposition was permitted to stand. Yet in East Germany the regime persisted with an old-fashioned, Soviet bloc-style stolen election in which intelligent people were expected to believe that barely one citizen in a hundred opposed the regime.

This was the first time West German TV played a serious role in the GDR's politics. Most East Germans watched – except around Dresden, where for some reason reception was unavailable. That area was called The Valley of the Clueless. The faces of many West German broadcasters were as familiar as those of the presenters on their own television. On the whole, people watched West German TV for entertainment; East German television was exceptionally dull and never showed any American soaps or films. West German news so far had made marginal impact, but that was now changing. Viewers could see alternative interpretations of East German reality beamed into their living rooms in their own language. If they wished – and increasingly many people did – they could watch a half-hour 7 p.m. news bulletin on West German ZDF, followed by the East's official news broadcast at 7.30 p.m. and then an 8 p.m. news and current affairs programme on the Federal Republic's ARD channel.

The availability of Western media in East Germany was to have a profound effect, starting with the stunned and angry response to the fraudulent election. Spontaneous, but peaceful, demonstrations erupted in the main cities, at first numbering just handfuls of people. Allegations of electoral malpractice poured into Party committees throughout the country. Government propaganda claimed they were 'groundless calumnies inspired by the Western media and agents of imperialism in an attempt to smear the State'. But the public knew which version of German truth to believe. In the church at Berlin Friedrichshain a week after the poll, 400 people gathered to formulate a letter asking the government to launch an official inquiry into the conduct of the elections. As they left the church, a Stasi truck appeared. Security guards attacked them with sticks and truncheons. Around twenty were taken to Stasi headquarters, where they were beaten up more thoroughly.

Later, Communist chiefs admitted the fraud. Some in the leadership had reckoned there would be a 'dissent' rate of 5 to 7 per cent. 'But district mayors were convinced that the Party wanted better results,' Günter Schabowski said. 'The tally was doctored. The officials accepted it . . . as their task in life and set about it. They did it out of habit and Party discipline.'[3]

The Party bosses in Berlin did not need an election to tell them that opposition was growing. Accurate Stasi reports about the level of discontent went to Mielke, though it is unclear how many of them he showed to Honecker. One, produced by a senior officer at the Stasi's Normannenstrasse headquarters, stated clearly that there had always been grumbling and complaints among workers but now,

> economic discontent is discrediting the regime . . . Workers are openly expressing their doubts about the objectivity and credibility of the balance sheets and economic results published in the mass media of the GDR. Frequently workers are demanding to be kept informed about problems and their solution . . . If they talk to West German visitors they deprecate the productive capacities of their own economy and condemn it . . . To an increasing extent manifestations of indifference and resignation are growing. GDR citizens who return from abroad on family visits glorify the West . . . and in general [talk of] the superiority of capitalism.[4]

One report that landed on Mielke's desk around the time of the local elections worried the Stasi boss. This did go to the rest of the top leadership. It said that there was an air of gloom and despondency within the lower and middle ranks of the Party itself. 'There is widespread demoralisation,' it said. 'People no longer believe in the goals of the Party and the regime. Such attitudes are especially evident among those who hitherto were socially active but have . . . become tired, resigned or have finally given up.' As apparently efficient as ever, the Stasi calculated opposition numbers in a report sent to Mielke and, on this occasion, circulated to Honecker a few days after the election. There were 160 scattered groups – 'including pacifists, feminists, environmentalists . . . 2,500 people are involved and 600 were in leading positions . . . 60 people are hard core activists'.[5]

It was an understatement, but not by much in the early summer of 1989. Nobody emerged as an inspirational figure like Lech Wałęsa or with the reputation of Václav Havel. Some Protestant pastors were politically active, such as Eppelmann in Berlin, a one-time bricklayer who went to jail for nine months for refusing army service. Like many young people who wound up in the East German clergy, he retrained as a theology student for pragmatic rather than spiritual reasons: 'I asked myself, what can you become for a contented, or even happy life in this country? The only answer which occurred to me was: pastor. Only the study of theology was able to offer me a little mental freedom.' Christian Führer, pastor at the beautiful and famous Nikolaikirche in East Germany's second city, Leipzig, had originally started a peace group in the mid-1980s to campaign for nuclear disarmament on both sides of the Iron Curtain. At first these peace groups were permitted, even encouraged by the regime, which thought they were harmless and were as great an irritant to the West as to the East. But Führer's congregation became a thorn in Honecker's flesh. Regular demonstrations began after prayers each Monday night from the week after the rigged election. At the beginning a few hundred attended; then, during the summer, numbers grew to thousands.

But the churches had been deeply compromised by the regime and only a few wanted anything to do with opposition politics. Biologist Frank Eigenfeld wished to set up a peace group in Halle, about 140 kilometres south-west of Berlin. 'We had basic problems with churches,' he said. 'We had problems finding rooms for people to meet in. We depended on parishes to support our efforts and help to provide rooms for grassroots groups. In most cases it was hard to get support. In Halle only three out of fourteen parishes provided any space for us ... Most churches wanted nothing to do with us.'[6]

The best-known secular group was the Initiative for Peace and Human Rights, established by the forty-three-year-old artist Bärbel Bohley and her partner Werner Fischer. In January 1988 they were arrested at a demonstration marking the anniversary of the murder of Rosa Luxemburg and Karl Liebknecht, two of the founders of the German Communist Party and heroes in the Marxist pantheon. Their offence was to unfurl a flag which in large letters quoted one of Luxemburg's most famous sayings: 'Freedom is the freedom to think differently.' Bohley was given the choice of remaining in jail or leaving the country. After around four hundred people marched in Berlin protesting at her treatment she reached a compromise with the Party that went right up to Honecker for personal approval. She would go to live in Britain for six months, as long as she was allowed to return. By May 1989 she was back in East Germany leading new protest groups and citizens' committees that the regime dismissed as 'illegal groupings'.

Yet few people were interested in negotiating with the Communists or reaching a compromise with them. Some enterprising young East Germans looked for a new way to show how they felt. Five days before the municipal elections, West German television had screened a special broadcast from the Hungarian border with Austria. Hungarian soldiers were cutting the wire fence – the Iron Curtain – and opening the border to the West. It was an extraordinary sight that showed some East Germans a way out of their prison nation. If they could not climb over the Wall, tunnel under it or fly over it, perhaps there was a way around it? In small numbers to begin with they started to make their way to Hungary, hoping they might never have to return to the GDR.

THIRTY-SIX

EXPULSION OF THE TURKS

Sofia, Saturday 20 May 1989

THE WINTER HAD BEEN one of the harshest on record in Bulgaria. The spring was proving no easier. Queues in the shops were the longest in living memory. Bread, milk, cheese, eggs, fresh vegetables of all kinds were hard to obtain for most families. After the oil price crashed in 1985–6, Bulgaria's ruse of selling cheap Soviet oil on to the West ceased to be profitable. Western bankers were refusing to lend further money. The country was bankrupt. Todor Zhivkov turned to a tried and tested tactic to deflect any criticism of himself: once again he unfurled the flag of nationalism. The country's problems, he said, were all caused by the foreigners within. So they would have to go. He announced that he would throw out all the ethnic Turks from Bulgaria. The decision was as bizarre as it was cruel. It triggered a reaction he had not predicted. Zhivkov thought he would strengthen his position on a wave of patriotic fervour. But this time his campaign was treated with disdain by the majority of Bulgarians, prompted a plot against him among his own clique of elite Communist officials in Sofia, and created an international outcry.

By 1989 all but a fraction of the ethnic Turks had been compelled to change their names, as the regime had been forcing them to do since the mid-1980s. Those who refused were either dead or had been jailed, but the bitterness among the minority population ran deep. From 9 May 1989, Turks in the north-east and south of Bulgaria began a series of demonstrations to coincide with the Conference on Security and Co-operation summit held in Paris. There were three marches – in Kaolinovo, Todor Ikonomovo and in Tolbukhin near Varna, organised by the Democratic League for Human Rights. This had been founded by Turks who had spent time on the prison island of Belen for refusing to adopt Bulgarian names. Demonstrators demanded the right to speak Turkish, the right to practise Islam and the restoration of their original Muslim names. The regime's response was brutal.

About 15,000 attended the peaceful, silent protests, and were met with the full force of the State. They were surrounded by troops and militia who used dogs, clubs, tear gas and helicopter gunships against unarmed civilians. The official figures put the casualty toll at seven dead and forty injured, but reliable witnesses insist the more accurate number was sixty dead and well over a hundred injured. About a thousand demonstrators were arrested. The towns and villages where the protests took place were sealed off by military roadblocks and communications were cut. Four-day curfews were imposed and soldiers patrolled the streets, beating and arresting people indiscriminately. They sought out those who joined the demonstrations for special treatment. Dozens more died over the next few days.

The government's first reaction was to make an example of the organisers and the Turkish community leaders. But then Zhivkov chose a different, far more radical, route. On this day he decided to get rid of the Muslim minority once and for all, though he would start with the troublemakers. He ordered Interior Minister Georgi Tanev 'to organise the quick expulsion of all the extremists and fanatics among the Turkish Muslims and to stimulate the emigration of the rest'. Tanev had been Communist Party boss in the predominantly Turkish area of Kurdjali in the mid-1980s and distinguished himself by the zeal he had shown in the earlier campaign to force the Muslims to change their names. Now, within a few days, 5,000 Turks were deported. They were mostly writers, journalists, artists and academics but included many doctors, engineers and teachers – a large proportion of the minority population's professional class.

A week later Zhivkov summoned his fellow Party chieftains and announced that all the Turks would be expelled speedily. 'It is absolutely imperative to expatriate . . . at least 300,000 from the Turkish population,' he declared. 'If we don't get rid of them, in fifteen years Bulgaria will not exist. Their population increases . . . Can you imagine what will happen in twenty years?' Inwardly, as they said later, some of the leadership were appalled by Zhivkov's pronouncement. But nobody opened his mouth to object.[1] The next day, 29 May, Zhivkov appeared on prime-time television. He accused Turkey of trying to foment a crisis in Bulgaria and of provoking the disturbances for their own 'expansionist' ends. He demanded that Turkey open its borders to every Bulgarian Muslim. Ethnic Turks were forced to leave, often with only a few hours' notice. Most were allowed to take with them no more than 500 leva, less than a month's average wages and in any case unusable currency outside Bulgaria. They were banned from selling their property before they left, or damaging it in any way, on pain of long prison sentences.

The Turkish Prime Minister, Turgut Özal, led the protests. For a while at least he opened Turkey's borders, albeit with great reluctance. The European Community halted talks on a new trade agreement with Bulgaria. The country was isolated – even within the Soviet bloc. The Russians sent formal protests. Gorbachev was furious when he met Zhivkov in Moscow in June. The Bulgarian tried to argue that he had 'no choice on the Muslim issue . . . if we don't act we will soon look like Cyprus'. But Gorbachev barely allowed him to finish the sentence. 'What you are doing is unhelpful and counterproductive at a time when we are seeking to improve our relations with Turkey. We cannot support you,' he said. From that moment he was determined to see the back of Comrade Zhivkov – and soon.[2]

The Turkish exodus was a disaster for Bulgaria. More than 350,000 fled within a few weeks, during the planting and sowing season. Even Zhivkov could see the damage it was doing to the land and desperately tried to backtrack. But it was too late. The regime said they could stay working their farms, and then leave later in the year when the harvest was safely gathered. In a desperate but vain effort to save the crucial tobacco crop in the south-west Gotse Delchev area local officials would issue only postdated passports. In six key villages there were demonstrations, strikes and protests, quelled by soldiers and militia who sealed off the area and forced the people back to work at gunpoint. Nevertheless, entire villages emptied, factories ground to a halt, crops and farm animals were left untended.

Senior Party officials were alarmed. Men like the Foreign Minister, Petar Mladenov, the Prime Minister, Georgi Atanasov, and the finance chief, Andrei Lukanov, had done Zhivkov's bidding for years. Now they were receiving international protests about Bulgaria's behaviour and they knew the old despot had gone too far. But they were scared of disagreeing with him or taking any action against him. Zhivkov still had the powerful state security service, the Durzhavna Sigurnost, and the People's Militia, another armed wing of the Party, on his side. It was dangerous to make any move to challenge him openly. There had been an attempt to force him to retire in the summer of the previous year. But he cannily outmanoeuvred his opponents. He summoned his ministers and cronies for a meeting of the Party leadership and declared that he was growing older and wearier and that he wanted to resign soon and lay down the heavy cares of office. Then, over the next few days, he held private meetings with some of them, at which they all pledged their fealty and assured him he had their support if there was any challenge. Lukanov explained what happened next. 'Of course, everybody knew this was a provocation. If you had answered "Yes, why not resign" you were finished. So, having interviewed everyone, he held a smaller meeting to inform them that everyone was in favour of him staying in office so he would defer to their wishes reluctantly. This kind of theatre was then represented by him as a serious attempt to retire.' There was a group of plotters ready to pounce against him, but they knew they had to wait until the time was right.[3]

This time Zhivkov faced opposition outside the Party to his ruinous and vicious campaign against the Turks. None of the minuscule dissident groups had previously raised their voices in support of the minority Muslims. As the leaders of some of them admitted, it seemed like a side issue for most Bulgarians. Challenging the regime on behalf of the Turks would not have furthered their cause with the majority population. But now human rights groups which had before been silent spoke out. At the end of May six activists were arrested, including three leading figures from the fledgling free trade union organisation Podkrepa and Father Kristopher Subev, an Orthodox priest from the Religious Rights Committee. They were accused of inciting the Turks to riot and faced long prison terms. When they went on a hunger strike in jail they were painfully force-fed. Their plight became a *cause célèbre* on the BBC World Service and Deutsche Welle. Though it was technically illegal to listen to foreign radio broadcasts, both stations were avidly heard in Bulgaria and had audiences as large as domestic radio. Though official state-controlled news barely mentioned the expulsion of the Turks, everyone in Bulgaria now knew about it.

The Club for the Support of Perestroika and Glasnost had been founded the previous summer. Originally it had around eighty members, nearly all of them prominent writers or academics and one-time Communists. The regime had kept a close watch on the organisation. Apart from Sigurnost surveillance, its launch meeting was attended by Goran Goranov, one of Zhivkov's best-known aides. It had tried to navigate a careful path. All its material 'was phrased to keep us out of trouble, or so we hoped. We deliberately used the slogans and ideas of perestroika and glasnost as political cover for ourselves. If Gorbachev, the most powerful Communist in the world, used them, who was the Bulgarian dictator to tell us that we could not?' said Ivan Stanchev, one of the Club's founders. The most influential member was Zhelyu Zhelev, a dapper, silver-haired fifty-four-year-old philosopher and long-time dissident, who had been thrown out of the Party in the late 1960s and spent six years in internal exile outside Sofia. Zhelev was the author of a clever and profound book, *Fascism*, in 1982, which again landed him in trouble with the regime, though he managed to stay out of prison. He had a shrewd flair for political tactics that matched his powerful intellect. His greatest early coup was in January 1989 when the French President, François Mitterrand, passed through Bulgaria on a fleeting visit. The French Embassy held a breakfast for him and wanted to gather twelve Bulgarian intellectuals to meet him. They asked Zhelev to compile the guest list. 'This was a recognition that we were a serious opposition group,' he said. 'But . . . [we] were monitored much more closely by the secret police.'

When Zhivkov expelled the Turks from Bulgaria, the Perestroika Club protested and presented a petition signed by more than 250 well-known figures of Bulgarian communism, including the distinguished research chemist Alexei Sheludko, who had once been the KGB's chief of operations in Sofia. There were a few arrests of Club members, though not the most prominent ones, and of activists from Ecoglasnost, who had made a film, *Breath*, about pollution levels near Bulgaria's industrial plants. It was a fairly muted response, but Zhivkov was planning more vigorous moves. He saw objections to his policy on the Turks as an attack on him personally.[4]

THIRTY-SEVEN

THE LANDSLIDE

Warsaw, Sunday 4 June 1989

SOLIDARITY'S ELECTION HEADQUARTERS were on the second floor of the Café Surprise, just off the main boulevard in the centre of the city. Late in the evening, union activists stared in disbelief at the TV screens as the first poll results began to be announced. It was clear that a revolution had taken place within the Soviet empire and it had happened, peacefully, in the polling booths of Poland. Almost nobody had expected the overwhelming scale of the Communists' defeat. As the night wore on it became a humiliation for the Party that had ruled Poland for more than forty years. The electoral procedure was highly complex, but according to some figures the Communists won between 3 and 4 per cent of the vote. The election had been turned into a referendum on Communist and Soviet rule. The people's verdict was a devastating indictment against the regime. In the first of two rounds of voting, Solidarity won thirty-three of the thirty-five seats that were up for free election in the Sejm. The Communists and their allies retained the uncontested 65 per cent of the seats reserved for them in the gerrymandered parliament. But that was little consolation to them. Solidarity won ninety-nine of the hundred freely elected Senate seats. Virtually the entire Communist leadership was defeated, including all the familiar names from the government that had ruled for so long: the Interior Minister Kiszczak, the Prime Minister Rakowski, the Defence Minister Florian Siwicki.

It was the Communists who had insisted on quick elections after the Round Table agreement was signed. They thought a snap poll would give them even more of an advantage and would wrongfoot Solidarity. The Party may not have had much experience in democratic electioneering, but it had money, organisation, staff and, most important of all, monopoly control of television, which it expected to use ruthlessly. During the Round Table talks Jerzy Urban, the deeply unloved chief spin doctor for General Jaruzelski, and for years the scourge of Western and domestic journalists, told the Solidarity activist Jacek Kuroń with his usual cynicism that 'we will give you the ZOMO [riot police] before we give you the TV'. Kuroń replied, 'We'd much rather have the television, thanks'. Urban orchestrated coverage of the election on all the national broadcasting networks, which had been wholly biased against the opposition. He was one of the most heavily defeated Communist candidates.

Solidarity had not wanted an immediate election. They would have to build an organisation from scratch, raise money, rent office space, hire staff, all within a few weeks. It would be a vast undertaking. Wałęsa complained repeatedly: 'These elections ... They're the terrible price we have to pay to get our union back.' He feared that the public, after so many years of apathy, would not respond and turn out to vote. His advisers thought that Solidarity would do well to win a quarter of the contested seats in the Lower House and perhaps two-thirds of the Senate. Yet, relying mainly on inexperienced volunteers, Solidarity improvised and was brilliantly effective. From 1 May when Wałęsa launched the campaign at St Brigid's Church in Gdańsk, his message was optimistic and upbeat. It was the Polish people's chance to 'tell them we've had enough', he used to say in his stump speech. He had his picture taken at the Lenin Shipyard with every Solidarity candidate. In the fortnight leading up to polling day these pictures were visible as posters everywhere, on trees, walls, windows in apartment blocks, along with the Solidarity logo in the national colours of red, white and blue. Underneath the picture was the message, in Wałęsa's handwriting: 'We must win'.

The Church had done well out of the Round Table agreement. Some of its property was returned gratis and it was allowed to buy back a great deal more. It could run schools and radio stations; priests could now qualify for state pensions. The Church was unashamedly campaigning for Solidarity, despite Cardinal Glemp's initial reluctance to alienate the regime, his dislike of the union and his contempt for Lech Wałęsa. While state-controlled broadcasting was in the hands of the Party, the BBC World Service and Radio Free Europe, which had Polish audiences of millions, made no effort to hide their support for Solidarity. With extraordinary speed Solidarity set up an excellent daily newspaper, *Gazeta Wyborcza* (*Election Gazette*), which was full of wit and sparkle compared to the plodding Party organs. It was edited by

Adam Michnik, but the vast majority of its journalists were talented young women.[1]

The Communists ran a dull, complacent campaign. The leadership was convinced it would do well against an apparently disorganised opposition. It hardly bothered electioneering in some districts which the Party thought it easily controlled. Party headquarters in Warsaw decreed that none of its posters or printed material should appear in red, so many other colours were tried. This was designed to confuse voters, though to what end was hard to see. The campaign colour that became most identified with the Communists was a faded blue. One of its most often used slogans simply stated 'With us it's safer', which as one foreign reporter remarked sounded more like an advert for condoms than a slogan for a political candidate. 'It was a hopeless, lifeless, lacklustre campaign,' one Party chieftain admitted halfway through. 'I don't think we understand what the concept is of seeking people's votes. We've been smug.'[2]

By polling day, the opposition appeared far better organised than the Party. Most priests throughout the country in their Sunday sermons that morning reminded congregants, 'I think you know who God would vote for in today's election.' When they got to the polling stations electors were presented with complicated ballot papers. They were thick sheets and voters were required to cross out the names of candidates they did not want. Solidarity realised these might bewilder many voters. So outside all of the country's 20,000 polling stations, the opposition set up information booths where voters were helped to cope with the lists. They displayed a mock ballot paper filled in to show which names – i.e. the Communists – should be deleted. Once voters got the hang of what to do, they reacted with alacrity. It was 'a complicated method, but uniquely satisfying to cross out the names you don't like', one observer said.[3]

Even on the morning of polling day the Communists were still convinced they would do reasonably well. Rakowski admitted that they did not anticipate the possibility of a big defeat, or imagine that, given the opportunity, the people would reject the Party outright. 'In May, after the Round Table talks, our opinion polls showed that 14 per cent would vote for us and our coalition partners while 40 per cent would vote for Solidarity,' he said. 'The rest were "don't knows". I don't know why we imagined the rest would vote for us. We were prisoners of the past when elections were not free. It just didn't register that the "don't knows" would not support us.' The Soviet Embassy and the

KGB were reporting back to Moscow that the likeliest outcome of the election was that Solidarity would do moderately well and it would gain a voice in government over the next few years. There would be a gradual move towards power-sharing and liberal reforms. These were just the kind of predictions that Gorbachev and his advisers wanted to hear. So no alarm bells had rung during the elections and the Soviets were relaxed about them.[4]

Among the few to call the result accurately before the votes were counted was the US Ambassador to Poland, John Davis. A sixty-two-year-old career diplomat, he had served in Warsaw for six years – unusually long for an American diplomat to stay in one posting. He had developed close links with the Solidarity leadership over the past months, since the Round Table talks began. Frequently, they would spend evenings together at the Ambassador's Warsaw residence 'socialising, watching recent American movies and eating large amounts of beef Stroganoff,' as he said. While senior Solidarity figures such as Geremek and Mazowiecki were pessimistic about the election outcome, Davis was reporting back to Washington that Solidarity 'will win – and win big'. On 19 April he had cabled to the State Department: 'The Communist authorities are ... likely to meet total defeat and great embarrassment.' On 2 June, two days before polling day, he predicted 'a nearly total Solidarity victory', which he said was not an entirely welcome prospect. There was a danger it could provoke 'a sharp defensive reaction from the government' that could destabilise the whole of Eastern Europe.[5]

Wałęsa was amazed by the size of his victory. 'I face the disaster of having a good crop,' he joked. 'Too much grain has ripened for me and I can't store it all in my granary.' But he had heard other news that disturbed him greatly. Earlier in the day, hundreds of unarmed Chinese students had been murdered in Beijing when troops and tanks had been dispatched to crush demonstrations in Tiananmen Square. It was unlikely, but not impossible, that the Soviets or the generals at the head of the Polish regime would react violently to the humiliating defeat at the polls. Geremek, one of the coolest of heads around Wałęsa, was also sounding warning hints: 'Yes, of course, we knew we had won. But ... we also knew they had all the guns.'[6]

Early the next morning the Party chieftains met in a state of shock for a post-mortem. 'The results are terrible, worse than we could have expected,' Jaruzelski said. 'I blame the Church. They are the main culprits. We will have to meet with the Catholic hierarchy urgently.' Stanisław Ciosek, who had played a prominent part in the Round Table talks and met the bishops frequently, agreed. 'We trusted the Church – and they have turned out to be Jesuits,' he said bizarrely. But then he went on to castigate the Party, as many of the Communist oligarchs did throughout the day. 'The guilt is on our side. We overestimated our strength and we have turned out to be completely without a base,' he lamented. Alexander Kwasniewski, the youngest and one of the smartest among the Polish leadership, said: 'There were large numbers of Communist Party members who were crossing out our own candidates.' Jerzy Urban, who had masterminded the publicity for the campaign, said that the second round of votes, due in a fortnight's time, for the few remaining contested seats could be an equal disaster. 'We could ridicule ourselves before our own base. The results prove that the Party has outlived itself . . . We face disintegration. This was not only an election defeat, but the end of an age.'[7]

Jaruzelski seriously considered imposing a new version of martial law. He called a meeting of the Military Council and the army General Staff. The Interior Minister, Kiszczak, was there and they spoke of announcing a state of emergency and calling the election null and void. 'We still had the levers of power in our hands,' Jaruzelski said. But he knew that it was too late for that sort of violent solution now. He had spoken with Gorbachev's aides in the Kremlin who were stunned by the election results, but knew that the Soviet leader would not support any military crackdown. It could not work. Moscow would continue to encourage a political settlement of a political problem, they told him. Jaruzelski announced that he would accept the election results and learn to live with them. But he was prone to self-pity and was sent into a dark gloom. His advisers claimed that he brooded deeply over a comment Rakowski had made early in the morning, which seemed like a straightforward reportage of fact: 'The people simply didn't want us any more.' Why? He felt that he had made the right choice to go down the path of compromise, that he had behaved properly, and he should not have been punished for it. Jaruzelski always thought he was a great patriot who acted in the national interest. Yet he had a poor understanding of the Polish people.[8]

His principal concern now, and that of his entourage, was to make sure that he was elected President when the new parliament was convened the following month. The electoral arithmetic made it a close-run thing. He needed thirty-five votes in the Lower House, which seemed unlikely without the acquiescence of Solidarity. There could be no effective government until the issue of the presidency was settled. The administration tried to limp on, but power was visibly slipping from the regime. It was an unwritten assumption of the Round Table talks that Jaruzelski would be elected President. The post was created with him in mind, as the negotiators from both sides knew. Some of the more cautious Solidarity leaders – Wałęsa in particular – feared that if they did not deliver that part of the agreement, the entire framework of the deal would come apart. The Communists were exerting pressure to ensure the General's election. Some senior army officers warned the government that they would feel 'personally threatened' if Jaruzelski was not elected and would 'move to overturn the Round Table agreements and the election results'. In other words, they threatened a coup against their own generals. Kiszczak met Cardinal Glemp and other Church leaders privately. He issued a stark warning: 'If Jaruzelski is not elected . . . we would face further destabilisation and the whole process of political transformation would have to end. No other President would be listened to in the security forces and in the army.'[9]

The General himself was doing some head-counting and began to hesitate. For three weeks he dropped vague hints that he would not run, if the country did not want him. At first he was grandstanding, according to his aides. He had held on to power for so long and with such determination that he had not imagined that he could simply retire. But if the numbers did not look right he would think again and decline the nomination. He told his advisers he 'did not want to creep into the presidency'. Nor did he want to face another public humiliation after the disastrous first round of the elections. By the end of the month he had decided that he was not prepared to risk losing another election – and more face. He decided to pull out of the race unless a rabbit was found from a hat somewhere and he could be assured of the nomination.[10]

THIRTY-EIGHT

FUNERAL IN BUDAPEST

Budapest, Friday 16 June 1989

BY 9 A.M. MORE THAN two hundred thousand people were already packed into Heroes' Square, an impressive neo-classical space, where most of Hungary's great men and women are commemorated in epic statuary. The crowd was growing all the time, spilling over into the broad Avenue of the People, and to the nearby City Park. For most of the last thirty-three years it had been taboo even to mention the name of Imre Nagy. Now the political leader of the Revolution of 1956, judicially murdered two years later, was reburied in a dramatic and emotional ceremony. It was a funeral of a long-dead man. But everyone who witnessed this extraordinary day could see it also buried an entire era of Hungarian history. On the same date a year earlier, when some of Nagy's old friends and family tried to hold a small protest march to mark the thirtieth anniversary of his death, truncheon-wielding police broke up the demonstration. Now Nagy's funeral had been turned into a great state occasion, given live coverage by the government-controlled television. The police co-operated with former dissidents, political activists and Nagy's relatives to ensure that the event was conducted peacefully and with due solemnity.

Nagy's original burial place after he was hanged in the Central Budapest Prison in Fö Street was a closely guarded secret. The regime did not want it to become a place of pilgrimage or for Nagy to turn into a martyr. In the dead of night, he and four of his closest comrades who had been executed around the same time were taken to Rákoskeresztúr municipal cemetery, an out-of-the-way spot in an eastern suburb of the city. Nagy, his Defence Minister Pál Maléter, his secretary József Szilágyi, his political aide Ferenc Donáth and one of the principal intellectual voices of the 1956 Revolution, Miklós Gimes, were buried by police in unmarked graves in the cemetery's Plot 301. The secret was unlocked by Miklós Vásárhelyi, who had been Nagy's press officer in the short-lived revolution and was jailed for four years after 1956. In the 1980s Vásárhelyi, a charming, avuncular, white-haired gentleman, became a father figure of the dissident movement, with excellent contacts in the Western press. He was told about the existence of Plot 301, and whose remains were buried there, by a friendly prison guard. He could not do much with the information while Kádár remained in power. Rehabilitating Nagy would have condemned the three decades of Kádár's rule. But after the old man was removed from office, he and the Nagy family established the Committee for Historical Justice to clear the name of Imre Nagy and the 329 other revolutionaries executed for their role in 1956.

The dead men posed a dilemma for the Party, which almost broke apart amid agonising internal debates about how to confront the greatest trauma of Hungarian communism. Reformers like Imre Pozsgay were convinced that the silence and denial of the last three decades could not continue. 'We had to face up to the issue,' he said. 'There was no way we could start anew, turn over a new leaf, without accounting for what happened in the past.' Pozsgay put himself at the forefront of radical changes within the Party to forge a grand compromise with the opposition. He more or less *was* the opposition, in the eyes of many old Party loyalists. He was partly motivated by ambition, imagining he could win power by presenting himself as the agent of change, and partly by conviction. He realised that communism was finished – and he could be well placed to pick up the pieces. Late in 1988 he established a Historical Commission of a dozen leading Communist academics and historians to study the Uprising. They were given unprecedented access to documents that shed a shameful light on the Party's actions at the time.

Their report early in January 1989 turned on its head Party history, which had maintained that 1956 was a 'counter-revolution' and that the Soviet invasion was necessary to save Hungary from reactionaries and imperialists. The Commission concluded that it had been 'a popular uprising against oligarchic rule that had debased the nation' and that it had been entirely unjustified for the Red Army to crush it. This was not an esoteric question of Communist theory or mere symbolism. As the conservatives in the dwindling Party ranks could see, the new line acknowledged that Communist rule during the last three decades had been illegitimate and that the Russians were an occupation force. It jettisoned comfortable orthodoxy to which people had grown accustomed, and the conspiracy of silence in which Kádár and his associates

The fortieth anniversary of the formation of East Germany turned into an embarrassment for the regime. All the world's most senior Communists, including Gorbachev, attended. At a torchlight parade organised by a Communist Youth organisation – the cream of the Party's younger generation – thousands of young people began chanting, 'Gorby, save us, save us!'

Günter Schabowski, East Berlin Communist Party boss, accidentally hastened the collapse of the Wall. On the morning of 9 November 1989 the GDR leadership decided to permit controlled border crossing from the next day. At an early evening press conference Schabowski misspoke and announced that the border with West Germany would be opened 'immediately'.

Within minutes of Shabowski's statement, thousands of Berliners had taken to the streets to see if it was true. Sheer numbers forced bemused and frightened border guards to open three checkpoints by 11 p.m. that night. After twenty-eight years dividing the city, the Berlin Wall was breached.

DAVID 89

Hilf

(*Above and inset, far right*) Every day for a fortnight vast demonstrations of more than a quarter of a million people brought Prague to a virtual standstill in Czechoslovakia's 'Velvet Revolution'. A characteristic sound could be heard throughout the city and its suburbs for hours: the jangling of keys as protesters told the Communist government: 'It's time to go home.'

(*Inset, near right*) The Czech regime fell on 24 November. Václav Havel and the former Communist Party leader Alexander Dubček, who had been ousted by the Soviets after Red Army tanks crushed the Prague Spring in 1968, were among the first to celebrate.

The fatal moment of weakness for Romanian dictator Nicolae Ceauşescu. On 21 December at a mass rally in central Bucharest designed by the regime to show his popularity, he was heckled. His startled and terrified reaction was the spark that began the revolt against him.

(*Above and facing page*) Romania was the only place where the Revolutions of 1989 turned violent. National troops who backed the new government and Securitate secret police loyal to Ceauseşcu fought on the streets of Bucharest and other Romanian cities. Around 700 people were killed, most of them civilians caught in the crossfire.

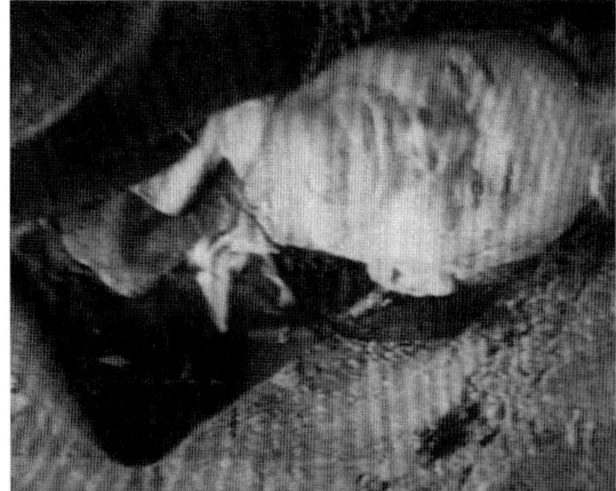

The trial and execution of Ceauşescu and his loathed wife Elena on Christmas Day 1989. Three days earlier they had been the most powerful people in the country, feared and worshipped in a paranoid and grotesque personality cult. Now they looked like a peevish and terrified old couple.

Full circle. When the Polish Cardinal Wojtyła was elected Pope John Paul II in October 1979, the KGB warned he would be a dangerous threat to communism. The Kremlin bugged his private office and apartments. Ten years later most of the Communist states collapsed. On 1 December 1989 Mikhail Gorbachev and his wife Raisa went to the Vatican for an audience with the Pope.

In the months after the 1989 revolutions, the roads east from the Soviet satellite states were frequently jammed with Red Army tanks and troops heading for home. It was the end of more than forty years of occupation.

had maintained peace in Hungary. The other big issue was: how would the Soviets react? Pozsgay carried the day in a series of bruising Party meetings. This was the only way for the Hungarian Party to purge itself, he argued, and it would never regain credibility 'unless we take this opportunity now'. There had been no official reaction from the Soviets. The statement on 1956 was a test of Gorbachev's reforms and of the 'Sinatra Doctrine', he said. 'Of course we watched for reaction from the Soviet Union and after we saw the lack of reaction, we would make another move forward. This was how we made our initiatives.'[1]

The government announced in March that it would allow the five bodies to be exhumed and a proper reburial to take place. Initially it had no idea of turning the occasion into a big public ceremony. The regime wanted a simple, private funeral, out of sight, which they thought could close the entire issue once and for all. But during the year, as the pace of change speeded up and the Party began visibly to die on its feet, Communist officials thought that a better way of dealing with it was to hijack the event. They had been holding informal talks with the opposition since mid-March. They had agreed that Polish-style Round Table talks would begin on 13 June, three days before the funeral. Party leaders insisted on being at the burial ceremony and making speeches. Though Vásárhelyi and the Nagy family were reluctant to let them, they felt they were in no position to refuse. Both the Committee for Historical Justice and the government appealed for 'calm and dignity' and asked that no political banners should be visible, only national colours or black flags. But the authorities were apprehensive that there might be unrest. And they were determined to use the occasion for their own political ends, as an extraordinary top-secret report by the Hungarian secret service shows. It reveals how the intelligence service had penetrated every opposition group and that its agents were active in persuading them to moderate their demands. 'Among agents operating in various alternative groups,' the report says, 'agents "Knotweed", "Passion Flower", "Rhododendron", "Agave" and "Sword Flag" will ... exert their influence on these ... [groups] to abandon the idea of initiating, or participating in a political demonstration ... "Bellflower" will explore the plans and ideas of the Hungarian Democratic Forum and its participation in the mass rally ... "Calla" will follow the co-ordination meetings of the Free Democrats'. Agents abroad will spy on the activities of expatriate Hungarian communities in the US and Europe and 'deliberately use the media ... to spread the suggestion that it will establish the maturity of the nation if the funeral proceeds in an orderly manner'.[2]

Stagehands and builders had been working for the last three days to turn Heroes' Square into a giant theatrical set. It had all been designed with much style by the architect László Rajk, one of the country's leading dissidents, whose father was the most prominent victim of the Stalinist show trials in the late 1940s. The columns were draped with black cloth. The grand façades of the buildings were covered with huge green, red and white tricolour flags, but with a hole in their middle, to remember the 1956 revolutionaries whose symbol had been the national flag with the hammer and sickle emblem hastily removed. On one side of the square, high on pedestals and flanked by tall flares, lay the six coffins. The extra one was an empty casket of the Unknown Insurgent. It was a powerful and moving ceremony. From the moment it began at 10 a.m., when the celebrated acter Imre Sinkovits read a letter to the Hungarian people from the Nagy family, emotions were raw. For two hours mourners filed past the caskets, while the names of every Hungarian who died in the revolution, and the cruel reprisals that followed, were read out. A large proportion of the 300,000 people who eventually attended were not even born in 1956.

The high point many remembered was the fiery speech delivered by the bearded, red-haired Viktor Orbán, twenty-six, wearing traditional dissident jeans. It was an inspiring performance which made him an instant name in Hungarian public life.* 'Young people fail to understand a lot of things about the older generation,' he said:

> We do not understand that the same Party and government leaders who told us to learn from books falsifying the history of the Revolution now vie with each other to touch these coffins as if they were lucky charms. We do not think there is any reason for us to be grateful for being allowed to bury our martyred dead. We do not owe thanks to anyone for the fact that our political organisations can work today ... If we can trust our ... strength, we can put an end to the Communist dictatorship; if we are determined enough we can force the Party to submit itself to free elections; and if we don't lose sight of the ideals of 1956, then we will be able to elect a government that will start immediate negotiations for the swift withdrawal of Russian troops.

* He went on, a decade later, to become Prime Minister.

The applause and cheers rang around Heroes' Square for several minutes. Even at this stage it was still daring at a big public event to call for the Soviets to leave Hungary.[3]

Among the mourners, Mária Kovács was moved to tears several times during the ceremony, particularly as she heard the cry through the square 'Russzkik Haza' – Russians Go Home. 'I was cautious about these changes,' she said. 'We had seen reforms from Moscow before. We saw reforms in Central and Eastern Europe in 1956, in 1968, in 1980–81 in Poland. In all these cases ... they began, to a large extent, in Moscow, or were permitted by Moscow, and continued for a while. Then, very suddenly, the reforms ended, sometimes violently.' She was cautious because the same thing could happen again, Gorbachev could be removed from power, the process he began could be reversed.

'And you must not forget the duplicity of the ... funeral. It was staged by the Communists. They were the same people who just a few years earlier had no trouble condemning Imre Nagy as a traitor to the Soviet system and to socialism. All the people from the Communist side who stood on the podium at the burial were the people who had gone through the ritual of condemning 1956 just a few years earlier. It sent the message that these people could change their minds if an opportunistic moment turned up.'[4] They included the Prime Minister Németh, Imre Pozsgay and the State President Mátyás Szüros. The Communists reminded mourners that they had a right to revere Imre Nagy as one of their own. Nagy had been a passionately loyal Party man all his life. His last words before he bravely faced the scaffold were to declare undying commitment to the party of the working class. It was not a message the thousands in Heroes' Square wanted to hear.

At 1.30 p.m. a funeral procession comprising the families of Nagy and his four comrades, along with a few close friends, returned to Plot 301. The men were laid to rest for the last time at a short private ceremony, but now had a monument and gravestones.

Soon after the Nagy reburial Hungarian immigration officials began to notice a phenomenon they had not seen before. Hungary was a major summer holiday destination for East Germans. Many favoured Budapest, which had the restaurants and fleshpots that did not exist in dull and staid East Berlin. Most, though, would head for Lake Balaton, where they could sunbathe on sandy beaches or take the curative waters in the excellent spas dotted mainly around its southern shore. It was a place where many German families could be reunited, if only for a few days, as large numbers of West Germans also visited Balaton. Usually, the visitors would return home after a fortnight or so of vacation. This summer it was becoming clear, even by mid-June, that many of the GDR visitors were staying and new numbers were steadily flowing into Hungary through Czechoslovakia, clearly with no intention of returning home. The movement along the highways seemed to be one-way. It was not a serious problem, yet, for the Hungarians. A few thousand families were easily accommodated with generous Hungarian hosts. But the government was aware it could grow into a major crisis soon and turn into a row with the East Germans, which they would prefer to avert if possible. The Party leader Grósz, Prime Minister Németh and the Foreign Minister Gyula Horn decided to do little for now and wait to see what happened. They sought some advice from the Kremlin, but aides to both Gorbachev and Shevardnadze said it was Hungary's decision, they would not interfere, and it was up to the comrades in Budapest to sort the matter out with the GDR.

The regime in Berlin was becoming uneasy. It was beginning to be noticed that many people were not returning to their homes and jobs after their summer holidays. It was a talking point everywhere, but never allowed to be mentioned in the press. The numbers increased considerably after items on television from China were screened, which regularly repeated the government's statement that it 'wholeheartedly congratulated the People's Republic of China for its prompt action in dealing with disturbances in Beijing that were instigated by Western imperialist agents'.[5]

This was the start of the 'Trabi trail', when East Germans filled up their cars with as much as they could hold and drove to Hungary and, they hoped, ultimately, to freedom. Invariably they drove in the Trabant, the box-like, 2-stroke-engine cars, partly made of plastic, which spewed exhaust fumes and were a spluttering symbol of East German life and industry. The Trabi was not elegant, but it functioned with relative efficiency. Production did not conform to the laws of supply and demand: customers of the 'people's car' could wait for seven to eight years for delivery, so when it arrived it was a prized possession. Six colours were supposed to be available, but only three were ever seen: white, a powder blue and beige. The speedometer went up to 130 kph but, in the great tradition of East German fib-telling, a motorist was lucky to get past 80. It belched out noxious fumes at four times the European average. East Germans told endless jokes about it. Yet most owners had an extraordinary affection for their

Trabi. Seldom, if ever, was a single mode of transport more closely identified with its country of origin.

After the Hungarians began dismantling their section of the Iron Curtain on 2 May, East Germans thought that if they reached Hungary they were already halfway to the West. They qualified for West German citizenship automatically. The problem was getting into Austria. They could obtain a West German passport virtually on demand at any FRG consulate. But East Germany had agreements dating from the early 1960s with all the Warsaw Pact countries not to honour a West German passport that did not contain a valid entry stamp. The rule was that if you did not enter Hungary on a West German passport, you could not leave on one. That was enough to ensure East Germans remained in the Soviet bloc. Now many thought that if they simply stayed in Hungary, eventually the government in Budapest would allow them into Austria and thence into West Germany.

Most of those who took the Trabi trail were professional, middle-class people in their twenties or early thirties with young families. 'It was no place to bring up children. There were no prospects, no hope. Just a sterile life of lies to look forward to,' one of them said. But almost everyone complained of something similar. 'We weren't malnourished or maltreated physically. It was a grinding oppression and we had to get out. We did not think the Hungarians would send us back, though of course that was a possibility. We thought we could sit and wait.'

The East Germans asked the Hungarians to keep to their agreement and not to allow their citizens to leave. The Hungarians pledged to stick to their Warsaw Pact Treaty obligations. Then Berlin demanded the return of their citizens. The leadership in Hungary unanimously refused and said the GDR should negotiate an agreement with the West Germans about the fate of people they now called, for the first time, 'refugees'. Berlin appealed to the Soviets for a ruling. Honecker met Shevardnadze for confidential talks in Berlin. The Soviet Foreign Minister refused to come down on either side and repeated the Kremlin line that the East Germans must reach a deal with Hungary. The East German dictator was furious and despaired of developments in the Soviet bloc. 'We see what is happening in Poland, following the elections. It is . . . unsettling. Socialism cannot be lost in Poland. In Hungary the processes are probably unstoppable. I remember well the events of 1956. Many comrades in Hungary fear that . . . with the reburial of Nagy counter-revolution will break out again. Is it possible to prevent the splitting-up of the Hungarian Party? If not Hungary will split further into the bourgeois camp.'[6]

A month after Imre Nagy was reburied, thousands of mourners attended another funeral in Budapest that laid Hungary's past to rest. János Kádár lived just long enough to see his old rival's reinterment, though he was so senile and ill by then that he could not grasp what was happening. He died on the morning of 6 July and the news of his passing was met with surprising but genuine grief. Hungarians may have grown to hate much that Kádár stood for – and much that they themselves had done with him over the decades in a conspiracy of silence. Yet they respected the man. His funeral on 14 July was also a political event, a sombre occasion attended by 100,000 people at Kerepesi, Hungary's national cemetery. Many had attended the Nagy funeral a few weeks earlier. Three million Hungarians watched live on television. The Hungarian leader for thirty-two years was buried in a section of the graveyard filled with other Communist 'heroes' known as the Pantheon of the Working Class. The inscription on his marble gravestone was intended as self-justification, but spoke for countless numbers of other Communists who fought for their cause during the twentieth century: 'I was where I had to be. I did what I had to do.'

THIRTY-NINE

A PRESIDENTIAL TOUR

Warsaw, Monday 10 July 1989

IT WAS THE AMERICAN REPUBLICAN George Bush who convinced the Communist General Jaruzelski to stand as Poland's President. Bush was worried that the pace of the changes in Poland and Hungary could career out of control and lead to serious instability. His tour to the two countries had been planned soon after his inauguration, but revolutionary events had happened since it had been arranged. He wondered to aides such as Condoleezza Rice if they 'weren't more than the market could bear'. Some of his advisers were surprised by the comment, but they understood the President's natural caution. Bush told the speechwriters who were preparing material for the visit: 'Whatever this trip is, it is *not* a victory tour with me running around over there pounding my chest ... I don't want to sound inflammatory or provocative. I don't want what I do to complicate the lives of Gorbachev and the others. I don't want to put a stick in Gorbachev's eye.' He was willing to take the risk of looking like a plodder, to achieve higher gains.

Repeatedly, he told his staff that he did not want to make the same mistakes as President Eisenhower in 1956: the US encouraged the Hungarian revolutionaries to rebel, but when Soviet tanks invaded the insurgents were left on their own. 'I wanted to be careful,' he said. 'The traumatic uprisings in East Germany in 1953, Hungary in 1956, and Czechoslovakia in 1968 were constantly on my mind ... I did not want to encourage a course of events which might turn violent and get out of hand and which we then couldn't – or wouldn't – support, leaving people stranded on the barricades. I hoped to encourage liberation ... without provoking an internal crackdown, as happened in Poland in 1981, or a Soviet backlash.' In Warsaw and Budapest on his coming trip, he did not want 'to foment unrest ... or stimulate it unintentionally ... If massive crowds gathered, intent on showing their opposition to Soviet domination, things [could] get out of control. An enthusiastic reception could erupt into a riot . . . with devastating consequences for the growing sense of optimism and progress that was beginning to sweep the region.'[1]

The President and his entourage had arrived the evening before – a sweltering, humid night, recalled the US National Security Advisor, General Scowcroft. 'The air conditioning system in our hotel was not up to the demands of the weather. The inside temperature was worse than outdoors and with the windows not designed to open, we had a real problem. I finally managed to get a window propped open and I pulled the bedding on to the floor where there was . . . a wisp of a breeze. The hotel explained that there was simply not enough . . . power for the system to run properly – a painful reminder of how backward the Polish economy was.[2]

After a sleepless night Bush saw Jaruzelski at the Belvedere Palace soon after 9 a.m. They had met two years earlier when Bush was Vice President and briefly passed through Poland. He had advised the General to legalise Solidarity and negotiate with it, but Jaruzelski baulked at the suggestion and declared that it would 'be suicidal for the Government'. Nevertheless Bush liked Jaruzelski, respected him and thought he was astute. He described him to his advisers as 'a real class act'. Now that the General had struck a deal with Solidarity, the US President did not want to see him and the Communist regime suddenly swept aside. Bush was convinced that Jaruzelski could 'be a force for stability'. The irony was obvious. The Americans had for nearly half a century wanted to free the satellite states from the Soviet orbit. They had spent many billions of dollars on defence, espionage and propaganda with that objective. Now some of these regimes, loathed by their subjects, were teetering on the edge of destruction. Barely a month ago, in their first taste of democracy for sixty years, Poles had resoundingly voted against their Communist rulers. Yet the American President wanted to keep them in power – at least for a while. The ultra-cautious Bush thought it was a way of preventing anarchy in Eastern Europe.

His conversation with Jaruzelski on this morning was bizarre. The General said he had thought long and hard but was now reluctant to stand for President and face possible humiliation. Defeat, he said, was 'unacceptable. I can't win without Solidarity support, and I don't think that will come. What role do you think I should play?' Bush replied instantly that he should seek the nomination: 'I told him his refusal to run might inadvertently lead to serious instability and I urged him to reconsider.' Bush admitted it was a strange feeling trying to persuade a senior Communist to run for office. 'But I felt that Jaruzelski's experience was the best hope for a smooth transition in Poland.' For the next day and a half he continually praised Jaruzelski's patriotic efforts to transform his country. The opposition was deeply disappointed. Most of the intellectuals in Solidarity were instinctively pro-American. Yet they showed their displeasure at the words they were hearing.[3]

They were yet angrier when they heard the details of a US$ 100 million aid package Bush had brought with him. The President was aware how meagre it was. Secretary of State James Baker, Condoleezza Rice and General Scowcroft had all urged much more generous assistance as a way of encouraging the democratic changes in Poland. But the US Treasury Secretary, Nicholas Brady, said the cupboard was bare. 'We can't throw good money down a Polish rat-hole,' he had said, and the President listened. Bush announced the aid at a speech to Solidarity parliamentarians, along with an additional offer of US$ 15 million to help clean up the pollution around Kraków. He was heard in silence. Government leaders and the opposition were united in their fury when they discovered that John Sununu, the President's Chief of Staff, had been telling reporters that more money for Poland 'would be like a young person in a candy store ... [who] lacked the self-discipline to spend it wisely'.[4]

The next day Bush flew to Gdańsk to meet Lech Wałęsa. The President disliked and distrusted the Solidarity leader, in contrast with his growing sympathy and fondness for Jaruzelski. He thought Wałęsa was too quixotic, too radical and not solid or reliable enough. When they had met two years earlier Bush was taken aback by Wałęsa's answer when he asked if Solidarity would be legalised. Wałęsa had said that if such an unlikely event occurred it 'would cause a lot of trouble for us' because Solidarity might then be blamed for the economic disaster in Poland. Bush and his wife Barbara had an uneasy lunch in the Wałęsas' modest flat – prepared by Danuta – which ended in a near-shouting match. The Pole complained about the 'pathetic, paltry' aid offer and declared that Poland deserved far more generous treatment. He demanded US$ 10 billion over three years to get the Polish economy moving. When Bush replied that it was impossible the union leader angrily said that there could be mass poverty and unemployment in Poland and then 'we will have civil war. We're at the end of our rope.'[5]

Glad to be out of Poland, the President received a rapturous welcome in Budapest. Air Force One landed in a tremendous thunderstorm. Thousands of people turned up to greet him, which buoyed him after his difficult time in Gdańsk. Bush rarely played the showman, but he sensed a good photo opportunity on this occasion and after he walked down the steps in the driving rain he offered an elderly woman his overcoat.* He was drenched after a walkabout, shaking hands on the tarmac. But when he settled down to business, as in Poland, he got on well with the conservative voices in the Communist regime, rather less so with radicals in the opposition. When he was handed a small piece of the barbed-wire fence, the Iron Curtain, which the Hungarians had dismantled in May, he declared himself moved to tears. He praised the government, which had ordered the fence removed, not the opposition, which had put pressure on the regime to remove it. Németh, Grósz, and the economist Rezsö Nyers, the trio now at the helm in Hungary, impressed him and he promised American support. Bush told them: 'We're with you. What you're doing is exciting. It's what we have always wanted. We are not going to complicate things for you. We know that the better we get along with the Soviets, the better it is for you too . . . We have no intention of making you choose between East and West.'[6]

Later the same day he met leading opposition figures at the residence of the American Ambassador to Hungary, Mark Palmer. The party did not go well. When Imre Pozsgay told Bush that the Communists would lose power the moment free and fair elections were called – 'My Party is doing too little, too late,' he said – Bush looked worried. Palmer had built good contacts with the dissidents and reform Communists over the last three years but the 'extreme caution' of his President and his boss at the State Department frustrated him. 'Bush and Baker kept cautioning these people . . . in my living room . . . not to go too far, too fast,' he said. When Bush told the former dissidents that their Communist government 'was moving in the right direction. Your country is taking things one step at a time. Surely that is prudent,' they did not pretend to hide their amazement. There was a culture shock, as Palmer described it. The godfather of underground dissident activity in Hungary, the philosopher János Kis, was at the Ambassador's reception. He was a highly influential man in opposition circles throughout the Communist world, and he looked precisely what he was: a Central

* Actually it belonged to one of his secret service guards, which the President had borrowed.

European intellectual. 'When I introduced the President and Jim Baker to János Kis,' said Palmer, 'it was, like, "who is this strange man with a beard who looks like Woody Allen?"' Bush told his aides afterwards: 'These really aren't the right guys to be running the place. At least not yet. They're just not ready.' He thought the Communists he had met were far better placed to introduce democracy and free markets to Hungary.[7]

Bush's influence was powerful with Jaruzelski, who announced soon after the Americans left Poland that he would run for President after all. The US Ambassador, John Davis, was influential in persuading Solidarity to help elect him. Wałęsa believed that the Soviets, as well as the Polish army and security forces, would accept no other candidate. So he made a deal with Jaruzelski that would guarantee the General's victory. But it was a close-run thing. Wałęsa had to strong-arm newly elected Solidarity MPs into abstaining during the vote. Many simply refused: they could not support the man who had jailed them and caused their families to suffer. But finally he persuaded seven of them to agree. 'Vote with your consciences,' he told them, and then explained that Solidarity needed this 'vital' deal. 'We held our noses, but went through with it in the end,' one Solidarity legislator declared. At a point during the voting when it seemed possible that the General might lose, Solidarity activists had to scour the bars looking for MPs to go through the lobby for Jaruzelski. He scraped home by just one vote. On 19 July General Jaruzelski, the man who had turned Poland into a military dictatorship, became the democratically chosen President of the country.[8]

One of the cleverest of the Communist chieftains in Poland was Janusz Reykowski, the former psychology professor from Warsaw and the chief negotiator for the Party at the Round Table talks. He said: 'There are plenty of Marxist-Leninist textbooks about taking power; but there are none about giving it up.' Over the next month of tortured negotiations, Poland experienced its first taste of real parliamentary democracy since the 1920s. It was not always a pretty sight. Jaruzelski was President, but he could not find a working government. He gave up his position as Party boss, but he had not abandoned the idea of ensuring that the Communists should retain power in Poland. On Tuesday 25 July he summoned Wałęsa and asked him to join a Communist-led Grand Coalition, as the General called it. The Party would hold the top positions, Solidarity could have four junior posts – Health,

Environment, Housing, Industry. 'Solidarity must grow into power,' Jaruzelski said. Wałęsa refused immediately and would not budge. A week later Jaruzelski appointed Kiszczak Prime Minister, but support for the Communists had drained away. The former head of state security could not form a government. Even some old Party stalwarts refused to serve with him or the other men in uniform, old familiar faces who he thought could lead Poland into a new democratic dawn.[9]

Wałęsa had not intended to take Solidarity into government, despite long consideration of the electoral position following the second round of voting on Sunday 18 June. Solidarity had lost just one contested seat in which it fielded a candidate for the Sejm and took 99 per cent of the seats in the Senate. The bizarre exception in the Upper House was an Independent, Henryk Stokłosa, an ex-Communist-turned-millionaire entrepreneur, who claimed he spent US$ 100,000 on his election, a fortune in Poland at the time. Wałęsa had said before the elections: 'We are a trade union . . . What we want is autonomy and independence from the government. Let the Communists govern.' That caution was partly for Soviet consumption. He was not sure the Russians would let Solidarity take power and he did not want to provoke them. Gorbachev had said all the right things, but Wałęsa could not trust the Soviets. They still had thousands of troops on Polish soil. Also, he was not sure that Solidarity was yet ready for power. Wide splits were opening up within the union. As one of its leading figures said, not entirely as a joke: 'Lech deserved a second Nobel Prize for keeping the peace within Solidarity.' There had been factions in the union from the beginning, but seldom was the infighting as intense as now, when the Communists were on the verge of defeat.[10]

Some of the leaders who had been influential figures from the start in 1980 were opposed to Solidarity forming a government. They were championed by the mild-mannered, intense, thoughtful Catholic intellectual Tadeusz Mazowiecki. A widower now aged sixty-two, he shared a small and untidy Warsaw flat with his two sons. He had hardly slept since the election campaign had begun in May, living on cigarettes and adrenaline. He was convinced the time was not yet right for Solidarity. They should stay in opposition, learn the parliamentary ropes and prepare themselves to take over after elections in four years. He believed it would be a mistake to enter into a government in which 'the police and the army are still in the hands of the ruling Party', and he thought that if Solidarity joined an administration now it would be blamed for the mess of the Polish economy. 'We had clever people with us, lots of them, intellectuals who knew a great deal about history, philosophy, literature, theology,' he said. 'But we didn't have people who knew how to run anything, how to organise things, run local governments, departments of state. We needed time to learn how to do this. I thought we were not prepared.' Always a moderate, sensible voice, he argued the case in the newspaper he edited, *Tygodnik Solidarność* (*Solidarity Weekly*) under the headline 'Make haste, slowly.'[11]

Adam Michnik, one of the most creative voices of opposition in Poland, profoundly disagreed. He thought Solidarity should grab what they could while they had the opportunity. The Polish people, who for years had wanted to see the back of Communists in government, would expect no less. Inflation was now out of control at nearly 500 per cent and no decisions were being taken while the constitutional crisis continued. He knew Solidarity had some bright young economists, led by Leszek Balcerowicz, who said that urgent, radical and painful measures – 'shock therapy' – had to be taken immediately, within days, to stave off economic collapse. Michnik came up with a formula put simply in a headline – 'Your President, our Prime Minister'. Solidarity should try to take the lead in a coalition and work with Jaruzelski as President. Wałęsa finally came down on Michnik's side. He knew too that the Pope was in favour of Solidarity taking the power they could. Pope John Paul thought it would send a message throughout Eastern Europe if the Soviet empire was defeated by peaceful, democratic means.

Wałęsa resolved the problem by looking at the parliamentary arithmetic. He acted in typically bold, unilateral fashion away from his advisers and aides, who he said sometimes confused him. He returned to his flat in Gdańsk and on the evening of 7 August made a statement to the Polish news agency inviting the two junior partners of the Communists, the Peasant Party and the Democratic Party, to break with forty years of slavish support for the Communists and to join Solidarity in forming a new government. Together, they would constitute 55 per cent of the Sejm. Wałęsa's announcement was a shock to the rest of the Solidarity leadership. He had talked the idea through with almost nobody in his entourage, but the dramatic coup worked. At first the Peasants' leader, Roman Malinowski, and Jerzy Jozwiak of the Democratic Party were highly dubious. Two grey old bureaucrats, they had been puppets of the Communists for years, obeying orders out of habit. They were unused to thinking independently. But their members persuaded them to accept the arrangement. They realised they would soon be sidelined entirely if they turned the offer down.

Jaruzelski did not like the deal. Rakowski, now Communist Party chief, advised him to reject it. The General's spokesman for years, the unpopular Jerzy Urban, told him that if the Communists went into opposition they would lose power 'altogether and forever'. But the General, a realist, knew he had no choice. 'Solidarity has burst over our life like a typhoon,' he had told the other Warsaw Pact leaders barely a fortnight earlier.

> We must attempt to solve the current crisis, without the use of violence, without bloodshed. We can't forever take a path that brings us into conflict with the working class . . . that tears open a rift which can be healed with great difficulty. The Party has been the guarantor of the strength of socialism. But the Party is no absolute monarch. I have to admit that is what we became, that is how we behaved, an absolute monarch, who was always right, who gives commands and orders. Yes, we have commanded the military apparatus, but we have suffered a political defeat.[12]

On the afternoon of Friday 18 August he told Wałęsa that he would agree to a Solidarity government on two conditions. 'Our anxiety, and that of the Soviets and the other Warsaw Pact countries, is that . . . you will leave the socialist bloc and then we don't know what may happen,' he said. The General also insisted that Communists must retain the Interior and Defence Ministries. Wałęsa agreed. That evening on television he declared, in a message directed at Moscow: 'Poland cannot forget where it is situated and to whom it has obligations. We are in the Warsaw Pact. That cannot be changed.' It was not the most ringing endorsement, but he had been assured by Jaruzelski that it would be enough to assure him of the Kremlin's blessing.

Wałęsa then dropped a bombshell. It had been assumed, during most of these negotiations, that he would become head of the new government. Mazowiecki, Kuroń and most of the Solidarity leadership urged him to become Prime Minister. When Solidarity legislators met to approve the new coalition, they thought they were voting to anoint him as Premier. But he announced he had no intention of taking the job. 'I wish to remain a worker . . . a man of the people. I stay with the masses, I am one of them,' he said with *faux naïveté*. The principal reason was probably that he knew that whoever led the new government was unlikely to be thanked or remain popular within a year or two. He did not wish to be directly associated with the pain that would inevitably be accompanied by 'shock therapy', which he could foresee would be closed factories and unemployment for many already badly-off Polish workers. Even the Lenin Shipyard was scheduled for partial closure under an austerity package being discussed by economists from Solidarity and the Communists. He would handpick a Prime Minister to take the difficult decisions in the first non-Communist government in the Soviet bloc for forty years. Then he could pretend to be above politics. He did not need a formal title. Lech Wałęsa was now the most powerful man in Poland – and everybody knew it.[13]

At around midnight on the day Jaruzelski agreed to allow a Solidarity government, the Soviet Foreign Ministry received an urgent telex from Bucharest. Nicolae Ceauşescu had been frantically cabling Warsaw Pact capitals urging them to intervene 'to rescue socialism in Poland'. He denounced Solidarity as 'the hireling of international imperialism'. The note to the Poles called on Jaruzelski to form 'a government of national salvation'. In the message to the Soviets, the man who twenty-one years earlier had denounced the Soviet invasion of Czechoslovakia as interference in a sovereign state's affairs now urged 'collective military action' against Poland. He demanded the presence of Eduard Shevardnadze in Bucharest for talks about a crisis in the 'camp' and wanted an immediate Warsaw Pact summit to plan an intervention in Poland.

He was not the only worried dictator in Eastern Europe. At the Warsaw Pact summit in Bucharest the previous month, Honecker, Ceauşescu and Miloš Jakeš, had formed a united front to urge Gorbachev to halt the drift in Poland and in Hungary. Honecker warned that there was a 'grave danger to communism – and to all of us here'. Gorbachev's response was: 'The fears that socialism is threatened . . . are not founded. And those who are afraid had better hold on because perestroika has only just begun . . . We are going from one international order to another.' The response left them indignant.

Most of the Soviet leaders were on holiday when the latest Polish crisis brewed. Gorbachev was at his seaside villa at Foros in the Crimea. He was more concerned with domestic issues than foreign ones, even developments as dramatic and revolutionary as were happening in Poland. He had given his blessing to Jaruzelski to do what he thought was best and was determined not to interfere. The policy was simply put by one of its architects, Alexander Yakovlev, and Gorbachev was essentially true to its spirit and letter. 'There never was a formal decision to refrain from using force in Eastern Europe,' he said. 'We simply stopped being hypocritical. For years we had told the entire world that these countries were free and independent, even though this was obviously not the case. There was no need to take a formal decision. We just had to implement what was formal policy.' When Gorbachev heard of the Ceauşescu demand he simply told his aides, 'Don't worry. Ceauşescu is just worried for his own skin', and then concentrated his mind on Soviet matters. Those were consuming him throughout the year, not events in the satellite states.[14]

Shevardnadze was holidaying in Georgia. His chief adviser, Sergei Tarasenko, showed him the cable while the Foreign Minister was sunbathing on the beach.

> He took it calmly. There was no way he was going to take any action. He said 'Forget about it.' We remained on the beach and started talking in general and posed a question to ourselves in our swimming trunks. 'Do you understand what is going to happen?' he said. 'We are going to lose our allies, the Warsaw Pact. These countries will go their own ways . . . yes we will suffer. We will lose our jobs.' It was no problem to project the collapse of the empire. Our empire was doomed. But we did not think it would come so soon.[15]

FORTY

TRAIL OF THE TRABANTS

Sopron, western Hungary, 19 August 1989

THE IDEA ORIGINALLY BELONGED to Otto von Habsburg, eldest son of the last Austrian Emperor and King of Hungary, Karl I. The seventy-seven-year-old von Habsburg was a staunchly conservative member of the European Parliament, who had fought the Cold War for decades with much passion and some flair for propaganda. He saw a way to publicise the plight of the East German refugees who were flooding into Hungary, and to embarrass the regimes which would not let them freely enter Austria. There were around 85,000 of them now, on top of the 35,000 or so Romanians fleeing the rigours of life under Ceauşescu. The swelling numbers were causing a humanitarian crisis within Hungary, and a political dilemma for the government. They could not decide what to do with the refugees and continued to dither for weeks. The Hungarian authorities hoped the problem would go away and they could avoid a more serious confrontation with their supposed fraternal socialist allies in Berlin. Clearly that was wishful thinking.

Von Habsburg had been barred from visiting Hungary until the autumn of the previous year. There were a few royalist supporters in the country. Their Habsburg flags and insignia could occasionally be spotted at demonstrations against the Danube dams and for better treatment of the Transylvanian refugees. It was a minuscule movement but the regime had taken no chances and kept him out of the country, for decades. Now von Habsburg could come and go as he pleased. Along with Hungarian human rights groups, and the opposition Hungarian Democratic Forum, he planned a 'day of celebration to say farewell to the Iron Curtain'. There was to be a giant symbolic gate built at the border near the baroque town of Sopron, attended by delegations from Hungary and Austria. At 3 p.m. the delegations would cross sides, to represent freedom of movement. The public would be encouraged to watch the ceremony, eat a meal and raise a glass to celebrate. The event was billed as the Pan-European Picnic where, on a sunny day in Central Europe, people could commemorate freedom near the spot where a few months earlier border guards began dismantling the electrified fence that had separated East and West. At that point it was a small-scale event that might receive some publicity in Austria and Hungary. But the stakes were raised when Imre Pozsgay became involved as the co-sponsor of the picnic. He came up with the suggestion that turned a modest, though interesting, commemoration into a worldwide media event that had profound effects on the entire Soviet empire.[1]

Pozsgay was the acknowledged leader of the reform Communists. It was in his political interests to be seen to support the refugees wholeheartedly. His boldness and compassion, or so he thought, would shame his erstwhile Party comrades in Budapest who displayed indecision and weakness. He negotiated a deal with the government that would keep the 'symbolic gate' open for four hours in the afternoon. He made an informal deal with his old friend and reformist soulmate, the Interior Minister István Horváth, that the border guards should turn a blind eye to East Germans trying to cross illegally – at least for a few hours during the day. It was not planned as a mass breakout from Hungary. Von Habsburg believed that if even just a few score refugees arrived safely in Austria his point would have been made and thousands would soon follow.

The Trabis were on the road again, from Lake Balaton to western Hungary near the border areas. With an entrepreneurial spirit not quite suppressed over the past four decades, garages throughout the country had specially stocked up on the fuel their inefficient 2-stroke engines used. More refugees were arriving each day now on trains and buses, carrying bedding, camping equipment, cooking utensils. Leaflets publicising the 'picnic' were printed in German telling the refugees where to go so they could 'clip off part of the iron curtain'. A convenient map guided them to the spot. In the few days before the picnic, large numbers – estimated at nearly 9,000 – began to appear in campsites and bed and breakfast guest houses around Sopron, said the head of the Hungarian border guard, Gyula Kovács. 'The whole town appeared to be filled with East Germans . . . It was also a serious sign when the Austrian Red Cross and other Austrian officials put up tents on the other side of the border . . . They were obviously expecting a large number of East Germans to cross.'[2]

The West German Foreign Minister, Hans Dietrich Genscher, had dispatched scores of extra consular officials to Sopron 'to assist fellow Germans any way they could'. They acted as a form of pressure on the border guards, who would be more circumspect if they knew their actions were observed by foreign diplomats. Not that it was needed. The border guards, mostly young conscripts, had no intention of using force against the refugees. Kovács issued his men clear orders. 'We gave instructions that there should be no border patrols in the area immediately next to the picnic site,' he said. 'In the areas beyond the picnic, if the patrols came across any East Germans trying to cross the border they should instruct them to stop and turn back. If they turned back, fine. If they didn't then ... OK, we should just count how many went across and then carry on with normal duties.'[3]

Nevertheless, the East Germans who planned to escape were nervous and scared. They could not know what orders Hungarian soldiers had been given. Up to now the Hungarian people had been remarkably generous. But the regime, while expressing sympathy for their plight, had done little to help them. At least they had not been sent back to East Germany. Berlin teachers Sylvia and Harry Lux had left their home just over a month ago with their seven-year-old son Danny. As soon as they had heard about the Pan-European Picnic they were determined to try to make it into Austria this day. They arrived by train in Sopron, 120 kilometres west of Budapest, in the early morning. 'Outside the railway station there were two or three taxis with their doors already open ... it was all planned so perfectly that you wondered how it was possible,' Mrs Lux said;

> Then we were taken to a hotel and up to a room where we had to wait in hiding ... We had to wait until 3 p.m. when the leaders of the festival were to join the picnic for the gate-opening ceremony. We were worried sick and shaking and time seemed to drag on forever. Then we were driven straight to the picnic ... But there were so many different people from all nationalities there that we thought that we were too late ... that it had happened ... But we made our way away from the picnic, deeper into the countryside where we thought the border was, according to the map. When we crossed some high ground we saw a man from the West German Consulate in Budapest, whom we recognised and who knew us by ... sight and said, 'Ah, the Lux family, hurry up, there are some kind border guards up ahead and they've lifted up the wire fence for you. Good luck.' My husband took Danny in his arms and we started off again and there really were

border guards there and the barbed wire was lifted so you could crawl through.

She stopped for a short while just in front of the gap, watched by some Austrians on the other side. 'I was not able to grasp that this really was it. And then one of [them] said, "Come on you can do it" . . . grabbed hold of me from the other side and pulled me through . . . and on the other side he shook my hand and said, "You're free now." I asked, "Is that true, they really can't come and take me back?" We all cried and hugged each other.'[4]

More than 600 made it to Austria that day through the 'symbolic' gate and around 1,400 through the borders nearby. It was not a huge number; they were replaced within a couple of days by new refugees pouring into Hungary. East German television reported, without any pictures of the scenes at the picnic, that some 'GDR citizens had been seduced and paid to emigrate by the Federal Republic in order to slander our state'.

The Hungarian government realised it could not sit on its hands and do nothing for much longer. That was graphically driven home to the Prime Minister, Miklós Németh. 'I was visiting a friend of mine who happened to live near the West German Consul General's house. I had to step over bodies lying on the pavement waiting for the Consulate to open in the morning . . . to get West German passports. I could see the problem with my own eyes, we had to have a clear-cut solution.'

Minor disturbances had broken out in some parts of Budapest and a decision could not be delayed much longer. The East Germans wanted to send planes and trains to Hungary to take their citizens back: 'We refused. We told them it was absolutely out of the question for you to hunt them here in Hungary and take them,' Németh said. But they were allowed to send 'diplomatic observers'. These turned out to be Stasi officers who kept a watch on the refugees. At one of the refugee centres in a church on the Buda side of the River Danube run by Csilla, Baroness von Boeselager and the Catholic priest Imre Kozma, a Stasi captain asked her for the names of everyone who was in the building or who had passed through it over the past weeks. She refused, outraged, but she agreed they could run an office in a van on a side street outside the gates. The intelligence agents started taking photographs of people entering and leaving the centre and an angry crowd gathered, shouting at them and pelting stones. Local police had to be called to keep the peace. The next night the van was vandalised and the following day it was withdrawn.[5]

The Hungarians were put under intense pressure from the West to let the East Germans go. The Americans turned the screws. The US Ambassador, Mark Palmer, demanded to meet the Foreign Minister, Gyula Horn. 'I told him they could forget about trade and investment from the US if they sent the East Germans back,' he said. But despite all the encouraging signals the Hungarians had been receiving for months, they were still unsure what the Russians would do if they allowed the East Germans to head West. It would have serious implications for the Soviet bloc.[6] 'We were very worried about how the Soviets would react,' said László Kovács, Hungary's Deputy Foreign Minister. 'We knew that the East German reaction would be virulent. We expected economic reprisals and we made contingency plans for that. But we were troubled by the response from Moscow.' After several weeks' hesitation they sent a note to Shevardnadze discreetly suggesting that they were considering opening the border. 'We got a reply back quickly saying very simply that "this is an affair that concerns only Hungary, the GDR and West Germany".'[7]

In Berlin the government was paralysed by the serious illness of Erich Honecker. On 8 July, at the annual Warsaw Pact leaders' summit held this year in Bucharest, he had collapsed in agony clutching the right side of his abdomen and his back, shortly after making a speech to his peers warning of the great perils facing communism. He was rushed to the best hospital in the city, reserved for the top Party officials, where he was diagnosed with stones in his gall-bladder. After one night, he was flown back to Berlin. There it quickly became obvious that his condition was more serious: he had cancerous tumours in his bladder and surgeons had to operate urgently. Honecker was out of action for weeks and the extent of his illness was kept from the public. In dictatorships like the GDR nothing of importance could be decided without the supreme leader's authority. 'For a long time we were unable to say anything about the refugee crisis because of Honecker's absence,' Günter Schabowski said. 'We were insecure about it, but we felt helpless. So we said OK let's wait until he returns.' But he was ill the whole of the summer and all efforts in the leadership to talk about the biggest issue facing the country were shelved until late September.

The East German Foreign Minister, Oskar Fischer, sent diplomatic notes to Budapest demanding the return of the East German citizens who had 'illegally overstayed their visa regulations'. He reminded his counterpart, Horn, that apart from the Warsaw Pact agreement that all member states would honour each other's travel laws, there was a treaty between the two countries signed on 20 June 1969 repeating the pledge. Horn said that an international treaty, like the Geneva Convention on Refugees, superseded bi-party agreements. They had reached an impasse. Fischer began talking to West German officials, but those negotiations broke down too.

The Exodus, as East Germans called it, was the main topic of conversation throughout the country. 'Within every family there was at least one person asking the question: do we go, or do we stay here and keep hoping? The choice was agonising for people who may have hated the regime, but still had friends, families, jobs they liked, homes. The Exodus dominated life,' Matthias Mueller, a history student in Berlin at the time, said. It dominated West German television news. Every day there were reports from Hungary about the refugees and footage from the Trabi trail with interviews of the mainly young families who were leaving.[8] On East German TV it was hardly ever mentioned. Orders came from above to keep silent, said radio journalist Ferdinand Nor. 'Then when it was no longer possible to hide the vacant apartments, the empty desks in offices and at schools, we began to denounce the refugees as politically illiterate and "criminal elements".' Instructions were given in the summer to journalists on *Neues Deutschland* from the Party leadership:

> Our task is the propagation of the values of socialism and the effective revelation of the crimes of capitalism. Do not publish material on conflicts with foreigners in the country ... We will deny ourselves any comment on shortages ... The theme of 'Exodus' should not dominate daily conversation in the GDR. The events are damaging our image. With the aid of the media in the West the unimaginable successes of 40 years of socialist policies in the GDR are being disputed because the GDR does not fit into the picture of communism in crisis. We will not let ourselves be provoked ... We will report nothing of those returning from the West to the GDR.[9]

The Soviets were not prepared to help the East German regime. They thought the refugee crisis was a 'good thing' because it might make Berlin rethink, remove Honecker and spur it on to reform. Fischer met Shevardnadze privately. The Soviet Foreign Minister told him to allow free emigration. 'It will not be bad. It will ease your economic burdens, too,' Shevardnadze said. 'You should talk to opposition groups as comrades are doing elsewhere.' When he returned to Berlin, Fischer told his colleagues that they should expect no help from Moscow in this crisis of existence for the East German state.[10]

FORTY-ONE

A GOVERNMENT OF DISSIDENTS

Warsaw, Thursday 24 August 1989

IN HIS ROLE AS KINGMAKER, Wałęsa considered three candidates for Prime Minister. All had served time in jail for varying periods as subversives. The presence of any of them as head of a Warsaw Pact government would have appalled Ceauşescu or Honecker, who had now given up any hope that the Soviets would step in and halt the collapse of socialism in Poland. The prospect of dealing with any of them would have shocked almost every Communist Party official in Moscow just four years earlier. Now, shortly after eight minutes past one, when Tadeusz Mazowiecki was officially elected Polish Premier, the first message of congratulations he received was from his Soviet counterpart in the Kremlin.

Mazowiecki seemed an uninspiring choice for such a historic role. Yet it was precisely his virtues of modesty, humility and solidity that thrust his name forward, so different was he from Lech Wałęsa. The other options would have been riskier – particularly fifty-five-year-old Jacek Kuroń, one of the founding fathers of Polish opposition, who had been an active dissident since the 1960s. He had a brilliant analytical mind and shining integrity, but Wałęsa thought he would have been too radical a choice. Bronisław Geremek, now fifty-seven, was moderate enough and had been an influential adviser to the independent trade union since Solidarity was founded. Latterly an academic, for a short while he followed a diplomatic career and was dispatched, as a young official, to the Polish Embassy in Paris. But he became disillusioned with the Party and returned to his fourteenth-century manuscripts. He was a shrewd political tactician and a tough negotiator, but argumentative and quick to take offence, thought Wałęsa.

Mazowiecki was a safe bet. He was widely respected in Poland and abroad. After his release from jail in 1984 he had been allowed to travel and he was a powerful advocate in the West for Solidarity's cause. The clinching factor was that, unlike the other two, he was a devout Catholic who had excellent contacts at the Vatican and with the Polish episcopate. There was one problem, though. Mazowiecki was publicly against Solidarity forming a government. Generally he had good relations with Wałęsa, even when they disagreed. Sometimes he thought the former electrician was too high-handed and dictatorial, but he invariably trusted his judgement about people and strategy. Wałęsa felt sure he could work his charm and persuade Mazowiecki that a Solidarity government was now the only sensible course and that he, Mazowiecki, was the right man to lead it.

The seduction, as Mazowiecki once described it, not entirely as a joke, took place on the evening of 18 August at a dinner in the dismal restaurant of the faded but once grand Europejski Hotel, on the edge of Warsaw's Old Town. Initially, Mazowiecki made a show of not wanting the job, and insisted that Wałęsa should take it. Then he said he would accept the post on condition that Wałęsa would allow him a free hand and would 'not try to run things from behind the scenes'. He did not want the entourage around Wałęsa trying to place pressure on him either. He wanted to be his own man. He insisted on choosing his team of ministers, with nobody looking over his shoulder. Wałęsa agreed to keep in the background, but said he would always be available to co-operate.[1]

Jaruzelski was still brooding about being the Polish Communist who lost power. He remained a True Believer, even though the entire edifice of Soviet authority which he so admired was falling apart. He accepted Mazowiecki's appointment. He respected him. Jaruzelski insisted that his two close friends and associates, Generals Kiszczak and Siwicki, retain their posts at the Interior Ministry and Defence. Cardinal Glemp strongly approved of the choice and the Pope was delighted. He invited the new PM for an audience at the Vatican to receive a blessing.

Rakowski, Poland's last Communist Party leader, had a thirty-five-minute telephone conversation with Gorbachev on the morning of 22 August. He had once told Jaruzelski during martial law in 1982 that the Party could not maintain its position for ever and 'sooner or later we'll have to live with them, I'm afraid'. Most Communists would have thought he was talking nonsense, back then. Now it was Gorbachev who told him, 'You must learn to live with them. There is no other alternative but to accept the new government. Maybe we aren't very happy about it, but it has to be done. We will support the line of agreement pursued by Jaruzelski.' Policy would change only if Solidarity – which throughout the conversation he continued to call 'the opposition' – specifically turned on the USSR, which he did not think likely. He said he was 'astonished' by the Polish Party, 'which has shown itself to be crap. You'll have to rebuild it entirely from the bottom up. You'll never accomplish anything with the lot you have now.' Rakowski asked if he could go to Moscow for a meeting. This was a normal request for a new Communist Party chief in one of the satellite states and was usually granted as a matter of course. But things had changed. Gorbachev said, 'That's not a good idea now. It would look as though we are trying to interfere in Polish affairs.'[2]

Mazowiecki changed his mind about governing with Party men still in control of the army and police. 'Is it more dangerous to have a Communist general in your house, or leave him out of doors? It was clear to me that if the Party was not represented one way or another in the government ... reforms could not be carried through in a peaceful manner.' The rest of the team was mostly made up of former dissidents, like the economist Balcerowicz, who became Finance Minister, determined to institute his 'shock therapy'. The emotion of the moment when Mazowiecki became the first post-Communist Prime Minister of a Soviet bloc country nearly overcame him. He wept as he shook the hand, politely, of every member of the old government of Party officials. Most of them looked bemused. Then he kissed Geremek, newly elected leader of the Solidarity group of MPs, on both cheeks. At his home in Gdańsk, Wałęsa was filmed watching the event. It had taken nearly ten years, but power had irreversibly been wrested from the Polish Communists – and from their Soviet masters. He beamed an enormous smile from behind his walrus moustache and flashed a V for Victory sign.

In a clever move, the philosopher Jacek Kuroń, an inspirational figure behind the KOR group and Solidarity, was appointed Minister for Labour. He had first been jailed in 1969 for writing samizdat articles attacking the regime. Early on the morning after his appointment, as he was shaving, Kuroń received an urgent phone call from a neighbour warning him that a car was spotted outside his apartment building on Mickiewicz Street, a fashionable part of Warsaw. This had happened many times in the last twenty years. Invariably the car was a secret policeman's and the telephone call was to give Kuroń some time to put a few things in a bag before he was arrested and taken away to prison. Kuroń was surprised. He had only been in government for a few hours. Surely they might have given him longer than that before locking him up. This time it turned out to be his ministerial car and his chauffeur.[3]

FORTY-TWO

REFUGEES

Schloss Gymnich, Bonn, Friday 25 August 1989

SOON AFTER 7 A.M., amid the utmost secrecy, the Hungarian Prime Minister, Miklós Németh, and the Foreign Minister, Gyula Horn, flew from Budapest to Bonn. They wanted as few people as possible to know their destination: a medieval castle twenty-five kilometres south of the West German capital, where the FRG government often conducted high-level diplomatic conferences. Two days earlier, Németh had asked the Hungarian Ambassador to Bonn, István Horváth, to set up a meeting for him as soon as it could be arranged with the West German Chancellor, Helmut Kohl. 'We didn't say what it was about,' Németh said. 'All we told them was that it was very important, not only to us, but to them.' The Hungarians made a further request – for absolute discretion. In particular, they did not want the East Germans to hear until later that the meeting had taken place.

After dithering for several weeks, Németh had finally made a firm decision about how he would handle the refugee crisis confronting Hungary. He wanted the West Germans to be the first to know. He got to the heart of the matter straight away. His opening words to Kohl were: 'We have decided to allow the GDR citizens to leave freely, mainly on humanitarian grounds. It seems you may have to deal with 100,000 or even 150,000 new citizens arriving very quickly.' At first Kohl and West Germany's long-serving Foreign Minister, Hans Dietrich Genscher, were sceptical. It was too good to be true, or so they thought, a vindication of West German policy for forty years and a hammer blow to the regime in Berlin.

Németh explained that there were powerful domestic reasons for the decision, as well as humanitarian considerations. Hungary could not cope with the weight of numbers arriving into the country. 'We cannot wait for a decision much longer and this is our best option. Already some refugees have been clashing with our border guards,' he explained. Undoubtedly there would be more incidents of the kind unless action was taken speedily. The West Germans were partially persuaded, but needed more convincing. Genscher had suffered a heart attack just five weeks earlier and had left his sick-bed for these talks. He had vast experience of negotiating with officials from the Eastern bloc and he asked the crux question: did the Soviets know? 'No they don't know, yet, and we won't inform them until you tell us that preparations have been made on your side,' Németh replied. He told them that he was sure the Soviets would make no objection. When the Russians said the border question was a matter for us to deal with they meant it, he insisted.

The two West German politicians began to believe the extraordinary news they were hearing. Most Germans, from East or West, had longed for the day the Wall no longer divided them. The moment was fast drawing nearer. Invariably an ebullient figure, Kohl started to beam good cheer. Genscher recalled later that his convalescence speeded up once he became convinced that the Hungarians were genuine. They began to discuss the details. Németh told them that his government would make one final effort to persuade the East Germans to grant the refugees permission to leave, but he did not expect much success. If they refused, his lawyers said, Hungary could 'suspend' the bilateral Berlin/Budapest agreement on travel permits, arguing that conditions had materially changed since it was signed. The West Germans pledged that they would hastily organise reception centres and transport for the refugees. They would even make an exception in this case, and allow Trabis into the country, which under normal circumstances would fail West German pollution regulations.[1]

The big controversy about the Schloss Gymnich conference has been over the question: did Hungary receive money to open the border for the East Germans? The claim has persisted that a DM 1 billion loan on generous and flexible terms was agreed. There is nothing in the records of the meeting to suggest that it was and the Hungarians have always denied it. Németh said that 'two or three times at the meeting the Chancellor asked me, "Now what do you want as a gesture from me?" I felt, he thought I was asking for money, so I said "No, no money, I am not asking you".' In fact, Németh said, he asked the West German government publicly to rescind a loan agreement the Hungarians were at that time negotiating with FRG banks. 'I did not want it to be perceived by the public – Hungarian or international – that we were doing this for money. We were not.' Nevertheless, five weeks later a line of credit up to DM 1 billion was made available to Hungary – DM 500 million from the Federal government and the rest from the provincial government of North Rhine-Westphalia.[2]

Immediately after the meeting Kohl spoke to Gorbachev. He was satisfied the Hungarians were telling him the truth as they saw it, but he wanted to make sure there was no misunderstanding. He did not wish to provoke a confrontation with the USSR over the East German refugees. Would the Soviets really accept this arrangement that breached the Iron Curtain? Gorbachev acquiesced in a roundabout way and offered this observation about the refugee crisis: 'Yes, the Hungarians are good people.'[3]

Breaking the news to the East Germans was altogether less agreeable, from the Hungarian perspective. Six days after the Schloss Gymnich talks, Foreign Minister Horn went to Berlin for a showdown with the GDR government. Honecker was still recovering from surgery and the Prime Minister, seventy-five-year-old Willi Stoph, was also unwell. Horn met Oskar Fischer, his East German counterpart, on the morning of Thursday 31 August. From the first, the encounter did not go well. Horn had built a liberal reputation, from the summer of 1989, based on his role in opening the border for the East German refugees. But initially the canny fifty-seven-year-old was ambivalent about letting them leave for the West. For many weeks he prevaricated and hedged his bets. He was an ambitious man, a moderate, who was persuaded that it was the right thing to do only when he was convinced the majority in the Hungarian leadership approved the idea. Then he sold the policy enthusiastically and believed it was his own.

When they met, Fischer insisted that Hungary must stick to the spirit and letter of the 1969 Treaty between the two countries. Horn replied that it would be best if East and West Germany came to an agreement. Then Fischer repeated the pledge that if the refugees returned of their own volition to East Germany now 'they would face no punishment'. Horn said that 'the refugees do not believe your government'. When he added that the Hungarians would within a few days let all the refugees leave for the West, Fischer exploded. 'That's treachery. You are leaving the GDR in the lurch and joining the other side. This will have grave consequences for you.' Later in the day Horn had an equally bitter meeting with the East German economics chief, Günter Mittag, at which he said that Hungary did not want poor relations with the GDR but there could be 'no inhumane solutions to this problem'.[4]

The East German regime vented more steam. It fired off angry notes to Budapest and to Moscow. But it realised there was little it could do if the Russians would not come down on the GDR's side. Fischer suggested that all the Warsaw Pact foreign ministers go to Berlin and together they could lean on the Hungarians. But the Poles flatly refused and Shevardnadze did not want to go. Without the Soviets, there was no point in holding the summit. When the Berlin Party chieftains met on the morning of Tuesday 5 September there was a mood of bitterness and of capitulation. The Stasi chief, Erich Mielke, thundered: 'Hungary is betraying socialism.' Prime Minister Stoph was still unwell but rose from his sickbed to fume that Hungary was playing an active part 'in a long-term FRG plot of subversion'. When Defence Minister Heinz Kessler suggested that perhaps young people may have some reason to complain about life in East Germany, as they saw real opportunities in the West, others were indignant. Horst Dohlus, the head of the Party organisation, said: 'How can we allow ourselves to be kicked around? We must guard against being discouraged . . . More and more people are asking, how is socialism going to survive here?'[5]

By the time Gyula Horn officially announced on Sunday 10 September that all border controls would be lifted from midnight, scores of buses had been sent by the West German government to ferry the refugees through Austria and into Bavaria, where they were given automatic West German citizenship. On the first day 8,100 people poured across the frontier. Within three days there were more than 18,000.

On his flight back to Budapest from Castle Gymnich, Németh had been in contemplative mood, wondering whether he had done the right thing. 'One of my advisers came up to me and said "You know, the importance of this decision will perhaps not be recognised immediately, but within five to ten years it will."' Its significance was felt throughout Eastern and Central Europe within a few weeks.[6]

The opposition in East Germany was strengthened. From a few isolated peace groups and Church organisations, kept under permanent surveillance by the Stasi, the numbers of people now emboldened to challenge the regime swelled. 'We saw the border opening and Hungary's behaviour as a sign of weakness in the GDR regime – it *was* a sign of weakness,' said Dr Matthias Mueller, a post-graduate student at Berlin's Humboldt University. 'The government seemed no longer to be entirely in control of events. It was a big psychological change in a lot of people, a key moment.' Yet the opposition was still polite, orderly and well mannered in an old-fashioned and traditional East German way. New Forum, which over the next few weeks became one of the largest of the opposition groups, was founded on 11 September, the day after the Hungarians allowed the refugees to leave. All it sought, to begin with, in the most moderate language, was 'dialogue' with the government. The first thing it did was to make an application in the courts for legal status, as though it was seeking permission to start a revolution. The culture of obedience in the GDR ran deep. The ruling went against them: 'The goals and purposes of the applicant . . . contradict the constitution of the GDR and represent a platform hostile to the State . . . and [the application is] thus illegal,' stated the verdict. There were still some prominent members who thought the best tactic was to continue the legal course and mount an appeal. 'We had to be careful. Our aim was to form an association,' said Reinhard Schult, one of New Forum's founders. 'We did not want to set up a party, nor could we found one.' Yet within a few days 150,000 people signed a petition calling for talks with the regime. It was as though the entire country had at last woken up. 'In no way did we imagine that could possibly happen,' said Schult at the time. 'It overwhelmed us a bit. We have no office, no telephones, only our apartments . . . And most of us have to work – put in our eight and three-quarter hours a day at the plant, or the institute.'

Jan Lässig, a New Forum organiser from Leipzig, said that over the last few years he was used to a few dozen people turning up at meetings – familiar faces belonging to various groups. 'Now, suddenly, so many people were joining our movement that it was not simple. A thousand people would come to a meeting and they wanted to do something. And we didn't really have a programme, a concept of what do.'[7]

Monday night demonstrations began again at the Nikolaikirche in Leipzig, after a break for August. East Germany's second city was choking to death from neglect. The regime was allowing it to rot. It had once been a big industrial centre of more than 700,000 people, but around 20 per cent of Leipzig's population had deserted the city over the last five years. Most had gone to other towns in the GDR, though recently significant numbers had headed to the West. Outside the city centre, scores of abandoned shops were boarded up, houses were derelict and the roads were full of potholes. It resembled an urban wasteland. There was a small and still-beautiful centre, with many impressive buildings circled by a broad inner ring road. This was where the demonstrators lit candles and marched for an hour or so, invariably in silence, beginning at around 6 p.m. They were a solemn sight, calling for peace and disarmament. Occasionally demonstrators would hold placards protesting about the environment.

Even by East German standards, Leipzig was a filthy place. Millions of tons of sulphur dioxide were spewed into the atmosphere nearby each year. The water in the reservoirs and rivers was massively polluted. An official government report, kept strictly secret, revealed that the city's water supply contained twenty substances available only on doctor's prescription, and ten times West German levels of mercury. Journalists and scientists who had investigated the high levels of cancers, respiratory ailments and skin diseases around the city were arrested when they established that the problems were caused by the nearby lignite mines which produced more than two-thirds of East Germany's electricity.

From September, thousands of people who had never attended the demonstrations before joined them. Leipzig became the focus of opposition throughout the country. The regime had no answer. Honecker's illness left a power vacuum that was never filled. On 18 September around 15,000 people attended the Monday night march that started from the Nikolaikirche. It was the largest unofficial demonstration in East Germany since the troubles in 1953. As usual it was an entirely peaceful procession by candlelight, though slightly more noisy than before. Police and plain-clothes Stasi men arrested around a hundred demonstrators they had heard shouting anti-regime slogans. The police vans that carried them away drove straight into the crowd, badly injuring around a dozen people. The incident opened a rift within the ruling Party. Most of the leadership was unwilling to begin a violent confrontation with the demonstrators – especially three weeks before the fortieth anniversary of the founding of the East German state. Huge ceremonies had been planned to celebrate the success of 'actually existing socialism', in front of distinguished guests from the entire Communist world who would include Mikhail Gorbachev.

The Stasi chief was one of the few who had the stomach for a fight. Mielke continually urged violent measures 'to deal with a counter-revolution that's brewing in the GDR'. In a speech he kept secret from his fellow Party chieftains, he told his highest-ranking Stasi officers to take tough measures against protesters: 'Hostile opposing forces and groups have already achieved a measure of power and are using all methods to effect a change in the balance of power.' He said East Germany now was in a similar position to that of China two months earlier. 'The situation here now is comparable and must be countered with all means and methods. The Chinese comrades must be lauded. They were able to smother the protest before the situation got out of hand.' He told some of his commanders, according to his head of counter-intelligence, Rainer Wiegand, that they should prepare a plan to form special squads to attack the demonstrators, split them into three groups and arrest their leaders.

His officers on the ground were telling him that feelings in Leipzig were running high, not only among the demonstrators, but in offices and factories throughout the city. The Stasi commander in Leipzig, Lieutenant-General Siegfried Gehlert, told Mielke: 'The situation is lousy, Comrade Minister . . . There are many discussions about all the justified – and unjustified – problems that we have. What is particularly relevant is that these lousy currents exist within the Party organisation. As to the question of power, Comrade Minister, we have the situation in hand, but extraordinarily high vigilance is required. From an accident here or there . . . just a spark would be enough to bring about serious problems.' When, among other Party chieftains he proposed violent measures against the Leipzig protesters, he was voted down.[8]

Earlier in the summer Erich Honecker had declared: 'I will not shed a single tear for those who want to leave the country.' The opposition shed many. 'There were always good friends who were leaving, people to whom I had been very close,' said Ulrike Poppe, one of the founders in the mid-1980s of the Democracy Now human rights group. 'We missed them. On the other hand we could understand why they left, because there were so many reasons why they couldn't stand being in the GDR. We always thought about how long we could stay and we set ourselves a limit. I said that if I had to go to prison, that would be the time to leave. Or if they took our property away, as we did have a small property, or if they took away the kindergarten that we had organised for children. All of that happened, but we always decided to stay primarily because we felt there were others who wanted the same things as us and we had to stay to keep trying. Somewhere there was always hope.' After the Hungarians helped to breach the Wall, the main rallying cry at demonstrations was 'We Are Staying' and that gave the opposition groups hope.[9]

Many East Germans still dreamed of leaving the country, though. After the Hungarians opened their border to GDR citizens, Czechoslovakia closed its frontier with Hungary to GDR citizens, following pressure from Berlin. They regretted it quickly. East Germans stranded in Czechoslovakia headed straight to Prague and besieged the West German Embassy, the baroque Lobkovitz Palace in the Castle District of the city. The Czechs did not want a diplomatic incident with East Germany, and its neo-Stalinist leadership had sympathy with the regime in Berlin. But they did not see that it was their problem to police East German refugees. They had tried to prevent the refugees reaching the Embassy, but quickly gave up the attempt. Scores of Trabants were left abandoned on the streets of Prague as around 3,000 people had crammed into the Palace. It was big and elegantly spacious, but not built for anything like that number. The weather was mild, so large numbers could camp out in the large garden. Soon conditions were becoming unpleasant and unhygienic, though the West Germans refused none of the refugees admission.

The Czechoslovak Party chief, Miloš Jakeš, told Berlin that he did not need this problem. He had troubles of his own. Late the previous month riot police had arrested scores of demonstrators in Wenceslas Square as 4,000 people were marking the twenty-first anniversary of the Warsaw Pact invasion to crush the Prague Spring. Václav Havel had been released from prison at the end of May, after serving about half his original nine-month sentence. Immediately, he continued where he had been interrupted on the day of his arrest, writing about conditions in the country for the Western media. Within a fortnight he had produced a manifesto for the Czech opposition – 'A Few Short Sentences' – calling for talks between the opposition and the regime and the release of all political prisoners. Now Havel and other human rights campaigners were demanding that the East Germans be allowed to leave freely for the West.

Among the refugees inside the Embassy was teacher Birgit Spannaus, who had decided to leave because she did not want her daughter to grow up in East Germany. She told nobody that she was going to Czechoslovakia and she bought a return train ticket at the station. As soon as they arrived in Prague she and her daughter headed for the West German Embassy:

> We had watched the TV reports and could see that the building was well guarded. Behind the garden was a park, though. We waited until the evening . . . and went to the park, pretending to take a walk. We saw the fence at the Embassy . . . and climbed up. We didn't know what would happen to us. We weren't sure if there were Czech police inside the compound, or even Stasi people. That was a fear. We thought it had been so easy to climb the fence. We saw people inside the Embassy who said 'Do you want to come in? Wait a minute. We'll get a ladder.' Then we climbed over . . . and were in the Embassy grounds. There were people everywhere . . . They were sleeping on the stairs. Every room was crammed full of beds. There were many infants crying. The air was bad. It was noisy. Everybody was nervous . . . We found a room in the attic with another family and their three children. They had been there weeks. There was hardly any room on the floor, which was full of mattresses.

She felt full of hope, but never safe, as they waited for the politicians to find a solution.[10]

Erich Honecker was back at his desk in the third week of September. Surgeons had discovered another cancerous tumour, in his colon. They removed the growth and declared him well enough to take his place at the helm of the forthcoming fortieth anniversary festivities. He began immediate negotiations with the Czechs about the Embassy refugees. Miloš Jakeš told his East German counterpart that the GDR must reach an agreement with the West Germans 'that will get us Czechs off the hook and your people out of Prague. This is not our concern. We can help, but it has to be done quickly.' The third party to the deal was Hans Dietrich Genscher, who was in New York attending the UN General Assembly. Reluctantly, Honecker eventually said he was willing to let the 'traitors' in the Embassy leave for the West. They could have gone directly to West Germany on normal passenger trains. But Honecker stubbornly insisted that they had to go through East Germany first, so it would look as though the GDR was throwing them out. He demanded that they must leave on sealed trains. While in transit East German officials would formally take their ID papers and withdraw their GDR citizenship from them. It was designed to humiliate them and make it seem as though the regime was still in control of events. An editorial in *Neues Deutschland*, which the Party's propaganda chief, Joachim Hermann, said was dictated by Honecker personally, stated that 'by their behaviour they have trampled on all moral values and excluded themselves from our society'.[11]

Honecker's Party colleagues knew nothing of the agreement he had concluded with the Czechs and the West Germans. On the evening of Friday 29 September, most of the senior officials were at the State Opera House on Unter den Linden at a gala performance to celebrate the anniversary of the founding of Communist China. Honecker, still visibly in pain but assuring everyone he was fit, summoned them into the ornate Apollo reception room where the Party Secretary told them of 'information regarding a matter of the highest urgency'. He outlined the plan as though it was a triumph of diplomacy, whereas most of them could see straight away, said Günter Schabowski, that it was a bad mistake. 'Many of us saw this exodus, organised by ourselves, as evidence of the country's helplessness.' From that point on a group within the top rung of the regime realised that it was imperative that Honecker had to be replaced soon. But they did nothing. 'It was pointless to prevaricate so long. But we did,' said Schabowski.[12] The next day Genscher flew to Prague to tell the refugees about the deal he had negotiated with Honecker. It was one of the most difficult and emotional duties he had ever had to perform. 'I must say I arrived ... with my emotions totally churned up,' Genscher recalled. 'How do I put this to the people who on the one hand will be overjoyed at being able to leave. But on the other I have to tell them that the journey will pass for several hours through East Germany. Will they accept my assurances of safe passage?' They realised that they had little choice. They could not stay at the Embassy indefinitely.[13]

When, early in the afternoon of Monday 2 October, the first few hundred of the refugees were placed on coaches at the start of their journey, the mood was tense. They were driven to one of the small suburban stations outside Prague and told to wait. 'We waited for a couple of hours until a train arrived, and then there was some panic,' Birgit Spannaus recalled. 'At first some people said "We are not going. This is a betrayal. We're too scared." A West German official tried to calm us down. He said he would travel with us and each train leaving from Prague would have one of his colleagues aboard, for security reasons.' Soon after the convoy reached East Germany 'the train stopped. Two men opened the doors. "Good day, we are from State Security and we'll collect your identity cards now." I will never forget how they had to bend down to collect these documents because the people threw them at their feet. The feeling was "you can't threaten me any more".'[14]

East Germans waved and cheered the refugees along the route until the eight sealed trains reached Dresden, the first major city across the border. A trail of torn-up identity papers, East German passports and worthless East Marks littered the side of the track. People had been told they must not greet the refugee trains. More than 1,500 demonstrators, mainly youngsters, ignored the order, broke through police lines and desperately tried to climb on board. The police could barely contain the crowds, which threw bricks and stones. Practically every window in Dresden station was smashed, much of the concourse was destroyed and dozens of people were injured. One protester fell under a refugee train as it left. Both his legs had to be amputated. The demonstrations grew after all the trains had departed. Ordinary factory workers and older people joined the youngsters. They were ordered by the police to disperse but they refused. There was a stand-off for several hours, but, significantly, the police took no further action. At the candle-lit Leipzig protest later that night around 12,000 demonstrators were allowed to march peacefully around the city's inner ring road.

When the refugee trains arrived in Hof, Bavaria, ecstatic crowds of West German well-wishers welcomed their brothers and sisters from the East. It was a highly charged, emotional ceremony televised live on the Federal Republic's TV and beamed to Eastern homes. Within hours, thousands more Berliners and Leipzigers had filled up their Trabis and Wartburgs and headed east to Czechoslovakia.

FORTY-THREE

THE BIRTHDAY PARTY

East Berlin, Saturday 7 October 1989

THE LAST THING THE SOVIET LEADER WANTED to do this weekend was to go to Berlin. He had complained about the trip numerous times to his foreign policy adviser, Anatoli Chernyaev, but it was clear that there was no way of avoiding it. The Soviet Communist Party boss could not fail to attend the fortieth birthday party of the East German state. Gorbachev still thought the existence of the GDR worthwhile, if not as important to the interests of the USSR as it once was. But he loathed the atrophied country it had become and, in particular, he despised its leader and the Stalinist henchmen around him. Gorbachev had heard through the KGB that despite his illness, Erich Honecker had been talking about seeking a new term as East German Party Secretary from the following year. Gorbachev thought that could not be allowed to happen, though he was insistent that the Soviets would do nothing directly to remove him. He was determined, this time, that when he went to Berlin he would show what he thought of Honecker and his cronies.[1]

Elaborate celebrations had been planned for the big anniversary. Most of the leading figures of world communism would be in attendance. To Honecker, this was a huge event, another of his crowning achievements, and further recognition of the GDR as an important state. Never known for his modesty, he was determined that nothing should go wrong with the celebrations, nor that his own role in the shining success of the GDR should go unnoticed. Over the last few days, the Stasi had arrested some known troublemakers in Berlin, opposition elements who might, if unchecked, have tried to spoil the party by holding demonstrations. He was assured that there would be no unanticipated problems.

Gorbachev had arrived the evening before and had talks with Honecker. They did not go at all well, according to Joachim Hermann, who sat in on the meeting: 'It was as if two people were talking to each other but speaking about entirely different things. It was a dialogue of the deaf.' Honecker was bitter at the way the Soviets were treating East Germany, that 'suddenly, they renounced [our long] . . . friendship and dropped us in a manner you wouldn't wish on your worst enemy', Hermann said. Gorbachev met the rest of the leadership at an encounter that both the Russians and the Germans said was 'painfully embarrassing'. Gorbachev made one of his wide-ranging speeches about 'new thinking', the changing shape of a transformed world and the end of the Cold War. It was a typical 'big picture' performance. He gave a pointed look at Honecker when he said that 'Life punishes those who fall behind.' Its meaning was clear to everyone.[2]

Honecker replied with a sonorous list of statistics to show the unique success of the GDR as one of the world's great economies and how East Germany was moving from triumph to triumph. The proof 'is that soon we will be producing, in our modern and high-technology industry, a four-megabyte computer chip'. Members of his own leadership team began whispering to each other and looking dumbfounded. As the GDR's State Planning chief, Gerhard Schürer, said: 'We couldn't believe this . . . here was Gorbachev talking about the fate of the world and here's our General Secretary talking about computer chips.' Others were in despair: 'We were assholes,' said Schabowski. 'We acted like dummies. We should have banged our fists on the table and said "Erich, you can't do that." But of course that's pure fantasy. We would have been put out of action immediately. It would have created a scandal.' A serious plot to oust Honecker began on this day, but it was far too late.[3]

The high point of the celebrations was a huge torchlight procession through Berlin. Tanks and weaponry and military bands passed the dignitaries on a raised podium, followed by column after column of strapping members of the Communist Youth group, the Frei Deutsche Jugend (FDJ), in blue shirts and red scarves. These were supposed to be the most obedient sons and daughters of the nomenklatura, born and raised in the bosom of the Party. Now many were heard to shout 'Gorby, help us. Gorby, help us.' The Polish Communist Party boss, Mieczysław Rakowksi, was sitting next to Gorbachev. He asked the Soviet leader whether he understood what they were saying. Gorbachev said he did not know German well but he thought so. 'They are demanding Gorbachev, rescue us,' Rakowski said. 'And these are supposed to be the cream of Party activists. This is the end.' Honecker was plainly nonplussed at first, but then began to grasp what was happening. Then he looked hurt rather than angry at the humiliating public insult.

As he was leaving Berlin, Gorbachev gave a clear blessing to East German Party officials to act against Honecker. The Soviet Ambassador to the GDR, Kochemasov, told Gorbachev that he knew that 'comrades were planning' to remove the old man. Gorbachev told him to watch and listen, but not to become directly involved. 'What is to be done about him?' Gorbachev said, according to the Ambassador. 'He doesn't take anything in. Then let him look to the consequences for himself. But it is not going to be done by our hands. They have to do it themselves.'[4]

There were 380,000 Soviet troops on East German soil. They were the force which the GDR leadership had thought would be the ultimate protection of the socialist state – and of themselves if there was ever a real danger of 'counter-revolution'. Gorbachev wanted to make absolutely sure that Soviet soldiers would not be drawn into any potential conflict between the regime and its own citizens. Late in the evening, the Ambassador called General Boris Snetkov, commander of Soviet forces in East Germany. Snetkov was a wheezing sixty-five-year-old, a veteran of World War Two, who was coming up to retirement. He was popular with his men. He had little wish to use them fighting against demonstrators crying out 'Gorby, save us'. He was delighted by the request the Ambassador was now making. 'We have to think about how we're going to react to possible unrest on the streets,' Kochemasov said. 'The matter is very serious and I ask you immediately to give orders for all troops to go back to barracks as soon as possible. You should stop all manoeuvres and stop all flights of military planes if possible. Do not interfere in any way with internal GDR developments. Let them take their course.' Like a good officer, Snetkov double-checked with the Soviet General Staff and was issued the same orders from his superiors in Moscow.[5]

Within an hour of Gorbachev's departure that evening demonstrations erupted in towns and cities all over the country. The authorities reacted with the brutal force they had rarely used in the last few weeks. In the Prenzlauer Berg district of East Berlin, thousands of people gathered to shout the day's catchphrase, 'Gorby, save us'. As they marched towards the ornate state council building, they were stopped in their tracks by a convoy of police trucks. Seconds later Erich Mielke, now eighty-one, appeared from his own bullet-proof car in a state of high agitation. Accompanied by his head of domestic counter-intelligence, General Günter Katsch, he screamed at the police: 'Club those pigs into submission.' They waded into the crowd, beat up scores of the demonstrators and arrested many more. Elsewhere in the city, the police and the militia attacked protesters with dogs and water cannon, and broke up a candle-lit march outside the Gethsemane Church, where nine young people were in their fourth day of a hunger strike. Altogether in Berlin 1,067 people were arrested that night and the next day. Many reported later that they faced a long night of abuse and beatings at the hands of Stasi interrogators.

Around 200 demonstrators were arrested in the centre of Dresden. They were driven to the barracks of the riot police and mercilessly beaten up. Student Catrin Ulbricht was among them: 'When we got out of the lorries, we were separated, women to the right, men to the left,' she said. 'There I saw some sort of garage and watched as men were placed against the wall legs apart and they were being beaten. We women were taken off to a kind of shower room, and that was pretty brutal.'[6]

The main trial of strength was on the following night, 9 October, in Leipzig, where the epicentre of protest had been for the past weeks. Despite the violence of the police and Stasi over the weekend, the opposition was determined to go ahead with the regular Monday night 'event'. As usual, the plan was to begin the march at the Nikolaikirche and head clockwise around the inner ring road. They hoped this would be the biggest rally so far, in a mass display of defiance. 'Of course we were scared at this time,' said Ulrike Poppe, one of the founders of the Democracy Now organisation. 'I was not courageous. But I was angry and hard-headed . . . There were many who feared that there might be a Chinese solution – that they would use weapons. That could never be excluded as a possibility. And sometimes we thought that Soviet troops might appear. There was fear, because our army, police and State were so well armed and prepared that we had to reckon with there being a violent reaction.' But numbers at the marches had been growing so quickly that the opposition now called the GDR 'The German Demonstrating Republic'.[7]

The regime was divided. Honecker wanted a tough response against the demonstrators. But he issued no specific instructions at any stage that the army or the Stasi should open fire on them. By now his authority was visibly draining away. 'He would not have got an order through even if he had given it,' one of his aides said. His wife, Margot, was fond of saying, 'We have to defend socialism with all means. With words, deeds and, yes, with arms.' But she had limited power in the land.[8]

Mielke did issue draconian orders that gave his men the power to shoot 'troublemakers'. Without consulting anyone else in the leadership he issued secret Directive No. 1/89 on the morning of Sunday 8 October.

> There has been an aggravation of the nature and associated dangers of the illegal mass gatherings of hostile, opposition, as well as ... rowdy-type forces aiming to disturb the security of the state. I hereby order 1. A state of 'full alert' ... for all units until further notice. Members of permanently armed forces are to carry their weapons with them constantly, according to the needs of the situation ... Sufficient reserve forces are to be held ready, capable of intervention at short notice ... for offensive measures for the repression and breaking-up of illegal demonstrations.[9]

For the last two weeks the East German army had been put on heightened alert, although so far troops had not been used at any of the demonstrations. Unusually, the conscripted men were cut off as much as possible from the outside world. 'It was an absurd idea, but the senior officers reckoned they could keep information like that away from the men,' said Klaus-Peter Renneberg, a captain in an infantry regiment. His rank was a 'political officer' – a Party job as well as a military one, with the task of ensuring ideological orthodoxy and obedience in the ranks. 'They were not allowed to use radios, they didn't receive letters, they were discouraged from using the telephone to contact family or friends. The television set in the mess was removed. It was ridiculous because everybody knew what was going on in the country. The official line was that there had been some outbreaks of trouble with counter-revolutionaries who were out to destroy the State.' Troops were given double their normal issue of ammunition – 120 rounds instead of 60 – and were each issued with an extra first aid kit. Overnight a crack paratroop regiment was dispatched to Leipzig with orders to hold a position just outside the city centre. The hospitals had been emptied of routine patients and had been sent extra supplies of blood and plasma. The local Party newspaper, *Die Leipziger Volks-*

zeitung, ran an editorial declaring: 'We will fight these enemies of our country, if necessary with arms.'[10]

When all the pieces seemed in place for a violent showdown in Leipzig later in the day, it was a musician who orchestrated a peaceful outcome. The conductor Kurt Masur was one of the most renowned celebrities in East Germany. Artistic director of the world famous Leipzig Gewandhaus Orchestra, he was a favoured son of the regime, which heaped awards on him. He had never been a Communist Party member, but he had kept a studied silence about politics while he became one of the most brilliant interpreters in the world of German Romantic music. He had gone along with official propaganda referring to him as one of the stars that made the GDR shine so bright. Now sixty-two, distinguished-looking with his neat white beard, he was beginning to speak out occasionally. When some street musicians in Leipzig had been arrested in the summer, he protested. He was appalled at the prospect of a bloody confrontation in Leipzig. If conflict erupted it could happen outside the delightful, neo-classical Gewandhaus concert hall on the city's main ring road. On past Mondays the demonstrations usually marched past there at around 7.45 p.m., often while he had been conducting.

Masur spoke to other prominent Leipzigers in an attempt to prevent bloodshed. He called the Protestant pastor Peter Zimmermann and the actor Bernd Lutz Lange, both of whom were involved with moderate opposition groups in the city. Local Party chieftains were equally desperate to avoid a bloodbath. The Leipzig Party boss, Helmut Hackenburg, was ill, but two other high-ranking officials, Wilhelm Pommert and Roland Wötzel, went to meet Masur and the opposition activists, which in itself was a revolutionary act. Policy had always been to have no dialogue with them, so they did not tell Party headquarters in Berlin about the meeting. They hammered out the text of an appeal for peace and calm, signed jointly, which was repeated on the radio every half-hour from about 3 p.m. onwards in Kurt Masur's voice. 'We all need a free exchange of views on the future of socialism in our country. Therefore ... we today promise to lend our strength and authority to ensure that this dialogue will be conducted not only in Leipzig but with our government. We urgently ask you for prudence, so that peaceful dialogue will become possible.'

It was not clear that the appeal would be heeded. The army was still preparing to move on to the streets. Hans Illing was an NCO with an infantry regiment based at the main army barracks on the edge of

Leipzig. By early afternoon the men knew that they had been ordered to take up positions by Leipzig railway station, directly on the route of the demonstration. It was his job to hand out weapons from the armoury. 'I issued rubber truncheons and shields and helmets, then gave the officers their handguns – 9mm Makarov pistols, with live ammunition. Each officer got at least two magazines ... Then the company commander came and gave the order to hand out Kalashnikovs which were loaded on to the lorries ... There were pretty bad scenes, with young men lying on their beds and crying because they knew their wives and parents would be on the demonstration. So feelings were not good.' He knew his mother and stepfather would probably be on the march. 'I rang my parents to warn them that they shouldn't go out that day ... because it was so dangerous, there'd be live rounds fired.'[11]

More than seventy thousand demonstrators had gathered outside the Nikolaikirche by around five p.m. 'and the atmosphere was extraordinarily tense', said one of them, Aram Radomski. 'None of us knew what was going to happen, whether the shooting would begin. We just knew that if we were not there, it would be a sign that we had given up, which we could not do.'[12]

In Leipzig Party headquarters, they were still waiting for instructions from Berlin. 'We rang repeatedly. We told them of our appeal and we tried to persuade the bosses but they gave no immediate answer,' said the Leipzig Party's second Secretary, Roland Wötzel. 'We got hold of Egon Krenz personally. He said he would call back. So we waited. But things were getting absolutely critical. The march was reaching the railway station, where most of the army forces were concentrated, and still we had no instructions. Finally Hackenburg gave the order to pull the troops back and let the demonstrators past peacefully. It was touch and go.' At the same time General Gerhard Stassenburg, the Leipzig police chief, told his men to let the march go ahead without interference and only to shoot in self-defence.[13]

Egon Krenz continually maintained later that he was the saviour of the day and it was his decision to let the demonstration proceed. He spoke to the Soviet Ambassador, Kochemasov, who advised him to let the march go ahead. But he did not call the Leipzig Party officials back until about half an hour *after* they had already made the decision not to intervene. He hesitated briefly when he spoke to Hackenburg, but then said he had made absolutely the correct decision and the Party approved. This was the turning point, when the people knew that the regime lacked the will or the strength to maintain its power.

Erich Honecker survived in place for another week. Plotters had been sharpening a stiletto, but it was the demonstrators in Leipzig who sealed his fate. There had been no public criticism of him for eighteen years. Now there was a tide of complaints within the ruling Party that came from all directions. The officially approved Writers' Union called for 'revolutionary changes', insisting that what must be feared 'is not reform, but fear of reform'. Its President, Hermann Kant, one of the foremost East German Communists, wrote an open letter calling on the leadership to show 'self-criticism'. The Communist Youth paper, *Junge Welt*, took a giant step by printing it. He urged Honecker to talk to the opposition and 'grasp the nettle, even if we do not like the individuals involved, or, as Communists, feel ill at ease with some of their ideas'. The mayors of Dresden and Leipzig called for dialogue. Honecker was unmoved. 'Everything will collapse if we give an inch,' he said.

Why did it take so long for Honecker's colleagues to turn against him? There had been moves to oust him the previous February, but the plot fell apart. Planning chief Gerhard Schürer, one of the most powerful of the oligarchs in the regime, discussed removing Honecker with Krenz, who seemed like the only obvious successor acceptable to a majority of the old guard. 'I'll make you a suggestion,' Schürer had said. 'I'm an old man and in any case close to retirement. I'll leave some time soon. I shall demand that Honecker ... be removed. Of course you can't intervene and say "I want to be General Secretary". But I can propose you. I'm prepared to do this because otherwise the GDR will go *kaputt*.' The two men discussed it for three hours at Schürer's country retreat in Thuringia, Dierhagen. But finally Krenz said he was not prepared to unseat 'my foster father and political teacher. I can't do it. There'll have to be a biological solution to this problem.'[14]

Krenz could have made a move while Honecker was ill, but he felt constrained. He decided to wait until after the fortieth anniversary celebrations 'which were so desperately important to him' were over. This was not because Krenz was a sensitive and caring soul. He was deeply ambitious. His caution was because he was unsure of his own strength. Now he realised there could be no delay. He could not afford to wait for the 'biological solution' offered by Honecker's death, which could take many years. He had to act now. 'There were too many things that can happen by accident,' Schabowski said. 'At a demonstration someone throws a stone, it hits a soldier, another soldier gets scared or trigger-happy and then the shooting starts. If that happens I thought we could all say goodbye – they'd come at us Party men and we'll all be hanging from trees.'[15]

The other plotters were Siegfried Lorenz, Party boss in Karl-Marx-Stadt and a crucial, though unexpected supporter, the Stasi chief Erich Mielke, who was looking out for his own position. The head of the East German trade unions, Harry Tisch, a powerful man in the state, was behind the coup. So was the Prime Minister, Willi Stoph. Tisch visited Moscow and tipped off Gorbachev's entourage that the move was imminent. Gorbachev's immediate reaction was extraordinary for a Soviet leader. He told Shevardnadze, but no other Communist magnates in Moscow. Nor did he consult any other leading figures in the 'socialist commonwealth'. According to his chief adviser on Germany, his first thought was to discuss it with Kohl and Bush.[16]

On Monday 16 October, most of the country's top Communists were in a meeting room at the Party headquarters watching live footage on West German TV from Leipzig, where this time a vast crowd of at least 120,000 people, no longer scared that violence would be used against them, demonstrated. This was one of a dozen protests in other towns and cities throughout the GDR that evening. They were chanting 'Gorby, Gorby', 'Wir sind das Volk' and – for the first time that Honecker was aware – 'Down with the Wall'. Honecker repeatedly said, 'Now, surely something has to be done.' The army Chief of Staff, Colonel-General Fritz Streletz, refused point-blank to bring out his men against peaceful demonstrators. 'We can't do anything. We will let the whole thing take its course peacefully.'[17]

The leadership was due to meet at the Party headquarters the next morning, Tuesday 17 October. At dawn, Mielke rang the Stasi officer in charge of security in the building and ordered him to make sure that the main meeting room was surrounded by reliable men. He did not want Honecker to summon his own personal bodyguards at the time his political assassination was taking place. The plotters had planned everything to the last detail. At ten, while the meeting was coming to order, Stoph began. 'Please, General Secretary, Erich, I suggest a new first item be placed on the agenda. It is the release of Erich Honecker from his duties as General Secretary, and the election of Egon Krenz in his place.'

Honecker expected none of this. He thought he still had time left. But he did not allow his face to change expression. As if nothing had happened, he simply ignored the Prime Minister's comment and said 'Let's get on with the agenda.' Several voices protested. Then he cleared his throat and said, 'All right then, let everyone have their say.' First he called the old guard, people he expected would support him. But one by one they all turned against him. They had done his bidding for years, obediently. Now, not a single voice spoke up for him. When the vote came it was unanimous. In the time-honoured way of Communist Parties, he performed his final duty and put his hand up to vote against himself. The industry chief Mittag and propaganda chief Hermann were ousted at the same time and Krenz was unanimously elected General Secretary.

Without saying a word Honecker left the room and returned to his office to make two phone calls. The first was to the Soviet Ambassador: 'Hello, Comrade Honecker here,' he said. 'I want to tell you straight away ... that it has been decided to relieve me of my duties. The decision was unanimous.' A few minutes later he called his wife. 'Well, it has happened.' He collected some personal items and then asked his driver to take him to his villa in Wandlitz. He never entered the building again.[18]

FORTY-FOUR

PEOPLE POWER

East Berlin, Tuesday 31 October 1989

THE PLOTTERS WHO REMOVED Erich Honecker from power believed they would earn the people's gratitude and respect. They were badly mistaken. The new Party boss, Egon Krenz, had for many years been the second most hated man in the country. In the forty-six days he was to survive in office, he achieved the distinction of reaching top spot. The first big demonstration calling for his resignation took place on the evening that he replaced Honecker. Though he now attempted to present himself as a reformer, a man who had always wanted liberal changes in the GDR, nobody believed him. They remembered that he had been crown prince in the GDR for many years, and behaved like one. They remembered that he was the man who just a few months ago had praised the clearly fraudulent election results as an example of democracy in action. Many East Germans still had a mental picture of him in Beijing, which he visited soon after the Tiananmen Square massacre, shaking hands with Deng Xiaoping and praising China's firm action to quell unrest.

Jokes about him quickly began to appear in Berlin: 'Q: What's the difference between Krenz and Honecker? A: Krenz has a gall bladder.' Crude caricatures of him were carried on protest marches, many showing him as the wolf in Little Red Riding Hood, with the caption 'Why, Grandmother, what big teeth you have.' The satirist Wolf Biermann, as usual, summed him up pithily as 'a walking invitation to flee the Republic'. Igor Maximichev, the Soviet Union's Deputy Ambassador to the GDR, had dealt with him frequently. 'Egon Krenz was ... devoid of any charismatic qualities. He wasn't accepted by the people. He wasn't attractive. He couldn't find the words to speak to the people because he only spoke in Party jargon.'[1] He showed what he was made of in his first address as the leader. 'We ... have no other interest than that of the people ... Our historical optimism results from the knowledge of the ineluctability of the victory of socialism founded by Marx, Engels, Lenin.' East Germans' response was to take to the streets in even greater numbers, to call for Krenz to go; for the right to travel and for the Berlin Wall to come down. During the week after he succeeded Honecker more than a million people took part in a series of demonstrations in towns and cities throughout East Germany.

This was the first day Krenz heard the full truth about the catastrophic financial position in which Honecker had left the country. The facts had been hidden from all but the regime's economics tsar, Günter Mittag, the freebooting financier Alexander Schalck-Golodkowski, Stasi chief Erich Mielke and the State Planning chief Gerhard Schürer. Now the rest of the leadership were told. They were left in a state of shock. Bankruptcy was staring them in the face within a few days. East Germany did not possess enough cash to pay interest payments due on foreign loans and was likely to default. A top secret 'Report on the Economic Situation of the GDR, With Consequences' was presented to Party chieftains by Schürer, who now revealed the unvarnished figures of the national accounts. The previous May Schürer had tried to persuade Honecker to think seriously about the debt crisis – 'or we will become insolvent' soon. But the leader refused to confront it, saying the time was not right. Both he and Mielke told him 'to make sure you shut up about this'. Schürer remained silent, as he was ordered to do, but now he spoke up and declared that in truth the country was insolvent already.[2]

All the propaganda about the GDR's success was based on lies, the report said. The stark reality was that under 'actually existing socialism', nearly 60 per cent of East Germany's entire industrial base could be written off as scrap and productivity in factories and mines was nearly 50 per cent behind the West's. Most damning of all, debt had increased twelvefold in the last fifteen years to DM 123 billion and was rising at around DM 10 billion a year – 'extraordinarily high for a country like the GDR', said Schürer. He pointed out the illegal deceptions that were required to hide the facts from Western governments and banks, the short-term loans taken out to pay interest on long-term credits. If the financial markets realised how brazenly the GDR was lying about its assets, loans from the West would cease instantly. It was probably too late for the country to stop borrowing. Schürer said that if some radical action to reduce debt had been taken five years earlier, that might have helped. But now things had gone too far. 'Just to avoid further indebtedness would mean a lowering next year of living standards by 25 per cent to 30 per cent, and make the GDR ungovernable.'[3]

Krenz and the others looked aghast at this. Their chances of political survival were slim at best. That would reduce to zero if one of their first actions was to announce painful austerity measures. But the immediate problem was critical: how to raise the money to meet the next interest payment? 'It is absolutely necessary to negotiate with the FRG government financial assistance of two to three billion Marks as a short-term loan beyond the current limits,' they were told. If they could not raise it within two weeks there 'could be a damaging confrontation with the International Monetary Fund'. Once that happened, the GDR's reputation as a creditworthy nation would disappear. Schürer and his team of economists came up with a bold and desperate idea: in effect, they proposed to 'sell' the Berlin Wall and use it as a bargaining chip for more loans. 'We should put the currently existing form of the border on the table,' the report said. It was an extension of the sale of people to the West, which the regime had been doing for years. The West Germans may be prepared to go along with it, Krenz was told. Reunification would be ruled out in any negotiations, or even a confederation, but there could be promises of much more co-operation on a range of issues. 'In order to make the Federal Republic conscious of the GDR's serious intentions, it must be declared that such conditions could be created, as early as this century, that will make the border that exists between the two German states superfluous.'[4]

Krenz and the others embraced the idea enthusiastically and wanted to approach the West Germans immediately. Who better to handle such a sensitive political and financial transaction than the regime's colourful but utterly discreet wheeler-dealer Alexander Schalck-Golodkowski, who had so often before done delicate business with the West Germans? He was ordered to head for Bonn, with the utmost secrecy, to sound out the FRG's government about the deal. Initially, the West Germans were not wildly enthusiastic. Schalck-Golodkowski talked to Rudolf Seiters, head of Helmut Kohl's Chancellery, who laid out strict terms for any agreement. Neither he nor Kohl believed the East Germans were serious so he told Schalck-Golodkowski that, even before detailed discussions could begin, the Communist Party had to relinquish its monopoly on power, allow independent political parties and hold guaranteed free elections. 'Then Chancellor Kohl would be prepared to talk about a completely new dimension to our economic assistance.' Schalck-Golodkowski said he doubted business could be done on that basis, but he would return to Berlin and see what the Party bosses would say.[5]

The next day, 1 November, Krenz went to the Kremlin to pledge fealty to Mikhail Gorbachev. It was an awkward meeting. The Soviets had wanted a different figure to succeed Honecker. Gorbachev neither liked nor respected Krenz, who was far too closely associated with his predecessor and had a reputation as too obsequious and untrustworthy. The Soviet leader, and the KGB, would have preferred the Dresden Party chief, Hans Modrow, to take over in East Germany. By GDR standards the silver-haired, witty and subtle fifty-one-year-old Modrow was a reformer and an able administrator. He was one of a few Communist officials openly to disagree with Honecker, who subsequently sidelined him to posts in the provinces. He had excellent contacts in the Soviet Union, though, which is why Gorbachev had come to hear of such a relatively obscure East German Party apparatchik. The news Krenz brought to Moscow troubled Gorbachev greatly. The German told Gorbachev about the GDR's financial crisis, in the hope of touching him for a loan. The Soviet leader was silent for a moment and then declared, 'I'm astonished. We had no idea here. Are these figures secret? We had never imagined things had become so precarious. How could they have got so bad?'

Krenz said he had not known the details, nor had most of his colleagues. All the figures were a closely guarded secret of Honecker and Mittag, who ran the GDR economy themselves, he told Gorbachev. 'There's no mistake about the figures. Just to pay the interest will require US$ 4.5 billion, around two-thirds of our foreign currency earnings.' He then made a direct plea for financial help. 'After all, the GDR is in a sense the child of the Soviet Union and one must acknowledge paternity of one's children.' Gorbachev looked pained. He said: 'We are in no position to offer assistance, not in the USSR's present condition.' Then he told Krenz that his only choice was to be more open with his own people – 'who we can see are leaving in their thousands' – and tell them that they cannot continue to live in the manner they had become used to, above their means. Krenz again asked for financial support, or the regime might not survive. Gorbachev said he should not rely on the Soviets for help.

Krenz warned that there could be trouble if mass demonstrations on the Leipzig scale began in Berlin. He said: 'Measures must be taken to prevent any attempt at a mass breakthrough across the Wall. That would be awful, because then the police would have to intervene and certain elements of a state of emergency would have to be introduced.' Gorbachev took that as an attempt at political blackmail and told Krenz plainly that he and his colleagues could not expect to be bailed out militarily by the Soviets. 'You will have to solve the problem of what to do about mass emigration of your people and about the Wall. But if you don't do it soon there will be big problems for you, from your own people.' When Krenz left, Gorbachev's foreign policy adviser, Anatoli Chernyaev, quipped, 'There goes the Committee for the Dissolution of the GDR.' But Gorbachev was in a serious mood. Soon afterwards he issued a reminder to his generals that Soviet troops must not, under any circumstances, become involved in conflicts between the regime in Berlin and East German citizens. 'This is an absolute priority,' he told aides. 'I don't want anything to start there by accident involving our soldiers.'[6]

Krenz returned from Moscow empty-handed, but with no intention of resigning, or of dissolving the GDR. On the day he was in the USSR, the government reopened the East German border with Czechoslovakia, which Honecker had closed three weeks earlier in an attempt to stem the flow of the Exodus. Predictably, huge numbers headed in their Trabis towards the Czech border. The regime in Prague did not want another refugee crisis on their soil so it simply let them go straight on their way west through Czechoslovakia's frontier with the FRG. More than 50,000 people left East Germany along that route in three days. There were now two breaches through the Iron Curtain, through Hungary, and, for East German citizens, through Czechoslovakia. Yet Krenz was determined that the Wall would stay. 'I can see no circumstances under which the Wall will be removed,' he declared at the beginning of November. 'It is a bulwark against Western subversion.' Nor was he willing to concede free elections or to give up the Party's monopoly on power.[7]

In Poland there had been a Solidarity-led government for more than two months. In Hungary, the Communist Party had ceased to be at the end of September. Members had meekly voted it out of existence and formed a new Socialist Party. Its monopoly power was removed, most of its money and property was sequestered and it was banned from organising in the workplace, where much of the Communists' power had existed. Under an agreement with the opposition in Budapest reached six weeks earlier, there would be democratic elections held next March, which a right-wing party was heavily tipped to win comfortably. On 23 October, Hungary had officially ceased to be a People's Republic. It was renamed, simply, a Republic, and there was no mention in a new constitution of the Communist Party retaining a 'leading role' in the political life of the nation. Yet in East Germany the regime was still offering the people elections on the basis of one-party rule, a poll which a Party resolution stated 'can be democratic but must not entail opening the door to bourgeois party pluralism'.

Even some of the leaders of the regime felt a sense of unreality as they met now. Vast demonstrations were taking place in most towns almost every day and it had become clear they would not be suppressed by violence. The Party leaders had lost the will to fight for power, and the strength to govern, but they still spoke like Communists, especially Egon Krenz. In a cynical resolution on 4 November, some leading Party figures were deputed to meet the opposition and were 'instructed to appear to differ from the official Party line in order to gain the trust and confidence of the population . . . Comrades must be prepared not to proclaim the words of the Party, but rather to give the appearance of being thoughtful and realistic in order to win back our credibility.'[8]

The Party 'is not prepared to be dictated to by the Street', the leaders resolved on the morning of Saturday 4 November. Yet later that afternoon in Alexanderplatz, around 700,000 Berliners tested that resolve. A huge placard in the middle of the square was painted with the slogan 'Wir Sind Das Volk' ('We are the People'). The atmosphere in the country had changed, suddenly, over the last few days. It was more optimistic and good-humoured, still angry but less resentful. 'As for the opposition,' said Ulrike Poppe, one of the organisers of the demonstration, 'we had changed. We were no longer prepared to look for a dialogue. Now it was confrontation, not with violence . . . but we were questioning their authority. Now we were posing the question of who shall have power.'[9]

This was the most extraordinary of all the big rallies of *die Wende*, 'the Turn'. For the first time prominent figures in the regime appeared on the platform along with founders of opposition groups and dissidents. When Stefan Heym, whose books had been banned in East Germany for the last decade, appeared and declared 'Dear friends and citizens. It is as if someone has opened a window after all these years of spiritual . . . stagnation', he received rapturous applause. Soon afterwards, Günter Schabowski, the Berlin Party chief, tried calmly to assure the crowd that new liberal measures were on the way. He was a cheerful, ebullient figure, attractive in many ways, with a reputation as a reformer. But he was not the acceptable face of communism. He was loudly booed off the stage. One of the regime's best-known apologists, the officially approved writer Christa Wolf, was heard politely, but with little warmth.

At this time, throughout the Soviet bloc, many Communists with dubious past records, but with high ambitions, were hastily repackaging themselves as secret reformers who had always worked behind the scenes from within to change the system. The most bizarre of the born-again democrats was the spy chief Markus Wolf, who until the previous year had been head of the Stasi's foreign intelligence service, where he had scored many famous coups and was admired as a master of the espionage black arts. A man of impressive chutzpah, he imagined he could use the crowd for his political advantage and emerge clean and unharmed from the wreckage that he realised would engulf his country. When he stood up to speak, the crowd saw through him, as his own unintentionally comic account of his performance makes clear. 'I tried to persuade . . . the rally and the millions more watching on television not to resort to violence, but as I spoke, protesting the atmosphere of incrimination that made every member of the state security organisations scapegoats of the policies of the former leadership, I was dimly aware that parts of the crowd were hissing at me. They were in no mood to be lectured on reasonable behaviour by a former General of the Ministry for State Security.'[10]

Mielke had kept his position – as a reward for his part in the conspiracy against Honecker. But now, he thought, it was not so much a question of saving the state as saving himself. Anger against the Stasi was openly shown for the first time. Mielke had given up trying to persuade his colleagues to fight back against their opponents, but he warned the other Party leaders that big demonstrations were forming outside Stasi buildings, and some of them were looking ominous. He told them: 'People are shouting things like "Burn the building down", "Out with the Stasi swine", "Kill them" and "The knives are sharpened, the nooses are prepared".' On 7 November Mielke sent secret orders to provincial Stasi chiefs to destroy as many sensitive documents as they could, especially information that might identify informers. But it would require a Herculean effort. Thanks mainly to Mielke and his mania for keeping everything on paper, the volume of files was immense. Many heads of districts and departments burned a few files about agents in sensitive positions, but ignored Mielke's instruction, thinking it was now 'every man for himself'. Many officers held on to files, thinking they could be of advantage to them later.

Krenz replaced his entire government on the same day Mielke's order to burn the files was issued. Modrow was made Prime Minister. All the principal leadership figures in the Party, apart from Krenz, resigned the following day. Yet none of these measures relieved the pressure on the regime. As always in East Germany, emigration was the key issue. Krenz had promised a new travel law, but when it was published on 6 November it was treated with public derision. It allowed people to travel for thirty days a year, as long as they had permission from the Interior Ministry. But the process would take a month, and people were allowed to take with them only DM 15 once a year, about enough for a beer and a sandwich in West Berlin. So hundreds of thousands of people in the German Demonstrating Republic went out on the streets again, in Leipzig, Berlin and Dresden, chanting 'Around the World in Thirty Days – but how to pay?' Krenz knew he must devise something better. He ordered four officials from the Interior Ministry, including two Stasi colonels, to work on more plausible new visa regulations to deal with the immediate crisis. And he demanded urgent haste. He gave them less than two days.

FORTY-FIVE

THE WALL COMES TUMBLING DOWN

East Berlin, Thursday 9 November 1989

THE HELPLESS EAST GERMAN GOVERNMENT opened the Berlin Wall by mistake. It was not meant to happen – at least not today, and not in the way that it did. 'In one of the most colossal administrative errors in . . . history,' as one leading diplomat put it, the East German state effectively ceased to exist at around 10.45 p.m. It seemed a fairly normal late autumn morning in Berlin, grey, a little misty, around 10°C, with a slight smell of sulphur in the air from the pollution that often overwhelmed the city when an easterly wind was blowing. There had been an atmosphere of crisis in East Germany for many weeks now, but nothing seemed to suggest that this would be the critical moment. The regime was limping along, improvising day by day. The people were in permanent revolt – but in an orderly fashion. They did their eight hours' work first, and made revolution later, in the evenings. Not a single day's production was lost during *die Wende*.

The country was haemorrhaging people. They were leaving through Czechoslovakia, which, unable to cope with the volume, was now threatening to close its side of the border with the GDR. The exodus of East Germans was inspiring unrest among Czechs against their own Stalinist leaders. People in Prague and Bratislava were watching events in Berlin with eager anticipation.

Opposition figures in the GDR were worried about the number of their compatriots who were leaving. There were the usual jokes – 'Will the last one left, please turn off the light' – but now basic services were becoming severely stretched. In Berlin some schools had closed because so many teachers and children had gone. Hospitals were short of doctors. This morning *Neues Deutschland* carried an urgent appeal by moderate, dissident voices – usually castigated in the paper's pages as dangerous counter-revolutionaries – asking people to remain in East Germany because they were needed: 'We are deeply uneasy. We see the thousands who are daily leaving the country. We know that failed policies have fuelled mistrust in our community. We are aware of how helpless words are against mass movements, but we have no other means but our words. Those who leave diminish our hope. We beg you, stay in your homeland, stay with us.'[1]

Officials – including the two Stasi men – had worked overnight to prepare a new travel law, which the regime hoped would be a release valve. It had to be rewritten at the last minute because originally it covered only people who were seeking permanent emigration, not those who wanted to cross the border temporarily to see their relatives in West Germany, or take brief holidays. The final draft did not declare the Wall open. It stated that anybody with a passport and visa could leave permanently or for a short visit via any border crossing point between East Germany and either West Berlin or the Federal Republic. East Germans would still have to apply for an exit permit at a pass office, so it was designed to ensure some measure of state control. It said clearly that the new law would come into effect on Friday 10 November.

Krenz saw the wording for the first time late on Thursday morning. He gave it a cursory read and seemed content. He saw nothing in it that could possibly mean any East German citizen could go to a checkpoint at the Berlin Wall and be allowed through. People still had to apply to a bureaucrat for permission to go. He was not ecstatic about the proposal. But he thought that it would buy time, defuse the emigration issue, and that next day there would be orderly queues at the pass offices grateful to Egon Krenz for permitting them to travel to the West. He discussed the proposed new law with the top Party chiefs at around 4 p.m. at the Communist Party headquarters in Werderscher Markt. He told them that the Russians would go along with it – though he had not informed them about any of the details – and he thought that it was the best they could produce under the time pressure. 'No matter what we do in this situation, we'll be making the wrong move,' he said. Then, as he recalled later: 'I read it out sentence by sentence, read it slowly, read it emphatically so that nobody could say they didn't understand it.' It was accepted unanimously.[2]

At around 5.40 p.m. Günter Schabowski walked into Krenz's office. For the past two and a half weeks since Honecker was removed, Schabowski had been holding daily press conferences, as part of the GDR Communists' new-found glasnost policy. He was usually a reliable performer, safe, fluent and relatively quick-witted. He had not been at any of the meetings earlier in the day that approved the new travel regulations, though he was aware they were being discussed. He told Krenz he was shortly heading off to the press conference and asked whether there was anything he thought should be raised. Krenz handed him the full text of the decree and a press release about it. He recalled: 'Krenz showed me these papers and said "Here, friend, this is something that will do us a power of good" ... I took it along, skimmed through it again during the drive to the press conference and put it away amidst my other papers.'[3]

He arrived at Berlin's International Press Centre on Mohrenstrasse just before six, exhausted. He was beginning to feel the tension of the last few weeks during which he was surviving on little sleep, little food and lots of adrenaline. Although he had now appeared at a dozen of these press conferences, he was still a little nervous about performing before so many Western journalists and television cameras. Proceedings started punctually at six and most of it was concerned with dull, mundane matters about administrative reforms and ministerial changes in the government. It was nearly an hour before Schabowski got around to the travel regulations and he began to read out the text of the decree, which he explained 'would make it possible for every citizen of the GDR to leave the country using border crossing points of the GDR'. At this point, he had no idea of the storm that was about to break. He was asked to clarify and he put his half-moon spectacles back on his nose and began reading the press release: 'So, private travel to foreign countries can be applied for without presentation of existing visa requirements, or proving the need to travel or familial relationships. The travel authorisations will be issued within a short period of time ... The responsible departments for passport and registration control of the People's Police district authorities ... are instructed to issue visas for permanent exit without delay'.

This was still unclear. Many journalists have subsequently claimed that they were the one who asked the crucial question that breached the Berlin Wall. But by general consent now it was the American NBC network's Tom Brokaw who, amidst a gaggle of noise, inquired "When will this new regulation come into effect?'. Schabowski was sweating profusely at this point and was uncertain. He checked the papers in front of him and then scrambled around in the other sheaves of documents he was holding. After a few seconds' pause he replied: 'As far as I know, that is, uh ... Immediately, without delay.' He had not seen that the regulation came into effect next day – or that the news was supposed to have been embargoed until the next afternoon.[4] Various colourful and intriguing conspiracy theories have been suggested to explain Schabowski's misstatement: he was paid by the CIA, paid by West German media corporations, paid by rogue elements in the Kremlin. 'No one within the upper reaches of the Communist Party could believe it was a simple cock-up,' one SED official in charge of drawing up the travel law said. Yet that is what it was.

Immediately the press conference finished just after 7 p.m., Schabowski agreed to a live interview with Brokaw. He was still bemused and uncertain about the new regulations and during the interview he asked his assistant to show him the text once more. But he made the same announcement, that it came into force 'immediately'. Brokaw asked specifically: 'Is it possible for people to go through the Wall?' Schabowski said: 'It is possible for them to go through the border.'[5] Quickly, Schabowski's hesitations and evident confusion were edited out. By 7.30 p.m., news agencies throughout the world carried a line about the border opening in Berlin but West German TV was strangely hesitant for the first few minutes. ZDF's *Today* carried an item about new travel arrangements in East Germany as its sixth item. Then, at 8 p.m., West Germany's ARD, watched by millions in the East, announced that 'this is a historic day'. News anchor Hans Joachim Friedrichs, widely trusted on both sides of the frontier, declared: 'The GDR is opening its borders ... The gates in the Berlin Wall stand open.'

By the time the broadcast was finished scores of East Germans had arrived at the main border posts to see if the reports were true. The biggest crowd was at the Bornholmer Strasse, in the north of the city, which was within walking distance of a large residential area. Some apartment buildings overlooked the checkpoint into the French sector of Berlin. The border guard commander at the checkpoint, Lieutenant-Colonel Harald Jäger, had not seen the press conference and had heard only fleeting snatches of the news. When people turned up at the gate and demanded the right to travel 'as Schabowski said we can', he rang his superiors for advice. 'I told them that it was not possible because according to our regulations they needed a passport and a visa, without which they couldn't go. I told them to come back the following day and a few went away.' But most stayed and waited, shouting 'Open the gate, open the gate. The Wall must go.'[6]

These were not people with thoughts of emigration. 'We just

wanted to see whether we could go through, what life was like on the other side,' said Rüdigger Rosendahl, a chemical researcher, who lived near the checkpoint. 'People were saying to the guards, "It's OK, we won't go for long, we just want to see the Ku'damm, then we'll be back." The important thing was that we were not scared. Things had changed here in the last few weeks. For the first time our habitual fear of people in a uniform was gone. It was extraordinary, to see people arguing with soldiers and Stasi officers, demanding to be given the rights that we were told we now possessed.'[7]

After about half an hour Jäger was given orders which showed that the harsh, deceitful and arrogant face of East German officialdom had not yet disappeared. He was told to seek out the 'more aggressive' people at the checkpoint, note down their names and let them through with a special stamp on the photograph. This would mean that they could not return home to East Germany. The state was, in effect, withdrawing their citizenship. Jäger obeyed, and took the precaution of 'allowing a few "non aggressive" people to leave too'. At around 9.20 p.m. between 250 and 300 people were let through, but thousands more behind them were pressing at the gate, becoming angrier as they waited.

Three kilometres away, at Checkpoint Charlie, one of the great symbols of the Cold War, recognisable from a myriad of spy movies, the mood was equally tense. This was in the centre of the commercial part of Berlin, but there was a U-Bahn metro station just a few metres from the checkpoint where throngs of people were arriving. When they left the metro station, they were funnelled along a narrow lane. It was the checkpoint into the American-controlled sector of Berlin, one of the few places where soldiers of the US army and an East bloc army, still trained to see each other as mortal enemies, could stare into each others' eyes. Colonel Günter Möll, the border guard commander at Checkpoint Charlie, was frantically calling around army command for orders, but was continually told to wait. All he had been told was that some reinforcements would be sent and he was to maintain order. By 9.30 there was a crowd of about 2,000 people in a narrow street. 'I deployed the reinforcements in a line to hold the people back,' said Möll. The American commander looking at them from the other side, Major Bernie Godek, was 'very tense'. He said: 'They were acting as they normally would. They stood back from the white line – separating both sides – in typical formation, with cold faces. They seemed almost to be not bothered about what was going on in front of them. We had seen ... that before, but we were concerned about potential developments because we didn't know what they were going to do.'[8]

Nor, at first, did Egon Krenz and the other Party leaders. They were taken entirely by surprise. They had not thought that anything they decided earlier that day should start a stampede of people to the border. Krenz retreated, alone, into his office at Communist Party headquarters and waited. Reports came in that all the six border checkpoints in the city were besieged. He could see that trying to hold back the tide was impossible, but he gave no instructions of any kind. East German TV was making regular desperate announcements: 'At the request of many citizens, we inform you again of the new travel regulations . . . trips have to be applied for.' The announcement was ignored. East Berliners understood instinctively that something extraordinary and wonderful was going to happen. 'We had been told on the Western TV that the wall was down,' said Rosendahl, standing at the Bornholmer Strasse gates. 'We could see that in reality it wasn't, but I knew the momentum was unstoppable, that we wouldn't have to wait for long.'[9]

By 10.30 p.m. at least 20,000 people were crammed behind the Bornholmer Strasse checkpoint. Many had brought their cars, which they had simply abandoned on the street, blocking an exit route. Lieutenant-Colonel Jäger decided that things 'were impossible and we could not go on as we had'. Every time he asked for orders, he was told to wait. But things were too urgent. 'All I was thinking about now was to avoid bloodshed. There were so many people and they didn't have space to move. If a panic started, people would have been crushed. We had pistols. I had given instructions not to use them, but what if one of the men had lost his nerve? Even a shot in the air ... I cannot imagine what reaction that would have provoked. I told my superiors that I couldn't hold the checkpoint any longer.' He ordered two of his men to lift the red and white gate – and waved the crowds through, to rapturous applause. At Checkpoint Charlie, an hour later, Günter Möll made the same decision – independently, as none of his superiors were giving orders. It was when a flashbulb went off – one of thousands – and he could see a young soldier twitch nervously that he told his men to withdraw behind the Wall. 'We were totally surprised,' said the American commander Major Godek. 'The guards did not look aggressive, but they did not have a clue what was going on. You could see that quite clearly. They did not withdraw in formation, first a few at a time, then a wave.' A few minutes later Möll opened the Checkpoint

Charlie gates, wondering what he had been doing standing there for the last two decades.

Vast crowds had been forming on the Western side of the Wall, waiting joyously with open arms, flowers and champagne to greet the arrivals from the East. At the Invalidenstrasse checkpoint the first crowds from the East met cheering Westerners surging in the other direction in what had minutes earlier been No Man's Land. A few dozen West Berliners climbed on to the Wall at the Brandenburg Gate, originally built in the late eighteenth century as a symbol of German unity, and began to taunt the Eastern border guards. That morning they could have been shot if they had attempted to get so close to the Wall. Now they were ignored. By midnight all the six checkpoints were open and the 12,000 border guards had been ordered to return to barracks. The people had seized power and they repossessed their city. A group of East German youngsters joined the 'Wessis' at the Brandenburg Gate at around 12.15 a.m. They danced together on the Wall. When East German police turned a hosepipe on them to force them down, one of the revellers nonchalantly unfurled an umbrella. It was an astonishingly powerful image, beamed live around the world on television – the medium that had contributed so much to the revolutionary moment in Berlin. 'We Germans are now the happiest people in the world,' the usually uninspiring Mayor of Berlin declared. He captured the mood exactly right.

'Most of us, I think, did pretty much the same thing,' Rosendahl said at the time. 'As soon as we got across the border that night, when we stepped over the white line, we would look up at the heavens and take a deep breath. The air didn't smell much different. But we knew everything was different. Then we'd forget the sentimentality, took the offer of free champagne from the Westerners ... and went a bit wild.'

It was the biggest street party in the world, but not for everybody. Most of the Party chieftains were holed up in their Wandlitz compound and in bed by midnight. Schabowski's Russian-born wife, Irina, noticed that there was barely a light on in any of the thirty or so houses. She would have liked to have talked with her husband about how he had triggered the fall of the Wall by a chance remark, but he was one of the few top Party men in the city. The others were asleep. Her elderly mother woke at one point and asked her what all the fuss was about on the television.

'They've opened the border,' she was told.

'Does that mean we'll have capitalism now?'

'Yes, it probably does.'

'Well, in that case I'll hang around for a few more years and see what it's like.'[10]

For four decades the Soviet Union had regarded Berlin as the most prized possession in its empire. It had cost the most blood to win, in the Second World War, and it stood as a supposedly solid symbol of Soviet power. It was thought central to the Soviets' strategic interests. Nothing of importance was supposed to happen in East Berlin without the Soviet Union knowing about it beforehand – and approving it. Yet Berlin was not uppermost in the minds of any of the top leaders in Moscow on the day East Germany slipped peacefully out of the Soviet orbit. Mikhail Gorbachev did not know the Berlin Wall had fallen until he woke up the next day. Amazingly, no one in the Kremlin had thought to tell him earlier. The KGB had one of its biggest stations in Berlin, but nobody there warned Moscow Central that by the end of the day Moscow would lose control of Berlin. In the afternoon, the most senior Soviet Communists met in the walnut-panelled room for a routine session of the Party leadership. East Germany was not even discussed. They talked about possible changes to the Soviet constitution, moves towards separatism in Lithuania and a series of minor items that were soon to be debated at the Congress of People's Deputies. But Moscow had not anticipated a crisis in Berlin. Rather, East Germany was always in crisis these days; they had not anticipated an imminent threat, within hours, to the existence of the state.

Krenz's aides told the Soviet Ambassador, Vyacheslav Kochemasov, about the plan to let East Germans head to the FRG directly, rather than go through Hungary or Czechoslovakia. The Ambassador told the Soviet Foreign Ministry, which had no objections. But the Embassy knew nothing about the plan to let East Germans go back and forth across the Wall. That was so sensitive, Kochemasov thought, that the Soviet government was bound to be aware that it had been proposed. It affected the four-power status of Berlin, under which, in theory at least, Berlin was still divided between the Soviet Union and the three Western Allies. Kochemasov assumed that the issue had been discussed by Krenz and Gorbachev when they had met the previous week, without the Embassy knowing about it, or between the two leaders on the direct phone link between Berlin Party headquarters and the Kremlin. Nevertheless, he wanted to check.

After the Schabowski press conference he tried to call both Gorbachev and Shevardnadze to discuss Berlin. But he was told that both were too busy to talk to him. So he simply watched events unfold on the television. According to the Deputy Ambassador, Igor Maksimichev, at about 5 a.m. Berlin time (7 a.m. in Moscow) the Embassy received a call from a panicky-sounding official in the Soviet Foreign Ministry in Moscow. 'What is happening there at the Wall?' The Embassy political officer said they assumed Moscow knew all about it. 'But has all this been agreed with us?' the man from the Ministry asked. Apparently, in that day of errors and accidents in Berlin, nobody had kept the Soviets informed. Shortly after 6.15 a.m. Ambassador Kochemasov was called by a senior official from the East German Foreign Ministry. 'Last night's decision was forced upon us,' the Ambassador was told. 'Any delays could have had seriously dangerous consequences.'[11]

When Gorbachev was given the news the next morning he was surprisingly relaxed, say aides. Berlin was not at the forefront of his mind, but he had not expected the Wall to tumble down, certainly not in the dramatic way it did. He told Krenz, 'You made the right decision because how could you shoot Germans who walk across the border to meet other Germans . . . the policy had to change.' Later in the morning he grew more concerned, though. He did not want to see a united Germany. He thought his own people would not accept it and would put him under great pressure to halt it. He had often said a reunited Germany was unlikely for several decades, if at all. He had told Willy Brandt, the former West German Chancellor, and Mayor of Berlin for much of the 1950s, so in a private conversation just a few weeks earlier. He had said something similar in a speech the previous month. Now it looked like a distinct possibility, soon. Mid-morning, he sent a note to Helmut Kohl warning him 'not to destabilise the situation in Germany'. And he sent another anxious and top-secret message to Bush, Thatcher and Mitterrand: 'If statements are made in the FRG . . . that seek to generate emotional denials of the postwar realities, meaning the existence of two German states, the appearance of such political extremism cannot be viewed as anything other than attempts to destabilise . . . the GDR and subvert the ongoing process of democratisation . . . not only in Central Europe but also in other parts of the world.' Two of the recipients agreed with him – Margaret Thatcher and the French President. But Gorbachev's advisers, even that morning, were telling him that if the Germans wanted reunification, there was very little, short of war, that the Soviets could do to reverse the process.[12]

President Bush's reaction the previous day to the astonishing drama in Berlin amazed many Americans. Never renowned as an orator or a phrase-maker, he gave a lacklustre performance even by his prosaic standards. Over the years, his predecessors had found noble and uplifting words hoping for this great, world-transforming event. Now that it had happened, Bush, the leader of the Free World, could say nothing to inspire, or even to sound happy. Unusually, his press office hand-picked a few reporters to come to the Oval Office to interview him. His spin doctors asked for much of it to stay off the record. He mumbled and bumbled his way through a farcical half-hour. A reporter asked if this meant the end of the Iron Curtain. The President said, semi-coherently: 'Well, I don't think any single event is the end of what you might call the Iron Curtain, but clearly this is a long way from the harshest Iron Curtain days – a long way from that.' Had he ever imagined such a development? 'I didn't foresee it, but imagining it? Yes.' Told that he did not sound very elated, Bush said: 'I'm not an emotional kind of guy . . . I'm very pleased. And I've been pleased by a lot of other developments . . . And so the fact that I'm not bubbling over – maybe because it's getting along towards evening, because I feel very good about it.' Bush knew he had flunked the opportunity. But he explained later that his first priority was not to overreact or sound triumphalist, for fear of provoking a reaction from the Soviet Union. 'The stupidest thing that any President could have done then would have been to go over there, dance on the Wall, and stick his fingers in the eye of the Soviets. Who knows how they would have reacted?'[13]

Bush confessed privately to his advisers that it was only when he was watching the Wall fall on TV that he realised the Soviets genuinely intended to relinquish their empire. 'If . . . [they] are going to let the Communists fall in East Germany, they've got to be really serious.' Throughout the evening NSC staff – including Condi Rice – were in constant touch with the CIA to find out the latest news from Berlin. The Agency could not provide any, admitted its senior analyst on the Soviet bloc, Milt Bearden: 'The harsh fact is that we didn't have any spies in place who could give us much insight . . . into plans in East Germany, or, for that matter, in the Kremlin,' he said. 'It [was] CNN rather than the CIA that would keep Washington informed of the events in Berlin. The fall of the Berlin Wall was the first shot in an unspoken competition between the CIA and CNN that would continue throughout the closing years of the Cold War. The CIA had no human intelligence on events . . . none of our assets in the capitals of Eastern Europe, and in the Soviet Union, were in a position to tell us what was going on.'[14]

Helmut Kohl was in Warsaw when the Berlin Wall fell. Earlier in the day he had talks with the new Polish Prime Minister, Tadeusz Mazowiecki and, separately, with Lech Wałęsa. The Chancellor got on well with Wałęsa, though they had a mild disagreement as they were discussing East Germany. Wałęsa said, 'You know, the Wall will come down soon. I don't know when, but I really think very soon, maybe weeks.' Kohl laughed one of his big belly-laughs and replied, 'No, really, I don't think so. You're young and don't understand some things. There are long historical processes going on and this will take many years.' That evening Kohl cut short his visit – 'I'm at the wrong party,' he quipped – and went via Bonn to West Berlin, where the celebrations had only just begun.[15]

FORTY-SIX

THE COUP

Sofia, Friday 10 November 1989

IT HAPPENED ON THE MORNING of the night before. While the rest of the world's eyes were on Berlin, the news emerged that the Bulgarian dictator for three decades had been removed in a neatly planned *coup d'état*. It was not people's power on the streets that brought down Todor Zhivkov, as in Berlin. He did not negotiate his power away, as the Communists had done in Poland and Hungary. He lost his throne in a palace revolution led by a small clique of his most senior henchmen. It was said of Zhivkov, by one of his former toadies who joined the plot against him, that he had the 'instinct for danger of a wild boar'. But the decaying despot in Sofia did not take the conspiracy against himself seriously, or he would have tried to avert it. In the end he went meekly, fearing for his skin. Fittingly, the crumbling old Communist institution in Sofia was toppled about two hours before the Wall in Berlin fell. Both were far weaker than they appeared.

Pressure from outside the top rung of the regime played a part in Zhivkov's downfall, but no more than a supporting role. The rulers were divided about how to deal with opposition groups, which had grown in strength, though they were still a minor irritant to Zhivkov, not a revolutionary force against him. Civil rights campaigners seized a chance for maximum publicity when a Conference on Security and Co-operation in Europe (CSCE) summit on the environment was scheduled to be held in Sofia for two weeks, starting on 16 October. 'We saw that as a great opportunity to get more widely known,' said Krassen Stanchev, one of the founders of Ecoglasnost. 'There would be foreign politicians, civil servants and journalists here and the police and security services couldn't keep us away from these delegates. We were still campaigning on environmental issues, like the hydroelectric dam project and Rila Monastery. But these were a pretext, our activities were really anti-regime in general and everyone knew it.'[1]

For the first time Ecoglasnost was given permission to mount press conferences with Western and domestic journalists. It was allowed to hold public meetings, though they were sparsely attended. They organised demonstrations against the appalling pollution levels in the Black Sea and held screenings of the film *Breath*. In a popular spot in the centre of the city, the Crystal Garden, they were allowed to set up a table where they could collect signatures for an environmental petition. For twelve days they were watched carefully by the security services but were left alone. Then, on Thursday 26 October, Zhivkov lost patience. Durzhavna Sigurnost officers told the Ecoglasnost activists and their supporters to move from downtown Sofia to a remote spot in the suburbs. They refused. Shortly after midday uniformed militia and DS thugs savagely broke up the demonstration, beating up and arresting forty people in full view of American and French diplomats, conference delegates and foreign journalists. They then rounded up and assaulted around three dozen other opposition activists, drove them out to the countryside and left them to walk back to Sofia. One woman was severely wounded in the stomach. Most of them were charged with minor offences, but one, Lyubimor Sobadijev, faced prosecution for espionage, which carried a possible death sentence. This level of state violence had not been seen in Sofia for decades and shocked citizens who were used to submission and apathy, but not to bloodshed on their city streets.

The reaction from the foreign dignitaries at the conference was predictable and swift. Every government represented at the CSCE – including the Soviet Union – protested. Delegates threatened to walk out of the conference. Zhivkov had not bargained for an international outcry that threatened to isolate Bulgaria. The Environment Minister, Nikolai Dyulgerov, was forced to make a grovelling public apology the next day when he admitted that the security forces 'had overstepped the mark'. The damage had been done, though. There were unprecedented murmurings within the rank and file of the Party that it was time for Zhivkov to go. At one research institute staffed entirely by Communists, Party members tabled a resolution urging him to resign – an impermissible offence just a few weeks ago. The security service did nothing, a sure sign of weakness from the man at the top.

The conspirators saw that this was the time to strike. The most active among them was the Finance Minister, Andrei Lukanov, a sharp, silver-haired fifty-one-year-old, fluent in seven languages and for years a favourite of Zhivkov, whom he used to flatter outrageously. Born in the USSR, he slithered upwards in the Sofia regime largely through sycophancy on an epic scale but also through his powerful contacts in the Kremlin. Lukanov was chief fixer in the plot, but it was decided that Zhivkov's successor would be Petar Mladenov, a moderate technocrat aged fifty-three, popular in the Party, who burnished an image as a reformer. He had been Bulgaria's Foreign Minister for nearly twenty years, admired on the international circuit as a cool head, who could present a plausible face to the outside world. Prime Minister Georgi Atanasov had seemed a mere cipher of Zhivkov, a pen-pusher whose abilities were average but whose ambitions were not. The key player, though, was the Defence Minister for the last twenty-eight years, Dobri Dzhurov, whose role was to ensure that Zhivkov was in no position to fight back. A long-time crony and drinking companion of Zhivkov, the gruff, uncouth seventy-three-year-old was one of the few men the dictator felt he could trust. All the plotters thought the only way of saving their own positions was to remove Zhivkov, as the Hungarian Communists had ousted Kádár, and the East Germans Honecker. But they had another, personal reason. They were convinced that the dictator was planning to appoint as his successor his son Vladimir, aged forty, whom he had been fast promoting up the Party hierarchy over the last few years. Zhivkov had groomed his bright and interesting daughter Ludmilla for high office, but she had unexpectedly died in mysterious circumstances aged thirty-nine in 1981 and since then all his hopes rested on Vladimir, who, as Atanasov said, 'we all regarded as half-witted'. Jealousy and ambition motivated the plot.[2]

The quartet had been conspiring in a vague way since Zhivkov launched his campaign in May to expel the Turks. But they had to tread with care. They could not meet in the open because Zhivkov's personal spies would be suspicious. 'We were living in a glasshouse, closely observed,' said Lukanov. 'Everyone knew that everything we said was bugged, so we only talked about business or personal things when we knew we were being overheard. We used to write notes to each other and slip them across the desk. Obviously it was impossible to phone each other. We couldn't trust anyone else.' They had to engineer meetings outside in the street, where they were unlikely to be overheard. That was where Dzhurov's final, crucial agreement to join the conspiracy was reached – on a pavement.

Lukanov and Mladenov were convinced that they needed Moscow's blessing to proceed. That had to be handled with great care. Gorbachev was personally told about their intentions by Mladenov at the Warsaw Pact summit in Bucharest on 7 July. The Bulgarian took a copy of one of Gorbachev's books and during a break in the proceedings he went up to the Soviet leader and asked him to sign the volume. 'Then Gorbachev said, "I want to talk to you." We went into a corner where there was nobody else,' Mladenov recalled. 'In . . . our system it was inconceivable to have the Foreign Minister, rather than the First Secretary, talking to Gorbachev. I was not authorised to have private discussions with him . . . I told Gorbachev that we intended to carry out this change . . . he said "This is entirely your business. You have to sort it out yourselves." Probably Zhivkov knew what we were doing. He had strong intuition. But . . . it was another thing to have proof.'[3]

Three people in the Soviet Union were kept informed all along: Gorbachev, Yakovlev and Shevardnadze. In Sofia the Soviet Ambassador, Viktor Sharapov, knew about the plot. But they did not play an active role, apart from wishing the conspirators well. The KGB was deliberately kept in the dark, for fear of a leak. Nobody in the Lubyanka was told and General Vladilen Fyodorov, the KGB's Resident in Sofia, did not know until the next day from the TV news. The Soviet and Bulgarian intelligence services were exceptionally close – they had co-operated on numerous operations, such as the murder of the writer Georgi Markov. The conspirators wanted to be especially sure that the Sigurnost should have no inkling of the plot.

The final act began on 24 October, when Mladenov suddenly resigned as Foreign Minister. Zhivkov was deeply concerned. He tried to talk Mladenov out of it but his charm failed to work on this occasion. Mladenov sent the letter to all the senior Communist Party oligarchs, knowing it would soon be widely leaked throughout Sofia. It was a devastating indictment of Zhivkov's leadership and personality. He wrote:

> Todor Zhivkov . . . has led our country into a deep, economic, financial and political crisis. He knows that his political agenda, which consists of deviousness and petty intrigues designed to keep himself and his family in power at all costs and for as long as possible, has succeeded in isolating Bulgaria from the rest of the world. We have even reached the point where we are estranged from the Soviet Union, and we find ourselves entirely on our own, in the same pigs' trough as the dictatorship of Ceauşescu . . . Zhivkov has forced Bulgaria outside currents of the age. Do you think it is easy being Foreign Minister of

> such a state, headed by such a leader? The world has changed . . . and if Bulgaria wants to be in tune with the rest of the world, it will have to conduct its affairs in a modern way. Like all of you, I think I have a realistic picture of Todor Zhivkov's moral character. I know that he will stop at nothing, not even the most outrageous crimes, when what he holds most sacred – his power – is impinged upon . . . I do not even rule out his trying to take physical retribution against me, or members of my family . . .[4]

Mladenov had taken the precaution of sending a copy to Gorbachev 'because I wanted to have a record there for history if something were to happen to us', he said. Zhivkov wanted to be assured of the Soviet Union's support and on 31 October he sent a message to Gorbachev asking for an urgent meeting in Moscow. Gorbachev refused, saying he was too busy to see him and that he was 'neutral' about internal issues in Sofia, which were entirely the business of Bulgarians.[5]

Zhivkov was drinking more heavily than usual and sleeping poorly. He had been a strong man all his life, though now he began to look physically weak. But he was not yet broken. He met Dzhurov at around ten on the morning of Wednesday 8 November, who delivered a heavy blow. His old friend told him that it was time for him to step down and that there were enough members of the top leadership ready to vote him out of office if he did not resign. But he played for time, hoping that he could organise a counter-coup against the plotters. 'When I tried to go a year ago and asked all the others whether I should resign they all said No,' he said. 'Now you all say Yes. What's happened in a year? I am prepared to resign, I'll go soon, but not just yet. I need to do a few things first.' The plotters knew 'that it would have to be now or never', according to Lukanov. 'We can't afford any postponement,' he told Atanasov and Dzhurov. Mladenov was in China and would not return until late the following night. 'If you give Zhivkov a week everything could be finished, and we could be finished too.'

Zhivkov tried to round up support that night, but it drained away. Dzhurov had tight control of the army. The leaders of the militia and even the Sigurnost, which been loyal to Zhivkov for decades, said they could not back him. A leadership meeting at the Party headquarters in central Sofia was called for 5 p.m. on 9 November. The conspirators gave him a last chance to resign. At 4 p.m. Dzhurov told the leader that army units loyal to the Defence Ministry were guarding the exits to the building and warned him that if he continued to resist the obvious and refused to resign voluntarily, there would be a resolution not only to remove him from office but to execute him. He finally caved in, amid floods of tears. An hour later he took the chair of the Communist oligarchs of Bulgaria for the last time. He said he was old and ill and wanted to be relieved of the cares of duty. He resigned, but tried to play one final card. He recommended Atanasov to replace him. Zhivkov lost that trick too. Atanasov declined and nominated Mladenov.

The next day, at a larger Party meeting, his resignation was officially accepted and Mladenov was formally elected in his place. At the end he was standing, alone, at the lift, waiting to leave the building. The man who had held power for thirty-five years, removed thousands of his enemies, and had allegedly stashed away upwards of US $100 million in Swiss banks for himself and his family, cut a pathetic figure. Mladenov went to him to try to say a consoling word. Zhivkov brightened up for a minute and stayed true to his character. 'He started making several demands . . . could he continue to stay in his official residence, in Banyka, near Sofia . . . could he have a smaller residence . . . he asked about his pension . . . I said he could do as he pleased,' said Mladenov.[6]

Zhivkov's dictatorship was over. But the Communists tried to keep their monopoly on power. Mladenov made it clear that he proposed to stay in office and so would all the Party chieftains. It seemed that the principal beneficiaries of the coup would be the conspirators who ousted Zhivkov. Bulgarians felt cheated. They had watched Soviet TV and seen the crowds on the streets in Berlin. A wave of protests swept through the country on a scale never seen before. 'The coup had worked for them,' said Stefan Tafrov, a spokesman for the hastily formed Union of Democratic Forces, and later an Ambassador to the UK and to Paris. 'We had to find something that would work for us.' Massive demonstrations over the next three weeks forced Mladenov – like the East Germans before him – to cave in, start serious talks with the opposition and agree to democratic elections the following spring.[7]

FORTY-SEVEN

THE VELVET REVOLUTION

Prague, Friday 17 November 1989

IT WAS RITA KLIMOVA who invented the phrase 'Velvet Revolution'. A petite, blonde, one-time politics lecturer at Prague's ancient Charles University, she was the formidably erudite spokeswoman for the opposition that bustled the Communists out of power in Czechoslovakia. Klimova spoke impeccable English, but in a Manhattan accent with West Side idioms; she had been to school in New York where her father, the left-wing writer Batya Bat, had fled to escape the Nazis in 1938, when she was an infant. The family returned to Prague soon after the war. Her story was fairly typical for a Czech dissident of the 1980s. She had been a convinced Communist, like her husband Zdeněk Mlynář, who had shared digs and a close friendship with Mikhail Gorbachev at Moscow State University in the 1950s. He rose high in the ranks of the Party, and she in academia, until the Prague Spring was crushed. Then they both lost their jobs – and their idealistic faith that communism could offer any hope for mankind. In the harsh years of 'normalisation' she found work as a translator, became active in Charter 77 and was a firm friend of Václav Havel.

The fiercely intelligent Klimova could occasionally look stern and forbidding, but at fifty-eight she had a large girlish streak and a sense of fun. As Klimova used to say, it was fun that characterised the Velvet Revolution and made it so different from the others in Central Europe in the summer and autumn of 1989. Defeating the Communists was a serious matter. Nobody doubted that. But in Czechoslovakia it was done with plenty of music, wit, humour, laughter and a little absurdity, much of it scripted by a celebrated playwright. It happened with astonishing speed. As the acute observer on Central Europe Timothy Garton Ash pointed out, 'In Poland it took ten years; in East Germany ten weeks; in Czechoslovakia ten days.' Barely a month earlier, in mid-October, the Czech Communist

Party chief, Miloš Jakeš, was assuring his fellow Communist oligarchs that 'we'll be all right. As long as the economy holds up here, and there's food on the shelves.' He was fooling himself. Like his peers in Berlin and Leipzig, by the time the hapless Jakeš and his colleagues in Prague Castle grasped what was happening to them it was too late to do anything about it.[1]

For a week after the Wall fell there had been an uneasy quiet in the Czech capital. Everyone had seen the pictures from the Brandenburg Gate, just 200 kilometres away. Communism in East Germany had collapsed. The Party had been defeated and was now negotiating the details of its capitulation. The comrades in Prague still imagined that somehow they could cling on, that the 'infection', as Vasil Bil'ak, one of the leading neo-Stalinists in the Czech leadership, called it, would not spread. They did not seek to negotiate with the opposition. Instead, they put the riot police and the StB on full alert. A secret report to the Czech Deputy Interior Minister in charge of security, Rudolf Hegenbart, written after the Wall was breached, detailed the preparations the security forces were making 'to protect peace and stability against enemy elements, rowdies and counter-revolutionary forces'. Round-the-clock patrols in known troublespots in the centre of the city would increase. 'We were living in a different place from the rest of the world's population, in a bubble of our own,' said one old comrade, who confessed that he did not see what was about to happen, despite all the evidence in front of him.[2]

Students sparked it. They had been given permission, through the official Communist Youth organisation, the SSM (Socialist Union of Youth), to hold a rally marking the fiftieth anniversary of the death of Jan Opletal. The regime had wanted to ban the march. But it could find no plausible reason. Opletal had hero status in People's Czechoslovakia. The Communists had used his name in anti-fascist propaganda for four decades. He was shot by the Germans at a demonstration against the Nazi occupation, after which 1,000 of his fellow Czech students were sent to concentration camps and all Czech universities were closed for months. Three weeks before the anniversary march, a route was agreed between the SSM organisers and the police which avoided the centre of the city and would end at the National Cemetery at Vyšehrad, burial place of Dvořák, Smetana, a host of other Czech notables, and Jan Opletal. More than 50,000 well-behaved people had joined the march. The shouts heard most often were 'Remember 68', 'Down with the Commies', 'Forty years are enough' and 'Perestroika, here'. A huge banner was unfurled halfway through the march bearing a saying attributed to Gorbachev in large red letters: 'If not now, when?' The police did nothing. They let the march go ahead.

According to the agreement with the authorities, the demonstration should have ended at the cemetery and most of the people left, particularly the older ones. It was now about 5.30 p.m., a freezing winter late afternoon and that familiar dense, foul, sulphuric fog had descended over Prague. A core of about 3,000 people, all students or young workers, stayed at the cemetery, standing around in the cold, doing nothing in particular At around 6.30 p.m. a few of them shouted 'To Wenceslas Square' and they turned back, hastening towards the centre of Prague. As they reached the Czech National Theatre on Národní Street, which leads to the Square, they were confronted by riot police wearing white helmets and carrying plastic shields and by anti-terrorist squads in red berets wielding heavy truncheons.

The students sat down in the street and started singing – hymns, the national anthem, old Beatles hits, 'We Shall Overcome'. 'We chanted "We have no weapons". The only things we had with us were candles and flowers, which we gave to the police. They used loudhailers and shouted "Go home", but they had blocked our path,' said Charles University economics student Pavlina Rousova. Another squad of riot police had come up behind the students. They could not move.

They continued to sit in the freezing cold, wrapped in their coats, hugging each other to keep warm, and out of fear. They waited, singing, for around two hours, staring at the riot squad behind their shields. Occasionally one of the students would get up and try to ask an officer to release them from the trap and let them go home. They were ignored. Just after 9 p.m. a riot squad van appeared from behind the line of police. It deliberately rammed into the crowd, causing panic. The police attacked the students, beating them with truncheons as they scattered. 'There was blood everywhere and I could hear bones cracking,' said student Dasa Antelova, who managed to hide in a narrow alleyway and later make a getaway. 'They selected people from the first row of the demonstration, and they beat them mercilessly. They would not let the young people go. They brought in buses and arrested them all.'

There was no hiding any of the evidence of brutality. A British journalist, Edward Lucas, watching the riot police laying into the students, was led away by two officers. As they did so, a plain-clothes StB man knocked him, unconscious, to the ground. Philip Bye, a news cameraman from Independent Television News, was beaten up. At around 9.45 the violence stopped, almost as abruptly as it had started. Wounded and bloodied young people picked themselves up from the ground and staggered home, or to a hospital casualty unit. Five hundred and sixty-one were injured. Around 120 were carted off in police vans, where they were beaten again. One young man was left lying on the cobblestones on Národní Street appearing lifeless. He was covered with a blanket and stretchered away in an ambulance.[3]

This is where the Czechoslovak Revolution enters the murky, looking-glass world of Kafka and *Švejk*, spiced with a hint of John le Carré. Rumour travelled fast in Communist capitals and it was generally believed, certainly more so than the official media. Within hours, the word was that the prone body seen lying on Národní Street was that of a mathematics student, Martin Šmíd. It was spread mainly by the dissident Charter 77 activist Peter Uhl, who daily provided information from the opposition underground to journalists from the West. Uhl had been told about the death by a woman calling herself Drahomíra Dražská who claimed to be an old friend of Šmíd. Uhl immediately told Radio Free Europe, the BBC and Voice of America, which reported the death of Martin Šmíd as fact. There was public fury throughout Czechoslovakia. The regime denied that anybody had died in the 'riot' and the next day managed to produce two Martin Šmíds, both of them alive. One, who had been on the demonstration, appeared on nationwide TV breathing and talking. It did little good. Nobody believed the regime's denials.

That weekend huge spontaneous demonstrations erupted in Prague on an unprecedented scale. An archway on Národní Street where many of the police beatings had taken place was turned into a shrine visited by scores of thousands of people. Someone had painted a cross on a wall nearby and passers-by lit candles. 'The news about that death changed everything, not just for us, but for our parents' generation,' said Dasha Antelova. 'They had been silent since 1968, terrified of what they could lose. But now they were as enraged as we young people were. Mothers and grandmothers joined students and ordinary workers on the rallies. It was all good-humoured, and wonderfully exciting, but determined.' The government could think of no response, other than to arrest Peter Uhl for spreading false rumours.[4]

The regime was deeply split. The Martin Šmíd story is evidence. The Party's own 'sword and shield' was working against its leadership. Often, conspiracy theories can be discounted, even in Central Europe under communism, where they abounded. But occasionally there really were conspiracies behind the theories. This is an example. The Czech secret service, the StB, faked the 'death' of Martin Šmíd in order to create a groundswell of popular anger that would remove Jakeš, Prague Party boss Miroslav Štěpán and other hardliners and replace them with Gorbachev-type reformers. It seems far-fetched, but evidence which established the conspiracy as genuine, rather than a plot in a spy movie, was provided later in a commission of inquiry set up by a post-Communist government.

The plan was the brainchild of General Alois Lorenc, head of the StB, and a small group of Party reformers who looked at events in Poland and Hungary and thought the only way of maintaining their own positions was to find a means of negotiating from strength with a divided opposition. At the same time, the other essential step in the operation – codenamed Wedge – was to infiltrate the dissident movements and find opposition figures willing to do a deal with reform Communists. It was convoluted, ill-judged and entirely misunderstood the Czech opposition and character, but undoubtedly it was bold. The details were worked out when the StB knew that there would be a big student demonstration on the anniversary of Opletal's death. A key player was Lieutenant Ludvik Zifčák, a young StB officer who, under orders, had infiltrated the student opposition underground. In a classic 'provocation', he was one of the leaders of the main march to the National Cemetery, and when that ended in the afternoon he was one of the students shouting at the top of his voice 'To Wenceslas Square'. He knew there would be a trap when the students arrived. He kept his head down as far as possible when the violence began. He lay on the ground and pretended to play dead. Drahomíra Dražská, who subsequently disappeared, was another agent. She had orders to pass on the news to Uhl that a student had died.

It is still unclear exactly how much the Soviets knew about the plan – or which Soviets. While the riot police were beating up students in central Prague, General Lorenc was dining with the KGB's head of station in Czechoslovakia, General Gennady Teslenko, and the deputy head of the KGB, General Viktor Grushko, who had arrived in Prague a few days earlier. They then drove together to the gloomy sludge-grey concrete and glass StB headquarters on Bartolomějská Street, not far from Wenceslas Square. But he socialised with KGB officers as a matter of course. That does not prove direct Soviet involvement. It is not the kind of operation that the men around Gorbachev would have recommended. It was far too risky and its main purpose opaque. The plotters had picked out their candidate to take over the leadership: Zdeněk Mlynář, who they thought would start Prague Spring-type reforms, which they could learn to support. But Mlynář was no longer a Communist, had lived in comfortable exile in Vienna for some years, and wanted nothing to do with the plot. Seldom can a conspiracy have been so elaborate, so wrong-headed, and turned into such a spectacular failure. The Czechs did not rise up to remove the excesses of neo-Stalinism. They wanted rid of the Communists, and especially the Russians. As the 'corpse' Lieutenant Zifčák said, he and the other conspirators had tried to save communism. Instead, they hastened its end.[5]

While a make-believe revolution was taking place in the minds of secret police officers, the real thing was happening on the streets of Prague and in a box-like theatre just off Wenceslas Square called the Magic Lantern. Václav Havel had been at his country house in Bohemia when the students were beaten up. He did not return to Prague until Sunday 19 November. He knew when the Berlin Wall fell that the Czech regime had only limited time left in power, but he did not know when or how it would go. It needed a push. When he arrived back in the city, already there was a group of friends, dissidents and opposition activists at his cluttered but elegant flat on the riverbank with a sweeping view towards the Castle. They were looking to him for leadership. From that moment he took command of the Velvet Revolution. He no longer seemed like a shy intellectual plagued by self-doubts, but appeared a strong and decisive man of authority. He was a formidable political tactician. To most Czechs he was still unfamiliar. 'Havel was ... more or less unknown, or known as the son of a rich capitalist, even as a convict,' said the Czech novelist Ivan Klíma, who had known Havel for years and did not always agree with him. 'But the revolutionary ethos that seized the nation brought about a change of attitude ... In a certain atmosphere, an individual suddenly identifies himself with the prevailing mood and state of mind, and captures the crowd's enthusiasm ... Within a few days Havel became the symbol of revolutionary change, the man who would lead society out of its crisis.'[6]

The priority, he told his associates, was to form a unified group, one voice that could represent the opposition and, when the time came, negotiate with the regime about a peaceful transfer of power. The first task was to remove the totalitarian system, Havel maintained. They could all disagree later when a working democracy was established. Havel called Rita Klimova and asked her to translate for him at an impromptu press conference with foreign reporters. It was a shrewd move. He spoke English, but with a heavy accent, and he thought her part New York, part Central European cadences, as well as her wit, would play well to Western audiences. He was right. 'The ideals for which I have been struggling for many years and for which I have been imprisoned are beginning to come to life as an expression of the will of the people,' he said. At last the Czechs were beginning to wake from their torpor.

First, they needed a headquarters. The previous day actors had declared a strike – as did students. So the playwright directed operations from a theatre. At ten that night he took up residence at the Magic Lantern. Performances of Friedrich Dürrenmatt's expressionist classic *The Minotaur* were cancelled while the Czechs brought down their government. By midnight they had agreed on a name, Civic Forum, and produced the first of a series of proclamations and demands. The group claimed to be a 'spokesman on behalf of that part of the Czechoslovak public which in recent days has been profoundly shaken by the brutal massacre of peacefully demonstrating students'. At first there were four demands:

- The immediate resignation of the Communist leadership responsible for crushing the Prague Spring and for the 'normalisation' purges, including Husák and Jakeš.
- The resignation of the ministers who were presumed to have given the orders for the attack on the students two days earlier, starting with the Prague Communist Party boss Miroslav Štěpán.
- The establishment of an official and independent inquiry into the demonstrations of 17 November.
- The immediate release of all political prisoners.[7]

Shortly after it was published, Havel quipped only half in jest that it was time for another Russian invasion – now, he said, the men in charge at the Kremlin would be more on his side than on the regime's.

For the next six days vast demonstrations filled Wenceslas Square every evening. Most people went after work. As in East Germany, it was a well-ordered revolution and well-mannered. When professional footballers called a strike, they made sure they continued 'working' for ninety minutes on Sunday afternoon, so supporters would not miss matches. 'Each day people felt stronger and stood up straighter,' said the musician Ondřej Soukup. 'It was as though the weight of the previous twenty years was being shed. We Czechs had not felt good about ourselves. We had been so submissive. But now we were beginning to feel proud. It was extraordinary.'[8]

The police took no action as the numbers grew. There were at least 300,000 on Monday 20 November, in the freezing cold. The odd snowflake fell, which did nothing to dampen the enthusiasm or the good humour. People talked to each other with trust about their hopes and dreams for the first time in two decades. Occasionally speeches were made, more often there was music. A rock band formed by the hugely popular Czech artist Michael Kocáb, a friend of Havel, set up a loudspeaker system. When the music stopped the most commonly heard sound was the shaking of keys, which frequently echoed around Wenceslas Square and through the whole of central Prague. Addressed to their Communist masters for the last forty years, it meant 'Goodbye, it's time to leave'. Similar huge demonstrations were taking place in towns and cities throughout the country, like Brno and Ostrava, where there had been almost no opposition political activity for the past twenty years. In Bratislava, Charter 77's sister organisation, VONS, the Committee in Defence of the Unjustly Persecuted, had existed since the late 1970s, but with a minuscule membership. It became Civic Forum's central branch in Slovakia, where Alexander Dubček again emerged as a political figure. When he sent a message of support to the demonstrators in Wenceslas Square, cheers erupted around the whole city.

In the Magic Lantern there was a constant hum of excited activity. It was a varied crowd. As Timothy Garton Ash, who spent many intense hours of conversation and laughter there said, 'The room smells of cigarette smoke, sweat, damp coats and revolution.' Havel had managed to bring together people of entirely opposed views with one purpose: to remove the totalitarian regime. There were Trotskyists, reform Communists, environmentalists, feminists, right-wing Catholics, Calvinist pastors and rock musicians who wanted to make the music they liked. People in jeans or overalls would come into the Magic Lantern for a while at lunchtime or early evening and then return to their paying jobs. During the Prague Spring they had been lawyers, published writers, Communist Party officials or academics. They had been fired. Now they were part-time political activists, and full-time factory workers, electricians or minor office clerks. One of the leading figures in Civic Forum, the trim, sparklingly original Jiří Dienstbier, had been among Czechoslovakia's best-known journalists, a campaigning foreign correspondent, until he was fired in the autumn of 1968. He had since found a job as a janitor. Every now and then he left meetings at the Magic Lantern to stoke up the boiler at the building where he worked.[9]

The Czech Communists divided into chaos. Jakeš, the Prague Party boss Štěpán and old Stalinists like Jan Fojtík wanted to continue with tough police action. They considered imposing martial law on the morning of 19 November. At first the Defence Minister, Jaroslav Václavík, suggested a 'military solution' that involved moving tanks to key locations on the edges of cities. The Czech air force would be put on high alert. But it was not a realistic prospect at this stage. No soldiers were ever ordered out of barracks during the Velvet Revolution. Jakeš held a series of meetings of the hardliners at which the threats they made sounded bloodcurdling, but no strong action followed. 'Force has to be met by force,' Jakeš said to his colleagues. 'We cannot helplessly watch the activities of groups acting ... outside the law and incited from abroad. Attempts to manipulate ... sections of Czechoslovak youth could lead society into a crisis with unforeseen consequences.' One of the other old Stalinists said later that 'we looked at what had happened in Berlin. They sat on their hands and took no action – and we could see what followed. Some of us were determined we had to do something.' But the Party was disintegrating.[10]

On the morning of Wednesday 22 November Jakeš decided that he would call out the People's Militia to attack the demonstrators. This was the Party's private, part-time army, 20,000-strong, recruited from ultra-loyalists, mostly factory workers who were paid considerable extra money for voluntary duty at weekends and a few evenings a month. They were not officially part of the army or the state security service, but it was always thought they would come to the aid of the Communists in the last resort. The militia refused. Štěpán tried to rally workers and militia against the students at a big steel plant in the Prague suburbs. 'We do not intend to be dictated to by children,' he declared. 'We are not children,' they roared back. Civic Forum called a general strike for Monday 27 November, but, in the typically Czech way, only for two hours, between midday and 2 p.m. It was designed to be a symbolic test of strength. When it became clear that almost every Czech worker intended to join the strike, the old guard's will evaporated. Marián Čalfa, the Deputy Prime Minister, sat listening to the hardliners, flabbergasted by their lack of realism and common sense, and by their indecision: 'The whole police and security apparatus was at our disposal. The key factor was that nobody appeared with the guts, instinct, character, call it what you will, to use force, or to convince others that it was appropriate.'[11]

Jakeš had heard in direct terms from a senior figure in the Kremlin that he could not expect help from Soviet forces, or any political support, to stay in power. Gorbachev had dispatched Valeri Musatov, an influential figure as head of the Communist Party's international department, to Prague with orders to watch events. The Kremlin wanted accurate information because, as Musatov said, the Soviet Ambassador in Prague, Viktor Lomakin, was a deeply conservative figure who had no contacts among Communist reformers, let alone among the opposition. 'He spoke only to what used to be called "healthy sources", which was not of great use to us in these circumstances,' Musatov said. On the other hand Musatov, in an unprecedented move for a senior Soviet official, went to a Civic Forum meeting at the Magic Lantern. That was seen as a great blow against the regime in the Czech Party and to Jakeš personally. The hardliners, in effect, raised the white flag on the evening of 22 November, when Defence Minister Václavík declared on television that 'the army will not fight the people. We will not become involved.' The reason was obvious: the soldiers would not have obeyed their senior officers if ordered to fire on unarmed civilians.

Each night the demonstrations continued to grow. People were now going for amusement as well as political fervour, even though temperatures in Prague were well below freezing in the evenings and a nasty influenza bug, which most people called 'revolution flu', was going around the city. As Party control was losing its grip, state-owned television grew more daring. For the first time, it televised the Wednesday demonstration live, though such glasnost was short-lived. The next morning police raided the office, sacked the senior management and installed a flunkey of Jakeš, Deputy Prime Minister Matej Lucan, as director. Staff demanded that coverage of the demonstrations continue, though. A strange half-censorship was agreed on. The protests were screened, live but for a limited time, when the screens would go blank and dance music would be played for a short while before the broadcast of the demonstration would start again. Not that it made a great deal of difference. As in East Germany, most Czechs could receive foreign broadcasts and even if they could not easily understand the language, people grasped what was happening.

The most emotional of the demonstrations was that Friday evening, a week after the students had been beaten. There was a crowd estimated at around half a million. Suddenly, without any announcement, a stooping, grandfatherly-looking gentleman with a kindly, beaming face, still rather good-looking for sixty-eight years old, appeared from a balcony above the square. For some moments few people realised who the man could be. Then they saw that it was Alexander Dubček, who had that morning arrived in Prague from Bratislava. The cheers were deafening: 'Dubček na hrad, Dubček na hrad' ('Dubček to the Castle' – meaning 'Dubček for President'). The hero of the Prague Spring enjoyed his moment of vindication. He embraced the other man on the balcony receiving cheers of his own, Václav Havel. It was an intoxicating evening of high drama. Dubček spoke as though the last two decades had not existed, about socialism with a human face. 'Twenty years ago we tried to reform socialism, to make it better,' he said. 'In those days the army and police stood with the people and I am sure it will be so again today.' There was resounding applause, but slightly more muted than before. 'We hadn't thought he'd still be a Communist,' said Ondřej Soukup. 'It wasn't a disappointment so much, he was a hero because he stood up to the Russians. But by then we were not Communists, and we didn't want to hear people telling us how great communism could be if only the circumstances were right.'[12]

That is what Dubček persisted in saying for the rest of the evening. An hour after appearing before the crowds, Dubček and Havel spoke at a press conference at the Magic Lantern. The former leader of the Czech Communist Party looked as though he had stepped out of a black-and-white photograph, as one observer commented. He spoke about the 'reformability of socialism – as long as we depart from everything that is wrong with it'. Havel appeared uncomfortable, as did most of the Civic Forum activists. 'Socialism is a word that has lost its meaning in our country,' Havel said. 'I identify socialism with men like Mr Jakeš.' Seconds later a young man in jeans and sweater went on to the stage to whisper a message to Havel and Dubček, who smiled at each other. The news had just been announced that Jakeš and the entire leadership of the Communist Party had resigned. The applause was deafening. A bottle of Sekt appeared from somewhere. Dubček and Havel embraced and Havel raised a toast – 'Long live a free Czechoslovakia'. They downed the wine in one gulp. There was not a dry eye in the house.[13]

Senior StB officers and the moderates in the Party leadership were desperate to make a deal with the opposition. Prime Minister Ladislav Adamec, sixty-three, the best-known of the Communist reformers, was the man who negotiated the end of Czech communism with Havel. They knew they could not save the regime, and in any case they had not believed the ideology they had been spouting for many years. Adamec was a careerist first, a cynic second and a Communist third, though he had never been a brute. He and his associates wanted to save themselves, in particular from possible prosecution after the opposition took over. At first the talks were secret – Adamec did not want his colleagues to know he was meeting Civic Forum. Havel wished to negotiate openly only when he knew he was dealing with the right man and when he was certain an agreement could be reached. Havel used an emissary, the composer Michael Kocáb, one of his friends, who had met Adamec socially a few times and knew some members of his family. Kocáb, a tall, rangy thirty-five-year-old, was Czechoslovakia's biggest rock star. He had not been overtly political, but he had found ways to show the public how he felt about the regime, while staying just within the law and outside prison. 'Both sides knew from the start that it was time to talk, but wanted to work out some basic ground rules first,' Kocáb said. The initial, confidential, meeting was the day after Civic Forum was formed on 20 November. 'It was amazing that it needed a musician to oil the wheels in this way, but this is Czechoslovakia. The moment Havel knew they were ready to talk seriously, he knew it was the end for the Communists. But he had to know they were serious. Adamec wanted to continue playing a role in Czech politics, and talking with Havel was the only way he could.'[14]

Kocáb met the reform Communists secretly several times. He set up the first official talks on Sunday 26 November, which began with some hilarious formality. Havel and Adamec, both grinning nervously, sat opposite each other at a crowded table in a packed, smoke-filled room. They then both rose at the same time, with the same thought. 'Hello, we haven't met, my name is Havel.' 'No we haven't. Mine's Adamec.' Over the next several days of hard bargaining a peaceful transfer of power was negotiated, while vast crowds occupied the streets of Prague. Within two weeks, the Communists promised free elections the following spring, gave up their 'leading role' and much of their wealth and Husák had resigned the presidency.

Adamec tried to salvage something of his career but failed lamentably. Because the crowds had become so immense, demonstrations were moved from Wenceslas Square to Letná Park, outside the city centre. Adamec appeared at the first of these, on the evening before the talks commenced. He had spun himself as a great reformer and people were cheering him loudly before he began to speak. In his first sentence he declared that the government accepted the demands of Civic Forum and he was applauded wildly. But then came the ifs and buts. In fact he promised nothing and started speaking in Marxist-Leninist jargon. He was booed off-stage and had to be spirited away for his own safety.

Havel had no official role but, in effect, the new government announced on 7 December was picked by him. The Interior Minister was the Slovak dissident and civil rights campaigner Ján Čarnogurský, now in charge of the secret police, who until a few days earlier had been their guest in custody. The janitor, Jiří Dienstbier, was made Foreign Minister. The Prime Minister, though, was the Communist Deputy Premier Marián Čalfa. Havel explained that Czechoslovakia needed a few people in government who had run things, as well as a few intellectuals. 'Čalfa can get things done,' he said, when colleagues appeared doubtful. Havel easily defeated Dubček for the presidency. There was never, in fact, a real contest. When, in early December, Civic Forum tacticians began to consider potential candidates, there was barely a debate. The Trotskyite Petr Uhl and the Conservative Catholic Václav Benda both said the same thing, almost at the same time: 'It might as well be Václav.' Dubček was widely respected, but he was sounding increasingly out of date. He became Speaker of Parliament. Havel had guided the revolution and the immediate transformation almost as though he were giving stage directions.[15]

FORTY-EIGHT

THE MOMENT OF WEAKNESS

Timişoara, Romania, Sunday 17 December 1989

ROMANIA COULD NOT REMAIN forever immune. Ceauşescu had done his best to isolate the country from the rest of the world. But even there people had heard that the Berlin Wall had fallen and that neighbouring countries had toppled their Communist regimes in a dizzying few months of revolution. Covertly, Romanians could tune into the BBC or Radio Free Europe and hear Czechs, East Germans and Bulgarians discuss the merits of democracy and describe their former rulers as corrupt thugs. Yet Ceauşescu appeared to be carrying on as though nothing had happened. At the end of November he had been unanimously re-elected Romanian Communist Party leader for another term, as he had so often before. The occasion was marked by the usual rituals. He stumbled his way through a dreary three-hour speech which was interrupted thirty-four times when the audience 'spontaneously' rose in rhythmic applause lasting several minutes. The loudest cheers erupted when he said that 'Socialism has a long future. It will die only when pears fall from apple trees.' Ceauşescu still controlled all the forces of repression that had kept him in power for a quarter of a century. He seemed still to be unassailable. Unlike his peers in Berlin, Prague and Sofia he had the will and the authority to fight and kill for his position. Yet when the end came, the most powerful and feared dictatorship in Europe collapsed within five days.[1]

Seldom can a revolution have begun in a bleaker place. The Transylvanian city of Timişoara had a tiny medieval centre, which had once been pretty but was crumbling away, and a few fine baroque buildings from the period before 1919, when it was a Hungarian city called Temesvár. Now it comprised mainly hideous new apartment blocks for a quarter of a million inhabitants, so badly constructed they were already falling apart. Like all Romanian towns it was unremittingly poor and heavily polluted, from nearby chemical and engineering works and agriculture that spewed dangerous fertiliser into the water supply. A canal which might once have been charming ran through the town. Now it was filthy and smelly and children were warned not to play anywhere near it. Around a third of the town's population came from the Hungarian minority. Despite traditional hostilities that ran deep, and Ceauşescu's attempts to suppress Hungarian culture and heritage, on the whole the two communities rubbed along reasonably well together and suffered together.

A shy but inspirational pastor lit the spark. László Tőkés, a tall, dark-haired thirty-seven-year-old, had a diffident and quiet manner that hid a steely determination. He had been the priest in charge of the Hungarian Reformed Church in Timişoara since January 1987. For a long time considered a troublemaker by the regime and by the Church hierarchy, which like all the religious organisations in Romania had collaborated closely with the Communists for decades, Tőkés had been removed from his previous parish in Dej. The authorities, spiritual and secular, thought he was showing too much overt support for the Hungarian minority's cultural demands, such as education in Hungarian for their children. He was given the post in Timişoara on a probationary basis and told to steer clear of politics.

The parish had fallen on hard times. The congregation had dwindled to little more than a handful. Tőkés blamed his predecessor, Leo Leuker, whom he called 'a Red Priest' for collaborating with the regime. Quickly, he established a reputation as a powerful preacher and the church began to fill with new or returning congregants, impressed by their pastor. He was in regular conflict with his bishops. Oddly, on one occasion, his offence was to quote from the Book of Daniel: 'To you it is commanded, O people, nations, and languages, That at what time ye hear the sound of the cornet, flute, harp, sackbut, psaltery, dulcimer, and all kinds of musick, ye fall down and worship the golden image that Nebuchadnezzar the King hath set up: And whoso falleth not down and worshippeth shall the same hour be cast into the midst of a burning fiery furnace.' His superiors thought it could be taken by the congregation as a criticism of Ceauşescu and they gave him a warning.

He found himself in deeper trouble in September 1988 when he publicly supported a letter written by a congregant to the Bishop of Arad, László Papp, one of the most senior men in the Reformed Church's hierarchy. The letter criticised the regime's systemisation policy, which it was rumoured would destroy hundreds of Transylvanian villages. Tőkés was arrested and interrogated by the Securitate and told to stay out of politics. The final straw as far as the bishops were concerned was when Tökés proposed to hold a joint, ecumenical Reformed Church/Catholic service in Timişoara for young people from both faiths.

In March 1989 Bishop Papp started legal proceedings to fire the pastor from his living and evict him from his home. But he defended himself through the courts, which turned into a long process that was starting to receive some coverage in the religious press, the BBC World Service and Radio Free Europe. One night in late November, just a few days before his final appeal was scheduled to be heard, four masked men armed with clubs and knives broke into his house. Pastor Tökés was beaten, while his three-year-old son, Maté, looked on. His pregnant wife, Edit, shouted for help from the uniformed police outside, who had been keeping the family under surveillance for months. But they did nothing while the men inside, clearly Securitate officers, performed their duties. He lost the legal appeal on 7 December and in his last sermon on Sunday 10th he asked his congregation to witness his eviction from home the following Friday, 15 December.[2]

The church and attached parsonage was a nondescript slab-grey late-nineteenth-century building close to the centre of town. It was in a small square, but easily visible from the main road and within a few metres of a tram stop. At first around thirty-five of Tökés's congregation stood outside, while the Tökés family remained in the church. Then an unprecedented thing happened. As word spread throughout the city about a demonstration, they were joined by ever-increasing numbers. 'At the beginning, it was only members of our parish,' Tökés said. 'But then, hour by hour, people joined from the whole of Timişoara, whether they were Hungarian, Romanian, Orthodox, Baptist or whatever religion. People from all communities joined together. They forgot the original reason for their resistance and in general terms just opposed the regime itself.'

As the numbers swelled, local Party bosses were unsure how to react. The Mayor, Petre Mot, sought instructions from Bucharest and was initially told to play for time and to negotiate in the expectation that the crowds would disperse. They did not. The weather was extraordinarily mild for mid-December, still above freezing. Many Romanians have said that it was the warm weather that made the revolution. They were not entirely joking. It is unlikely that the crowd around Pastor Tökés's church would have grown overnight if it had been much colder. During most of Saturday there was an uneasy stand-off. The

Mayor returned in an attempt to disperse the protesters. He promised to reinstate the pastor, but when he refused to put the pledge in writing the crowd booed and catcalled him. They were now no longer calling for bread or meat or in support of László Tökés. They began repeating 'Down with Ceauşescu' and 'Down with tyranny', 'We are the People' and 'Freedom now'. By mid-afternoon, the police and Securitate formed a line on the boulevard within sight of the square. But after an hour or so they left. 'That was the first time we felt we had power,' said one of the demonstrators, Lajos Várga. 'We had driven the Securitate away. It was like living a wild dream, a forbidden fantasy.'[3]

Ceauşescu himself had given the orders to let the demonstration go ahead. He thought it would run out of steam. Now the orders were reversed. The next morning, Sunday, the police and Securitate began to make some arrests, on the fringe of the crowd. The mood turned uglier and angrier. There were at least 2,500 protesters by now in a country where spontaneous demonstrations had been practically unheard-of for a generation. Most of them left the church and marched to the centre of the city, along one of the main boulevards towards the Opera House and the headquarters of the Communist Party, the seat of the tyrant's power. There they were met with a line of troops, riot police and a fire engine. They turned water cannon on the crowd but the protesters rushed the building, forcing the security forces to withdraw. They ransacked the ground floor, throwing as much Party property as they could on to a fire. For the next several hours the demonstrators were in control of the centre of Timişoara, but they had no plan of action. They looted bookshops and burned the works of Nicolae Ceauşescu. They threw petrol bombs at official-looking cars. They set fire to the town hall and destroyed thousands of official files.

After most of the demonstrators had left the Hungarian Reformed Church, the Securitate seized the pastor, seven-months-pregnant Edit Tökés and their son. The pastor was badly beaten around the body and face. With a split lip and black eye he was taken to Ion Cumpănaşu, head of the Department of Religious Denominations, and threatened with violence against his wife unless he signed a blank piece of paper which effectively accepted his dismissal and eviction. They were taken in separate cars to Minev, an isolated village in Sălaj County, which had been designated his residence.*

* László Tőkés subsequently became a bishop and one of the leaders of the Hungarian Reformed Church in Romania.

When the Ceauşescus were told that a riotous mob had taken over the centre of Timişoara, they were incandescent. Late on the Sunday afternoon, 17 December, the President summoned into his presence the heads of his various security services. Interior Minister Tudor Postelnicu, Iulian Vlad, head of the Securitate, General Vasile Milea, head of the army, and the Defence Minister. While Communists throughout the rest of Eastern Europe were negotiating with their opponents, this extraordinary meeting shows that Ceauşescu was determined to shoot them. He would offer no quarter – and nor would his wife.

CEAUŞESCU: I think the foreign groups outside are involved in the organisation [protecting Pastor Tökés]. It is known that both East and West have said that things in Romania must change. Some elements have come together and caused disorder. The police and army have done a very poor job. I talked to comrades in Timişoara and told them to put on a show of power with tank units in the centre of the city. My impression is that the units of the Interior Ministry, the regular police and the Securitate were unarmed.

POSTELNICU: Except for those who were border guards, the rest were unarmed.

CEAUŞESCU: Why? I told you that all had to be armed. Why did you send them unarmed, who has given them this order? When I understand that the Securitate troops are going somewhere it is clear to me that they are going armed. You sent them to beat people with fists. What kind of interior units are they? And the militia [police] have to be armed. That's the law.

POSTELNICU: Comrade General Secretary, the militia is armed.

CEAUŞESCU: If it is armed, it has to shoot, not let people attack it. How is such a situation [ransacking of Party HQ in Timişoara] possible? What did your officers do, Milea? Why didn't they intervene? Why didn't they shoot?

MILEA: I didn't give them ammunition.

CEAUŞESCU: Why didn't you give them ammunition? If you don't give them ammunition you might as well send them home. What kind of a Defence Minister are you? What kind of an Interior Minister are you, Postelnicu?

ELENA: The situation is very grave . . . The Minister of Defence and the Minister of the Interior did not act properly.

CEAUŞESCU: Some few hooligans want to destroy socialism and you are making it child's play for them. Fidel Castro is right. You do not quieten your enemy by talking to him like a priest, but by burning him.

ELENA: They are cowards.

CEAUŞESCU: They are more than cowards. As supreme commander, I consider that you have committed treason against the country's interests and against the people's interests and against the interests of socialism. In this moment . . . we are dismissing the Defence Minister, the Interior [Minister] and the chief of the Securitate troops. From this moment, I'll take command of the army. Prepare the decree to take force this evening. They've got to kill the hooligans, not beat them. [To the three officials] Do you know what I'm going to do with you? Send you to the firing squad. I have realised now that you cannot create order with batons. I will give right now the order that all will have guns and ammunition.

ELENA: You should shoot them so they fall and put them in Securitate basements. Not one of them should see the light of day again. We've got to take radical measures. We can't be indulgent.

CEAUŞESCU: We'll fight to the last.

VLAD: We thought it was a limited problem and we could solve it without ammunition.

CEAUŞESCU: I didn't think that we should shoot with blanks. Those who entered the Party building should not leave the building alive.

All of them grovelled and accepted they were in the wrong and pledged to act more decisively in future. 'I assure you . . . that such a situation does not occur again,' said Postelnicu. 'Please place this trust in me.' Milea pleaded, 'I did not appreciate the danger from the beginning.' Vlad assured his leader that from now on 'I will proceed in such a way as to merit your faith.' Grudgingly, Ceauşescu reinstated them to their jobs but continued with his sarcasm and abuse. 'Very well then . . . So shall we try once more, comrades?'[4]

Later that evening army units with live ammunition took control of the streets of Timişoara, shooting at civilians mercilessly. The Securitate made more than 700 arrests. The next morning Ceauşescu went on a long-planned visit to Iran, one of the few countries that would now accept him as a visitor. But he did not leave before being told from his army high command and the Securitate that Timişoara was quiet. As usual, he left his wife in charge of Romania while he was away. Around sixty civilians died that night in Timişoara. It was the single bloodiest protest against communism there had yet been in Romania. But rumour spread fast that a horrendous massacre had taken place. Radio Free Europe, widely trusted among covert listeners in the country, put the death toll at anything between 4,000 and 20,000. Of course, the official media had not mentioned anything about Timişoara, so Romanians believed what they heard on foreign radio broadcasts and from the grapevine. 'We all believed that a terrible genocide had happened in Transylvania,' said teacher Alex Serban. 'It aroused a kind of desperation we had not felt before. It took us out of complete torpor, but still we needed more of a push before we could do anything.'[5]

Nicolae Ceauşescu arrived back in Bucharest from Iran at about 3 p.m. on Wednesday 20 December. From the moment he returned he made a series of critical misjudgements. The first was his hasty decision to hold a giant rally in the centre of Bucharest the following day that would show the world that he was still the beloved leader of his people. He remained convinced of his popularity to the end. All he needed to do was to speak to Romanians as their leader, demonstrate his power and authority over them, and they would listen, applaud and obey as always. Neither he nor his wife had a clue how detested they were. The bootlickers and flunkeys surrounding him had an idea of the truth. But nobody dared to contradict him or even to suggest that perhaps a big public appearance along traditional lines was not the wisest course.

The Bucharest Party worked overnight to ensure a huge, adoring crowd for the appearance of the Conducător in Palace Square. The organisation for these occasions was a well-oiled machine to force the attendance of a loyal crowd. Early in the morning of Wednesday 21 December Party officials in factories and offices mobilised workers. They selected participants by work units. Anybody who refused to go faced the sack. They were bussed to downtown Bucharest where they were issued with red flags, placards of Ceauşescu's picture and banners in praise of socialism. Then they marched in a column to Palace Square. On arrival they were usually screened to weed out any potentially disruptive elements. On this occasion, though, many passers-by along one of Bucharest's main streets, the adjoining Calea Victorei, were press-ganged into turning up in order to swell the numbers. The hard-core loyalists carrying photos of the leader and banners were at the front. Ordinary people were at the back. There was a big Securitate presence, but widely spread out amidst a crowd of 110,000 people.

The mood was subdued when at noon, in bright winter sunshine, the warm-up speakers, little-known Party apparatchiks, began. The dictator appeared on the balcony of the Party headquarters at 12.31 p.m. with Elena at his side, and a bank of four microphones in front of him. At first everything went as usual. Ceauşescu was cheered and rhythmic applause regulated his mundane utterances. But then, eight minutes into his speech, something unheard-of happened. From the rear of the crowd there were unmistakable sounds of booing and catcalls and the low chant TI-MI-ŞOA-RA. It started faintly at first, then grew louder and more confident. Ceauşescu looked nonplussed for a second or two, and tried to continue reading from his script about 'fascist agitators who want to endanger socialism'. But the boos continued, now accompanied by whistles. Romanian TV had been ordered to screen the rally live and continued filming. The great leader froze, his mouth open. It was the moment of fatal weakness and the crowd sensed it.

People began shouting 'Ceauşescu, we are the People' and 'Down with the killer'. He put up his right hand in a gesture of irritation. That incensed the crowd further. Elena urged him loudly, but off-microphone: 'Speak to them. Offer them something.' Ceauşescu looked panicked as he announced pension and family allowance increases of 2,000 lei (around two US$ 2 a month). Then he dried up completely. The catcalls grew louder. The director of TV made an executive decision and halted transmission. The picture went blank, apart from a caption that read 'Live transmission'. Ceauşescu's burly personal bodyguard, General Marin Neagoe, bustled the leader from the balcony. Many have claimed credit as the first to jeer the dictator. For some years it was thought to have been student Nica Leon, but his claims have since been doubted. One of the first barrackers was certainly a taxi driver, Adrian Donea, who said: 'We could see he was scared. At that moment we realised our force, that we had strength.' The first to chant 'Timişoara' were workers from the Turbomecanica power plant outside Bucharest.[6]

Most popular revolutions are characterised by confusion. The crowd in Palace Square had seriously wounded the dictator, without firing a shot. But now they had no idea what to do. If the Securitate had attacked in strength at that point and forced the protesters from the streets of Bucharest, the course of the Romanian Revolution might have been entirely different. But they did not. Soon the demonstrators were joined by thousands of people who had watched Ceauşescu on television transform himself in an instant from an omnipotent tyrant into a weak old man. Others had heard what had happened and rushed on to the streets to see if it was true. Was Ceauşescu seriously being challenged? Rioting erupted that afternoon at three main points in the centre of Bucharest: at University Square, dominated by the Intercontinental Hotel, where foreign journalists did not need to travel far to see the disturbances; at Palace Square and at the Romanian TV station in the north of the city. For a few hours Ceauşescu's formidable security forces did nothing. They let the demonstrators run riot. Pavel Câmpeanu, the aged Communist who had once shared a prison cell with Ceauşescu but broke with him decades earlier, said: 'At this point, even then, he could have chosen to talk – to the students and the dissidents and to the reform-minded Communists. But . . . he would have had to leave his familiar world, which he was unable to do.'[7]

Instead, he chose to fight and to use the same tactics as in Timişoara a few days earlier. From about six in the evening Securitate troops and police units began firing indiscriminately at demonstrators, whose only defence was Molotov cocktails, stones and makeshift shields provided by cars overturned on the main boulevards. 'There was uproar everywhere, pandemonium,' said one of the revolutionaries. 'But our determination was to stay on the streets that night, to show defiance at least that long, and then to see what happened.' No regular soldiers had taken part in any of the fighting. They had stayed in barracks. The few who had been sent out on duty, mostly young conscripts, were not sure at whom they should be shooting.

Inside the Communist Party headquarters on Palace Square, Ceauşescu was making his second big mistake. He was a man so conscious of his security that he employed a praetorian guard of eighty highly trained Securitate troops, pampered and well paid to be ultra-loyal. There was a network of underground passages which linked this building to many of his other Bucharest residences. He could easily have made a getaway from the city and tried to muster his supporters elsewhere. Nobody knows for sure why he did not make the attempt. Throughout the afternoon and evening Ceauşescu was holed up with his aides and officials. Once he told his entourage of courtiers that 'I'll stay and fight . . . I won't be forced to run away, and my wife agrees.' Nobody tried to talk him round. Some had already turned coat and had plans to save themselves. Others stayed silent from habitual fear.[8]

The people held the streets overnight. There had been sporadic fighting, around thirty-five people had been killed, but the Securitate and the riot police had disappeared before dawn. A vast but peaceful crowd occupied Palace Square. 'We were expecting something, but we didn't know what,' Alex Serban recalls. Romanian TV was on air again and broadcasting the demonstrations live. Nobody had given an order not to film, but it still required bravery to keep the cameras running.[9]

Inside, at around 9 a.m., the dictator made the decision that turned the army against him and ensured his defeat. Someone had to be blamed for the riots in the city. Ceauşescu chose the Defence Minister, General Vasile Milea. He said it was 'treachery' that Milea had not ordered the soldiers to fire on the demonstrators and sacked him. What happened next is still uncertain. According to Milea's family, friends and some of his junior officers, shortly before 10 a.m., on Ceauşescu's orders, a Securitate detail took the General upstairs to his own office and shot him. Another account, backed up by a different group of officers, is that Milea was escorted to his office and killed himself. An official broadcast at 11 a.m. said that 'General Milea was a traitor and has committed suicide'. Either way, the news had a profound effect. A huge resounding boo echoed around Palace Square when it was announced. A paunchy sixty-two-year-old, Milea had for years been one of Ceauşescu's most serpentine of sycophants. He had commanded some respect from his senior officers, but the lower ranks had thought little of him. Instantly he was turned into a martyr of the revolution. The commanders of all three services gave up Ceauşescu as a lost cause, and their men eagerly joined the side of the rebels. Soldiers took the magazines from their guns and waved them at the crowds. A few tanks had been dispatched on to the city's main boulevards early that morning. Their turrets opened and soldiers stood up, waving at passers-by. The resounding cry went up in Palace Square and throughout the city: 'The army – with *us*.'[10]

At around 11.30 a.m. a white helicopter landed on the roof of the Communist Party headquarters, to the jeers of the people below. Ceauşescu tried one last time to talk to the crowd but it was a fiasco. He stepped out on to the first-floor balcony, where he had spoken the previous day. People began hurling stones and anything they could lay hands on in his direction. His guards bundled him and Elena away and into a lift. One group of protesters had managed to break down the great steel doors of the building, overpower the guards and take their weapons. They ran up the stairs, where Ceauşescu's bodyguards put up some resistance, but after a fierce fight for a few minutes they surrendered. The insurgents rushed through Ceauşescu's office and on to the balcony, where thousands of people cheered from the square below, hailing them.

None of the rebels realised that at this point they were standing just a few metres from the loathed ruler. He was stuck in a lift and escaped only by luck. His Securitate detail had decided against going to the basement, where the presidential party could have used the network of underground passageways to make their getaway. They went to the roof, but the electricity failed during the fighting and the lift halted just before it reached the top floor. After a struggle of several minutes, the bodyguards managed to force open the lift doors and the President and his wife, breathless and agitated, clambered up on to the roof. They were accompanied by two of the dictator's most loyal henchmen, the Prime Minister, Emil Bobu, and a Deputy Premier, Manea Mănescu, one of Ceauşescu's many brothers-in-law. The rotor blades of the French-built Ecureuil helicopter were turning – and decisions had to be made quickly. They were met by the burly, forty-six-year-old Lieutenant-Colonel Vasile Maluţan, the Ceauşescus' personal pilot for the last eight years, who had not wanted this assignment. 'I was sent to the roof of the building to wait,' he said. 'Originally there had been four helicopters, three to pick up the government. But the mission of the other three helicopters was cancelled. I toyed with the idea of flying away . . . without picking anyone up. But I could see some Securitate sharpshooters on adjacent rooftops and feared that if they saw me taking off empty they might try to shoot me down. I radioed my base: "Do I stay here?" The answer came back: "Yes, stay and wait."'

Maluţan knew what was happening below – his base was providing him with a running commentary of what Romanians were seeing for themselves live on television. When he saw the size of the entourage Maluţan said: 'There are far too many of you.' But by then some demonstrators were already on the roof and could have rushed the helicopter in seconds. The pilot was ignored and his passengers climbed up to the helicopter. When he took off, the helicopter was barely able to clear the roof. 'Had we been on the ground I don't think we would have been able to make it,' he said. It was 12.10 p.m. There were nine people inside the aircraft, including three crew. It was so packed that one of the crew had to sit on a guard's knee. Elena was in floods of tears. Ceauşescu looked crestfallen. After a few moments in the air Maluţan turned to Ceauşescu and asked, 'Where to?' He was not sure. He and Elena argued briefly and finally Ceauşescu said, 'To Snagov,' 60 kilometres north-west of Bucharest, where the Ceauşescus had a lakeside palace.[11]

Joy erupted in Palace Square when the presidential helicopter was spotted heading away from the capital. Everywhere, Romanian tricolour flags of red, blue and yellow appeared with a hole in the centre; the hammer and sickle emblem had been removed. Singing began, most often to the tune of a football chant heard everywhere soccer is played:

Ole Ole, Ole, Ole
Ceauşescu unde é?
(Where's Ceauşescu?)
Ole, Ole, Ole, Ole
Ceauşescu nu mai é!
(There's no more Ceauşescu)

Hundreds of insurgents occupied the Party HQ, ordinary people who believed that as they had forced their way into the building, it was they who had brought down the dictator. It was a disparate group that had come together only because they had been there at the right time. They were factory workers, taxi drivers, office clerks, teachers. One of the first into the central lobby had been a 'bar hostess' at the tourist hotel, the Intercontinental. In the enormous office on the first floor that used to be occupied by Ceauşescu there were hours of talk, but no organisation. None of them had any experience of government, or of opposition. Everybody had an opinion. Nobody had power.

Amidst the confusion, power lay elsewhere. Television played a vital role in the Romanian Revolution. But it was not foreign broadcasts that made the difference. In the first chaotic day after Ceauşescu fled, the Romanian broadcasting studios became a seat of government. As Gelu Voican-Voiculescu, who became one of the first post-Ceauşescu leaders, admitted: 'Our success lay in the successful exploitation of television.'[12]

From the morning of 22 December, anybody in Bucharest with influence, or who thought they had influence, went to the headquarters of Romanian TV, an ugly modern concrete building on one of the city's main boulevards. Ion Iliescu, known in Communist Party circles as a cautious opponent of Ceauşescu, noticed that around mid-morning the Securitate tail who had been following him for years had disappeared. He went straight to the TV studio. General Victor Stănculescu, who had been made Defence Minister that morning to succeed the late General Milea, and who had advised Ceauşescu to flee by helicopter, went to the TV studio, accompanied by other senior officers. The dissident poet Mircea Dinescu had been under house arrest at his home in Bucharest for the last six months after he gave an interview to the French newspaper *Libération*. He went straight to the TV studio, by a method typical of the Romanian Revolution. 'On that Friday morning, 22 December, a neighbour called to tell me the armed Securitate men who had always been outside my door weren't there any more,' he said. 'I went outside to look and walked around a little. It was true. I wandered into town. Then a crowd of people came up to me and lifted me into the air. I was put on an armoured vehicle and people said to the soldiers "This is Dinescu, take him to the TV station." It was like a bad film about a revolution.'

The National Theatre actor Ion Caramitru, one of the most popular artists in the country, was taken to the studio on the top of a tank. For an hour after Ceauşescu fled, amidst the confusion and unsure what to do, the management halted broadcasts. But from 1 p.m. live transmission started again and the first people viewers saw were the poet and the actor beaming and happy. 'The dictator has fled,' Dinescu announced. By the end of the day the poet would be a government minister. For millions of Romanians outside Bucharest this was the first news they had heard of a revolution in Bucharest. Silviu Brucan, the dissident intellectual, opponent of Ceauşescu and tireless gossip, went to the studio. 'The sense of liberation and of excitement after all these years was intoxicating,' said Caramitru. 'But we were innocents. How were we going to form a government? I am an actor. I didn't have any conception of myself as a President or anything like that.'[13]

There were those who understood better the nature of power. Ion Iliescu and his accomplices saw the opportunity to take control of the revolution – and they seized it. When he arrived at the TV station there was chaos. 'All kinds of people were there talking, showing enthusiasm,' said Iliescu. 'But I felt something had to be put in order, because just enthusiasm and general sentiment could lead to anarchy.' He and a few Communist officials passed over for promotion by the Ceauşescus, a large number of generals and a few dissident academics established a government from the ruins of the Ceauşescu dictatorship. It is an enduring myth that there was a well-organised plot to take power. It is widely believed in Romania and elsewhere. The appearance in the future government of so many unreconstructed Communists, and the country's difficult transition towards democracy afterwards, seem to give the various stories credibility. But there is no documentary proof. The conspiracy theories are so heavily dependent on a mass uprising and a fleeing dictator, unpredictable circumstances, that an elaborate and carefully calculated plan prepared months in advance sounds implausible.

Yet some others, including General Nicolae Militaru, who became Defence Minister in the new government, insist that there was much pre-planning. He said there had been a plot to overthrow Ceauşescu scheduled for February 1990. Ceauşescu would be taken prisoner while he was away from Bucharest and put out of action by tranquilliser guns, while the army and members of the apparat declared a coup. The guns would not be delivered until the middle of January, though, so the revolution overtook the conspirators. The new government would call itself the National Salvation Front and be led by Ion Iliescu.

It is denied by Iliescu and other leading figures of the post-Ceauşescu administration. 'Many people discussed things about the future, ways out of the disaster we were in,' Iliescu said. 'I spoke with military men. But were we prepared to implicate ourselves in action which could eliminate the Ceauşescu regime? To have a plan you need to have the conditions to put it into action. We discussed what could be done, but ... it became clear – from people inside the army and other institutions – that it was not possible to organise anything.'[14]

When Iliescu spoke on television that afternoon he looked like a figure of power and authority as he promised to bring the man who had inflicted such misery on Romanians 'to the reckoning before the public'. He said that the immediate task was to restore order. It was not yet certain that Ceauşescu would not fight back. And he called on all 'responsible people' to form a Committee of National Salvation. By 6 p.m. that evening the army had effectively installed Iliescu as leader of a new government, shaky, weak, born amidst uncertainty and confusion. It had one urgent primary task: to fight a civil war.

*

The shooting began at 7 p.m. Small groups of Securitate officers loyal to Ceauşescu started firing indiscriminately on the streets at people celebrating liberation. It went on ferociously for a day and two nights and sporadically for another day after that. Often it was difficult to know who was shooting at whom or for what. Much of the violence seemed entirely wanton, like the deliberate shelling of the beautiful neo-classical National Library when nobody was inside the building. Hundreds of ancient and irreplaceable volumes were destroyed. The Securitate operated under an order – number 2600 – which was supposed to deal with a foreign invasion or a serious uprising. It is unclear who activated the order as the most senior Securitate officers, including General Vlad, had gone over to the revolution. The tactics did not seem to have a military purpose, but were designed to sow as much terror in the civilian population as possible. The army was unsure how to respond. The soldiers were mostly raw conscripts, barely trained, who had never before fired a shot in anger. Differentiating friend or foe was hard, made even more so as thousands of civilians were handed weapons by soldiers at military barracks. Often the Securitate 'terrorists' would wear civilian clothes, or army uniforms. In small groups, they used the underground passageways and sewers to move around Bucharest, attack army units or civilian targets, and then just as suddenly disappear.

At 9 p.m. on 22 December they attacked the TV station, but not in a serious attempt to take over the building, which by then was ringed with tanks. The defending troops had received less than two months' training and wore heavy armour better-suited to the open battlefield than to fighting guerrilla actions in the streets of a city. Fighting raged for about an hour and sixty-two people were killed, mostly civilians caught in the crossfire. The studios were attacked several more times over the next few days. Rumours spread that the casualty figures were in their thousands and Bucharest had turned into a bloodbath. Fighting was intense. Throughout Romania the death toll was 1,104, of whom 493 died in Bucharest and about a third were Securitate 'terrorists'. There were 3,352 wounded, 2,200 of them in the capital. The worst single incident was a case of 'friendly fire'. Early in the morning of Saturday 23 December, troops guarding Otopeni, Bucharest's airport, fired at a truck bringing fresh reinforcements to join their own side.

According to Valentin Gabrielescu, chairman of the Senate inquiry that later looked at the fighting in the revolution, most of the deaths were civilians, 'innocents caught in the crossfire between panic-stricken soldiers and civilians firing at terrorists'. He concluded: 'As well as the army and the police, thousands of civilians were armed and under the stress of false rumours and false dangers . . . everyone fired at everyone else. It was chaos.'[15]

The Ceauşescus' getaway attempt was tragicomic. By mid-afternoon the couple were left abandoned, on their own and under arrest. After escaping in the nick of time from the rooftop at Party headquarters, they reached their forty-room villa in Snagov within twenty minutes. But they did not stay long. Ceauşescu made a series of phone calls to local Communist Party secretaries to see if there was any region willing to take him in. They ruled out trying to flee the country. He frowned as he was told the revolution had spread everywhere. They went up to their apartment on the first floor. There they searched through all the cupboards, emptied the drawers and turned over the mattresses. They put everything into blue bags, including two loaves of bread.

Within fifteen minutes, at around 1.20, they hurried back to the waiting helicopter. They sent their two unwanted passengers, Prime Minister Bobu and his deputy Mănescu, off by car to fend for themselves. As they left, Mănescu knelt and kissed the President's hand. Now the Ceauşescus were accompanied only by their two bodyguards, Lieutenants Florian Rat and Marian Rusu. The helicopter pilot was desperate to offload the President and his party, but the guards kept pointing their guns at him and told him to do as he was instructed by the President. Maluţan said: 'When they were all back on board Ceauşescu asked me, "Whose side are you on? Where are we going?" I answered "You give the orders." We took off at 13.30 hours. The bodyguards were very nervous. They kept their machine pistols pointed at me. On my headphones I could hear my commanding officer saying to me "Vasile, listen to the radio – this is the revolution." After that, Ceauşescu ordered me to cut all radio contact with my base. I wanted to persuade him to let us land . . . but I was on my own, cut off from the world.'[16]

He was told to head for Piteşti, in the south-west of the country, and he deliberately flew high 'so we could be seen by radar'. But one of the guards spotted the manoeuvre and said, 'Vasile, what are you up to?' The pilot answered Ceauşescu himself. 'We've been spotted by radar,' he said. Both of the Ceauşescus looked terrified and Nicolae barked 'Let's go down, land near the road.' The pilot put the helicopter down in a field, four kilometres from Titu, outside a village called Salcuta. It was 1.45 p.m. Marian Rusu hailed two passing cars. The Ceauşescus and Florian Rat got in one. Rusu, who had been Elena's personal bodyguard for many years, got in the other, promising to follow close behind. But he deserted them immediately.

The Ceauşescus were in a red Dacia driven by Doctor Nicolae Deca. He realised immediately who was in his car and he tried to get rid of his passengers as soon as possible. He said he was running out of petrol, which was a lie, but plausible in Romania at the time. Rat hijacked another driver, thirty-five-year-old Nicolae Petrisor, outside the front door of his house. Ceauşescu told him to drive to Târgovişte, where there was a showcase Potemkin village-type factory which he had visited several times with foreign dignitaries. They were privileged workers, loyal Communists, surely they would be welcome there, he told Elena. She looked doubtful.

When they arrived in Târgovişte the town was in uproar, celebrating the news of the revolution. They abandoned Rat on the outskirts. Fearful of being recognised, they kept their heads down as far as they could. Petrisor was ordered to drive to an agricultural plant which they had also visited many times. The director, Victor Seinescu, let them in, but at around 2.45 p.m. called the local militia to inform them of the identity of his guests. The Ceauşescus were taken away by two uniformed militiamen, but it was not until three hours later that they were handed over to the army, even though the barracks were only 450 metres away. Like so many senior officials that afternoon Seinescu was deciding whose side to be on. Eventually he chose to hand them over and just before 6 p.m. they were taken to the barracks at Târgovişte, where an anti-aircraft artillery regiment was based. It was difficult getting the couple to the barracks without anyone seeing who they were. The Ceauşescus were bundled into an armoured personnel carrier, shielded from the public's gaze, and taken by a roundabout route to the barracks. The drive took five minutes or so. When they arrived they were taken to their last living quarters. An office had been transformed into two cubicles, separated by standard-issue desks. Two army beds were placed in the corners of the room, with blankets but no sheets. There was a large porcelain stove in another corner and a cold-water-tap washbasin next to it. This ground-floor section of the barracks was placed off-limits for all but a few hand-picked officers and NCOs. Major Ion Secu spent the next two and a half days with the couple.

At first, said Secu, 'Ceauşescu behaved as though he was still the Commander-in-Chief. His first words were: "Well what's the situation? Give me your report." I said "We are here to protect you from the mob, but we must obey the authorities in Bucharest." This enraged him and he launched into a long tirade against the traitors who had engineered this plot against him. Only gradually did he adjust to the fact that he was the prisoner.' His mood alternated between bouts of deep, silent depression and intense excitability when he would rant about 'traitors'. The commander, Lieutenant-Colonel Mares, was worried above all about security. There were 500 soldiers and forty civilians on the base. They had to be restricted from leaving in case news of the Ceauşescus' presence became known.

Sometimes Ceauşescu was wheedling. One of his twenty-four-hour guards said: 'He came up to me ... he put his hand out and said "I'll give you a million American dollars and any rank in the army you like if you help to get us out of here." But it never occurred to me to believe the offer was genuine. I thought that instead of a million dollars I would just get a bullet in the back of the neck. So I said to him "nothing doing".'

From Elena there were three days of nagging. 'She complained all the time,' her guard said. 'She was scared, but in a state of constant fury and her rage was terrifying. Because he was diabetic, Ceauşescu had to make frequent visits to the foul-smelling lavatory at the end of the corridor. She refused to use the lavatory so we had to bring her a chamber pot. Whenever I addressed him she snapped at me "How dare you talk to the Commander-in-Chief like that?"'

That first night, recalled Secu, they shared a single bed, huddled together – two old people in each other's arms. 'They talked in whispers and though they kept hugging each other they kept bickering softly. At one point Nicolae said, "If you'd only told me what was going on I could have got rid of that Iliescu. I could have finished him off last summer. But you didn't let me." And she whispered at one point: "It's all your fault; we shouldn't have come here in the first place. That was your responsibility."'

They refused to eat anything but bread and apples and drank only unsweetened tea. Meals were brought to them from the officers' mess. But they were left untouched as though they feared the food was poisoned. On their first morning, officers tried to put them in army clothes – to make them more difficult to find should the barracks be stormed. Ceauşescu was told to take off his dark overcoat and fur hat and wear an army uniform. Elena refused. Guards removed her fur-collared coat by force, placed an army greatcoat around her and thrust an army cap on her head.

That night Ceauşescu made another attempt to talk his way out of his predicament, according to Major Secu. 'He saw me dozing off. Elena was watching everything from her bed, wide awake and attentive. He said to me "Are you tired? You have every right to be tired." He then asked about my family. I told him I was married with one child and lived in a small apartment. "That's tough," he said. "You deserve something better than that. Listen, I could get you a villa in Kiseleff [a fashionable district of Bucharest]. Seven or eight rooms, more if you like, and a garage. And the car inside the garage needn't be an ordinary Dacia" ... I didn't reply and he began again. "You wouldn't be risking your life for nothing. If you get me out of here and take me to the TV station where I can address the people, I would see that you got one million, no, two million dollars."'[17]

On Christmas Eve the Securitate troops finally worked out where they were held and took up positions outside the building. Soon after midnight they opened fire, but were forced back. An hour earlier, the Ceauşescus had been told to put on their greatcoats, were hurried into an armoured car parked in a sheltered place outside the building and told to lie face-down on the floor. They remained there for the next five hours until the firing died down. They were then taken back to their room in the barracks. It was there that they spent their last night.

The new government needed to assert its authority. By late afternoon on Christmas Eve fighting in Bucharest, and in large towns like Sibiu and Braşov, was less ferocious, but there were still sporadic battles and mounting casualties. The more moderate of the revolutionaries hated the name National Salvation Front. It sounded too Stalinist. But Iliescu and the other long-time Communists in the new regime thought it had a patriotic ring. They met at around 5 p.m. on the 24th to reach a decision on the fate of the Ceauşescus. It was a sombre, bad-tempered occasion. They had hesitated for two days. But now the soldiers wanted a swift execution. They felt sure that would immediately halt the shooting. If Ceauşescu was dead there would be no rallying point, nothing to fight for. Iliescu was at first doubtful. He did not want blood on his hands. When Militaru suggested with heavy sarcasm that 'Yes, that might look like a bad start to your reign,' Iliescu angrily replied, 'What do you mean, my reign? This is not a reign.' Some voices suggested that holding a kangaroo court in a rush, without proper evidence, would cause derision internationally. But the generals were adamant, and Brucan supported them. He said Romania needed to be assured that the Ceauşescu dictatorship was dead and gone and there was no better way 'than to show them the body'. Iliescu, finally, was convinced. 'It would be better to have a proper trial and allow all the evidence to be presented,' he said. 'But circumstances don't allow it. Let's proceed with a trial tomorrow.' The sentence was decided by a handful of people after that meeting and nothing was put down on paper. But Iliescu, Brucan, Militaru, Voican-Voiculescu and Stănculescu all decided on a firing squad immediately after the trial.[18]

There was hardly a murmur of protest. The poet Anna Blandiana objected. In the first euphoric hours of the revolution she had been given a position within the Front to show that it was a 'government of all the talents'. But she had not been informed of the decision to execute Ceauşescu and she was appalled by it. She resigned immediately he was shot. It was the first of many open splits in the movement that emerged later. One of the few voices from outside the country against the execution came from Eduard Shevardnadze. He said he understood the circumstances. 'But still it left a bad taste in the mouth.' Many Romanians are convinced the Soviets inspired and took part in a coup against the dictator. The evidence, it is said, was the presence of the *éminence grise* Silviu Brucan in Moscow in November. But there is no evidence. Brucan frequently visited Moscow to see contacts and he often asked the Russians if they could intervene, but they declined. He always denied there was a plot – 'In the circumstances in Romania it was simply impossible to organise anything like that. We complained to each other and hoped for his death. The whole nation longed for his death. But we didn't do anything,' he said.[19]

Gorbachev had decreed that there should be no direct Soviet involvement in Romania, and the evidence is that he was obeyed. 'We knew something would happen there,' said one of Gorbachev's key foreign policy advisers, Valentin Falin. 'We knew there would be victims ... something was inevitable because the regime was not only rotten but intransigent. Even then we didn't foresee the bloody bacchanalia that came to pass. Romania had no other way out. We therefore ... watched.'[20]

The dénouement in Bucharest was full of irony. At the height of the fighting, the Americans became seriously alarmed that violence might spread in the Balkans. Lawrence Eagleburger, the Assistant Secretary of State, told his boss, James Baker, that he was worried the Romanians might turn their weapons on ethnic Hungarians and wondered if the Soviets should intervene to stop it. US objections to the Brezhnev Doctrine should not apply in this case. On Christmas Eve Baker formally suggested 'that the Soviets have the incentive and the capability to do something to stop the bloodshed'. He said the US would not object 'if the Warsaw Pact felt it necessary to intervene' in Romania. This was almost exactly the tenth anniversary of the Soviet invasion of Afghanistan. It seemed an extraordinary suggestion for an American Secretary of State to make. He told the American Ambassador in Moscow, Jack Matlock, to sound out the Soviets, who reacted with mirth. Shevardnadze said the idea was not sinister 'but merely stupid'. He was 'categorically opposed' to any outside intervention. The Romanian Revolution was 'their business'. Any kind of Soviet intervention might 'make a martyr out of Ceauşescu'. Besides, the fighting stopped immediately after he was executed.

Late on 24 December, Matlock had an uncomfortable meeting in Moscow with one of Shevardnadze's officials, Ivan Aboimov, who repeated that the USSR would not intervene. The Americans, he pointed out, had just a few weeks earlier invaded Panama to remove a hated dictator, Manuel Noriega, from power there. He was brutalising his people and involved in a drugs-running cartel that smuggled cocaine into the US. 'We'll leave that sort of intervention to you,' said Aboimov. 'You mentioned the Brezhnev Doctrine. From our side, we will give you the Brezhnev Doctrine as a gift.'[21]

FINALE

Vatican City, Friday 1 December 1989

The motorcade of twenty black vehicles, with motor-cycle outriders, had created havoc in the congested streets of Rome for the previous day and a half. Wherever Mikhail Gorbachev went, outside the USSR, he attracted vast and enthusiastic crowds. This was no exception, though the occasion was unique. At about 10.30 a.m. the Soviet entourage reached the Gate of Bells at the side of St Peter's Basilica and turned right down a narrow cul-de-sac. Gorbachev's Zil limousine halted at the entrance to the papal apartments in the courtyard of St Damasus, one of the secret gems inside the Vatican closed to the public. He was greeted with a halberd salute from a detachment of Swiss Guards in their maroon- and mustard-coloured uniforms and by a group of senior Curia officials, including a clutch of four cardinals. Both delegations stood in sombre silence for a few minutes to savour a historic and bizarre scene. The Vatican band played the *Internationale* – and by all accounts, despite their unfamiliarity with the tune, played it beautifully – followed by the Papal Hymn. The first meeting was about to take place between a leader of the Communist Party of the Soviet Union and the head of the Roman Catholic Church.* The representatives from both sides were profoundly aware how pregnant with symbolism was the encounter.

Raisa Gorbachev caused a minor sensation. According to Vatican protocol, women at formal papal audiences are supposed to wear black. Raisa had been aware of this for several weeks. It was her husband who had desperately sought the Vatican visit, which was sandwiched between a formal state visit to Italy and the summit due to begin the next day in Malta with President Bush. According to his advisers, the

* Indeed, it was only the second meeting ever between a pope and a Russian leader. The last had been in December 1845 when Tsar Nicholas I visited Rome and was received for a brief audience by Pope Gregory XVI.

Pope had originally been doubtful, thinking the Russian leader might receive too much favourable publicity, and approved the meeting with the utmost reluctance. But since then a Catholic intellectual had become Prime Minister in his own homeland, the Berlin Wall had fallen, the Czech regime had collapsed. The Pope felt vindicated – and thought Gorbachev deserved the publicity.

When Mrs Gorbachev turned up in a bright red trouser suit flattering enough to demonstrate that at fifty-six she was still an attractive woman, Vatican officials showed only the briefest hint of surprise, continuing as though nothing unconventional had happened. She was given a tour of the art treasures of the Vatican while her husband was ushered into the Pope's private library, where the two spoke for seventy-five minutes with just their interpreters present. This was a room that had been bugged by the KGB when one of Gorbachev's chief mentors, Yuri Andropov, had been the Soviets' main spymaster. It had been Andropov who had predicted eleven years earlier that Pope John Paul's election could foreshadow disaster for the Soviet empire. He had been prescient. Gorbachev was an exceptionally confident man, though he admitted he was 'very nervous' as he was preparing to meet the Pope. He did not often use irony, but – though he repeatedly denied it – he must have smiled inwardly at his presence in a Bishop of Rome's chambers. The meaning of his comment afterwards – that if it had not been for Pope John Paul none of the transformations in Europe would have happened – was open to several interpretations. The conversation between them at the Vatican rambled into generalities and nothing of significance was agreed. But the important thing was not what they talked about, but that these two men spoke to each other at all. It showed the world how profoundly things had changed.

Similarly, little of significance was agreed at the summit in Malta two days later. Bizarrely, it took place at sea – or just outside Valetta harbour – jointly on a pair of American and Soviet naval vessels during one of the worst winter storms in the Mediterranean for several years. Many of the participants, including some key aides of both George H.W. Bush and Gorbachev, were so violently seasick that they could barely take their place at the talks, let alone at any of the formal dinners and receptions that had been scheduled over two days.*

Bush had proposed the summit in a private note to Gorbachev in

* The venue, controversially, had been suggested by the US President's younger brother, the entrepreneur Billy Bush, who had visited Malta, had various business interests on the island and told his brother George how wonderful the weather was.

the early spring. His intention had been to hold as informal a meeting as possible, with only a few aides and minimal media attention. The idea was to discuss a range of East/West issues, disarmament and, most particularly, Eastern Europe. By the time the summit took place the map of Europe had been transformed and, as both of the main players recognised, there was far less to talk about. Both agreed the Cold War was over. Condoleezza Rice, Bush's senior adviser on Eastern Europe, was in the room at the most dramatic point in the summit, when she realised that 'the world had changed, utterly . . . It was when Gorbachev said something I never imagined I would hear from a Soviet leader. He said matter of factly, without a hint of rancour, that he regarded the United States as a European power, and as a partner. That, for us, was a revolutionary change.'[1]

On New Year's Day 1990, three days after he was elected President of Czechoslovakia, Václav Havel spoke to an enthusiastic crowd of a quarter of a million people outside Prague Castle. It was a polished performance from a man who had little experience of appearing at great public gatherings. When he mounted the podium the shout 'Havel – Havel' rang throughout the city. He began, typically, in his measured, well-constructed, closely argued way, still the philosopher as much as a practising politician. He was cheered when he said that among the principal faults of the Communist regime was 'the way that, armed with an arrogant and intolerant ideology, it reduced Man and nature to mere tools of production . . . to nuts and bolts in a monstrously huge and stinking machine'. Then, halfway through his text the mood of his audience began to change and Havel noticed that some people were beginning to shift uncomfortably. He even heard the odd catcall as he warmed to his theme, that Czechs had lived in 'a contaminated moral atmosphere. I am talking about all of us. We had all become used to the totalitarian system and accepted it as an unchangeable fact. This helped to perpetuate it . . . We are all – though clearly to different extents – responsible for the operation of the totalitarian machinery. None of us is just its victim. We are its co-creators.'[2]

Havel was being honest as usual. But few of his listeners in Prague, or elsewhere in the newly liberated lands of Central Europe, appeared to share his angst – yet. Disillusion might come, but not now. People seemed to want less introspection and more celebration, before the work of creating a new future began. Epic parties continued throughout December in the capitals of countries where for decades citizens had seen little hope or cheer. After the Brandenburg Gate in Berlin – symbol of German nationhood – reopened on 23 December, celebrations went on for three days and nights. For ten days in Bucharest a 'revolutionary committee' occupied the suite of offices formerly used by the Ceauşescus. On New Year's Eve the late dictator's possessions were divided in a ceremony that combined wild joy with pure greed. Everyone knew there remained plenty of unfinished business: Romanians and Bulgarians would quickly discover that their revolutions were half-complete; the momentum for German reunification was unstoppable, despite early efforts by Mikhail Gorbachev, Margaret Thatcher and François Mitterrand to halt the process. And what should be done with leading figures in the old regimes?

In Prague towards midday on 1 January the playwright-turned-president was finishing his speech. The crowd was now back on his side after he spoke about optimism rather than guilt. As Poland had done two days earlier, Czechoslovakia would immediately drop the 'People's Republic' label and in a new constitution would simply be called a Republic. 'People,' Havel declared: 'Your Government has returned to you.'

REFERENCES

APRF – Russian Presidential Archives, Moscow
BA SPMO – Bundesarchiv, Stiftung Archiv der Parteien und Massenorganisationen der DDR
CPCD – Centre for the Preservation of Contemporary Documents, Moscow
CWIHP – Cold War International History Project, Woodrow Wilson Center, Washington DC
GF – Gorbachev Foundation Archive, Moscow
LHCMA – Liddell Hart Centre for Military Archives, King's College, London
OHCW – Oral History of the Cold War, Russian Academy of Sciences, Moscow
USNSA – US National Security Archive, George Washington University, Washington DC
For titles referred to by the author's name only, see Bibliography

PROLOGUE

1. Victor Stănculescu, 'Nu Vă Fie Milă, au 2 miliarde lei in cont' ('Show no mercy, they have 2 billion lei in the bank'), *Jurnalul National*, Bucharest, 22 November 1990
2. John Sweeney, *The Life and Evil Times of Nicolae Ceauşescu* (Hutchinson, London, 1991), pp. 157–8
3. Trial transcript, *Romania Libera*, Bucharest, 25 January 1990
4. Ibid.
5. *Jurnalul National*, Bucharest, 18 December 2006

ONE: THE WORKERS' STATE

1. Heins, *The Wall Falls*, pp. 114–20
2. Ibid.
3. Volkogonov, pp. 166–72
4. Davies, *Europe: A History*; Robert Service, *Comrades: A History of World Communism* (Macmillan, London, 2003) and Torańska all have penetrating analyses of the Soviet system
5. 'Cold War Endgame' debate at 1996 Princeton University conference,

and published (ed. William Wohlforth, Penn State University Press, 2003), p. 178

6. Kornai, *The Socialist System* and *Politics of Shortage* (Elsevier, 1981) is superb on Marxist economic realities.
7. Ferenc Vali, *Rift and Revolt in Hungary* (Oxford University Press, 1961), p. 126
8. Partos, p. 132
9. Vasili Mitrokhin and Christopher Andrew, *The Mitrokhin Archive: The KGB in Europe and the West* (Allen Lane, London, 1998), p. 673. The entire archive can be found at CWIHP.
10. Jacques Lévesque, *The Enigma of 1989* (University of California Press, 1997)

TWO: A MESSAGE OF HOPE

1. *Mitrokhin Archive*, pp. 326–35
2. Ibid.
3. Nigel West, *The Third Secret: The CIA, Solidarity and the Plot to Kill the Pope* (HarperCollins, London, 1999), pp. 25–135
4. George Weigel, *Witness to Hope: The Biography of Pope John Paul II* (Cliff Street Books, New York, 1999), pp. 280–90 and O'Sullivan, p. 58
5. Weigel, *Witness to Hope*, pp. 175–80
6. Quoted in Davies, *God's Playground*, pp. 440–41
7. *Mitrokhin Archive*, p. 369
8. Quoted in Dobbs, pp. 134–5
9. O'Sullivan, p. 215

THREE: SOLIDARITY

1. Shana Penn, *Solidarity's Secret: The Women Who Defeated Communism in Poland* (University of Michigan Press, 2005), pp. 97–125
2. Wałęsa, *The Struggle and the Triumph*, p. 263
3. Jacqueline Hayden, *Poles Apart: Solidarity and the New Poland* (Cass, London, 1994), p. 38

FOUR: THE ELECTRICIAN

1. Garton Ash, *The Polish Revolution*, p. 135
2. Ibid, pp. 140–42
3. Ibid.
4. Background on Lech Wałęsa from Wałęsa's autobiography, *The Struggle and the Triumph*, and Boyes, *The Naked President*
5. Dobbs, pp. 121–5
6. Michnik, *Letters From Freedom*, p. 213
7. Lech Wałęsa, *The Path to Freedom 1985–1990: The Decisive Years* (Editions Spotnakia, Warsaw, 1991), pp. 160–72
8. Author's Interview with Tadeusz Mazowiecki, Warsaw, October 1995

9. Background on Leonid Brezhnev from Volkogonov, and from Dobbs
10. Oberdorfer, p. 135
11. Volkogonov, pp. 351–4
12. Centre for the Preservation of Contemporary Documents, Moscow, TsKhSD, Politburo
13. Minutes 3 September 1980, APRF; Soviet Communist Party Politburo minutes for 29 October 1980
14. Central Archives of the Ministry of Defence, Moscow, TsAMO
15. Garton Ash, *The Polish Revolution*, pp. 247–51
16. Michnik, *Letters from Freedom*, pp. 146–7
17. Ibid., p. 92
18. Boyes, p. 197
19. Ibid., p. 206
20. APRF, f80, Brezhnev's notes on meetings with Kania.
21. Vladimir Kryuchkov interview quoted in West, *The Third Secret*, p. 138
22. *Mitrokhin Archive*, pp. 413–15

FIVE: CIVIL WAR

1. Wojciech Jaruzelski's memoirs, *Różnić Się Mądrze*, (Kziazka i Wiedza, Warsaw, 1999), and *Les Chaines et le refuge*
2. Riccardo Orizio, *Talk of the Devil* (Secker & Warburg, London, 2003), p. 127
3. Wałęsa, *The Struggle and the Triumph*, pp. 168–75
4. Boyes, pp. 102–6
5. Hayden, *Poles Apart*, p. 147
6. *Mitrokhin Archive*, pp. 460–66
7. Wałęsa interview in CNN's Cold War series produced by Jeremy Isaacs, 1997, LHCMA box 11
8. TsKhSD, f89. op 42, d6, Moscow
9. Zubok, p. 390
10. TsKhSD, f89. op 42, d6, Moscow. Politburo minutes for 10 December 1980
11. Zubok, p. 393

SIX: THE BLEEDING WOUND

1. Interview transcripts for CNN Cold War series, LHCMA box 14
2. TsKhSD, f89. Per 14, doc 30, Moscow
3. Interview for CNN Cold War series, LHCMA box 12
4. Ibid.
5. Zubok, pp. 345–53 and TsKhSD, f89. Per 14, doc 31, Politburo minutes for 10 December 1990
6. Dobrynin, p. 232

SEVEN: THE POWER OF THE POWERLESS

1. Quoted in Gale Stokes, *The Walls Came Tumbling Down* (Oxford University Press USA, 1993), p. 235
2. Author's interview with Milan Hlavsa and other Plastic People, Prague, April 1999
3. Ibid.
4. Ben Lewis, *Hammer and Tickle: A History of Communism Told Through Jokes* (Weidenfeld & Nicolson, London, 2008), p. 208
5. William Echikson, *Lighting the Night* (Pan, London, 1991), p. 78
6. Václav Havel, *Living in Truth* (Faber & Faber, London, 1987), pp. 75–90
7. The original Charter can be read at the Open Society Archive in Budapest
8. The Treaty can be read online at www.state.gov/history/frus
9. Dobrynin, pp. 191–3
10. In conversation with the author, Budapest, December 1989
11. Interview in Cold War files at CWIHP
12. Henry Kissinger, *Diplomacy* (Simon & Schuster, New York, 1994)
13. Havel, *Living in Truth* and *Disturbing the Peace*, pp. 75–90
14. Ibid.
15. Keane, p. 134
16. Havel, *Living in Truth*, p. 167
17. In conversation with the author, Warsaw, 1995, and quoted in Stokes, *The Walls Came Tumbling Down*, p. 125
18. Vaculík, p. 14
19. Quoted in Stokes, *The Walls Came Tumbling Down*, p. 179
20. Gáspár M. Tamás, *From Liberal Values to Democratic Transition* (Central University Press, Budapest, 2003), p. 78
21. Michnik, *Letters From Freedom*, p. 180
22. Quoted in Garton Ash, *The Polish Revolution*, p. 318
23. Tony Judt, *Postwar: A History of Europe Since 1945* (Penguin, London, 2005), p. 497
24. Richard Rhodes, *Arsenals of Folly* (Knopf, New York, 2007), p. 186
25. Ibid., p. 245
26. Zubok, p. 338

EIGHT: ABLE ARCHER

1. Background on Yuri Andropov from Vladimir Solovyov and Elena Klepikova, *Andropov: A Secret Passage into the Kremlin* (Robert Hale, London, 1984); Sergei Semanov, *Andropov: 7 tain genseka s Lubianki* (Veche, Moscow, 2001) and Zhores Medvedev, *Andropov* (Oxford University Press, 1983)
2. Dobbs, pp. 95–100
3. Zubok, p. 278
4. Rhodes, *Arsenals of Folly*, p. 134
5. Ibid., p. 226

6. Ibid., p. 235
7. Aleksandrov-Argentov, p. 178
8. Rhodes, *Arsenals of Folly*, pp. 138–50
9. Interview with Osipovich, Cold War series, LHCMA box 18
10. Ibid. and Dobbs, pp. 101–9
11. Dobbs, p. 107
12. Interview with Tarasenko, March 1999, OHCW
13. Dobbs, p. 109
14. Centre for the Preservation and Study of Documents of Recent History, RTsKhIDNI. Politburo minutes for 2 September 1983, f3, op. 73, d 1152, 112–13.
15. *Izvestia*, 20 September 1983
16. Volkogonov, pp. 360–67, and Zubok, pp. 264–6
17. Melvyn Leffler, *For the Soul of Mankind: The United States, the Soviet Union and the Cold War* (Hill & Wang, New York, 2008), pp. 324–31
18. Rhodes, *Arsenals of Folly*, pp. 221–5
19. Ibid.
20. Author in conversation with Lord Powell, London, May 2007
21. Robert Gates, *From the Shadows* (Simon & Schuster, New York, 1997), p. 217
22. Ronald Reagan, *The Reagan Diaries* (HarperPress, New York, 2007), p. 346

NINE: AMERICA'S LEADING DOVE

1. Rhodes, *Arsenals of Folly*, p. 178
2. Dobrynin, p. 368
3. Ronald Reagan, *An American Life* (Simon & Schuster, New York, 1990), p. 417
4. Jack Matlock, *Reagan and Gorbachev: How the Cold War Ended* (Random House, New York, 2005), pp. 177–80
5. Weiner, p. 326
6. Ronald Reagan Library, Simi Valley, California, correspondence with Soviet leaders file.
7. Quoted in Rhodes, *Arsenals of Folly*, pp. 180–83
8. Matlock, *Reagan and Gorbachev*, p. 186

TEN: A PYRRHIC VICTORY

1. See Boyes, pp. 178–82
2. Ibid.
3. Hayden, *Poles Apart*, pp. 146–58
4. Michnik, *Letters from Freedom*, p. 93
5. Weiner, pp. 340–47
6. Gates, *From the Shadows*, pp. 378–85, and West, *The Third Secret*, pp. 186–200

7. Background on Father Jerzy Popiełuszko in Grazyna Sikorska, *A Martyr for the Truth* (Collins, London, 1985); Davies, *God's Playground*; and Kevin Ruane, *To Kill a Priest* (Gibson Square, London, 2004)
8. Boyes, pp. 240–46
9. *Mitrokhin Archive*, pp. 488–90
10. Michnik, *Letters from Freedom*, pp. 230–32

ELEVEN: THE NEW TSAR

1. Quoted in Matlock, *Reagan and Gorbachev*, pp. 45–8, Kaiser, p. 68, and Gromyko, p. 372
2. Kaiser, pp. 66–70
3. Anatoli Chernyaev diary at CWIHP, March 1985 and *She's lets Gorbachevym* (Progress, Moscow, 1993) (*My Six Years with Gorbachev*, Pennsylvania University Press, 2000), p. 62
4. Ryzhkov, pp. 88–90
5. Raisa Gorbacheva, *I Hope* (HarperCollins, New York, 1991), p. 93
6. Chernyaev diary, and in conversation with the author, Moscow, December 1993.
7. Matlock, *Reagan and Gorbachev*, p. 72
8. Background on Mikhail Gorbachev from Mikhail Gorbachev, *Memoirs*, (Doubleday, New York, 1996); Zhores Medvedev, *Gorbachev*; Dusko Doder and Louise Branson, *Gorbachev: Heretic in the Kremlin* (Viking, New York, 1990); Larisa Vasil'eva, *Kremlin Wives* (Arcade, New York, 1993) and Volkogonov
9. Anatoly Sobchak, *For a New Russia* (Free Press, New York, 1992), pp. 286–7
10. Lord Powell to the author, in a fascinating conversation on the Thatcher / Gorbachev relationship, May 2007
11. Grachev, pp. 64–8
12. Zubok, p. 366, and Bush and Scowcroft, p. 197
13. Jaruzelski, p. 276

TWELVE: THE SWORD AND SHIELD

1. In conversation with the author, Berlin, November 2007
2. The extensive files on Wolf Biermann – along with millions of others – are kept by the BStU, Bundesbeauftragte für die Unterlagen des Staatssicherheitsdienstes der ehemaligen Deutschen Demokratischen Republik (The Office for Preserving East German State Security files) in Berlin
3. Ulrike Poppe interview, Cold War series, LHCMA box 15
4. *New York Times*, 12 April 1992
5. Cold War series, LHCMA box 16
6. In conversation with the author, 2006, and *The Times*, 6 January 2007
7. Peter Siebenmorgen, *Staatssicherheit der DDR* (Bouvier Verlag, Bonn,

1993) and Stasi document collection, *'Ich Liebe euch doche alle . . .' Befehle und Lageberichte des MfS, Januar–November 1989*, ed. Armin Mitter and Stefan Wolle (BasisDruck, Berlin, 1989)

8. Quoted in Anne McElvoy, *The Saddled Cow* (Faber & Faber, London, 1992), p. 71
9. Background on Honecker from Pötzl, McElvoy, *The Saddled Cow*, Günter Schabowski, *Der Absturz* (Rowholt, Berlin, 1991) and Ed Stuhler, *Margot Honecker: Eine Biographie* (Ueberreuter, Vienna, 2003)
10. Wolf and McElvoy, p. 167
11. Partos, p. 126
12. Background on Alexander Schalck-Golodkowski from Pryce-Jones; Alexander Schalck-Golodkowski, *Deutsch-deutsche Erinnerungen* (Rowholt, Berlin, 2001); and Frederick Taylor, *The Berlin Wall* (Bloomsbury, London, 2006)

THIRTEEN: LENIN'S APOSTLE

1. Chernyaev, *My Six Years with Gorbachev*, pp. 26–7
2. Tarasenko interview, March 1999, OHCW, and Volkogonov, pp. 349–52
3. For the press and media in the USSR under Gorbachev, see Vitali Korotich and Cathy Porter, *The New Soviet Journalism* (Beacon Press, Boston, 1991); Pryce-Jones, and Remnick
4. Quoted in Jack Matlock, *Autopsy of an Empire* (Random House, New York, 1995), p. 133
5. Tarasenko interview, March 1999, OHCW
6. Quoted in Brown, *Seven Years that Changed the World*, p. 147
7. Quoted in Zubok, p. 278
8. Background on Yakovlev from his books *Striving for Law in a Lawless Land* (M.E. Sharpe, New York, 1995) and *The Fate of Marxism in Russia* (Yale University Press, New Haven and London, 1993) and Zubok
9. Boldin, pp. 138–47
10. Ibid.

FOURTEEN: SILENT MEMORIES

1. Cold War series, LHCMA box 7
2. Sándor Zsindely, in conversation with the author, Budapest, March 2003
3. János Vargha, speaking at Danube Circle demonstration, 8 February 1986
4. Miklós Haraszti, in conversation with the author, Budapest, April 2004
5. For background on János Kádár, see Victor Sebestyen, *Twelve Days* (Weidenfeld & Nicolson, London, 2006); Tibor Huszar, *János Kádár, Political Életrajza (A Political Biography*, Kossuth Kiadó, Budapest, 2005) and Roger Gough, *A Good Comrade* (IB Tauris, London, 2006)

FIFTEEN: 'WE CANNOT WIN'

1. Grachev, p. 86
2. Ibid., p. 90
3. Chernyaev diary in archive at GF and at CWIHP
4. Ibid.
5. Grachev, p. 96
6. For background on Eduard Shevardnadze, see Shevardnadze; Dobbs; Carolyn Eke Dahl and Melvyn Goodman, *The Wars of Eduard Shevardnadze* (Pennsylvania State University Press, 1997)
7. *Izvestia*, 18 July 1979
8. Shevardnadze interview, Cold War series, LHCMA box 4
9. George Shultz, *Turmoil and Triumph* (Macmillan, London, 1993), p. 287
10. Interview with Tarasenko, OHCW
11. Chernyaev diary, CWIHP
12. Transcript of Geneva Summit 1985 at USNSA, Cold War collection
13. Zubok, pp. 256–60, and Grachev, pp. 134–60
14. Cold War series, LHCMA box 9

SIXTEEN: 'LET THEM HATE'

1. Pavel Câmpeanu, 'The Revolt of the Romanians', *New York Review of Books*, 1 February 1990
2. *Jurnalul National*, Bucharest, 22 January 1991
3. In conversation with the author, Bucharest, October 2007
4. Quoted in Stokes, *The Walls Came Tumbling Down*, p. 198
5. Quoted in Sweeney, *The Life and Evil Times of Nicolae Ceauşescu*, pp. 132–4
6. John Simpson, *The Darkness Crumbles* (Hutchinson, London, 1992)
7. For background on Nicolae and Elena Ceauşescu, see Pavel Câmpeanu, 'The Revolt of the Romanians'; Vladimir Tismaneanu, *Stalinism for All Seasons: A Political History of Romanian Communism* (University of California Press, 2003); Ion Pacepa, *Red Horizon: The True Story of Nicolae Ceauşescu's Crimes*; Behr; and Daniel Cheroot, *Modern Tyrants* (Princeton University Press, 1996)
8. Mark Almond, *The Rise and Fall of Nicolae and Elena Ceauşescu* (Chapmans, London, 1992), pp. 148–53
9. Ibid.
10. *Nicolae Ceauşescu, Builder of Modern Romania and International Statesman* (Pergamon Press, Oxford, 1983), preface
11. Quoted in Behr, p. 136
12. Ibid., p. 148
13. For background on the Ceauşescu children, see Câmpeanu, 'The Revolt of the Romanians'
14. Gail Kligman, *The Politics of Duplicity: Controlling Reproduction in Ceauşescu's Romania* (University of California Press, 1998)

SEVENTEEN: CHERNOBYL: NUCLEAR DISASTER

1. Background on Chernobyl: Grigori Medvedev; Nicholas Daniloff, 'The Political Fallout of Chernobyl', *Demokratizatsiya*, Moscow, Winter 2004; Dobbs, pp. 153–69, and Piers Paul Read, *Ablaze: The Story of Chernobyl* (Mandarin, London, 1994)
2. Daniloff, 'The Political Fallout of Chernobyl', pp. 5–9
3. Dobbs, pp. 160–64
4. APRF, Politburo minutes for 28 April 1986
5. APRF, Politburo minutes for 3 July 1986
6. Zubok, 'Gorbachev's Nuclear Learning', CWIHP briefing paper

EIGHTEEN: ETHNIC CLEANSING

1. Robert Crampton, *A History of Modern Bulgaria* (Cambridge University Press, 1997), p. 274
2. In conversation with the author, Sofia, September 2007
3. Author in conversation with Andrei Lukanov, Sofia, April 1990
4. For background on Todor Zhivkov, see Pryce-Jones, pp. 215–18; Echikson, *Lighting the Night*, pp. 122–5
5. Crampton, *A History of Modern Bulgaria*, pp. 257–80
6. Chernyaev diary, May 1986, CWIHP
7. Author in conversation with Krassen Stanchev, Sofia, October 2007
8. *Le Monde*, 18 January 1989

NINETEEN: HUMBLED IN RED SQUARE

1. 'A Dubious Diplomat', *Washington Post*, 27 May 2007
2. Akhromeyev and Kornienko, *Glazami Marshala I Diplomatia*, p. 265
3. Ibid.
4. *Washington Post*, loc. cit.
5. Chernyaev diary, May 1987, CWIHP
6. APRF, Politburo minutes for 30 May 1987
7. Dobrynin, pp. 367–8

TWENTY: THE GANG OF FOUR

1. Grachev, p. 168
2. Ibid., pp. 176–80
3. It was Gerhard Schürer, head of the GDR's State Planning Commission, who, according to Chernyaev, made this comment immediately after the meeting
4. Gorbachev, *Memoirs*, p. 348
5. Musatov, as quoted by Grachev, p. 89, and also Gorbachev, *Memoirs*, p. 352

TWENTY-ONE: GORBACHEV'S VIETNAM

1. Quoted in Leffler, *For the Soul of Mankind*, p. 286
2. Weiner, pp. 365–7
3. Chernyaev diary, May 1986, CWIHP
4. APRF, Politburo minutes for 13 November 1986
5. APRF, notes from Politburo, 23 February 1987, and Chernyaev diary, February 1987, CWIHP
6. Quoted in Dobbs, p. 178
7. Leffler, *For the Soul of Mankind*, p. 228
8. Chernyaev diary, February 1987, CWIHP

TWENTY-TWO: OLD MEN'S TALES

1. Günter Schabowski interview for 1999 Fall of the Wall TV series, LHCMA box 6
2. Cold War series, LHCMA box 17
3. Wolf and McElvoy, p. 198
4. Partos, p. 136
5. Maier, p. 96
6. McElvoy, *The Saddled Cow*, p. 156
7. Author in conversation with Ondrej Soukoup, Prague, August 2007
8. Garton Ash, *The Uses of Adversity*, and author in conversation with Michael Kocáb, Prague, 2007
9. Václav Havel, letter to Mr Husák in *Open Letters*, pp. 86–8
10. Author in conversation with Jacques Rupnik, Prague, August 2007
11. Author in conversation with Miklós Haraszti, Budapest, June 1992
12. For the coup against Kádár, see Huszar *Jáhos Kádár, Politikai életrajza*; Gough, *A Good Comrade* and conversation with Haraszti, Budapest, September 1990
13. Interview with Horst Teltschik, Cold War series, LHCMA box 9, and Gyula Thürmer, *Nem Kell NATO* (Progressio, Budapest, 1995)
14. Németh interview, Cold War series, LHCMA box 8

TWENTY-THREE: ENDGAME IN POLAND

1. Micknik, *Letters From Freedom*, p. 157
2. Alina Pieńkowska interview in Cold War series, LHCMA box 12
3. Author's interview with Jerzy Urban, Warsaw, October 1995
4. *Mitrokhin Archive*, pp. 695–8
5. Strawomir Cenckiewicz and Piotr Gontarczyk, *SB a Lech Wałęsa* (Rok, Warsaw, 2008)
6. Author's interview with Rakowski, Warsaw, October 1995, and also Rakowski, *Jak To Şie Stało*

7. Pryce-Jones, p. 256, and author's conversations with Geremek, October 1995
8. Stanisław Ciosek speech at University of Michigan at Ann Arbor, conference on Solidarity, April 1999

TWENTY-FOUR: PRESIDENT BUSH TAKES CHARGE

1. Author's interview with James Baker, Houston, September 2007
2. Gates' memo to Reagan, Beschloss and Talbott, p. 135
3. National Intelligence Estimate 11/12–9–98, USNSA, Cold War files
4. Gates, *From the Shadows*, p. 178
5. Author's interview with James Baker, Houston, Texas, September 2007, and Bush and Scowcroft, pp. 93–9

TWENTY-FIVE: TRIUMPH IN MANHATTAN

1. Quoted in Dobbs, p. 216
2. Gorbachev, *Memoirs*, p. 387
3. Nikolai Ryzhkov in off-the-record interview with several Western journalists, Yerevan, Armenia, 9 December 1988
4. Dobrynin, p. 328
5. Chernyaev diary and Beschloss and Talbott, p. 257
6. Gromyko, p. 380
7. Volkogonov, pp. 478–80
8. Chernyaev diary, December 1988, CWIHP
9. APRF, Politburo minutes for 24–5 March 1988
10. Shakhnazarov memo to Gorbachev, 6 October 1988, CWIHP
11. Ministry of Foreign Affairs Archive, APRF, Moscow, report to Minister, 24 February 1989.
12. Chernyaev diary, December 1988, CWIHP

TWENTY-SIX: THE WAR OF WORDS

1. *Népszabadság*, 3 May 1988
2. In conversation with the author, Budapest, April 2004
3. *Scînteia*, Bucharest, 1 September 1988
4. *Népszabadság*, 4 October 1988
5. Thürmer, *Nem Kell NATO*

TWENTY-SEVEN: HAVEL IN JAIL

1. General Alojs Lorenc, report on security operations 1988–1989, Vol. 4/II, Úřad Dokumentace a Vyšetřování and at CWIHP
2. *Rudé Právo*, 11 January 1989
3. Havel, *To the Castle and Back*, p. 173
4. Quoted in Stokes, *The Walls Came Tumbling Down*, p. 278

TWENTY-EIGHT: THE ROUND TABLE

1. Wałęsa, *The Struggle and the Triumph*, p. 238
2. Janusz Reykowski quoted in Simpson, *The Darkness Crumbles*, p. 184; Mieczysław Rakowski in conversation with the author, Warsaw, October 1995
3. Hayden, *Poles Apart*, p. 146
4. Author in conversation with Rakowski, Warsaw, October 1995
5. Pryce-Jones, p. 168
6. Michnik, *Letters from Freedom*, p. 139
7. Ibid., pp. 141–9

TWENTY-NINE: SHOOT TO KILL

1. For background on Chris Gueffroy and his attempted escape, see Deutschland radio's *Chronik der Mauer*, website www.chronik-der-mauer.de, Taylor, *The Berlin Wall*, and Christopher Hilton, *The Wall* (The History Press, London, 2002)

THIRTY: THE FRIENDSHIP BRIDGE

1. Chernyaev diary, January 1989, CWIHP
2. *International Herald Tribune*, 16 May 1988
3. Gromov, pp. 190–204; Chernyaev, diary and *My Six Years with Gorbachev.* Also Dobbs, pp. 396–404; Artyom Borovik, *The Hidden War* (Grove Press, New York, 2001)
4. Gromov, p. 178
5. Russian State Archive for Contemporary History, RGANI, Moscow, f89.10. doc 25. st 1–3

THIRTY-ONE: THE CURTAIN FALLS

1. Minutes of meeting at GF; Gorbachev talks with Hungarian leaders, 1989
2. Cold War series LHCMA, box 11
3. Quoted in Pryce-Jones, p. 231
4. MOL (Hungarian National Archive), Budapest M-KS-288–11/4458
5. Chernyaev diary, January 1989
6. Németh interview, Cold War series, LHCMA box 8 and Tarasenko interview, March 1999, OHCW
7. Interview in Fall of the Wall series, LHCMA box 3

THIRTY-TWO: THE CAUTIOUS AMERICAN

1. James Baker in conversation with the author, Houston, September 2007, and Gates, *From the Shadows*, p. 298
2. Baker in conversation with the author, Houston, September 2007

3. Beschloss and Talbott, p. 156
4. Bush and Scowcroft, p. 86
5. Quoted in Weiner, pp. 349–53
6. Beschloss and Talbott, pp. 158–60
7. Record of Gorbachev/Thatcher conversation at GF, and also author in conversation with Lord Powell, London, May 2007
8. Beschloss and Talbott, p. 160
9. Bush and Scowcroft, p. 94
10. William Wohlforth, *Cold War Endgame*, (Penn State University Press, 2002)
11. NIE 11–4–89: Soviet Policy Towards the West, USNSA

THIRTY-THREE: THE LOYAL OPPOSITION

1. Quoted in Boyes, pp. 192–6
2. Hayden, *Poles Apart*, p. 137
3. Pryce-Jones, p. 180
4. Hayden, *Poles Apart*, p. 160

THIRTY-FOUR: THE DICTATOR PAYS HIS DEBTS

1. In conversation with the author, Bucharest, October 2007
2. Brucan, in conversation with the author, Bucharest, April 1990, and Almond, *The Rise and Fall of Nicolae and Elena Ceaușescu*, pp. 160–64
3. Peter Siani-Davies, *The Romanian Revolution of December 1989* (Cornell University Press, 2007), p. 139

THIRTY-FIVE: A STOLEN ELECTION

1. *Neues Deutschland*, 8 May 1989
2. Garton Ash, 'Sketches from Another Germany', essay in *The Uses of Adversity*
3. Maier, p. 72
4. *'Ich Liebe euch doche alle . . .' Befehle und Lageberichte des MfS* p. 113
5. Maier, p. 89
6. Dirk Philipsen, *We Were the People* (Duke University Press, Durham, NC, 1992), p. 93

THIRTY-SIX: EXPULSION OF THE TURKS

1. Archive of the Bulgarian parliament, Communist Party Central Committee files, May 1989
2. GF, files on talks with Bulgarian leaders.
3. Pryce-Jones, p. 246, and also Lukanov in conversation with the author, Sofia, April 1991
4. Roumen Danov and Krassen Stanchev in conversation with the author, Sofia, September 2007

THIRTY-SEVEN: THE LANDSLIDE

1. Garton Ash, *We the People*, and author in conversation with Tadeusz Mazowiecki, Warsaw, October 1995
2. Ibid. and author in conversation with Jerzy Urban, Warsaw, October 1995
3. Garton Ash, *We the People*, p. 36
4. Hayden, *Poles Apart*, p. 168, and author in conversation with Rakowski, Warsaw, October 1995
5. Ambassador Davis's telegrams to State Department at USNSA, Poland briefing papers
6. *Gazeta Wyborcza*, Warsaw, 5 June 1989, p. 1, and quoted in Dobbs, p. 268
7. Polish Communist Party (PZPR) Secretariat files, Institute of Political Studies, Polish Academy of Sciences, Warsaw
8. Author in conversation with Rakowski, Warsaw, October 1995
9. Author in conversation with Mazowiecki, Warsaw, October 1995, and as reported by Ambassador Davis in cable to State Department, 11 August 1989, USNSA
10. Author in conversation with Rakowski, Warsaw, October 1995

THIRTY-EIGHT: FUNERAL IN BUDAPEST

1. Hungarian National Archives (Magyar Országos Levéltár), Budapest, M-KS-288/1050; Pozsgay interview, Cold War series, LHCMA box 9
2. János Kenedi, *Kis Allambistonsági Olvasokonyvy* (*A Secret Police Reader*) (Magvet, Budapest, 1996)
3. BBC World Service radio report, 18 June 1989
4. In conversation with Maria Vásárhelyi and Miklós Haraszti, Budapest, April 2004, and Maria Kovács interview, Cold War series, LHCMA box 11
5. *Neues Deutschland*, 11 June 1989
6. BA SPMO, ZK, JIV2/2A/3225

THIRTY-NINE: A PRESIDENTIAL TOUR

1. Beschloss and Talbott, pp. 186–8, and Bush and Scowcroft, pp. 144–50
2. Bush and Scowcroft, p. 152
3. Ibid., p. 157
4. *Gazeta Wyborcza*, 11 July 1989
5. Author in conversation with Tadeusz Mazowiecki, Warsaw, October 1995, and Beschloss and Talbott, pp. 170–72
6. Bush and Scowcroft, p. 157
7. Palmer interview in Foreign Affairs Oral History collection of the Association for Diplomatic Studies and Training, Library of Congress, Washington DC

8. Author's conversation with Mazowiecki
9. Timothy Garton Ash, 'Poland After Solidarity', *New York Review of Books*, 13 June 1991, and author in conversation with Jerzy Urban, Warsaw, October 1995
10. *Gazeta Wyborcza*, 3 August 1989
11. Author in conversation with Mazowiecki, Warsaw, October 1995
12. Record of Jaruzelski's speech in Malcolm Byrne and Vojtech Mastny (eds), *A Cardboard Castle? An Inside History of the Warsaw Pact*. (Central European University Press, Budapest, 2005)
13. Bronisław Geremek, *Rok 1989 – opowiada, Jacek Żakowski pyta* (*The Year 1989 – Bronisław Geremek Advocates, Jacek Żakowski Asks*, translated into French as *La Rupture*, Seuil, Paris, 1991)
14. Quoted in Dobbs, p. 288
15. Tarasenko interview, OHCW, March 1999

FORTY: TRAIL OF THE TRABANTS

1. Otto von Habsburg interview, Fall of the Wall series, LHCMA box 6
2. Author's conversations with Miklós Haraszti and Agnes Gergely, April 2004, and Fall of the Wall series, LHCMA box 4
3. Author's conversation with Maria Vásárhelyi, and Fall of the Wall series, LHCMA box 4
4. Cold War series, LHCMA box 9
5. Ibid., box 4
6. Palmer interview, Foreign Affairs Oral History collection, Library of Congress, Washington DC; Kovács quoted in Lévesque, *The Enigma of 1989*, p. 187
7. Fall of the Wall series, LHCMA box 3
8. Author in conversation with Dr Matthias Mueller, Berlin, November 2007
9. Quoted in McElvoy, *The Saddled Cow*, p. 168
10. BA SPMO, Krenz's office mIV 2/2.039/77

FORTY-ONE: A GOVERNMENT OF DISSIDENTS

1. Author in conversation with Mazowiecki, Warsaw, October 1995; Geremek, *Rok 1989*, pp. 116–8, Boyes, pp. 191–200
2. Author in conversation with Rakowski, Warsaw, October 1995, and Stokes, *The Walls Came Tumbling Down*, p. 227
3. Author in conversation with Mazowiecki, and Boyes, p. 196

FORTY-TWO: REFUGEES

1. *Dokumente zur Deutschlandpolitik: Deutsche Einheit, Sonderedition aus den Akten des Bundeskanzleramtes, 1988/1989*, document 28, and Miklós Németh interview in Cold War series, LHCMA box 9

2. Ibid., Németh interview
3. GF, record of Gorbachev phone conversation with Kohl, 25 August 1989
4. BA SPMO, Krenz's office IV 2/2.039/76, and Günter Schabowski, *Das Politbüro* (Rowholt, Reinbeck, 1990)
5. BA SPMO, Krenz's office, transcript of 5 September Politbüro meeting, IV 2/2.039/77
6. Németh interview, Cold War series, LHCMA box 9
7. Author in conversations with Matthias Mueller and Reinhard Schult, Berlin, November 2007, and Maier, p. 168. Jan Lässig interview, Fall of the Wall series, LHCMA box 5.
8. *'Ich Liebe euch doch alle . . .' Befehle und Lageberichte des Mfs*, pp. 450–66
9. Poppe interview, Fall of the Wall series, LHCMA box 7
10. Fall of the Wall series, LHCMA box 11
11. *Neues Deutschland*, 12 September 1989
12. Schabowski, *Das Politbüro*, p. 127
13. Fall of the Wall series, LHCMA box 4
14. Cold War series, LHCMA box 7

FORTY-THREE: THE BIRTHDAY PARTY

1. Chernyaev diary, October 1989
2. Hermann interview in Cold War series, LHCMA box 6; Schabowski in Fall of the Wall series, box 6
3. Schabowski in conversation with the author
4. Chernyaev diary, October 1989
5. Interview in Fall of the Wall series, LHCMA box 5
6. London *Observer*, 22 October 1989
7. Cold War series, LHCMA box 6
8. Quoted in McElvoy, *The Saddled Cow*, p. 168
9. Order MfS, ZAIG, Nr 451/89 quoted in *'Ich Liebe euch doch alle . . .' Befehle und Lageberichte des Mfs*, pp. 372–5
10. In conversation with the author, Berlin, November 2007
11. Fall of the Wall series, LHCMA box 7
12. In conversation with the author, Berlin, November 2007
13. Fall of the Wall series, LHCMA box 9
14. Maier, p. 157
15. Schabowski, *Das Politbüro*, pp. 79–96
16. Chernyaev diary, October 1989
17. Pötzl, pp. 323–6
18. For the coup against Honecker, see Pötzl; Schabowski, *Das Politbüro*; Krenz

FORTY-FOUR: PEOPLE POWER

1. Cold War series, LHCMA box 9

2. See Pötzl, pp. 310–12
3. See Uwe Müller, *Supergau Deutsche Einheit* (Rowohlt, Berlin, 2006), pp. 56–70
4. Cold War files at USNSA and BA SPMO, Krenz's office IV 2/2.039/79
5. Hans-Hermann Hertle, *Der Fall der Mauer* (Westdeutscher Verlag, Opladen, 1999), pp. 108–10
6. BA SPMO, DY30/JIV2/SA/3225 and, for Gorbachev's private comments, Chernyaev diary
7. *Neues Deutschland*, 2 November 1989
8. Hertle, *Der Fall der Mauer*, pp. 467–75
9. Fall of the Wall series, LHCMA box 4
10. Wolf and McElvoy, p. 210

FORTY-FIVE: THE WALL COMES TUMBLING DOWN

1. *Neues Deutschland* 9 November 1989
2. Krenz, pp. 130–34, and interview in the Fall of the Wall series, LHCMA box 6
3. Schabowski interview, Fall of the Wall series, LHCMA box 5
4. A full transcript of the press conference is available from CWIHP
5. From several journalists present, and as recorded in the USNSA Cold War files
6. Cold War series, LHCMA box 6
7. In conversation with the author, January 2008
8. Cold War series, LHCMA box 7
9. In conversation with the author, January 2008
10. As quoted in McElvoy, *The Saddled Cow*, p. 189
11. Ambassador Kochemasov interview in *Moscow News*, 29 November 1992 and Igor Maksimichev in *Nezavisimaya Gazeta*, 10–11 November 1993
12. GF, telegrams to Helmut Kohl
13. Beschloss and Talbott, pp. 257–61
14. Milt Bearden, *The Main Enemy* (Century, London, 2003), pp. 206–7
15. USNSA, End of the Cold War file

FORTY-SIX: THE COUP

1. Author in conversation with Krassen Stanchev, Sofia, October 2007.
2. Pryce-Jones, p. 325, and author in conversation with Lukanov, Sofia, April 1991, and with Rumen Danov, Sofia, October 2007
3. Lévesque, *The Enigma of 1989*, pp. 217–20
4. Archive of the Bulgarian Parliament, Communist Party Central Committee, October 1989 file, Sofia
5. Lukanov, in conversation with the author, Sofia, April 1991
6. Pryce-Jones, pp. 325–30, and author in conversation with Lukanov

7. Author in conversation with Stefan Fratrov, Sofia, November 1989, and with Ionni Pojarleff, Sofia, October 2007

FORTY-SEVEN: THE VELVET REVOLUTION

1. Garton Ash, *We the People*, p. 121
2. Czech Interior Ministry archive, Documents of Defence Mobilisation Measures, OV-00174/S-89 and at CWIHP
3. All in conversation with the author, Prague, December 1989
4. In conversation with the author, Prague, August 2007
5. The commission of inquiry report into the demonstration is in the Czech National Archives, Prague. Accounts of the 'conspiracy' in BBC Radio 4's *Pushing Back the Curtain* series, and Simpson, *The Darkness Crumbles*.
6. Ivan Klíma, *The Spirit of Prague* (Granta, London, 1998), p. 95
7. USNSA, End of the Cold War file
8. Soukup in conversation with the author, Prague, August 2007
9. Kocáb in conversation with the author, Prague, August 2007
10. Fojtík, as told to Jacques Rupnik in conversation with author, Prague, August 2007
11. Pryce-Jones, pp. 323–30
12. In conversation with the author, Prague, August 2007
13. BBC World Service report, 24 November 1989
14. In conversation with the author, August 2007
15. Kocáb in conversation with the author, and Simpson, *The Darkness Crumbles*, p. 345

FORTY-EIGHT: THE MOMENT OF WEAKNESS

1. *Scînteia*, Bucharest, 22 November 1989
2. Background on László Tökés, see Tökés, *With God, for the People* (Crossways Books, New York, 1992); Petru Dugulescu, *Ei mi-au, programat moartea* (Ecclesia, Timisoara, 1991); Marius Mioc, *The Anticommunist Romanian Revolution of 1989* (Editura Marineasa, Timisoara, 2002) and Siani-Davies, *The Romanian Revolution of December 1989*
3. Lászlo Tökés, pp. 148–57
4. The transcript of some of the meeting was published by *Romania Libera*, 1 February 1990. The full transcript is at the National Central Historical Archive, Bucharest, 70/89.2.33.
5. In conversation with the author, Bucharest, October 2007
6. Author's conversations with participants Gheorghe Peletrescu, Andrei Oisteanu, Bucharest, December 1989. Accounts by Pavel Câmpeanu, Marius Mioc and the *Romania Libera* journalist Romulus Cristea. Simpson, *The Darkness Crumbles*, pp. 302–10. Ruxandra Cesereanu, *December 1989, Deconstructia unei revolutii* (Polirom, Iasi, 2004) pp 98–103

7. Pavel Câmpeanu, 'The Revolt of the Romanians', *New York Review of Books*, 1 February 1990
8. Victor Stănculescu, 'Nu Vă Fie Milă, au 2 miliarde lei in cont', *Jurnalul National*, Bucharest, 22 November 1990
9. In conversation with the author, Bucharest, October 2007
10. See Stănculescu, 'Nu Vă Fie Milă', and Siani-Davies, *Romanian Revolution*, p. 193
11. Interviewed in *Romania Libera*, 14 January 1990
12. Quoted in Siani-Davies, *Romanian Revolution*, p. 213
13. Dinescu at press conference in radio station, 26 December 1989, and in Cold War series, LHCMA box 13, and Caramitru quoted in Pryce-Jones, p. 284
14. Radio Free Europe interview, 31 December 1989, and Ion Iliescu, *Revolutia Traita* (Redactia, Bucharest, 1995), p. 96
15. Quoted in Siani-Davies, *Romanian Revolution*, p. 237
16. Maluţan interview, *Romania Libera*, 14 January 1990
17. *Romania Libera*, 14 January 1990
18. Brucan in conversation with the author; Stănculescu, 'Nu Vă Fie Milă'; Militaru, BBC interview with John Simpson, 12 January 1990
19. Brucan as quoted in Siani-Davies, *Romanian Revolution*, p. 286, and in S. Brucan *The Wasted Generation: Memoirs of the Romanian Journey from Capitalism to Socialism and Back* (Westview, New York, 1993), pp. 293–6
20. GF, Falin reports on Romania.
21. APRF Diplomatiecheski vestnik 1995-91, Moscow, pp. 74–9, doc 149

FINALE

1. Transcript of Malta Summit, CWIHP
2. BBC World Service news report, 2 January 1990

BIBLIOGRAPHY

Akhromeyev, Sergei, and Kornienko, Georgi, *Glazami Marshala I Diplomata* (Mezhdunarodnye Otnosheniya, Moscow, 1992)

Aleksandrov-Argentov, Aleksander, *Ot Kollontai do Gorbacheva* (Mezhdunarodnye Otnosheniya, Moscow, 1994)

Arbatov, Georgi, *The System* (Times Books, New York, 1992)

Arendt, Hannah, *The Origins of Totalitarianism* (Allen & Unwin, London, 1958)

Arendt, Hannah, *On Revolution* (Penguin, London, 1977)

Ascherson, Neal, *The Polish August* (Penguin, London, 1981)

Baker, James, *The Politics of Diplomacy* (Putnam, New York, 1995)

Bauman, Zygmunt, *Stalin and the Peasant Revolution* (Leeds University Press, 1985)

Behr, Edward, *Kiss the Hand You Cannot Bite* (Hamish Hamilton, London, 1991)

Bellow, Saul, *The Dean's December* (Harper and Row, New York, 1982)

Benda, Václav et al., 'Parallel Polis, or an Independent Society in Central and Eastern Europe', *Social Research*, 55:1–2, Spring/Summer 1988

Beschloss, Michael, and Talbott, Strobe, *At The Highest Levels* (Little, Brown, New York, 1993)

Boldin, Valeri, *Ten Years that Shook the World* (Basic Books, New York, 1994)

Boyes, Robert, *The Naked President* (Secker and Warburg, London, 1994)

Bozóki, András, 'The Democratic Charter One Year On', *East European Reporter*, November/December 1992

Brown, Archie, *The Gorbachev Factor* (Oxford University Press, 1996)

Brown, Archie, *Seven Years that Changed the World* (Oxford University Press, 2007)

Brzezinski, Zbigniew, *The Grand Failure* (Macdonald, New York, 1990)

Bush, George H.W., *All the Best: My Life* (Scribner, New York, 1999)

Bush, George H.W., and Scowcroft, Brent, *A World Transformed* (Knopf, New York, 1998)

Chazov, Yevgeni, *Zdorov'ye I Vlast* (Novosti, Moscow, 1992)

Dahrendorf, Ralf, *Reflections on the Revolutions in Europe* (Random House, New York, 1990)

Davies, Norman, *Europe: A History* (Pimlico, London, 1997)

Davies, Norman, *God's Playground: A History of Poland* (Oxford University Press, 2005)

Dienstbier, Jiří, *Od Snění K Realitě* (Lidové Noviny, Prague, 1999)

Dobbs, Michael, *Down With Big Brother* (Bloomsbury, London, 1997)

Dobrynin, Anatoly, *In Confidence* (Times Books, New York, 1995)

Dubček, Alexander, *Hope Dies Last* (Kodansha International, New York, 1993)

Falin, Valentin, *Politische Erinnerungen* (Droemer Knaur Munich, 1993)

Gaddis, John, *The United States and the End of the Cold War* (Oxford University Press, 1992)

Gaddis, John, *We Now Know* (Clarendon Press, Oxford, 1997)

Gaddis, John, *The Cold War* (Allen Lane, London, 2006)

Gaidar, Yegor, *Collapse of an Empire: Lessons for Modern Russia* (Brookings Institution Press, Washington DC, 2007)

Ganev, Venelin, *Preying on the State: The Transformation of Bulgaria* (Cornell University Press, 2007)

Garton Ash, Timothy, *The Polish Revolution* (Jonathan Cape, London, 1983)

Garton Ash, Timothy, *The Uses of Adversity: Essays on the Fate of Central Europe* (Granta, London, 1989)

Garton Ash, Timothy, *We the People* (Granta, London, 1990)

Garton Ash, Timothy, *The File, A Personal History* (HarperCollins, London, 1997)

Garton Ash, Timothy, *The History of the Present* (Penguin, London, 1999)

Gierek Edward, and Rolicki, Janusz, *Przerwana Dekada* (FAKT Publishing, Warsaw, 1990)

Grachev, Andrei, *Gorbachev's Gamble* (Polity Press, Cambridge, 2008)

Gromov, Boris, *Ogranichennii Kontingent* (Progress, Moscow, 1994)

Gromyko, Andrei, *Memoirs* (Doubleday, New York, 1989)

Haraszti, Miklós, *A Worker in a Worker's State* (Penguin, London, 1977)

Haraszti, Miklós, *The Velvet Prison* (IB Tauris, London, 1988)

Havel, Václav, *The Power of the Poweless* (Hutchinson, London, 1985)

Havel, Václav, *Letters to Olga* (Faber & Faber, London, 1988)

Havel, Václav, *Disturbing the Peace* (Knopf, New York, 1990)

Havel, Václav, *Open Letters 1965–1990* (Faber & Faber, London, 1991)

Havel, Václav, *To the Castle and Back* (Knopf, New York, 2007)

Heins, Cornelia, *The Wall Falls: An Oral History of the Reunification of the Two Germanies* (Grey Seal, London, 1994)

Jaruzelski, Wojciech, *Les Chaines et le refuge* (Lattes, Paris, 1993), *Stan Wojenny Dlaczego* (BGW, Warsaw, 1992)

Kaiser, Robert, *Why Gorbachev Happened* (Simon & Schuster, New York, 1991)

Keane, John, *Václav Havel: A Political Tragedy in Six Acts* (Bloomsbury, London, 1999)

Kis, János, *Turning Point in Hungary: A Voice from the Democratic Opposition, Dissent* magazine, New York, Spring 1989

Kis, János, *Constitutional Democracy* (Central European University Press, Budapest, 1993)

Kiszczak, Czesław, *General Kiszczak Mówi* (BGW, Warsaw, 1991)

Klaus, Václav, *Renaissance: The Rebirth of Liberty at the Heart of Europe* (Cato Institute, Washington DC, 1997)

Kochemasov, Vyacheslav, *Meine Letzte Mission* (Dietz, Berlin, 1994)

Kołakowski, Leszek, *Modernity on Endless Trial* (University of Chicago Press, 1990)

Konrád, György, *Antipolitics* (Harcourt Brace, New York, 1984)

Konrád, György, 'Chance Wanderings: Reflections of a Hungarian Writer', *Dissent*, Spring 1990

Konrád György, 'A Colourful Scene Ahead', *East European Reporter*, Spring/Summer 1991

Kornai, János, *The Socialist System: The Political Economy of Communism* (Princeton University Press, 1992)

Kornai, János, *By Force of Thought* (MIT Press, 2006)

Krenz, Egon, *Herbst '89* (Neues Leben, Berlin, 1999)

Laba, Roman, *The Roots of Solidarity* (Princeton University Press, 1991)

Ligachev, Yegor, *Inside Gorbachev's Kremlin* (Pantheon Books, New York, 1993)

Maier, Charles, *Dissolution: The Crisis of Communism and the End of East Germany* (Princeton University Press, 1997)

Medvedev, Grigori, *The Truth about Chernobyl* (Basic Books, New York, 1991)

Michnik, Adam, *Letters From Prison* (California University Press, 1985)

Michnik, Adam, *Letters From Freedom* (California University Press, 1999)

Miłosz, Czesław, *The Captive Mind* (Penguin, London, 1980)

Mlynár, Zdenêk, *Night Frost in Prague* (C. Hurst & Co., London, 1980)

Musil, Jiří, *The End of Czechoslovakia* (Central European University Press, Budapest, 1995)

Oberdorfer, Don, *The Turn: How the Cold War Came to an End* (Jonathan Cape, London, 1992)

O'Sullivan, John, *The President, The Pope, and the Prime Minister: Three Who Changed the World* (Regnery, Lanham, MD, 2006)

Partos, Gabriel, *The World that Came in from the Cold* (Royal Institute of International Affairs, London, 1993)

Patapievici, Horia-Roman, *Flying Against the Arrow: An Intellectual in Ceauşescu's Romania* (Central European University Press, Budapest, 1999)

Pond, Elizabeth, *Beyond the Wall* (Brookings Institution, Washington DC, 1993)

Pötzl, Norbert, *Erich Honecker: Eine Deutsche Biographie* (Deutsche Verlags-Anstalt, Stuttgart, 2002)

Pryce-Jones, David, *The War that Never Was* (Weidenfeld & Nicolson, London, 1995)
Rakowski, Mieczysław, *Jak To Şie Stało* (BGW, Warsaw, 1991)
Remnick, David, *Lenin's Tomb* (Random House, New York, 1993)
Roth, Philip *The Prague Orgy* (Jonathan Cape, London, 1985)
Ryzhkov, Nikolai, *Perestroika – Istoria Predatel'stv* (Novosti, Moscow, 1992)
Shcherbak, Yuri, *Chernobyl: A Documentary Story* (Macmillan, Basingstoke, 1989)
Shevardnadze, Eduard, *The Future Belongs to Freedom* (Free Press, New York, 1991)
Šik, Ota, *For a Humane Economic Democracy* (Praeger, New York, 1985)
Šik, Ota, *Socialism Today?: The Changing Meaning of Socialism* (Palgrave Macmillan, London, 1991)
Šimečka, Milan, *The 'Normalisation' of Czechoslovakia 1969–76* (Verso, London, 1984)
Şimşir, Bilâl, *The Turks of Bulgaria* (K. Rustem, London, 1988)
Tellkamp, Uwe, *Der Turm* (Suhrkamp, Frankfurt, 2007)
Thatcher, Margaret, *The Downing Street Years* (HarperCollins, London, 1993)
Tismaneanu, Vladimir, 'The Tragicomedy of Romanian Communism', *East European Politics and Societies*, 3:2 1989
Tismaneanu, Vladimir, *Reinventing Politics: Eastern Europe from Stalin to Havel* (Free Press, New York, 1992)
Tökés, Rudolf, *Hungary's Negotiated Revolution* (Central European University Press, Budapest, 1996)
Torańska, Teresa, *Oni: Stalin's Polish Puppets* (Collins Harvill, London, 1987)
Vaculík, Ludvík, *A Cup of Coffee with My Interrogator* (Readers International, New York, 1987)
Velikov, Vadim, 'The Political Economy of Protection Rackets', *Social Research*, 67, Vol. 3, Fall 2000
Volkogonov, Dmitri, *The Rise and Fall of the Soviet Empire* (HarperCollins, New York, 1998)
Vulkanov, Velko, *Na Kolone pred istinata* (Bulvest, Sofia, 2000)
Wałęsa, Lech, *The Struggle and the Triumph* (Arcade Publishing, New York, 1994)
Weigel, George, *The Final Revolution. Church Resistance and the Collapse of Communism* (Oxford University Press, 1992)
Weiner, Tim, *Legacy of Ashes: The History of the CIA* (Allen Lane, London, 2007)
Westad, Odd Arne, *The Global Cold Ear* (Cambridge University Press, 2005)
Willey, David, *God's Politician: John Paul at the Vatican* (Faber & Faber, London, 1992)
Wolf, Markus, with McElvoy, Anne, *Man Without a Face* (Times Books, London, 1997)

Yakovlev, Alexander, *Predislovia; Obval; Posleslovie* (Novosti, Moscow, 1992)
Zaslavskaya, Tatiana, *A Voice of Reform* (M.E. Sharpe, New York, 1989)
Zelikow, Philip, and Rice, Condoleezza, *Germany Unified and Europe Transformed* (Harvard University Press, 1995)
Zemtsov, Ilya, *Chernenko: The Last Bolshevik* (Transaction, Brunswick, NJ, 1989)
Zubok, Vladislav, *A Failed Empire* (University of North Carolina Press, 2007)

INDEX